W9-BAX-069

Books by Richard O'Connor

❦ ❦ ❦

Fiction

GUNS OF CHICKAMAUGA

COMPANY Q

OFFICERS AND LADIES

THE VANDAL

Non-fiction

THOMAS: ROCK OF CHICKAMAUGA

HOOD: CAVALIER GENERAL

SHERIDAN THE INEVITABLE

HIGH JINKS ON THE KLONDIKE

BAT MASTERSON

JOHNSTOWN: THE DAY THE DAM BROKE

HELL'S KITCHEN

WILD BILL HICKOK

PAT GARRETT

BLACK JACK PERSHING

GOULD'S MILLIONS

THE SCANDALOUS MR. BENNETT

COURTROOM WARRIOR: THE COMBATIVE
CAREER OF WILLIAM TRAVERS JEROME

JACK LONDON: A BIOGRAPHY

JACK LONDON

JACK LONDON

A Biography

RICHARD O'CONNOR

With Illustrations

LITTLE, BROWN AND COMPANY • BOSTON • TORONTO

LIBRARY OF CONGRESS CATALOG CARD NO. 64-21486

FOURTH PRINTING

The author gratefully acknowledges permission from Doubleday & Company, Inc., to quote from FINAL VERDICT by Adela Rogers St. Johns. Copyright 1962 by Adela Rogers St. Johns.

Published simultaneously in Canada
by Little, Brown & Company (Canada) Limited

PRINTED IN THE UNITED STATES OF AMERICA

To the memory of Olga Converse Derby

and Augustin Derby

Contents

Illustrations

(*Between pages 242 and 243*)

❦ ❦ ❦

BOOK ONE

The Bay

I

The Childhood That Never Was

1. *In London Country*

IN A high green valley between the mountains and the sea, the aspirations that spurred Jack London on through a short turbulent life become almost tangible. It is the Valley of the Moon in the foothills of northern California where he lived and worked during the last half-dozen years of his life. If, as James Joyce believed, every man spends his life looking for the place he can belong to, this is the home of Jack London's restless spirit. He saw himself not only as master but benefactor of the valley, and intended to build an agricultural paradise of happy workers and bountiful fields that would last a thousand years.

Almost half a century later the land itself, lying green and fertile at the foot of Sonoma Mountain, testifies to the enduring value of his gift, saved from erosion by the thousands of trees he planted. There are vineyards on the slopes of the valley, fat cattle in the bottom lands, mountain meadows greener than anything this side of Ireland. Two miles above the village of Glen Ellen, north of San Francisco, stands the Jack London State Historical Park, established in 1960, on the site of his ranch. It is the number one tourist attraction of the countryside, visible testimony not only of California's regard for one of its unique native sons but of the continuing hold he exercises on the imagination long after his works have gone out of intellectual fashion. Few American writers have managed to create so compelling a legend about themselves as to draw tourists on a rainy Sunday.

Just inside the entrance of the park is the House of Happy Walls, built three years after his death by his second wife, Charmian. A large, solid and quite ugly stone building, it shelters many mementoes of a literary career filled with hard work and crowned by the sort of success he craved — the green eyeshades he and Charmian wore at their desks, rejection slips, newspaper clippings, many of the photographs he took in various parts of the world, old typewriters, a pioneer-model dictating machine, the four-tiered wire baskets which held manuscripts in work. The name given this house he never saw revealed something of the complex nature of the second Mrs. London, who spent almost forty years of widowhood as the jealous guardian of his legend and who declared that she built it as a monument to him. There are grounds for suspecting that, covert rivalry being part of their marriage, it may have pleased her to accomplish one thing he didn't.

Deeper in the park, reached by a narrow footpath through dark and quiet woods, is the wooded knoll looking down the Valley of the Moon on which he was buried. He lies behind redwood pickets, under a chunk of reddish-brown volcanic rock, securely fenced in and weighted down for all time. An average of perhaps twenty visitors a day stare down at the rock, wondering about him; he was a gregarious man and would not have resented the intrusion. Nothing, except possibly the continuing sale of his books throughout the world, would have delighted him more than the knowledge that a half-century after his death people would still be coming up the road from Glen Ellen to see him. Nearby are the graves of two children of pioneer settlers, "Little David Greenlaw and Little Lillie Greenlaw," who were buried on the same knoll in 1876, the year London was born. The coincidence pleased his sense of drama and his instinct for continuity.

Farther along the trail, a half-mile from the House of Happy Walls, are the ruins of Wolf House. Here was to have been the seat of London's rural dynasty. The man who preached revolution and derided the rights of property proposed to set himself up in much the same fashion as another extraordinary native son, William Randolph Hearst, in his wilderness castle, Wyntoon, to the north. Fate had it otherwise, as though decreeing that castles are for newspaper magnates but not presumptuous writers. Its walls, however, still stand, solitary, fire-blackened and somehow accusing.

Down in the cities around San Francisco Bay where he spent most of the earlier years of his life his name and his legend are also commemorated more than adequately. The passing generations have remembered him more as the writer and adventurer than as the man who hoped to foment a revolution in the streets of those cities, more as the picturesque swashbuckler than the troubled and troubling man he was. The name of Jack London has become respectable in the oddest places. On the wall of the American Trust Company at Third and Brannan Streets in San Francisco a bronze plaque solemnly attests that this was the site of the house where he was born, though his opinion of banking institutions was once regarded as inflammatory. During World War II, a Liberty ship named the *Jack London* sailed out of the harbor. Over in Oakland the Jack London Oak spreads its branches over the City Hall Plaza, where The Boy Socialist was once arrested and loaded into a paddy wagon for mounting a soapbox and denouncing capitalism as a system of organized robbery.

The city fathers, it appears, have long since forgiven him not only his political views but the reputation he earned as a saloon brawler, a libertine and a notably free spirit in the Bohemian circles of Piedmont Hills and Carmel, not to mention a record for juvenile delinquency that has seldom (if we take his own word for it) been surpassed.

Information on every detail of his career is cherished by the public library; at Oakland High School, which he briefly attended, his name is all but hallowed. And down on the Oakland waterfront, at the foot of Broadway, is the most striking testimonial of all to his posthumous respectability: Jack London Square. Just off the tide-lapped stringpieces the visitor is lured to London House, the Sea Wolf Restaurant, the Jack London Marina, and a little theater housing the London Circle Players. All dainty tourism now, where the slammerkins of the waterfront once drank and brawled. Among flower beds maintained by the park department a sign indicates the starting point of his South Seas cruise in the *Snark,* and as an afterthought that of Robert Louis Stevenson's *Casco.* A block away, below First and Webster Streets, Heinhold's First and Last Chance Saloon, where London often bent his elbow, is still in operation. This sailors' snuggery, not more than twleve by twelve feet and looking about as permanent as a shack in a hobo jungle, is regarded as one of Oakland's landmarks and has been lovingly preserved. It still looks as though London might drop in at any moment and buy a round for the house.

London Country, however, is wider than the cities of the Bay and the valley to the north; it encompasses the earth if his influence as a writer is taken into account. New printings of his more popular works come off the presses annually and recently a Jack London Book Club was formed with the sole purpose of distributing a complete edition of his writings. Abroad, now as during his life, he is perhaps even more widely read; in Great Britain and on the Continent he is regarded as one of the more durable American writers, a primitive Hemingway, a legitimate ancestor of Steinbeck, a foreshadowing of O'Neill (who acknowledged London as his chief source of inspiration). In Soviet as well as Czarist Russia he has always been one of the most widely read American writers. "This," as the Russian poet Ilya Selvinsky wrote in 1941, "is the first cigar we smoke in our youth." Nobody, the poet added, could consider himself a man until he had "soaked" himself in London's works.[1] During World War II, when most American books were dropped from the state publishing house's list, copies of London's work continued to roll off the presses by the hundreds of thousands. He has since been downgraded officially, his doctrine of Anglo-Saxon superiority having been re-examined and denigrated, but his popularity has not greatly suffered. It is still remembered that Lenin himself, on his deathbed, insisted on having London's stories read to him.[2]

The short but vivid life of Jack London seems to belong to another age, a flashback to vanished frontiers, sailing ships battling the wild seas, and untrammeled lands. Yet if his end had not been so untimely he could still be alive, an aged and revered titan of American letters. He was roughly contemporary to such vital and diverse men as Carl Sandburg, Upton Sinclair, Winston Churchill, Bertrand Russell, Herbert Hoover, Bernard Baruch and Albert Schweitzer. If he had survived, we might have been fascinated and enlivened by his reaction to the depression of the Thirties — he would have been only fifty-four when it began — and the monstrous but logical culmination of his ideas about Nordic superiority — he would have been in his seventieth year when Hitler killed himself in the ruins of Berlin — and to the much sadder fate of the proletarian revolution he also preached, for he would have been eighty years old when Russian tanks, in 1956, crunched their way over the barricades of Budapest.

Obviously a man in whose thought could be found the elements of latter-day Fascism and Communism, mingled with a peculiarly American dream of success, was suffering from a confusion of the intellect. It was a state of mind shared by most of his contemporaries. He was born the year Custer fell at the Little Big Horn and died during World War I. Thus his whole life was enclosed by the ironbound parenthesis that vexed and bewildered all thinking men of his generation, as Frederick Jackson Turner noted, the end of the free opportunity of the Western frontier and the necessity to find in American life some social and economic substitute for it. What distinguished him from most of his fellows was his questing spirit, which impelled him to wander over much of the world, to seek the truth in strange places, and to write books as diverse as *The Call of the Wild* and *The People of the Abyss, The Star Rover* and *The Little Lady of the Big House.* He was not only the author of enormously popular dog and outdoor adventure tales — a rival of Albert Payson Terhune, Rex Beach and James Oliver Curwood in the big-money stakes — but the man who wrote *The Iron Heel,* a startling preview of Fascism, and *John Barleycorn,* a sardonic track on alcoholism and its impact on his own life.

The motive force that drove him to produce fifty books in the sixteen years of his professional career, was an unquenchable desire for success and all its rewards. If he was attracted to Marx in his youth, he had also read Horatio Alger as a boy. He wanted to see a radically different and better world come into being, but meanwhile he was determined to enjoy all the material benefits of a society he believed to be rotten and corrupting. He was proud of being a Socialist, a revolutionary, but he employed a valet who addressed him as "Mr. God" without the slightest risk of being rebuked. He discussed the coming revolution over a baronial dining table. He would have his proletarian bread and, in the same mouthful, his capitalistic cake. The result was a predictable and fatal indigestion. For London was a ground-breaker in more ways than the purely literary, who, without intending it to be so, without wanting to prove through his own life that the fruits of a materialistic society can be bitter, showed it can also be true that nothing fails like success. He signalled a change in stereotypes. Before World War I, the successful man, it was widely believed, lived happily ever after. Since then, the heroes of the Success Myth have been condemned to a tragic, frustrated end; their struggles generally dissolve in alcohol and disillusion.

Of all the hero-victims of American success there are none more prone to psychological accident than writers. Hardly a major literary figure since the turn of the century has escaped this doom. Upton Sinclair has listed the celebrated writers known to him to have been maimed by what he calls "the claws of John Barleycorn," all of them acclaimed and many of them made wealthy by their talent, including London himself, George Sterling, Ambrose Bierce, O. Henry, Sinclair Lewis, Edna St. Vincent Millay, Eugene O'Neill, Dylan Thomas, Scott Fitzgerald, Ernest Hemingway, Theodore Dreiser, William Faulkner, Finley Peter Dunne, William Seabrook, Sherwood Anderson, Stephen Crane — hardly a famous literary name of the past sixty years is missing.

If there is a definitive reason for this phenomenon, this common blight on literary success, it may possibly be found in London's life and work. Almost everything he put on paper derived from his own experience. Very little of his life and thoughts was kept hidden from his public. He lived in a self-constructed aquarium and gladly placed himself on exhibit, night and day, during good times and bad, until the last hour of his existence.

It was his ability to undertake the transmutation of life into literature, the rugged and venturesome facts of his own existence, that keeps the library dust off Jack London's books today. No one has caught this quality of London's better than the English critic Stephen Graham, who wrote in *The Death of Yesterday*: "He is a living writer. His books will be read when many that are greater works of art will be dust-collecting. He is lesser than Conrad and greater. . . . He is a young man's writer. Between him and youth flies a living spark. He has power to animate and set moving that which is still and immature. . . . He wrote for the unfinished and not the finished America."

It was to the "unfinished" America, the nation capable of growth and change and self-improvement, that he dedicated the best that was within him. Only when it closes the books on itself will it stop reading him for a clue to a vital part of its national existence.

2. *Discarded Wife, Unwanted Son*

On January 14, 1876 the San Francisco *Chronicle* found considerable space for relating how 2616 Mormon women were petitioning Congress to repeal a law which denied them the "right of concubinage" and how a Market Street horsecar conductor was arrested for mistreating a drunken passenger who tried to hijack the vehicle and was twice thrown off before a policeman came to his assistance. A police judge freed the conductor and fined the drunk. Buried in the back of the paper was a tiny item of greater but unforeseeable significance under the heading of "Births":

"CHANEY — In this city, Jan. 12, the wife of W. H. Chaney, of a son."

Routine and unremarkable as the announcement appeared to be, it caused a certain amount of commotion in the city. The infant whose birth was recorded, somewhat inaccurately, had attained notoriety while he was still in embryo. He was to be known successively as John Griffith London and Jack London, and troubled to the end of his days by the fact that he never knew what his name should have been. The best evidence indicated that he was the son of William H. Chaney, a footloose astrologer and freelance philosopher, and Flora Wellman, a Spiritualist who often presided at séances, who apparently had neglected to undertake the formalities of marriage in their preoccupation with the zodiac and the spirit world.

If the newspaper seemed to be taking undue amount of interest in two quite obscure citizens, it was largely because the *Chronicle* had been campaigning editorially against the "religious quacks" and "free love cultists" who had been "flocking" into the city. On June 4, 1875, the *Chronicle* had published a half-column account of the sorry facts of the coming birth:

A DISCARDED WIFE
Why Mrs. Chaney Twice
Attempted Suicide
Driven from house for Refusing
to Destroy her Unborn Infant
— A chapter of Heartlessness
and Domestic Misery

Day before yesterday Mrs. Chaney, wife of "Professor" W. H. Chaney, the astrologer, attempted suicide by taking laudanum. Failing in the effort she yesterday shot herself with a pistol in the forehead. The bullet glanced off, inflicting only a flesh wound, and friends interfered before she could accomplish her suicidal purpose.

The incentive to the terrible act was domestic infelicity. Husband and wife have been known for a year past as the center of a little band of extreme

Spiritualists, most of whom professed, if they did not practice the offensive free-love doctrines of the licentious Woodhull.*

He has been several times married before this last fiasco of the hearthstone, but it is supposed that all his former wives have been duly laid away to rest . . .

The last marriage took place about a year ago . . . The married life of the couple is said to have been full of self-denial and devoted affection on the part of the wife and of harsh words and unkind treatment on the part of the husband . . .

The wife assisted him in the details of business, darned his hose, drudged at the washtub, took care of other people's children for hire, and generously gave him whatever money she earned and could spare beyond her actual expenses. She never told her sorrows . . . except to intimate friends. She says that about three weeks ago she discovered, with a natural feeling of maternal pleasure, that she was *enceinte*. She told her husband, and asked to be relieved for two or three months of the care of the children by means of which she had been contributing to their mutual support . . . some angry words followed.

Then he told her that she had better destroy her unborn babe. This she indignantly declined to do, and on last Thursday morning he said to her, "Flora, I want you to pack up and leave this house."

She replied, "I have no money and nowhere to go."

He said, "Neither have I any to give you."

A woman in the house offeerd her $25, but she flung it from her with a burst of anguish, saying, "What do I care for this? It will be of no use to me without my husband's love." This show of affection had no effect upon the flinty-hearted calculator of other people's nativities. He told the poor woman that he had sold the furniture (for which she had helped to pay) and it was useless to think of her remaining there any longer.

He then left her, and shortly afterwards she made her first attempt at suicide, following it up by the effort to kill herself with a pistol on the following morning. . . . Failing in both endeavours Mrs. Chaney was removed in a half-insane condition from Dr. Ruttley's on Mission street to the house of a

* The scandalized reference was to Victoria Woodhull, who with her sister Tennessee Claflin and other members of their family had toured their native Ohio in a wagon show giving Spiritualist demonstrations. Later the sisters turned up in New York and persuaded Commodore Vanderbilt to set them up in a brokerage. Two years later, in 1870, with a half-million in profits from acting on stock market tips from the smitten Commodore, they started *Woodhull's & Claflin's Weekly*, which promoted women's rights, birth control, Spiritualism and more liberal divorce laws. Miss Woodhull not only advocated "free association" between men and women but apparently practiced it herself. She shared her Greenwich Village quarters with both her ex-husband and a Colonel Blood.

friend, where she still remains, somewhat pacified and in a mental condition indicating she will not again attempt self-destruction. The story given here is the lady's own, as filtered through her near associates.

Who was this heartless wretch who cast a pregnant woman out on the streets because she would not consent to an abortion? A much different, much put-upon man, according to his own lights. The *Chronicle* reporter admittedly did not attempt to learn his side of the story, nor to characterize him beyond identifying him as a man who sold "cheap nativities," as horoscopes then were called, and observing that astrological information in San Francisco was in much greater supply than the demand warranted. If the reporter had been more diligent, he would have uncovered a fascinating character.

Chaney was a rather short man with a heavy torso and muscular shoulders, the build of a day laborer (though he shunned toil). At fifty-five he was still handsome, attractive to women, with a strong jaw, bright blue eyes and an engaging manner. He had the kind of masculinity, implicit in his confident smile and swaggering walk, that appealed to feminine susceptibilities. As a practicing astrologer, with a clientele largely composed of women, he was as dependent upon that charm as any matinee idol. For years he had been living by his wits, though he preferred to think of himself as an intellectual. He passionately resented being called a charlatan simply because the bearded dolts who controlled university curricula refused to recognize astrology as the exact science he insisted it was. In addition to his occult interests, he was well read in mathematics, philosophy and astronomy. The characteristics people found most striking about him were his charm on and off the platform, his appetite for controversy, and his willingness to mix it with his fists if anyone slighted or insulted him.

William Henry Chaney was born in a log cabin near what is now Chesterville, Maine, on January 13, 1821. His grandfathers, Sam Linscutt and John Chaney, were among the first to settle in the Sandy River valley; both were Revolutionary War veterans, members of a plain-living, hard-working yeomanry. His parents were William and Betsey Chaney, who also had four daughters. When he was nine, both parents died. His relatives took in his sisters, but William was bound out to a farmer in the neighborhood, one of those hardheaded Yankees who did not believe in pampering child labor.

Young William took poorly to the apprentice system. By the time he was sixteen, he had run away from seven different masters who had offered him a pallet in their lofts in exchange for sixteen hours of daily toil. The deacon of the church which served the neighborhood pronounced judgment on the boy as "one of the Devil's unaccountables."

Oddly enough, a touring phrenologist named Dr. Wheeling was inclined to agree with this verdict after taking a reading of the Chaney skull some years later. "Here is a strange man," was Dr. Wheeling's diagnosis, "with a strange disposition. He can be tender as a child, or as brutal as a savage . . . He remembers a kindness like an Indian; he holds a grudge like an Indian; he will seek revenge like an Indian, and, in short, he looks like an Indian." [3]

Late in his teens he abandoned the scant prospects of Down East farm life. His ambition was to become a river pirate of the Southwest such as he had read about in various paperbacked volumes kept in hayloft libraries. He shipped out on a fishing schooner for some months but found Yankee skippers even tougher than Yankee farmers and joined the U.S. Navy instead. Naval discipline, too, was hard to take, and after nine months he deserted from the receiving ship *Columbus* in Boston Harbor in July of 1840. None of this was getting him any closer to the unfettered life of a river pirate. He headed west, caught a flatboat headed down the rivers to New Orleans. Once again he was thwarted when a malarial fever laid him low and the owner of the flatboat tied up near Wheeling, Virginia, just long enough to put the sick and raving Chaney ashore.

Except for the fact that he settled down in Wheeling when he recovered from the malaria, and that he studied for the bar and was employed alternately as a lawyer and editor, little is known about this period. He took the first two of his six wives there; the first left him a widower, the second he abandoned when he departed Wheeling. (Not all of the six wives, of course, were taken in any legal formality; the term "wife" meant to him the woman he happened to be living with.)

He left Wheeling some time in the early 1850's to return to Maine, not because he yearned for the scenes of his boyhood but because, all those years, the memory of a certain heavy-handed farmer rankled and festered unbearably. Until he had avenged the beating given him as a bond servant, he knew, he would never be able to respect himself completely. He thrashed his old tormentor, then proceeded to Ellsworth, a lumber port on the Union River, to set up another law practice.

His temperament, it is clear, was not adaptable enough to make him a very successful lawyer. A good lawyer should never drop his mask of genial imperturbability, except perhaps to dramatize his case before the jury. Chaney, however, was wildly partisan. When he took a case, when he assumed a defense, he regarded his opponent, not as a fellow member of the court, but a mortal enemy to be flayed with insults; the judge was not an impartial arbiter but a black-robed monster every time he ruled against Chaney. He refused to be bound by the cozy etiquette of the courtroom or to be guided by the sacred writ of the statute books. Others lawyers disliked him, he explained, because "I wouldn't run in the old rut of precedence." He was the most unpopular man who ever practiced law in eastern Maine. Judge Hathaway once halted his flow of invective while Chaney was addressing a jury and casting bitter aspersions on his opponent by observing from the bench, "It's a filthy bird that fouls its own nest."

During his stay in Ellsworth, Chaney made himself even more notorious after taking over as editor of the Ellsworth *Herald* on June 10, 1853. The weekly *Herald* was dedicated to the views of the Know-Nothing Party, an organization that crusaded to keep the Anglo-Saxon element dominant in the United States, was violently anti-Catholic and bitterly opposed to the recent flood of immigrants from Ireland, driven out by the potato famine of the Forties, and from Germany, which thousands fled after the unsuccessful revolution of 1848. As editor of a journal advocating intolerance, Chaney found a cause worthy of his talents, though it boomeranged and directly involved him in what a local historian has called "one of the most deplorable acts of bigotry ever committed in the United States."[4] It brought him into collision with a man as stubbornly opinionated as himself, Father John Bapst, a Swiss-born Jesuit who took over the Ellsworth parish soon after Chaney assumed his editorial duties.

Under Chaney's editorship, the *Herald* soon was whipping up sentiment against the local Catholics. Every week Chaney published articles and editorials under such headings as "Danger of Employing Popish Servants in Protestant Families." "Immorality of Romanism," "The Dangers of Popery," "Morals of Nuns and Nunneries," and "Help

Wanted — No Irish Need Apply." Despite his drumfire of denunciation, Father Bapst succeeded in converting twenty local Protestant maidens to Catholicism. The news of that missionary triumph aroused the whole community, swinging it largely to Chaney's side. With no great amount of tact and even less sense of timing, Father Bapst immediately petitioned the Ellsworth School Committee to exempt Catholic pupils from being required to read the Protestant King James Version of the Bible in their classes.

Chaney launched a vituperative editorial campaign against Father Bapst's petition, rousing all the latent prejudice in the community and stirring up that "ape behind the mask" that slumbers all too lightly. He denounced Thomas White, the Jesuit's leading lay supporter, as "an Irish Papist" and "a black-hearted hypocrite," leading to a fist fight in which Chaney, who had served notice on taking up his duties at the *Herald* that he would not suffer readers who sought to remedy grievances by direct assault on the editor, wiped up the street with Mr. White.

When a suit was brought against the School Committee, which had refused Father Bapst's petition, Chaney's broadsides against the Church ("the Scarlet Beast of Rome"), the priest and all his parishoners grew so provocative that the local *Eastern Freeman* and other Maine newspapers condemned Chaney as an unprincipled opportunist stirring up trouble to increase his paper's circulation.

At a special town meeting called to raise six hundred dollars to defend the School Committee's stand before the Supreme Judicial Court of Maine a resolution drawn up by Chaney, who was also town clerk, was passed unanimously. It read:

"Whereas we have good reason to believe that we are indebted to one John Bapst, S.J., Catholic priest, for the luxury of the present law suit now enjoyed by the School Committee, therefore resolved, that should the said Bapst be found again on Ellsworth soil we manifest our gratitude for his kindly interference with our free schools and attempts to banish the Bible therefrom, by procuring for him and trying on an entire new suit of clothes such as cannot be found at the shop of any tailor and that when thus apparelled, he be presented with a free ticket to leave Ellsworth upon the first railroad operation that may go into effect." The new suit of clothes, of course, would be composed of tar and feathers.

By that time the priest's superiors had transferred him to Bangor, hoping the controversy would cool if he was removed from its center. Father Bapst, however, was no more inclined to let the dispute die down than his chief opponent. On a rainy Saturday night, October 14, 1854, he returned to Ellsworth announcing that he would celebrate Mass the next morning in his former parish, then boldly paraded down the main street. A drunken mob set upon him, stripped off his clothes, stole his money, dragged him naked through the streets, and then tarred and feathered him. A resident of the town rescued him and gave him shelter. Next day he said Mass as promised. He became a national hero, though a man less bent on martyrdom might have accomplished more with less disturbance. Meanwhile Ellsworth was being denounced throughout the nation for its violent bigotry.

The Bangor *Journal* described the tar-and-feathering as a "diabolical deed," and the *Eastern Freeman*, holding Chaney chiefly responsible, declared the rival editor was "insane" and "unscrupulous" in the bargain.

Chaney agreed that the mob's actions, suggested by a resolution he had drawn up as town clerk, were a "flagrant act" but boldly asserted that it was ridiculous to charge that the *Herald*'s eight-month campaign against Catholicism had anything to do with it. Furthermore, it was well known that "papists rule the white folks in Bangor," from which most of the criticism stemmed. The whole affair, he insisted, had been caused by Father Bapst's "insulting bravado."

No doubt he felt himself vindicated when the Supreme Court ruled in favor of the Ellsworth School Committee, holding that Bible reading in class was more of an educational than a religious function and citing the "literary" value of the King James Version in a decision which has often been quoted in subsequent suits over religious teachings in the public schools.

Chaney failed in his effort to disclaim responsibility for the outrage committed against Father Bapst. The more respectable townspeople, who had kept silent at the town meeting while Chaney's resolution was passed with a roar of approval, now found the courage to blame him for the shame which had fallen on Ellsworth. Both as a lawyer and an editor, he was given to understand, his presence was no longer welcome.

A short time later, of necessity, he resumed his wanderings and a long hazy period of odd jobs and drifting from city to city followed. In 1857 he is known to have worked in a Boston match factory for four dollars a week. The Civil War was fought without any active interference from Chaney. In October of 1866 he first met Luke Broughton, known as the founding father of astrology in the United States, and was so impressed by his theories that he decided to devote the rest of his life to spreading the word that the hour and date of birth, under planetary influence, govern a person's destiny. Broughton had migrated from his native Leeds in England, and had gained a certain amount of renown for having predicted, in 1864, the assassination of Abraham Lincoln a year later.

With Chaney as his chief disciple Broughton set up shop at 814 Broadway in New York City. Together they presided over the Eclectic Medical University, an institution which soon attracted an odd but lucrative following. The two savants, bestowing the title of "Professor" on each other, came under a certain amount of criticism in the newspapers in November of 1867 for claiming that their "astro-botanical" plants could heal or eliminate practically anything from warts to tumors.

The city was full of wizards, healers, warlocks, psuedoscientific practitioners, religious fanatics, occultists, mesmerists and spook-consorts of all kinds. Phrenologists thrived on their analyses of cranial bumps as psychoanalysts do today. A whole cult was formed around the solemn consumption of graham bread. Hordes of Spiritualists congregated nightly for communication with the other world.

The New York *Herald*, the mightiest of the country's newspapers, edited by the redoubtable James Gordon Bennett, Sr., singled out Broughton's and Chaney's "university" and its astro-botanical discoveries for attack. Bennett averred that he had never heard of Eclectic Medicine; the institution of learning at 814 Broadway was a "Ghoul's Garret," with a faculty of knaves and a student body of idiots. Chaney was identified in the *Herald*'s expose as "the Chief Ghoul of the den."

Newspaper attacks generally die away as soon as a new sensation comes along to replace them, but the *Herald* made serious trouble for Chaney and Broughton. The landlord of their building tried to get them off his property but the two educators refused to consider moving. In retaliation the landlord rented the floor above them to a quarrelsome band of Fenians, dedicated to freeing Ireland from British rule, who drilled with crashing boots while Broughton and Chaney tried to conduct their classes. Chaney had one of the Fenians arrested on a charge of disturbing the peace, which was a serious mistake, for the Irishmen were regarded with something more than indulgence by Boss Tweed's dictatorship at City Hall.

The Fenian was turned loose immediately but Chaney himself was arrested on a charge of false imprisonment. There was no appeal from the dictates of Tweed and his friends. For twenty-eight weeks Chaney languished in the Ludlow Street jail, denied bail, trial or the right to communicate with anyone outside. Then he was released without further formality.

He took his third wife and lived in New York until 1869, writing pamphlets, casting horoscopes and delivering lectures on astrology, but apparently without continuing the good work at the Eclectic Medical University or his partnership with Luke Broughton. His third marriage palled, and Chaney decided on desertion as the most feasible remedy. He went west without his wife, and from then until 1873 spent most of his time in Salem, Oregon. In his only known work between book covers, *Primer of Astrology and Urania,*[5] a hodgepodge of astrological lore, autobiography and self-justification, Chaney claimed that while in the Oregon capital he "privately" guided the careers of many leading politicians through studying their horoscopes.

A closer study of planetary influences in his own life might have preserved him from a fateful occurrence in San Francisco when, late in 1873, he stopped over in that city on his way back to New York. Someone picked his pocket, and he was unable to continue his journey. Instead he had to gather up a new stake by giving lectures on Astro-Theology in San Jose, writing for *Common Sense,* a magazine, and by setting up an astrological practice in San Francisco. He advertised himself as a true practitioner of the "celestial art" and denounced rivals "calling themselves Astrologers" who were "simple fortune-tellers who divine through a teacup or a pack of cards, and by their charlatanism have done much toward bringing genuine Astrology into disrepute."

In his *Primer,* Chaney covered the Flora Wellman period in two cavalier paragraphs: "By May, 1874 I had saved enough money to return east, but just before starting, received an anonymous letter from my wife . . . stating that she was divorced and could marry again, but if I ever married again she would have me imprisoned.

"This aroused my ire and on June 11, 1874 . . . three weeks later . . . I took another wife. We lived together till June 3, 1875 . . . then separated."

After the explosive separation from Flora Wellman, whom he claimed to have "married" merely to spite her predecessor, Chaney fled back to the Pacific Northwest as denunciations rained down on him for deserting Flora. Suffragette papers attacked him as "this uncouth yet erudite Ishmaelite." He published a pamphlet attempting to defend himself, to tell his side of the story and deny paternity of Flora Wellman's child, but public sympathy naturally went to the woman in the case, who was not shy about claiming it.

Chaney married again in Portland, Oregon, in 1886; but domestic harmony eluded him, largely because of his appetite for a good row, in or out of the home. He attacked his brother-in-law, a millionaire and business associate of the railroad magnate Henry Villard, for "being in cahoots" with the Northern Pacific in stealing timber from government land. As a further affront to his rich relatives, he joined the Greenback, Populist and Anti-Monopoly movements, all dedicated to curbing the acquisitive tendencies of people like his in-laws. Somewhat miraculously, that marriage lasted almost three years. It was terminated, as usual, by the departure of "Professor" Chaney for faroff places. His next stopping place was St. Louis, where he lived off the horoscope trade until the World's Fair of 1893 suggested a move to Chicago, as it did to thousands of other pitchmen, grifters, con men and bunco artists.

Astrology apparently continued to be the lodestar of his existence until the end of his days, which were enveloped in obscurity. In 1897 he was able to write, rather proudly, and more than a little pathetically, that "now I have a few friends who think me respectable." The following year, the Chicago *City Directory* listed him as having acquired his sixth wife: "Daisy F. and Wm. H. Chaney, astrologers, h. 3104 South Park Avenue." The last discoverable clue to him was contained in the 1902 *City Directory* when he was eighty-one years old and living alone again. There is no record of the date or place of his death.

To the end of his days, William H. Chaney denied having fathered Jack London. The most definitive denials he issued were to the young man alleged to be his son. In his twenty-first year, London wrote Chaney in Chicago asking the astrologer, then seventy-five, if he was his father. Very belatedly, apparently after much thought and soul-searching, Chaney replied:

I was never married to Flora Wellman but she lived with me from June 11, 1874, until June 3, 1875. I was impotent at the time, the result of hardship, privation, and too much brain work. Therefore I cannot be your father, nor am I sure who your father is. . . .

There was a time when I had a very tender affection for Flora; but there came a time when I hated her with all the intensity of my intense nature, and even thought of killing her and myself, as many a man has under similar circumstances. Time, however, has healed the wounds and I feel no unkindness toward her, while for you I feel a warm sympathy, for I can imagine what my emotions would be were I in your place. . . .

Chaney also stated that the *Chronicle*'s story of his having turned Flora out of their home had been picked up and published in the East, that "my sisters in Maine read it and two of them became my enemies. One died believing I was in the wrong. All others of my kindred, except one sister in Portland, Oregon, are still my enemies and denounce me as a disgrace to them."

He pointedly added that he was "quite poor."

London was still not quite satisfied, however, and wrote pleading for more information, sensing that Chaney was holding something back.

His putative father's reply could hardly have comforted him. Chaney wrote that the estrangement between him and Flora began when she asked him whether he would be willing for her to have a child by another man, since she wanted to enjoy the pleasures of motherhood and he was too old to help her conceive one, with the understanding that she would continue to be known as his wife. His reply, Chaney said, was that the father of any such child would have to support it. He continued:

A month or so later she said she was pregnant by me. I thought she was only trying me and did not think she was pregnant. So I made a great fuss thinking to warn her not to make the attempt. This brought on a wrangle that lasted all day and night. After daylight I got up and told her she could never be a wife to me again. She was humbled in a moment, for she knew I was in earnest. But I would not forgive her, although I still thought she was merely pretending to be in a family way. But her temper was a great trial, and I had often thought before that time that I must leave her on account of it.

When she left she went to Dr. Ruttley's house; went out in the backyard, soon returned, a pistol in one hand and a box of cartridges in the other, a wound in the left side of her forehead and the blood running over her face. In reply to Mrs. Ruttley, Flora said, "This little woman has been trying to kill herself and made a bad job of it."

A great excitement followed. A mob of a hundred and fifty gathered, swearing to hang me to the nearest lamp-post.[6]

Chaney also claimed that Flora had passed as the wife of one Lee Smith in the same lodging house, and that one day a number of fellow lodgers quit the place in moral indignation because she had successively been known as Miss Wellman, Mrs. Smith and Mrs. Chaney, all without benefit of marriage license. He also hinted that Flora was involved with two other men in the spring of 1875, when her son was conceived — not exactly a novel defense in cases of that kind.

Who, then, was Jack London's father? William Henry Chaney claimed he was "impotent" at the time of Jack's conception. He was fifty-five years old. No paternity suit was ever filed against him. The only logical verdict would be: not proven.

On the other hand, there was Flora Wellman's claim that he was the father, and the fact that San Francisco's *City Directory* showed that they lived as man and wife in 1874 and 1875, first at 314 Rush Street, then at 122 First Avenue.

And there is the significant but less than conclusive evidence that London and Chaney resembled each other quite closely in the physical sense, and shared certain traits of mind, personality and temperament — an appetite for controversy, a readiness with the fists, an intense interest in the mystic and esoteric, a weakness for pseudoscientific theory (Chaney's for astrology, London's for the racial doctrines of Nietzsche). Both had literary talent, though that is rarely an inherited characteristic. Both had wanderlust. Both were sexual anarchists. The parallels are, in fact, both impressive and suggestive.

Chaney probably was London's father. No one will ever know for sure unless one day a neglected attic in Chicago yields up a deathbed confession by a certain star-crossed astrologer.

Even in the most impeccable sources Jack London is generally identified as an Irishman, or half-Irishman, with all the wild and romantic traits often ascribed to the race. This is based on the belief that Chaney, as his presumed father, was Irish. Actually there wasn't a drop of Irish blood in Chaney's veins. Chaney, like most Down-East Yankees, was of English descent on both sides of his house.

Any Celtic influence on Jack London's temperament came from his mother, whose antecedents were Welsh. Though much more is known about her later years than Chaney's, the woman herself remains something of an enigma. Chaney complained of her hot temper and wayward passions; her son would be repelled by her cold indifference, her determined effort to make him feel unwanted. Little that people could remember of her contributed toward a full-length portrait with depth and perspective.

Perhaps much that was good in her, much that would have defined her as a human being, was lost or congealed in her flight from her own home, the shame and notoriety attending her only child's birth, the incessant struggle and privation of her life after that. The one thing she held firmly to, her beacon as astrology was Chaney's, was Spiritualism. As late as 1910, when she was sixty-four years old, she told a San Francisco *Call* reporter about receiving visits from her late husband during séances. "His visits have been visual. I have not only felt his presence, but have seen him distinctly as well."

Flora Wellman was born in Massillon, Ohio, on August 17, 1843, with every expectation of leading a sheltered and comfortable life. Her father, Marshall D. Wellman, was the local tycoon. He and his brother Hiram B. Wellman made their fortunes during the canal-building boom. Later, in the heyday of the Ohio Canal, they bought and stored large quantities of grain, giving Massillon the title of the "Wheat City," and were the leading merchants. The Wellman brothers also prospered through the invention of various domestic appliances, including the Wellman coal grate.

Both Wellmans built stately homes in the 1830's. Marshall's seventeen-room mansion at Main and Prospect Streets was a showplace long after adversity compelled him to seek more modest quarters, and it was not torn down until 1954.

During the financial upheaval of the 1850's, however, both brothers failed in business, according to a regional historian,[7] and after that the Wellmans lived on a less grand but still respectable scale. Their mansion was deeded to a bank receiver in 1859, and the local paper in September, 1863, referred to Marshall Wellman as a "former influential citizen." About all he had left was the royalties from the manufacture of the Wellman coal grate.

Flora was in her early teens when her father lost his fortune, but there was still sufficient income to give her all the advantages proper for a young lady of breeding, piano and elocution lessons, frocks from New York, tutors, and all the books she wanted.

Her four older sisters married and settled into comfortable middle-class lives, but Flora was the family rebel, and spoiled in the bargain. Very early in life she learned to dominate others by flying into rages and throwing tantrums. The fact that she was the youngest encouraged the family's indulgence, particularly since her mother, Eleanor Jones Wellman, the daughter of a circuit-riding preacher known as Priest Jones, died during her infancy. Her father remarried when she was four years old, and Flora seized upon this as a possibility for further emotional blackmail. Her stepmother was a kindly and sympathetic woman easily bullied by the demanding child. Flora, as a result, got everything she needed but discipline.

Throughout her life, thanks to an overly indulgent father and a stepmother naturally on the defensive, she applied the lessons of her childhood and got what she wanted through displays of temper. Self-centered, willful and domineering, she successfully bullied her husband, her son, her stepchildren — the only one who refused to be dominated was "Professor" Chaney, who simply walked out when she threw a tantrum.

Her employment of hysteria as an instrument of power apparently began when she suffered an attack of typhoid fever early in her girlhood. The fever was so severe that she almost died. It resulted in stunting her growth (as an adult she was two or three inches under five feet), ruining her eyesight and causing her hair to fall out, with traumatic effects on an already disturbed emotional system. Pitying her, the family abandoned all efforts to apply the checkrein. Resenting their pity, she used it to get her own way.

In 1851, when she was eight years old, the Abby Warner case, involving a young medium's public demonstration of her talent and something of a cause célèbre in the history of Spiritualism in America, caused an uproar in the community. It occurred just at the time that various forms of mysticism were beginning to grip the country. Northern Ohio was not slow in succumbing. Among the pioneer stock which settled across the Alleghenies, practical though the settlers were in displacing the Indians and carving out their homesteads, there was a dark absorption with hocus-pocus that ill accorded with their nominal Christianity. The Western Reserve, as that section was known, was anything but impervious to whispers from another world. In nearly every Ohio town there were "spirit rooms" where local devotees could congregate and listen in on the "spiritual telegraph," defying the thunder from nearby pulpits.

Spiritualism made considerable inroads in Massillon, with its followers gathering nightly for communion with the departed. One of the enthusiasts was the Widow Kellogg, who was caring for an orphan named Abby Warner, then about eighteen years old. Abby had suffered from neglect, could neither read nor write, and was believed to be subnormal mentally. Her one talent was serving as a bridge to the spirit world. According to Dr. Abel Underhill, "Abby Warner often gave at her circles three separate communications at once, one with her right, and another with her left hand, and a third through the rappings; these were well-written and correctly phrased." [8] Abby's talent as a medium attracted so much attention that a Dr. Ackley of Cleveland, under commission from the local poorhouse, which more or less supervised the care of orphans, examined Abby and recommended a brain operation to remove such tendencies. All dabbling in Spiritualism, added Dr. Ackley, who apparently believed that surgery was the best corrective for nonconformity, was a "profound humbug."

To demonstrate Abby's powers in the most dramatic way, his nonconforming colleague, Dr. Underhill, took Abby, along with members of his own family, to the services at St. Timothy's Episcopal Church on Christmas Eve, 1851. The congregation was soon disturbed by rappings in the pew occupied by Dr. Underhill and his protégé.

They continued despite a plea from the altar that "these knockings might cease." When the congregation began singing, the rappings beat time to the music. So far as people in the neighboring pews could observe, the rat-a-tat emanated from Abby's presence but not directly from her, for she kept her hands folded primly in her lap. The Christmas Eve service ended in a hubbub.

Next day Abby was arrested on charges of having "disturbed a Christian assembly in the solemn act of public worship." Two days later her trial began before Justice of the Peace R. H. Folger and attracted such crowds that the proceedings had to be transferred to Welker's Hall. Abby pleaded not guilty, maintaining she had no control over the spirits who manifested themselves through her. "Not a single witness," reported the Cleveland *Plain Dealer* on December 28, 1851, "could be found who could swear that they perceived the slightest movement in the accused party." After a three-day trial, Justice Folger dismissed the charges against the girl on the grounds that "the true source of this disturbance cannot be ascertained." Which tended to confirm the claims of the Spiritualists. Abby Warner's exhibition in St. Timothy's succeeded in "planting Spiritualism in almost every household on the Western Reserve," according to Emma Hardinge. One of those households was Marshall Wellman's, whose youngest daughter was greatly impressed by Abby Warner's fame. Flora Wellman had always insisted on being the center of attention, had marked tendencies toward self-dramatization, and in a later generation would probably have attempted a theatrical career. Instead she found an outlet for her dramatic instincts in the séance.

At the age of sixteen Flora ran away from home and lived with each of her married sisters in turn. During the Civil War, she later told her granddaughters, she attended many balls and was eagerly sought as a dancing partner. Yet she never married, and perhaps for that reason stayed away from Massillon, rather than have her family and friends cluck sympathetically over her spinsterhood. She earned her keep by giving piano lessons. Apparently she returned home for a time when she was in her late twenties, but to the scandal of Main Street she suddenly left in 1871 and went out into the world on her own. A serious dispute with her parents was the probable cause, for girls in that mid-Victorian day, at least not the daughters of respectable households, simply didn't venture away from home on their own. Her departure, at any rate, caused almost as much gossip in Massillon as Abby Warner's visit to St. Timothy's.

Whatever the reason, the break with her family was final. She never saw or wrote to her father and stepmother or her sisters again, nor did they communicate with her. She never told her son why she left home. The story she gave her granddaughters was that she accompanied an older woman to the Coast as her traveling companion.

Late in 1871 she turned up in Seattle, where she supported herself by giving piano lessons. A year later she decided Seattle was too dull for her and left for San Francisco and her meeting with "Professor" Chaney.

After they set up light housekeeping, she often took tickets at the door when he lectured at Charter Oak Hall or before the Philomatheans, a group of freethinkers with offbeat intellectual interests. From all appearances she was in love with the stocky little charmer, despite almost a quarter-century's difference in their ages, and she would probably have stayed with him if he had not been so experienced a hand at dealing with difficult women. Her suicide attempt, half-hearted or faked though it might have been, was proof of her desire to hang on to him at all costs.*

The months before Flora gave birth were spent in the home of W. N. Slocum and his wife Amanda at 615 Third Street, where Jack London was born.† Mrs. Slocum worked for a publishing company while her husband was a reporter for the San Francisco *Bulletin*. When she first met them, the Slocums were editing *Common Sense*, a periodical devoted to social and political reform, free thought, free love, women's suffrage and the labor movement. Chaney himself had contributed to *Common Sense* and probably had introduced her to the Slocums. Had it not been for their stanch and tolerant friendship, Flora's son would have been born in a charity ward.

* Chaney, in a pamphlet he published defending himself against Flora's charges, claimed that an investigating detective reported that the gun she used smelled of oil rather than burnt powder and that there were no powder burns on her face, and suggested she had gouged her forehead with a glass or metal splinter to simulate a bullet wound.

† The house was destroyed in the earthquake and fire of thirty years later.

3. *"So All the World Could See"*

The hungers, the passions, the aspirations and contradictions of Jack London, reflected as they were in every aspect of his personal and professional life, were deeply rooted in the troubled times that produced him. There are people you can imagine living in any age or place from Justinian's Constantinople to Hitler's Berlin without any essential changes in personality; people born to stand on the sidelines, salute and cheer when they are told. London was always too alive, sensitive and questioning to be anything but a man of his time. What it was stamped him indelibly. His life began and ended in a period of transition, the change from frontier and farm to city and factory. It was a time of ferment and upheaval, as the country struggled to adjust socially, economically and culturally to the facts of national life. In everything he wrote and everything he was, London reflected that turbulence, beneath which was the gnawing suspicion that a country as rich and energetic as the United States ought to be able to produce a better life for the submerged portion of its people.

The city of his birth was as deeply affected by that continuing upheaval as any, perhaps more than any other. It was, in many ways, the capital of the passing frontier. It has always been in the vanguard, the city most likely to reflect social change; its millionaires have always been the most spectacular, its labor leaders the fieriest, its artists (from the Bay Window Bohemia of the Nineties to the North Beach of the Fifties) the most fashionably disheveled. It was and is a volatile city, a quality fittingly conveyed by its best known writer.

San Francisco was just breaking through its geographic shell when London was born. Until a half-dozen years before his birth, it had endured in semi-isolation, reachable from other parts of the country only by steamer, via Panama, or overland by stage through hundreds of miles of Indian country. Then, at Promontory Point, Utah, the rails of the Central Pacific and Union Pacific were joined on May 10, 1869, opening the floodgates of migration from the East. Real estate boomed in San Francisco as promoters claimed the city would attain the million mark in population by 1880. Initially, however, their hopes were deflated. Not only was there no influx from the East, but the city's commercial life suffered a decline because Eastern goods consigned to the interior, which had formerly come by water for transshipment, now were sent directly overland by rail to their destination.

The most striking thing about San Francisco in those several years before London was born — and after it, for that matter — was the contrast between the very rich on Nob Hill and the "work beasts," as London was to call them, in the wooden-frame tenements terraced below. "The 1870's had brought a new silver splendor to San Francisco," as the city's social historian Julia Cooley Altrocchi has written, "overlaying its earlier gold, yielding more resplendent houses, costumes, jewels, manners, displays, entertainments." [9] But underneath this gorgeous silverplating there were grimy layers of resentment and class hatred. Even Gilded Age New York couldn't outdo San Francisco in the matter of excess.

Business life early in the Seventies was dominated by feverish speculation in silver stocks. The value of such mining issues shot up from $17,000,000 in January of 1872 to $81,000,000 in May of the same year. During the next month the bears got busy, sent silver stocks crashing and wiped out $60,000,000 in paper profits. This frightening collapse was quickly forgotten when the Comstock Lode, a Nevada mining property valued at less than $100,000 in 1871, developed into a $150,000,000 bonanza in 1873. Speculation now heightened from the merely feverish to the frantic. An estimated hundred millionaires sprang up overnight like mushrooms in wet woods. While ninety-five per cent of the population worked twelve hours a day just to fend off the landlord and the grocer, the city sprouted a garish crop of the newly rich classified as Bonanza Millionaires, the like of which would never be seen again, ex-miners and ex-laundresses displaying themselves in lordly mansions and formal gardens. There was a certain naïve charm in the way they encrusted themselves with possessions and competed in showing them off. A Chicago millionaire who wanted to gain social recognition built a college, as one sharp-eyed observer noted, but "when a San Franciscan gets to be immensely wealthy he builds a palace of a stable with marble halls, Brussels carpets and hot and cold water in every stall." [10]

Then came the panic of '73, spreading west from the New York Stock Exchange and bringing with it the tides of migration which had been expected several years earlier, 36,000 new residents in 1873 increasing to 64,000 in 1875. In mid-1875 the shock waves of economic depression finally reached San Francisco in full force; the market value of Comstock shares dropped $42,000,000 in one week, $100,000,000 by the end of the year. The Bank of California, believed impregnable, closed its doors. A promising diamond-mine boom collapsed with the discovery that the supposed field in Colorado had been salted. Half the Bonanza Millionaires lost their money, shirtsleeves to shirtsleeves in three or four years.

The working classes, which had not shared to any appreciable extent in the prosperity, were now commanded to commiserate with their employers by taking wage cuts of forty to sixty per cent. Bitterly unsympathetic, the workers began turning back to the trade unions organized shortly after the Civil War but allowed to wither away during the years since. Soon they made San Francisco one of the strongest labor cities in the country, with nearly all trades unionized and a spirit of militancy rising. Their animus was divided almost equally between the nabobs on the crests of the city and the 116,000 Chinese who formed a pool of cheap unorganized labor.

What promised to be a torch in the tinderbox, with the depression becoming more severe every year, was the self-propelled career of a picturesque Irish agitator named Dennis Kearney, now tenderly regarded as one of the city's authentic originals but then a mob-rouser of unequaled power. Still-wealthy men huddled in their libraries, recalling how the Communards had taken over the streets of Paris only a few years ago and waiting for the revolution to lap against their thresholds; Kearney inflamed his mass meetings every Sunday and led his followers on marches up Nob Hill as an after-piece. Charles Crocker, the railroad magnate, kept a rack of Springfields in his entry hall and proclaimed his intention of shooting Kearney the moment he came through the door.

Kearney threatened to "lynch and burn out the thieving millionaires, the hell-born, the hell-bound villains, the bloated bondholders," by which he meant such magnificoes as Huntington, Hearst, Mills, Crocker, Stanford, Hopkins.

Kearney was a terrific showman, a demagogue and above all an opportunist. He generally led his marches on horseback, pausing at street corners to deliver orations from the saddle. San Francisco's privileged class felt the hot breath of revolution on its collective neck. The sight of those brawny draymen, dock workers, steamfitters, coal heavers and ditchdiggers marching under the bow windows of Nob Hill only lent credence to Kearney's shouted slogans that "The Chinese Must Go" and "Judge Lynch Will Decide the Fate of Capitalism."

Then Kearney, carried away by his own oratory or inflamed by the hope that the thudding feet of his marchers were causing the foundations of capitalism to tremble, went a little too far in suggesting how his Workingmen's Party should finish off the job. He urged his followers to arm themselves with a rifle and a hundred rounds of ammunition each in preparation for Der Tag, proposed that bundles of dynamite sticks be dropped from balloons on Chinatown, that members of the State Legislature be hanged, and "disloyal [by which he meant fainthearted] members of the Workingmen's Party be suspended from the nearest lamp posts."

Many of his followers began to develop symptoms of faintheartedness despite his bluster. The Workingmen's Party split on the issue of how far it should go in asserting its rights and Kearney, disgusted at his followers' lack of spirit, went east to attempt the organization of a national party in 1878. When that failed, he tried to lead his followers into the shortlived Greenback Labor Party. The Workingmen's Party eventually merged with the Socialist Labor movement, a power in state politics for many years afterward. One of the main props of Kearney's program was shattered by the passage of the Exclusion Act of 1882, which shut off further Chinese immigration. Kearney himself was involved in scandals over his handling of party funds and his curious reputation as a big spender in capitalistic fleshpots.

The fire-eating demagogue who once made the city tremble at the crashing boots of his Sunday protest marchers was reduced to the point of merely proposing to elect honest men and lower the tax rates, "a remedy," as Henry George, then reading gas meters in San Francisco and working on *Progress and Poverty*, commented, "which belongs to the same category as the recipe for catching a bird by sprinkling salt on its tail."

Kearney had succumbed to the corruption which he had pledged himself to destroy, but in the mid-Seventies, when he was at the peak of his influence over the working class, his ardent spirit helped to create the atmosphere in which Jack London was raised and which permeated much of what he wrote.

The first problem which confronted Flora Wellman after the birth of her son was finding a man to support herself and her child. A good steady man, rather than an elusive metaphysician, was what she needed. To ensnare an honest provider Flora had little to offer in the way of physical charm. At thirty-three, illness and sorrow had left her few vestiges of youth. Her features were too large, almost those of a jack-o'-lantern; her complexion was puttylike, and she wore a black wig with sausage curls falling over her forehead to cover the baldness caused by the childhood attack of typhoid. Her disposition was erratic at best. Further it was widely known that the son she bore was illegitimate, even among those who might have missed the newspaper stories, because she had recited her grievances at Spiritualist meetings, big with child, while collections were raised to "help this poor little woman."

Inevitably the man she attracted was a widower with his own problems, some of which would be solved by a wife who could care for his motherless children. The man was John London, a native of Pennsylvania, a soldier in the Union Army, a farmer in Iowa, a sheriff, a section boss on the Erie, and many other things, but primarily a farmer who had come west looking for an easier life. He was in his middle forties, a gentle, rather ineffectual, even-tempered man with an apronlike beard and mild blue eyes. In the New West of shrewd, aggressive exploiters, he was not the man to make his fortune, would always be a marginal wage-earner, but he would do. He was available and he needed a wife. Until he met Flora, he had been living in a rooming house while supporting his two surviving daughters in the Protestant Orphan Asylum. Neither was in a position to be too particular.

So the match was made, and on September 7, 1876, eight months after the birth of her son, Flora married John London. She signed herself as Flora Chaney on the marriage certificate, and with that the name of the footloose "Professor" was dropped from the family history. Her son was given the name of John Griffith London.

His mother ignored him as much as possible; understandable, if not commendable, since she hated the man she claimed was his father, and the child was, as contemporary melodrama had it, her "badge of shame." Her maternal instinct, if it ever existed, had shriveled to the vanishing point. A Negro wet nurse named Mrs. Jenny Prentiss, who had recently lost her own baby, assumed one part of Flora's maternal duties, and eventually became one of the few sound feminine influences in his life. Mammy Jenny, as she was called, provided him with more than mother's milk. A large coal-black woman, with a warm and generous heart, she gave him the love his own mother could not supply. All through his life she was to be the woman he could cling to. Wherever the Londons moved in the Bay area, Mammy Jenny followed of her own volition to be near her "white child."

John London's elder daughter, Eliza, who was eight years old at the time of her father's marriage, also mothered the boy and looked after him.

While her stepdaughter and Mammy Jenny took over her responsibilities, Flora practiced the piano and trotted around to Spiritualist meetings, escaping into a world of table-rappings and spectral voices. For a time John London worked fairly steadily as a carpenter, then as a door-to-door salesman for the Singer Sewing Machine Company. The Londons took in a boarder, and the money he paid in was used to employ a Chinese servant, thus relieving Flora of all duties around the house. Obviously, at this stage, she wasn't much of a bargain for the man who married her. Both Johnny and his stepsister Eliza contracted diphtheria during an epidemic, and it looked for a time as though they would die. Flora, as Eliza later recalled, asked the attending physician whether it wouldn't be possible to bury both children in one coffin to save expenses.

Nothing seemed to pan out for the earnest, hard-working but luckless John London. When people stopped buying sewing machines as the depression grew more severe, he moved his family across the Bay to Oakland. He opened a grocery store at Seventh and Peralta Streets, with the family occupying the four rooms behind the store. For a time the enterprise prospered as London daily traveled to the farms and ranches outside Oakland to buy fresh fruits and vegetables and sell them a little cheaper than stores which depended on the wholesale market. Flora finally shouldered some of the family burdens and waited on customers in the store while her husband was out on his buying expeditions. Things went so well that Flora, who never could resist a smooth-talking slicker, persuaded her husband that they could do even better by taking in a partner and enlarging the store. The partner took charge of the till while London continued to buy the fruits and vegetables that were the basis of their success. One day, however, London returned from the country to find that his glib partner had skipped out with all the establishment's liquid assets, as well as selling the entire stock and fixtures.

Johnny, later Jack, always remembered one incident of those early years of his life and related it to his second wife as a warning against female hysteria. It was the one feminine tendency, he said, that he couldn't abide, because his mother had often inflicted her hysterics on the family. When he was three years old, he recalled, he came into the house with a flower he had picked and held it out to his mother. "I was brushed aside, kicked over, by an angry rebellious woman striding her egomaniacal way." He was too young to understand that he had been victimized by one of his mother's moods, and would never forget how he had been wounded by the incident. Until then, he said, he had believed that Flora was "the most wonderful woman in the world" because "she said so herself."

He was four years old when disaster struck the family grocery business and his stepfather, necessarily with Flora's approval, decided to quit the city in favor of farming a twenty-acre ranch outside Alameda. London was a diligent and experienced farmer and made a success of truck gardening for the Oakland market. The trouble was that Flora apparently had inherited something of her father's entrepreneur leanings, fancied herself a shrewd businesswoman and insisted on handling the money. Some of John London's hard-earned money was invested in Chinese lottery tickets. Her advice in financial matters, she declared, came from spirits summoned at séances she held several nights a week with a group of disciples gathered hand in hand in the London parlor.

There was a definitively Dickensian flavor to Jack London's recollections of the years he spent in the country, where life was just as bleak, though it was possibly healthier than in the streets of Oakland. Even Dickens might have hesitated to invent such a strange character as his mother. Often she pressed him into service as an aid to summoning the spirits at her séances and he would be placed on a table surrounded by Flora and her fellow believers as ghostly lights filled the room and disembodied voices spoke, allegedly, from the beyond. The effect on a five-year-old's nervous system may be imagined. The boy would fly into tantrums or fits of weeping, suffered from bowel trouble, brooded in corners and otherwise exhibited all the symptoms of a child deprived of maternal love. Flora ignored all those distress signals, too self-centered to care much about what might be troubling her son. Her attitude was that he was simply a willful child who must not be spoiled by paying any attention to his moods. It didn't contribute to domestic serenity that Flora when displeased would pretend to suffer a heart attack, usually at the dinner table, until she got her own way. At such times her husband, her son and two stepdaughters were required to gather around the couch to which they carried her and listen to predictions that her unappreciative family would be the death of her. Not surprisingly, she outlived the son of whose unfilial neglect she complained to the end of her days.

Of his early years London recalled in a biographical sketch prepared for his first publisher, Houghton Mifflin: "My life, from my fourth to my ninth years, was spent upon California ranches. I learned to read and write about my fifth year, though I do not remember anything about it. I always could read and write, and have no recollections antedating such a condition. Folks say I simply insisted upon being taught. I was an omnivorous reader, principally because reading matter was scarce and I had to be grateful for whatever fell into my hands."

In 1881 he was enrolled at the West End School in Alameda, located on ground now occupied by the Alameda Air Base. Life on a California ranch, he said, was not "very nourishing" to the imagination. Nor was there much effort in the back-country schools to kindle a love of learning.

A year later he changed schools when the family moved again, down the foggy peninsula to a farm near San Mateo. Here they spent two years on a larger place, seventy-five acres, on which John London raised horses and vegetables. His stepson always remembered it as a desolate period, lighted only by the few books available, which he read over and over again. These included Horatio Alger's *From Canal Boy to President*, a biography of President Garfield; Washington Irving's *Alhambra;* Paul du Chaillu's *African Travels,* and Ouida's *Signa,* as well as pulp stuff detailing the adventures of "poor but virtuous shopgirls." He was so impressed by Irving's book that he built an Alhambra of his own from bricks fallen from a chimney, with towers and terraces and chalked inscriptions. He was convinced that "there were only two clever people in the world — Washington Irving and myself."

There was little else to cheer him along the "bleak sad coast" on which the farm was located. Occasionally he and Eliza would gather clams and mussels on the rocky, fogbound beaches nearby. He had no playmates. Eliza was eight years older and usually occupied with household chores.

His other stepsister, Ida, was a more cheerful sort than the dutiful Eliza, but she was sent out to work at a tender age. A city directory listed her as "Ida London, laundress, Contra Costa Laundry." [11] She played a much less prominent part in Jack London's later life than Eliza.

Jack's daughter Joan remembers Ida as "a warm-hearted, loving person with a gift of laughter that could override her cares — a full-blown woman in those days when overweight was not frowned upon. I think she may have been pretty as a girl. She grew up (and lived all of her life) in the shadow of her energetic, domineering older sister whose quick, shrewd mind compensated for her lack of education . . . Our group of Londons — Flora, my mother and Mrs. Prentiss — always spoke of Ida with loving pity: 'Poor Ida,' they would say, 'but she never hurt anyone but herself.'" She drifted outside the family circle for some years, and when she reappeared it was with an infant in her arms.

Jack's daytimes, spent in a one-room schoolhouse on a hilltop near Colma, were no escape from rural dreariness. The schoolmaster was a drunkard whom the older boys would set upon and thrash when he was under the weather. In retaliation, the teacher would beat the younger and weaker boys.

Already he was conscious of the mysterious shadow on his birth. When he was six years old, as he recalled in notes for an autobiography he never quite got around to writing, he overheard a quarrel between his mother and his stepfather — whom he then believed to be his father and always loved as a father — about the circumstances of his birth. London reproached his wife for having borne a child out of wedlock. His mother wept and tried to defend herself on the grounds that "Professor" Chaney had promised her an easy life and she had been young and gullible enough to believe him.

Later came the gibes of his schoolmates, who apparently learned of his illegitimacy from overhearing their elders.

What he called the "clear, white light of alcohol" exercised an early fascination, as he recollected in *John Barleycorn*.* The first time he fell under its influence, he recalled, was when he was five years old. He had been sent with a lard pail to fetch beer for his stepfather, who was working in the fields. Rushing the growler, as it was called, gave him the idea of trying the beer himself. He took a number of swigs on the way back and by the time he reached his stepfather he was staggering. London gulped down the beer and continued with his plowing. His stepson stumbled after him, fell between the horse's hoofs and the plowshare, and would have been disemboweled if London hadn't snatched him away in time.

Two years later, when he was seven, he went to a party on a neighboring ranch attended by the Irish and Italian youth of the neighborhood, most of them older than he was. His mother had warned him that the "brunette races" were treacherous and would "stab you in the back" if you gave them half a chance, but he let his guard down among the merry Latins and bibulous Celts. An Italian boy persuaded him to join in drinking the wine that was being passed around. Glad to be the center of attention, he drank several tumblers of the sour red wine. On his way home he fell into a ditch. An Italian girl about his own age who had tried to protect him from the bucolic humor of the gathering, hauled him to his feet and helped him to his door.

All through his childhood, as he remembered it, he felt the "shame of being poor." Actually the Londons were no poorer than most of their neighbors, and better off than many. Perhaps it was his reading that convinced him that most other people led more comfortable and gracious lives than his family. At any rate it was the most insistent theme of his recollections, the barrenness and poverty of his childhood.

One of his sharpest memories was being given a store-bought undershirt when he was eight years old. Its value lay in that it had actually been bought for him, rather than handed down or fashioned from an old flour sack. He was so proud of it that he insisted on wearing it

* A partly autobiographical tract against liquor, particularly as it affected his own life, published in 1913 to the great delight of the Prohibition movement.

without a shirt. "For the first time I mutinied against my mother—mutinied myself into hysteria, until she let me wear the store undershirt so all the world could see." [12]

In those six words were the summation of his career as a writer, for in book after book he figuratively held up that pathetic little undershirt "so all the world could see." He never escaped those childhood memories, branded so much deeper on the psyche of a sensitive and perceptive child than those of his thicker-skinned fellows. Very early in life he found what was to be the central figure of his work. As with many writers of stature, it was himself.

4. *A Gentle Poetess*

When Jack was ten years old, the London family moved back to Oakland, never again to return to country living. Yet another rural venture had failed, an eighty-seven-acre ranch at Livermore, where John London worked hard for two years at a more diversified kind of farming, with a row of olive trees, a vineyard and fruit trees, in addition to raising produce for the Oakland and San Francisco markets. Those two years, the boy's seventh to ninth, were no happier than the preceding ones. His stepfather was still the mild, passive, tolerant man who yielded to Flora's neurotic demands, her simulated heart attacks and her domineering ways. The boy did succeed in growing closer, more sympathetic to John London during those years, following his stepfather into the fields and learning all he could about scientific farming methods. Farming was the one thing at which the elder London was effective, sure and capable, and from him the boy absorbed the dream of an agricultural paradise, where only the finest crops grew and the sturdiest livestock was bred, which years later was to lead him into the Valley of the Moon.

They might have prospered on the Livermore ranch, if John London had been allowed to proceed at his own pace, but there was always Flora and her schemes for getting ahead faster. She insisted that they must switch to raising chickens, having bustled over to San Francisco and made arrangements with a hotel manager who agreed to buy all the eggs and chickens London could supply. Even this might have worked out if it hadn't been necessary to lay out a considerable sum for coops and brooders. London had to mortgage the ranch; a short time later he was unable to make the interest payments, and the bank foreclosed.

So the Londons trekked back to the city, now minus Eliza, who, still in her teens, had married a middle-aged widower with three children and established her own home.

At ten Jack London was a rather silent, ingrowing boy well aware of the constant tension between his parents, of their struggle for existence; dimly conscious of something shameful about his birth, which made him shy and hesitant; his imagination rubbed raw by his mother's obsession with the spirit world and harrowed by the morbid sessions in the family parlor. A photograph taken of him at that age shows a sturdy enough lad with a mop of curly light-brown hair, a sensitive mouth, large blue eyes, and something tremulous, almost haunted, about his features.

The Londons rented two cottages near the California Cotton Mills in which they lodged and boarded about twenty girls brought over from Scotland and entrusted to the care of the mill owner. Flora managed the two houses, quite capably for a time, while John London took care of the marketing and maintenance.

The ten-year-old Jack, attending the Garfield School and learning to hold his own in schoolyard fights, made the discovery of his young life. It was the Oakland Public Library, where thousands of books were to be obtained for the asking. A new world opened up for him as it did for many other poor boys of his generation. No one has quite managed to pay sufficient tribute to the free-library system in the United States, particularly in the years when it sustained and gave hope to millions who had to leave school early and go to work. Jack, like many boys, found his university there.

Years later when he was a weary and jaded author something of the wonder of his discovery came back to him as he recalled that "on the shelves of the Free Library I discovered all the great world beyond the skyline." Here, he said, he found thousands of books as fascinating as those volumes of Irving, Alger, Ouida and du Chaillu he had read until they were tattered. "I read everything, but principally history and adventure, and all the old travels and voyages. I read mornings, afternoons and nights. I read in bed, I read at table, I read as I walked to and from school, and I read at recess while the other boys were playing . . ." [13]

Here in the cool dark interior of the Oakland Public Library, hidden among the bookshelves that towered above him, he found a refuge and a sanctuary, his first real home, his first intimation of a greater splendor beyond the dingy horizon of tenement roofs and factory smokestacks. He would explore other escape hatches from reality — women, drink, sport, travel, wars foreign and domestic — but none so satisfactory.

He would travel along the stacks caressing the bindings like some lascivious old bibliophile, stagger to the lending desk with an armload of books heavy enough to founder, physically and intellectually, someone twice his age.

That was how the head librarian, Miss Ina Coolbrith, saw him the first time, bright blue eyes peering over a stack of books.

Twenty years later he wrote the lady as a world-famous author to let her know how everlastingly grateful he was for her friendship and guidance. No other woman had ever affected him as she did, he said; she was a goddess to him as a child. He recalled that she had been the first person ever to praise him for his choice of reading matter, that the first time she spoke to him he had just taken out a book about Pizarro's conquest of Peru, and how proud he still was of that praise.[14]

Miss Coolbrith was a considerable personage, poet laureate of California, friend and associate of Mark Twain and Bret Harte in their San Francisco days, hostess of a literary salon in her Russian Hill apartment across the Bay. Although she is now chiefly remembered as the early mentor of Jack London rather than as a creative artist in her own right, she was just gracious enough, possessed of just that touch of self-effacing nobility, to be inordinately pleased by it. Through the eighty-five years of her life, as Oscar Lewis has written, she "wielded an influence on western letters that went far beyond her own writings . . . she had the faculty of gathering about her young men and women of talent and by tactful, sagacious counsel spurring them on to their best work." [15]

At the time London first knew her she was in her early forties, an attractive woman with candid gray eyes and classic features. Her verse, which had an austerity uncommon to poetesses of the day, had been widely published ever since she came to San Francisco during the Civil War. Born in Illinois, the daughter of Don Carlos Smith, a son of Joseph Smith, the founder of the Mormon Church, she was brought

West by her widowed mother in the first wagon train to cross the Sierra. At seventeen she married Robert Carsley in Los Angeles, but was divorced three years later. After that she adopted her mother's maiden name, and it didn't become known until after her death that she had ever been anything but Miss Coolbrith, that she was the granddaughter of the notorious or sainted Joseph Smith. Much as she concealed from the world in apparent distrust — perhaps caused by searing childhood memories of the persecution of the Mormons during their agonizing trek westward — she was remembered as a gay, high-spirited young woman generally surrounded by male admirers. But she never remarried. Beneath her composed exterior, undoubtedly, she bore psychological scars that made her all the more sensitive to a troubled boy like Jack London, all the more eager to help him.

Her days of glory came just after the Civil War when the *Overland Monthly* was founded with Charles Warren Stoddard, Bret Harte and herself presiding over its fortunes. They formed such a tight little clique that envious outsiders called them the "Golden Gate Trinity." Thanks to the eminence enjoyed by the *Overland* almost from its first issue, she knew and worked with such men as Prentice Mulford, John Muir, Mark Twain and Joaquin Miller. The *Overland* suspended publication for several years after Harte went east but was revived in the mid-1880's. Miss Coolbrith also contributed to the *Argonaut*, another of the Coast's lively literary journals, and for a time was the protégé of Ambrose Bierce, the periodical's star columnist.

In 1874, weary of the chancy literary game, she migrated across the Bay and assumed the head librarian's post in Oakland. Twelve years later Jack London first peered warily over his books at her. It was the beginning of an oddly balanced but very real friendship and tutelage that lasted until 1893, when she left her post at the library.

At first she helped him to find out what interested him most, stories of action and adventure, hazardous sea voyages, accounts of travel in far places. Gently, without pressing it, she interested him in other sectors of human experience. He began taking home with him the novels of Flaubert, Melville, Tolstoy and Dostoevsky. By the time he was twelve or thirteen he was as well educated, in a purely literary way, as most college graduates. His reading gave him something more than simply a literary education — the hope, the determination to find a better life than existed in the factory workers' section of Oakland.

He and Miss Coolbrith rarely saw each other after she left the library, when he was seventeen, but he always credited her with having guided his self-education.

5. *Boy Breadwinner*

In the 1880's prosperity returned to the cities of the Bay, sounder and more sensibly based than the silver boom of the previous decade. San Francisco was claiming its heritage as the commercial, financial, industrial and cultural center of the western third of the nation. The city passed the quarter-million mark in population and kept right on growing, with Oakland, always the little brother in its metropolitan shadow, sharing in the growth and prosperity to a lesser extent. Edwin Booth, Sir Henry Irving, Sarah Bernhardt, E. H. Sothern and Lawrence Barrett brought their companies to play in San Francisco, the only city west of the Rockies large enough to support more than a one-night stand. More wooden mansions, ornate with scrollwork, castellated to the last monstrous turret, sprang up on Nob Hill, which no longer quivered with the tramp of workingmen's boots on Sunday protest marches. Given a fairer shake for the time being, the wage-earners were drinking their beer on Sundays or taking their families on outings to the parks, the foothills and beaches.

In these comparatively easier times the Londons did not share, due more to Flora's mismanagement than her husband's chronic ill fortune. John London was something of a lost soul in the city; farming was what he knew and loved, but he did his best to keep his family solvent. Flora's waywardness as the family treasurer, however, cost them the two houses in which they boarded the Scottish mill girls. They had started to buy the houses from the landlord through mortgages arranged by a bank. Flora spent the income on something else; possibly her old weakness for the Chinese lottery had reasserted itself. When the mortgage installments fell due, they were unable to pay and were dispossessed.

Once more the family was adrift. They moved in and out of cottages at 411 Pine Street, 931 West Street, 1639 Twenty-second Avenue, always at the mercy of landlords demanding the rent money. They were decent enough small houses.[16] Most of them, in fact, are still standing and occupied by working-class families.

John London eventually found work as a night watchman on Davies wharf, with occasional daytime jobs swabbing the decks for members of the yacht club. Meanwhile, the eleven-year-old Jack had to bring home the money to keep food on the table.

He carried morning and evening newspaper routes before and after school, getting up while it was still dark to deliver the morning papers. Saturdays he worked as an iceman's apprentice, and Sundays he set up pins in a bowling alley. All these endeavors brought in about twenty dollars a month, which he turned over to Flora. On the side he was a hard-bitten trader in the picture cards given away with cigarettes and in postage stamps, minerals, marbles, bird's eggs and other curios — "thrifty and close-fisted," as he later characterized himself, neither of which qualities stayed with him during a notoriously open-handed manhood.

"I was famous as a trader. I was notorious as a miser. I could even make a junkman weep when I had dealings with him." [17] Other boys, recognizing his ferocity in making a deal, commissioned him to sell the junk they collected.

What he recalled most bitterly of those years on the Oakland streets was his constant hunger, particularly for meat. He could never seemingly get enough of it. In his last days, still haunted by that boyhood hunger, he continued to gorge himself on meat even when his physicians warned him that he was thereby killing himself.

Once as a schoolboy, he remembered, he stole a piece of meat from a girl's lunch basket. "I would have literally sold my birthright . . . for a piece of meat." When he saw his schoolmates throw away bits of meat sandwiches because they had eaten their fill, he could hardly prevent himself from pouncing on the scraps and eating them dirt and all.

Nor did he ever forget his disappointment when, as a newsboy, he was tempted to buy a hot tamale from a street vendor. All he knew about a tamale was that it had a core of ground meat inside the caked cornmeal; he had no idea the meat was spiced with chili and other condiments to which he was unaccustomed. He took one bite, felt the spice burning his mouth, and threw the tamale away in disgust. For years the memory of that wasted nickel irked him. Although he later grew fond of Mexican food, he could never eat another tamale.

At eleven he was a "work beast," and a hungry one, and an increasingly resentful one.

❦ II ❦

Man Among Men

1. *The Estuary and the Bay*

ESCAPE from drudgery, from the industrial slums and their crowded grimy streets, from the "pinch of poverty" in his home and the taunts of his fellows in the schoolyard was never very distant. A few blocks away, on the Oakland estuary, were the wharves and their constant traffic of whalers from the North Pacific, Chinese junks, Greek fishing boats, rust-flaked tramp steamers from every port in the seven seas, schooners from the South Sea trade, rows of houseboats, sloops and yawls and smaller craft. By the time he was thirteen Jack was frequenting the wharves, scrubbing decks and furling sails for yachtsmen, and learning how to handle boats.

"I never had a childhood," as he said and wrote many times in later life, but he had the wit and energy to find substitutes. At thirteen he graduated from grade school, and his parents decided that instead of attending high school he would have to find more work to supplement John London's inadequate income. He swept out the saloons at two of the local parks after busy Sundays, sold papers on the streets, hustled around after odd jobs of all kinds. The situation at home worsened when John London was seriously injured in a train accident and couldn't work. No landlord would trust the Londons, and young Jack couldn't bring in enough money for both rent and food. So they lived for months in a shack near the estuary.

Jack hoarded six dollars in pennies he held out from Flora to buy a battered old skiff, painted it, put a sail on it and oars in it, and began exploring the waters that opened out at the foot of Broadway into another world. He began sailing out of the estuary, into the bay, risking the rip tides and foul weather. A born sailor, he liked it best when the bay was rough and the winds gusty, when only his skill prevented the boat from capsizing or running aground.

At fifteen, with John London crippled and unable to provide for the family, he began working in a cannery near the estuary. There was no more time for sailing. As he labored at his machine he remembered with a bitter nostalgia recaptured years later in *John Barleycorn* all the sunrises and sunsets he would never see, the sweep of wind over the bay as it filled his skiff's sail, the sting of salt water in his nostrils and on his flesh, all the wild delights denied him. He worked a minimum of ten hours a day at ten cents an hour, often twelve or sixteen hours; once it was thirty-six hours at a stretch during the height of the canning season. Some months, by working all the overtime he could get, by denying himself all but a few hours sleep a night, he managed to bring fifty dollars home to Flora.

Somehow, determined as she was to get every last cent her son earned, even though she could afford to pay fifty cents a week to send out her washing rather than slave at the tubs herself, Flora found out that he had squirreled away five dollars which he wanted to spend on renovating his skiff. It had taken all of the fifteenth summer of his life to hoard that amount in pennies and nickels. Flora came to the cannery, stalked to the machine where he was working, and demanded the money he had held out on her. He handed it over without protest, perhaps a little guiltily, but that night he felt like killing himself. It was the first time he thought of suicide. If all that life promised was to be a "work beast," chained to his machine and his duty to his mother and stepfather, it wasn't worth the dreary effort.

What he feared most of all was that his spirit would be deadened, his mind would turn into the dull, hopeless vacuum he sensed behind the lusterless eyes of his fellow workers, and all his ambitions would be slowly killed. He had to save himself, even at the expense of his family. No one else would rescue him, or could even show him a way out of the trap.

A little honest ruthlessness was called for. He was strong enough and tough enough, he felt, to go out on his own. "At fifteen I was a man among men," he explained in a biographical sketch he wrote for the Macmillan Company in 1906, "and if I had a spare nickel I spent it on beer instead of candy, because I thought it was more manly to buy beer." He was determined to make his own living, and live for himself and by himself, on the water. "The adventure-lust was strong within me and I left home. I didn't run, I just left—went out on the bay . . ."

It wasn't quite that simple. He couldn't make a living at fishing for rock cod from his old skiff. He would need a craft more seaworthy and an occupation more lucrative.

What he had in mind was joining the oyster pirates, a hard-living polyglot band who raided the beds in the Lower Bay and sold their loot to peddlers and saloonkeepers at the markets behind the Oakland and San Francisco wharves the next morning. The oyster beds were privately owned and were guarded by the Fish Patrol, but at night the swift craft of the pirates slid in among the shoals and flats and looted them. It was a cutthroat business, you risked capture by the patrol or a knife in the back from one of your fellow thieves, but a nimble operator could make from thirty to fifty dollars a night. If you were caught stealing from the beds, you were liable to be convicted of a felony and sent to state prison. The penalty, to Jack, was not prohibitive. He reasoned that a prisoner had an easier life than a cannery worker. Nor did he consider himself too young; he had been fending for himself on the tough waterfront streets for several years and he accounted himself a better sailor than most men.

A man, even a fifteen-year-old man who had money in his pockets, could swagger into a saloon and be admired when he bought drinks for the house. Although he had been on the wagon since he was seven years old and got drunk on Italian wine, he had glimpsed the rowdy good fellowship behind the swinging doors. With a few dollars to set 'em up, he observed, you were treated like a prince; nobody asked to see your birth certificate, or sneered at your clothes, or made cracks about your dirty fingernails. It was a marvelous, if temporary, palliative for that gnawing sense of inferiority. "In the saloons life was different," as he noted in *John Barleycorn* in defining the attractions of drink. "Men talked with great voices, laughed great laughs and there was an atmosphere of greatness." For Jack London another escape hatch was opening, one that he would rarely shun in his lifetime.

2. *"Prince of the Oyster Pirates"*

An oyster pirate named French Frank, he heard, was willing to sell his tall-masted sloop for three hundred dollars. It was an inconceivable sum. His stepfather had never had that much money, in a lump sum, in all his life.

Who could he borrow it from? Well, who did he always turn to when he really needed help? Mrs. Jenny Prentiss, Mammy Jenny, who had nursed him. As usual she was living nearby, working steadily as a nurse, always available for "her white child."

He went to Mammy Jenny, asked her for the money — perhaps hinting at the desperation behind his appeal, or perhaps it wasn't necessary — and she gave it to him without question.

For what happened after he left Mammy Jenny's with three hundred dollars in twenty-dollar goldpieces clinking in his pocket, the only available testimony comes from London himself. There is no doubt that he became a pirate — or oyster thief, to put it more accurately — but there is a reasonable suspicion that his various accounts of those years when he was fifteen and sixteen assumed a romantic coloration in the telling. His inscription on a copy of *Tales of the Fish Patrol* (published in 1905) reads, "Find here, sometimes hinted, sometimes told, and sometimes made different, the days of my boyhood. . . ."

Straight away, he made a down payment on the sloop *Razzle Dazzle*, which was lying at anchor on the Alameda side of the estuary. French Frank took him below to meet some of his friends, who were gathered around a jug of wine. They included two sisters named Mamie and Tess, an oyster pirate named "Whiskey Bob" and another named "Spider" Healey. Spider was the *Razzle Dazzle*'s crew. The girl named Mamie was known as the "Queen of the Oyster Pirates," a rowdily amorous child of sixteen, who went with the boat, offering solace to whoever was its skipper. For three hundred dollars Jack would acquire a mistress, an employee, a sloop and an occupation. Also — as he later affirmed — he acquired the title "Prince of the Oyster Pirates" as consort of Mamie. At fifteen to be a pirate prince!

That day Jack drank wine and sang with his new friends. Queen Mamie took him on deck while the others were boozing below and made love to him. Later they all sat on deck and watched tugs scooting by, a sugar bark beating out to sea, schooners lined up waiting for the drawbridge to open. It must have been the greatest day of his young life.

In a short time he was involved in all the adventures he had dreamed of when he read Melville's South Sea novels and Captain Cook's accounts of his voyages. Without false modesty he would later recall that he was not the least daring of the oyster thieves who swooped down nightly on the shoals of the Lower Bay. In a matter of weeks, he claimed, he had become a waterfront legend — the youngest of the pirate skippers, the only one to have a female aboard, the bucko who brought in more stolen oysters than any other boat. He also told of how French Frank, regretting the bargain which deprived him not only of the *Razzle Dazzle* but the affectionate services of Mamie, tried to run him down in a schooner. Jack claimed he steered the *Razzle Dazzle* with his feet while keeping a double-barreled shotgun aimed at French Frank's wishbone and finally forcing him to sheer off. Quite a feat of seamanship. He also had to fight off other skippers who wanted to steal Mamie from him. He became noted, he said, for beating the other raiders back to the anchorage off Asparagus Island and getting his oysters first to the bustling Friday morning market. Once a rival set fire to his mainsail in the Upper Bay and he brought the *Razzle Dazzle* flying back under her jib.

None of these feats more solidified his popularity along the waterfront, or contributed more to his infant legend, than his openhanded swashbuckling in the saloons. He never drank while cruising around the bay, never thought of it, he said; but when the *Razzle Dazzle* was tied up, the night's skulduggery finished and the oysters sold, he headed for a saloon, often Johnny Heinhold's Last Chance, with the night's swag. Nothing so convincingly proved to himself that he was a man among men as bellying up to a bar and ordering drinks for such worthies as Joe Goose, Young Scratch, The Clam, Whiskey Bob, Big George and Nicky the Greek. Never mind that the back-slapping and the camaraderie were inspired by free drink, that his companions were thugs and ex-convicts who fought murderously among themselves out on the oyster beds, that most of them would stick a knife in his back for a sackful of shellfish. What counted at the moment was the admiration of his fellows and their awe at his generosity.[1]

Meanwhile he was also paying back Mammy Jenny the three hundred dollars he had borrowed from her and was taking money home to support his mother and stepfather, who apparently did not question the source of his sudden prosperity.

He would be gone for days at a time, but Flora did not concern herself about his disappearances. Sooner or later, she recalled for a San Francisco newspaperman years later, he would turn up, sometimes bruised and battered but nothing to get alarmed about. "I guess Jack was a pretty good boy when you come to figure it all out, but he fell in with bad company. He used to have terrible fights with the boys of the neighborhood. He got to going down to the waterfront. He became awfully bossy in the house. We couldn't stand him sometimes." [2]

No matter how diligently he glamorized the legend of his youth, he was simply the member of a band of petty criminals who committed burglary by boat. Undoubtedly it was more exciting than robbing a pea-patch or a pushcart. He and his fellows would sail out in a fog, approach the oyster beds as the tide was ebbing and leaving the shoals exposed, then walk across the beds picking oysters before the tide returned. In his recollections he managed to invest the wharf rats, free-lance whores and barflies of the Oakland waterfront with an aura of romance which compensated for the taunts of "bastard" and the shame he felt for his family's grinding poverty, particularly after they were forced to move into the shack near the estuary. This Bovaryism had become a psychological necessity.

There was no doubt that he was living dangerously as a member of a gang of seagoing delinquents and criminals. Some of his associates were killed or maimed in the knife, bottle and fist fights that broke out on the oyster beds or in the waterfront dives. Others ended their lives in nearby San Quentin Prison. Jack himself once was slugged during a drunken brawl and lay unconscious for seventeen hours outside a lodging house.

He considered this life "raw and naked, wild and free," yet at times felt the necessity of retiring from it, seeking solitude and night-long sessions with the books Miss Coolbrith reserved for him at the library, Zola's *Germinal*, Kipling's *The Light That Failed* and especially Melville's *Typee*. The hundreds of dollars he spent across the bar, buying fellowship and admiration, didn't give him half the satisfaction, he said, of a quarter's worth of candy and a long night with his books.

Another close brush with death, brought on by drink, served as a warning. Then in his sixteenth year, he was making Benicia, on the

Carquinez Straits, his temporary headquarters. He had been drinking heavily for weeks, as he told it, and one night he staggered back to the *Razzle Dazzle,* which was tied up at the end of a wharf, from a round of the local saloons. It was one o'clock in the morning and no one else was about. He stumbled aboard the sloop, lost his footing and fell overboard. The tide was ebbing out swiftly, the current was swift and inexorable. He was swept out far from shore, but being a good swimmer and possessing in addition the over-confidence bestowed by a skinful of whiskey, he wasn't alarmed.

Drifting out on the tide, floating on his back and looking up at the stars, a poetic vision of death took hold of him. Why not simply drift out to sea until he was sucked under? Maudlin with self-pity, he considered that he had little to lose by surrendering himself to death. He had never known a full measure of love from anyone; had missed most of the experiences other people regarded as their birthright; had thrown himself away on the company of thieves and parasites, and he saw clearly now that his life had been degraded and worthless. It was a "drug-dream," as he wrote of it in *John Barleycorn,* coaxing him to seek surcease in death, arguing against the instinct to save himself.

Later the cold water began to sober him, and he decided against yielding to the death-pull of the alcohol simmering in his system. He found himself caught in the shore-tide that swept under the Solano wharf and around the end of Dead Man's Island. He knew that he might be sucked under by the riptide that flowed into Turner's Shipyard Bight, and struck out with an overhand stroke to reach the greater safety in mid-channel.

Again he drifted along on his back, until it was almost daylight. By now he was sober, chilled to the marrow, and hadn't the slightest desire to drown. He hoped that the turn of the tide might bring him back before he was carried into San Pablo Bay.

By five o'clock, with dawn coming up, he was numb and frightened, fighting the tide-rips off the Mare Island light, where the ebbing currents from Vallejo and Carquinez Straits met and churned in combat. A dawn breeze sprang up, ruffling the surface of the water. He began swallowing water as the waves broke against him. He was close to succumbing now, his strength drained, his hope evaporated. Just when he was about to go under, a Greek fisherman headed for Vallejo with his night's catch bore down, sighted him floundering in the water and hauled him over the side.

It was a long time, he said, before he drank heavily again.

He began to consider the reckless futility of the life he had been leading, finally deciding he wanted more out of life than the endless round of thieving, brawling and drinking that apparently satisfied his associates. He shipped out on a schooner and tried his hand at salmon fishing for a time, and then, without any qualms, decided to try the other side of the law. He was recruited for the State Fish Patrol and assigned as a deputy patrolman, though as he later confessed his own crimes as a marauder of the oyster beds could have earned him "500 years in prison."

Most of his forays were not against the oyster-thieves but the illegal Greek salmon fishers and Chinese shrimp raiders, who used nets so fine the tiniest fish couldn't escape them. Most of his fellow patrolmen went armed, because their quarry often resisted violently when caught in the act of violating the fishing laws. "My only weapon on duty was a steel table-fork" but "I felt fearless and a man when I climbed over the side of the boat to arrest some marauder." [3]

Later his exploits as a patrolman, added to his experiences on the dark side of the law, furnished him with the material for *Tales of the Fish Patrol* and other stories. His adventures as a lawman, he related subsequently, were plentiful and included pitched battles by moonlight with the crews of Chinese junks engaged in illicit shrimp-netting. During one boarding party, he claimed, he stood off five Chinese armed with knives simply by reaching into his pocket as though about to draw a gun. Another time he was chased down the Martinez wharf by a mob of fishermen, enraged because he had just arrested two of their number.

Sometimes he worked under cover, joining a group of raiders to obtain information on their activities or evidence against them. In "A Raid on the Oyster Pirates" he told of pretending to throw in with such a band and agreeing to accompany them on an oyster raid in the south bay.

When the tide ebbed, Jack, another undercover operative and their temporary associates anchored their sloops and went prowling across the oyster beds. As soon as they were harvesting the shoals far enough away from the sloops, Jack and his colleague slipped away from them, tied the boats together and towed them away.

Near dawn, as the tide began rising, the poachers found themselves stranded on the shoals with the water swirling around their knees. They were only too glad to be rescued — and arrested — by the Fish Patrol.

3. *Before the Mast*

During the winter of 1892, when Jack was sixteen, about to turn seventeen, the sealing fleet which hunted the North Pacific was anchored in San Francisco Bay. In one of the waterfront saloons he met a seal hunter named Pete Holt, drank with him and formed an agreement that they would ship out together when the sealers set sail for the hunting grounds. For months he had been dreaming of sailing out the Golden Gate and into the wide seas beyond like the heroes of Melville's novels. He had become bored with the Oakland waterfront, its cramped opportunities and unimaginative routs and brawls.

Within a few weeks of making that decision he signed on the *Sophie Sutherland,* a three-topmast schooner of eighty tons, Captain Sutherland commanding. Once registered as the *Carmencita,* she bore a lurid reputation among seafarers. The schooner had once been a "pirate craft," had sailed under at least three other names and no one knew how many others unknown to Customs House officials. She was known to have participated in blackbirding raids in the Copper Islands — that is, snatching natives for forced labor on copra plantations.[4] A dozen years hence she would become celebrated as the background of Jack's novel *The Sea Wolf,* in which she was identified as "the schooner *Ghost,* bound seal-hunting to Japan."

Jack had just passed his seventeenth birthday when he signed on the *Sophie Sutherland.* He was husky, mettlesome and high-spirited, but he was taking on a life which had broken many men twice his age. All but one of the men in the *Sophie*'s forecastle had been at sea many years, having risen through the brutal school of the ordinary seaman. It was a merciless life inhabited by men engaged in a bloody trade. As deckhand and later as boat-puller, when the sealer reached the hunting grounds, he would be tried in every fiber of his being. There was no room for the weakling or incompetent. But that, he leaves no question in his writings on the subject, was just what he wanted.

Just as other men, one generation earlier, proved themselves on the frontier, he would establish title to manhood on the wild seas. It was one of the essentials of his existence that he must always outdo everyone else — endure more hardship, drink more liquor, conquer more women, write more books.

He not only wanted to be a man among men, he had to be a man above men. It was the only way he knew to rid himself of indefinable guilt, shame and fear that shadowed him from his first conscious hours.

In the forecastle of the *Sophie Sutherland* there were twelve men.[5] Ten were Scandinavians who had earned their able-seamen's ratings through long apprenticeship. Only he and a Missourian known only as "Bricklayer" had never been on salt water before. Yet Jack and Bricklayer had been signed on as able seamen, drawing the same pay as men who had learned their trade the hard way.

If he was not to be ground under heel, as he recognized immediately, he would have to prove himself their equal or "endure seven months of hell at their hands."

Thus at the beginning of a watch he was the first out of the forecastle and on deck; the first to go aloft when the topsails had to be taken in or furled out; the first to take on any difficult or dangerous task. At the slightest sign of weakness, he knew, the others would pounce on him like a wolf pack, so his temper was always on the point of explosion. At the slightest insult from a shipmate he would fly at the offender with flailing fists. One thing they respected was a berserker rage, the Nordic equivalent of running amok. Soon enough they stopped trying to bully him and paid him a measure of reluctant, watchful respect.

He got along so well with his mates, in fact, that after a few weeks he established a firm, fun-loving friendship with a Swede named Victor and a Norwegian named Axel, both among the younger members of the crew. They called themselves — or at least London called them — The Three Sports.

The Bricklayer didn't fare so well. He was a tall, powerful man of forty without even Jack's knowledge of shipboard routine, who was detested by everyone else becaue he was "vicious, malignant, dirty, and without common decency." The others made him the butt of all their resentments and sufferings, gave him the silent treatment, and continued to ignore him even when he lay dying of some unspecified malady in his bunk. The Bricklayer died, Jack wrote later in *The Human Drift,* knowing that his shipmates wanted him to die so they could be rid of his presence. Not a flicker of compassion was shown the man. A few hours after his death he was flung overboard sewn into the blankets in which he died with a gunnysack half full of coal to weight him down. The men of the *Sophie Sutherland,* Jack no less than the others, had become as brutal as the life they lived.

Jack claimed the Bricklayer's bunk, partly to show his defiance of a sailors' superstition that anyone who took a dead man's bunk wouldn't live to the end of the voyage, partly because less sea water leaked onto it from the deck and the light was better for reading. (He had brought a number of books along in his sea bag, including a history of the Orient, *Anna Karenina, Madame Bovary,* and several sea narratives.) That night the Bricklayer had his moment of retribution. Standing watch, Jack saw what looked like his ghost, come back to haunt the ship. Or was it the figment of a guilt-tinged imagination, an awareness that he had treated the Bricklayer as badly as any of his shipmates? Or was he more his mother's son than he had guessed, susceptible to visitations from the spirit world? It wasn't until late that night, after several more glimpses of the "apparition," that he learned it all a trick of light and shadow. It appeared when the moon was partly obscured by a thin cloud and its diffused radiance struck the fore-rigging of the mizzen-topmast to create a ghostly illusion. Later he would recall that lonely, haunted night watch in the middle of the Pacific as the most agonizing hours of his life.

They sighted their first landfall when the volcanic peaks of the Bonin Islands appeared off the *Sophie*'s bow. As they slipped in between reefs to anchor in the lagoon, Jack knew the journey had been worth it: there was a smell of the jungle in the wind, aborigines in outriggers clustered around the ship and Japanese in sampans were elsewhere in the landlocked harbor. Above the lava slopes could be seen the thick vegetation, drowsy palms and exotic flowers of a jungle island.

The Three Sports promised themselves they would hire a sampan from the Japanese and go fishing. A palm-thatched saloon distracted them from this worthwhile purpose. The trio found themselves belting down a potent native distillation, known to a later generation of Americans as jungle juice, out of square-faced Holland gin bottles.

Ten days of riot followed. Other schooners slipped into the lagoon, anchored and allowed their crews to go ashore for a last carouse before they headed north to the hunting grounds, where there would be month after month of slaughter and toil. Jack and his friends joined lustily in the round-the-clock wassail, with the main street of the harbor town jammed with hundreds of drinking, brawling sailors and hunters. The governor of the islands ordered the visitors to return to their ships by sunset and threatened to clear the streets forcibly, in which case the town would probably have been wrecked. His police and the reserves stood around powerless to restore order. Jack thought it was all wonderful, a throwback to the days of the Spanish Main or of the Viking sea-rovers celebrating their return from battle and pillage. Once during the saturnalia, as he would recall, he was sitting in a circle in front of the island governor's house passing a bottle of sake around with Japanese fishermen, Kanaka boatmen from the sealing vessels, a Danish sailor who had been working as a cowhand in the Argentine. The end of the debauch was fittingly dismal: he came to at dawn sprawled in the doorway of the home of the Japanese port pilot, whose wife was bending over him solicitously. He had been robbed of all his money, his coat, belt and shoes.

The *Sophie Sutherland* and the rest of the sealing fleet lifted anchor and proceeded northward along the Japanese islands to the cold sea and endless icy fogs off the Siberian coast, where they plunged into the slaughter. Jack and the other men of the forecastle handled the boats for the hunters. The killing went on for weeks during all the daylight hours. Each boat-puller and his hunter were engaged in a competition to see who could kill the most before the season was over. The decks of the *Sophie* reddened with gore as the slaughtered seals were brought back to be skinned, with the carcasses thrown overboard for the delectation of the glutted sharks. For weeks on end he and his fellows reeked of blood, smelled it in the cold moist air, tasted it in their stew, felt it seep into their pores. They waded in blood and blubber until it seemed there could be no more sleek sinuous creatures left in the Bering Sea; the hold was crammed with salted-down skins to keep society ladies warm and stylish in New York and London and Paris. Then suddenly the herd moved off, the season was over, the slaughter was ended.

The memory of that floating slaughterhouse in the Bering Sea, so far as his writings indicate, made no lacerating impression. It was hard, dirty work, that was all. What seared his conscience was the way he and the other deckhands had watched the Bricklayer die without showing him the faintest flicker of compassion.

The happiest memory, his "moment of highest living," came when the *Sophie* ran into a typhoon on the voyage home. With her sails reefed she scuttled before the roaring winds. Mountainous seas struck her broadside, causing her to rock in the trough as though in a gigantic cradle. Jack was summoned to take the wheel, though the sailing-master made no secret of his concern over whether he had the strength and skill to handle the job. Jack, however, managed to keep her running before the wind. A short time later, satisfied with the boy's performance, the sailing-master went below. All other hands were at breakfast. For forty minutes the destiny of the ship and all aboard were in his hands.

He had never known such exaltation.

4. *A Petition in Boots*

When he returned to San Francisco late in the summer of 1893, Jack found the Bay area, as well as the rest of the country, gripped once again by a depression. It had started with a Wall Street panic and spread from there, until now millions were out of work. Jack had hoped for a breathing space between jobs, a little time in which to read, rest and consider what to do with his life; what he found were the inexorable demands of his feckless family. Flora reported they were deep in debt, or as deep as people with their credit resources could be, and had been struggling along on a few dollars a week which her husband earned as a part-time constable.

Jack paid the bills and turned over what was left from his *Sophie Sutherland* wages to Flora. Back on the cheap-labor market, he found that Oakland employers had set a ten-cents-an-hour wage scale for all kinds of work, whether it was longshoring, coal-heaving, ditchdigging, or whatever; which meant that a man working the usual six-day week, twelve-hour day could earn $7.20 a week, if he was lucky enough to find a job. In seething resentment at this starvation wage-scale, Bay area workers began expressing themselves in sporadic strikes and in considering more radical solutions to their situation; it was this time of bitter discontent that Jack later described so vividly in his novel *The Valley of the Moon*.

Finally he found work in a jute mill, at the usual ten cents an hour (with a promise that he would be raised to $1.25 a day). He worked twelve hours a day. In other words, if he worked hard and stuck it out in an atmosphere made horrendous by clouds of lint that choked the respiratory tract he might win a thirty-cent-a-week pay raise.

Shortly after he began work at the mill, enabling his family to move into slightly better quarters on Twenty-second Avenue, his mother came across the announcement of a contest in the San Francisco *Call*. The newspaper was offering a twenty-five-dollar prize for the best descriptive article. Flora urged him to enter the contest. In that one intuitive moment she could almost be said to have made up for much of her failure and neglect as a mother, for she set him firmly on the path of what was to be his life work. Jack decided to write about the typhoon the *Sophie Sutherland* had endured off the Japanese coast. That night he wrote two thousand words before turning in for a few hours' sleep; the next night another two thousand words. The third night he cut and rewrote to bring the finished article under the two-thousand-word limit required by the contest rules. Then he sent it off to the *Call*, signing it "By Jack London, age 17. Address, 1321 Twenty-second Avenue, Oakland."

On November 12, 1893, the San Francisco *Call* published Jack's article as the winner of the first prize in its contest. For three nights' work, and not in the malodorous atmosphere of a jute mill, he had earned as much as he did in almost a month at a twine-spinning machine. Not only that, and this must have been the sweetest portion of his triumph, he won out over two students from the University of California and Stanford University — Jack London, who had finished his education with grade school four years before.

The prize-winning article, as the contest editor commented, showed a "steady force of expression" indicating the birth of a literary artist. From first to last, Jack was at his best describing what he had seen and known. In his article, he described the onset of the gale-force winds, the efforts of the crew to take in sail and batten down during the dark and windy night before the full force of the storm broke upon the *Sophie*, the weird light from the phosphorescent surface of the heaving sea. "A soft light emanated from the movement of the ocean. Each mighty sea, all phosphorescent and glowing with the tiny lights of myriads of animalculae, threatened to overwhelm us with a deluge of fire." His prose, surging like the tumultuous sea he was describing, had the instinctive rhythm of the born writer, rising to crescendo with the height of the storm: "The sea was a dark lead color, as with long, slow, majestic roll it was heaped by the wind into liquid mountain of foam. The wild antics of the schooner were sickening as she forged along. She would almost stop as though climbing a mountain, then rapidly rolling to right and left as she gained the summit of a huge sea . . . Like an avalanche she shot forward and down as the sea astern struck her with the force of a thousand battering rams, burying her bow to the catheads in the milky foam at the bottom that came on deck in all directions — forward, astern, to right and to left, through the hawse pipes and over the rail." It was a remarkable effort for a seventeen-year-old boy scribbling away at midnight after twelve hours of the most dreary labor, testifying to the vitality which was always the most striking feature of his work and his life.

This initial success, as he said later, "seriously turned my thoughts to writing," but his blood was "too hot for a settled routine." [6] He turned out a few fictional pieces for the *Call*, but they were rejected because the newspaper didn't publish that sort of material. Chasing the girls, with what energy he had left from the jute mill, was more fascinating. He and a friend named Louis Shattuck hung around the street corners, cigarets dangling from their lips, trying to make a pickup. They didn't have enough money to frequent the public dance halls, since most of their earnings went to their families. Occasionally they would make enough of an impression on the strolling shopgirls, laundresses, factory workers to cut a pair of them from the giggling herd and take them out to Blair's Park on the trolley for ice cream, a fling at high life that used up a week's allowance.

When the jute-mill bosses failed to keep their promise to raise his wage to $1.25 a day, he quit, deciding that unskilled labor would never pay enough to keep him and his family afloat and that he must learn a trade. Electricity seemed to be the coming thing; people were even beginning to light their homes with Mr. Edison's magic filament. He decided to learn the electrician's trade, and presented himself to the superintendent of the Oakland Street Railway's power plant, still laboring under the delusion that an honest, hard-working youth could work his way up like the heroes of Horatio Alger's fables, the "old myths which were the heritage of the American boy."[7] According to his sardonic description of the job interview, the power-plant superintendent positively beamed upon him when he recited his willingness to work his way up the ladder. The boss was so enthusiastic over Jack's possibilities that the youth wondered whether he wasn't already staking him out as a future son-in-law. Yes, Jack could learn the electrician's trade, but he would have to work his way up from firing a boiler in the engine room to oiler to apprentice under the carhouse electricians. In time, and with diligent effort, he would attain the journeyman status of electrician's helper. He might even some day become an electrician first-class.

When it came down to the actual terms of employment, Jack found himself back on the same old treadmill, or worse. Starting at the bottom of the electrical industry was, in fact, grimmer than working in a mill, the pay was no better than he had earned as a thirteen-year-old in the cannery. As a coal-passer, shoveling mountains of coal for the firemen on both the day and night shifts, he usually had to work twelve or thirteen grimy, sweat-soaked, backbreaking hours a day. He had to work every day of the week, Sundays and holidays included, with just one day a month off. And for this he was paid a flat thirty dollars a month — no overtime no matter how many hours a day he had to work to pile up enough coal for the firemen. He usually reported for work at six A.M. and rarely finished before eight P.M. His whole life was devoted to work and sleep; no more sessions with the library books, no more dates with the girls. The strain of handling the heavy shovel-loads and trundling a huge wheelbarrow between bunkers and boilers was so great that he had to wear leather straps constantly around his sprained and swollen wrists. The heavy straps, he said, were like "slightly flexible plaster casts."

Eventually one of the firemen got to know him and trust him enough to mutter a secret in his dust-blackened ear. Until the overly willing Jack came along, the smooth-talking superintendent had been paying two men a total of eighty dollars a month for the work Jack was doing for thirty dollars. The fireman told him he was simply killing himself to save the street railway company fifty dollars a month, and cheapening the price of labor as well as keeping another man out of work.

A short time later, having learned that one of the coal-passers he had unknowingly displaced had killed himself in despair at not being able to support his wife and three children, Jack turned in his shovel and gave up his hopes of a career with the street railway company.

He had decided that going on the bum was preferable to that kind of soul-killing bondage, just as earlier he had quit the cannery in preference for robbing the oyster beds. His family, once again, would have to get along without his pay envelope. His sense of responsibility always hung by a thread.

The spring of 1894, when Jack quit his job at the power-plant, was dark with foreboding. The "panic" of the previous year was not subsiding, after all. It was becoming a severe depression, and would last four years before the Canadian-Alaskan gold rush and the Spanish-American War brought back better times. Finley Peter Dunne's Mr. Dooley, whom the middle class considered a shrewd philosopher, soothingly commented that "the noise you hear in the land" wasn't the first gun of the revolution but the sound of the American people beating their carpets in their backyards. There were, however, more discomfiting noises in the land than mere carpet-beating.

Americans were beginning to sense that the days of free opportunity had come to an end, and sooner or later the nation would have to face the same problems which troubled the old countries of Europe. A character in Henry Blake Fuller's widely read novel remarked that faith in the old *laissez-faire* system had evaporated and "today we have all the elements possessed by the old world itself, and we must take whatever they develop, as the old world does. We have the full working apparatus finally, with all its resultant noise, waste, stenches, stains, dangers, explosions." [8]

In their own experience, however, there were no precedents for Americans to follow. Transcontinental settlement had been completed, and there was no outlet for the restless and ambitious, no new frontiers to absorb the malcontents and troublemakers. Nor was there any philosophic cushion to ease the shock of discovering that an industrialized United States faced many of the same problems that millions had migrated to escape. For the past century Americans had placidly assumed that, aside from a few economic groundswells that would cause minor distress at infrequent intervals, the land and the riches beneath it were so bountiful that there was plenty for all. Now countless numbers were starving in the midst of that plenty, causing many to wonder aloud, with increasing vehemence, whether there wasn't something wrong with a social system that didn't distribute its wealth more equitably.

Nowhere was the bitterness over the situation greater than in the Western states, whose people had traveled the farthest and suffered the most in pursuit of wealth and happiness, who believed themselves heirs to some vaguely promised legacy. The children of the pioneers deserved something better than bread-lines and soup kitchens. Hadn't old Dennis Kearney pointed the way to direct action, and hadn't the working people betrayed themselves by refusing to follow him in a violent overthrow of the social order? As one of the characters in London's *The Valley of the Moon* was to express it:

"We're the white folks an' the children of white folks, that was too busy being good to be smart. We're the white folks that lost out."

The more complex the economic dilemma grew, the wilder the remedies offered for it became. The West was rife with hot-eyed advocates of Populism, Free Silver and other more or less drastic theories. In the East arose "General" Jacob S. Coxey, a prophet from Flora London's hometown of Massillon, Ohio, with a scheme to alleviate the depression. Congress, he proclaimed, must issue five million dollars in greenbacks to finance a road-building project and give work to the jobless. This smacked of revolution to the middle and upper classes; the idea of the government providing employment for the "idle" was too radical to be considered; what would the shiftless proletariat be demanding next? His pleas and threats ignored, Coxey announced that there would be a march on Washington by his "Industrial Army." Its objectives were never quite made clear except that Coxey hoped the sight of marching men would convince Congress that he and his followers meant business. Forty-odd years later there would be echoes of the Coxey program when the Works Progress Administration functioned on a much grander scale than he envisioned.

The intellectual stimulus behind Coxey was an old collaborator of Dennis Kearney's, Carl Browne, who had edited Kearney's propaganda sheets and served as his secretary and gray eminence back in the Seventies. Since then, Browne, a painter of panoramas by profession, had dabbled in the Populist, Greenback and National Labor movements. "Humble Carl," as he liked to be called, was also something of a mystic and a follower of Theosophy. He held that Christ had been reincarnated many times; that Coxey was the cerebrum of Christ while he, Browne, was the cerebellum. Somehow, mumbo-jumbo and all, he not only insinuated himself as Coxey's chief adviser but persuaded Samuel Gompers and the American Federation of Labor to go along with Coxey's road-building program. He drew up the plans for the Industrial Army's organization along pseudo-military lines with all commanders, à la Kearney, to be mounted on horseback, and designed the army's banner with a picture of Christ and the legend beneath it, "Peace on earth, good will to men. He hath risen, but death to interest on bonds." It was largely due to his promotional genius that seventeen different brigades were raised for the march on Washington.*

Later it became a surefire vaudeville joke, but Coxey's army scared the daylights out of the privileged classes in the spring of 1894 as it started converging on Washington. There was unrest throughout the nation, in the farmlands as well as the cities. Banks were closing, railroads were going into receivership, and by 1894 wheat was selling for less than fifty cents a bushel. The working classes were inflamed by the brutal suppression of the Homestead strike. The South was enraged by "six-cent cotton." Mary Ellen Lease was causing an uproar at mass meetings of Middle Western farmers by challenging them to "quit raising corn and begin raising hell!" People with less acute revolutionary instincts than Humble Carl's began to believe that the country was reaching the explosive point.

In the cities around San Francisco Bay, plagued by unemployment and plummeting wage scales, the militancy matched or exceeded that of the rest of the nation. In Oakland, a self-designated "General" Charles T. Kelly, a young printer, organized one of the Western detachments for the assault on Capitol Hill. Kelly possessed a talent for leadership and a flair for the theatrical. His army of two thousand, organized into quasi-military companies, was to travel east in boxcars provided by the railroads, not so much out of sympathy for the movement as a desire to propel it eastward and rid the Western cities of restless troublemakers as quickly as possible. In Southern California another detachment under General Lewis C. Fry numbering six hundred set out for Washington. Hundreds of prospective marchers crossed

* Among other stopgap occupations, Browne had sold that famous old snake oil, Kickapoo Indian Remedy, at the Chicago World's Fair.

the Bay from San Francisco to join General Kelly. But there was a hitch: the Southern Pacific was refusing to provide transportation. Kelly and his agitators, holding forth at the Mills Tabernacle, which they had taken over as headquarters, were turning belligerent. The mayor of Oakland ordered them on their way even if they had to hoof it. Finally, one morning late in March, the Oakland police and fire departments, with the Fifth National Guard Regiment standing by in reserve, rounded up Kelly and most of his contingent, shoved them into comandeered boxcars and sent them on their way to Sacramento.

Jack and a friend named Frank Davis had intended to leave with Kelly and the rest but both were at home sleeping when the police rounded up their comrades. Jack wasn't particularly concerned with the purpose of the march on Washington, and certainly wasn't swayed by the "commonweal of Christ" propaganda put out by Carl Browne; right then a road-building job was the last thing he wanted. It simply offered an escape from the dreariness of Oakland, never the gayest city in the Western world; and as he looked back on the adventure later the life of a hobo, wandering the steel-tracked byways of The Road, was a worthwhile enterprise; especially for an eighteen-year-old known as Sailor Jack, eager to invade every new area of experience.

In the hoboes' world, as he wrote in *The Road,*[9] "the impossible happens and the unexpected jumps out of the bushes at every turn . . ." Respectable folk might shudder at the necessity of stealing transportation from the railroads via the "side-door Pullmans," begging for food at back doors in the towns, living in trackside jungles with outcasts and misfits, but Jack London never ceased to pride himself on his essay in vagrancy, on having been a Weary Willie who beat his way from coast to coast.

Jack and his friend Davis set out for Sacramento to catch up with Kelly's army, riding the cushions to the state capitol, unprofessional as it was to pay for the ride. Jack was rather oddly outfitted for the venture, wearing a chinchilla coat with a novel in each pocket, a cap pulled down over his brow, a flannel shirt, and well-worn trousers and shoes. They had not thought to equip themselves with food, blankets or extra clothing for the cold journey over the mountains.

In Sacramento, they learned that Kelly and his followers had already crossed the Sierras. They caught the Overland Limited, a fast express, and held it down as far as Truckee, where yard detectives tossed them off the blind baggage (the platform between the coal-tender and the first baggage car). Occasionally on the way east they separated, only to meet farther up the line. Part of the way Jack traveled with scattered detachments of Kelly's army, surviving rain, cold and hardhearted brakemen. The farther east they went, the more reluctant the railroads became to allow their rolling stock to be used to transport Kelly and his ragtag army on their pilgrimage. The hardships grew more severe. Frank Davis turned back to California because, as Jack noted in a diary he began keeping, "The Road has no more charms for Frank. The romance and adventure are gone . . ." Jack was determined to keep going, though at one low point in the journey across the Great Plains he scrawled in his diary the opinion that a person had the right to commit suicide whenever life became too dismal to be borne any longer. It was a thought that would occur to him again and again. Death always had a strong attraction for him, almost a fascination; it was the unseen companion, perhaps the guide and inspiration, of all his adventuring. The man who really loves life stays home, keeps his belly full, sleeps warm and plays it safe. The adventurer gambles with life to heighten sensation, to make it glow for a moment.

Jack and the rest of Kelly's brigade met with a varying reception on its eastward "march." In Grand Island, Nebraska, the authorities put them up in hotels and fed them in the restaurants. In Omaha, they arrested Kelly and quick-marched his followers across the Missouri River to Council Bluffs, Iowa. For days there, under torrential rains, the brigade lay helpless in the camping ground assigned to it in Chautauqua Park. The railroads refused to carry Kelly's two thousand any farther, and assigned a corps of Pinkerton detectives to ride the trains and keep them off.

Then the railroads stopped traffic on their lines running through Council Bluffs, and Kelly and his men were immobilized.

Very well, Kelly decided, they'd hoof it to Washington. The first leg of their march would be to Des Moines, 140 miles down a dusty wagon road. Kelly himself rode a "magnificent black charger," followed by a fife-and-drum corps, then his ragged infantry. Jack slogged along in the rear rank of the rear guard. In two days he wore the soles off his shoes and trudged along on blistered feet. But he and his comrades were cheered by Iowa's hospitality. In every little town along the way, the people turned out to welcome them, cheer them on, and feed them. When they camped for the night, townspeople and farmers from miles around would come out to mingle with the marchers and watch entertainments put on by them. On Sundays they played baseball, fielding a crack nine against the local team. Surely men who played baseball couldn't be the vanguard of revolution!

On the outskirts of Des Moines the brigade, thoroughly footsore and fed up with slogging it, squatted at a stove factory and announced they wouldn't take another step. They would throw themselves upon the humanitarian instincts of the city, which, of course, couldn't let them starve to death. On the other hand, it couldn't supply six thousand meals a day indefinitely. It was either that, said Kelly, or the city would have to float a municipal bond issue and buy them all railroad tickets to Washington. While the city fathers wrangled and money flowed out of the city treasury to feed the guests, some clever fellow came up with an alternative. Why couldn't the brigade float down the Des Moines River to Keokuk, three hundred miles away on the Mississippi? The marchers — "well-fed optimists" by now, as London observed — accepted the plan. A public subscription drive raised the money to buy lumber and other materials required to send the brigade on its way down the river. On May 9, after eleven days of levying on the municipal hospitality, they pushed off down the Des Moines River. Jack was assigned to the "advance boat," which was to tie up at every settlement along the way and collect coffee, tobacco, sacks of beans, butter, sugar, canned goods and sides of beef. "We never took more than we could get away with," as Jack candidly recalled.[10] The supplies were supposed to be turned over to commissary boats following them, but Jack and his fellow scroungers kept enough for themselves to take up any slack in their waistbands. They boiled their coffee in milk, and poured fresh country cream on top of that. Few had ever lived so well, until word seeped back to General Kelly that Jack and others in the advance guard were eating high off the hog while the main body of his brigade was missing meals. He sent two horsemen ahead to warn the people of the countryside not to contribute any more supplies to the "advance boat." In addition, he assigned three "police boats" to keep an eye on Jack and his rugged individualists and prevent them from making any sorties into the countryside on their own. Naturally they resented the surveillance. By the time the floating brigade reached Keokuk they were sorely disaffected, on the point of mutiny, and much less nourished.

In Keokuk, all the rafts were lashed together and towed by a steamboat down to Quincy, Illinois, where the vagabond army camped on Goose Island. Jack slipped away against orders in a dugout and "stemmed" the town, begging at back doors for money, underwear, socks and other items of clothing, which he brought back to his friends for equal distribution.

Later Jack recognized that Kelly and his chief lieutenant, "Colonel" George Speed, with whom he became better acquainted, were both "heroes" and deserved better from their followers. He confessed that he was sorry for "at least ten percent of the trouble" he'd caused them.

With disaffection spreading through the ranks, the brigade fell apart on Goose Island. Groups of men began deserting and heading back to California or going out on the bum. The picnic aspects of the march had vanished, and obviously it would be no fun at all walking all the way from the banks of the Mississippi to Washington, D.C. Jack himself was among the first to take off on his own.

Kelly and a few of his more loyal followers eventually made it to Washington, but by the time they arrived Coxey's army was in thorough disarray. Coxey himself was in jail. Just to show how revolutionists were treated in the United States, the Washington police arrested him on a charge of walking on the grass of the Capitol grounds. And that was the end of the Industrial Army, and a pointed lesson to people who thought the unemployed had some claim on their government.

As for Jack, not yet concerned with anything more high-minded than scrounging his next meal, he hopped the freights to Chicago. At the post office there he found a letter from Eliza containing four one-dollar bills, which he used to buy passage on a boat across the lake to St. Joseph, Michigan, and a restorative visit with his mother's sister, Mrs. Mary Everhard, who read the diary he had been keeping and told him he must become a writer.

From there he rode the rods to New York City, where he made the City Hall Park his headquarters. In the mornings he would beg enough food to last him the day; afternoons he spent reading books he bought for a few cents off the barrows of second-hand dealers. It was midsummer and a park bench usually served as his bed. One afternoon, however, the police raided the park and cracked down, literally, on the vagrants who had been homesteading there. Jack got whacked over the head with a nightstick, a blow which confirmed him in his contempt for established authority, but he managed to outrun the constabulary and escape a thirty-day jail sentence.

He left New York with a distaste for the metropolis that never vanished even when he returned years later as a celebrity; he could never forget his view of its underside, its casual brutality toward those who hadn't made the grade; its undeniable beauty was reserved for the successful and powerful.

His luck ran out altogether when he took the boxcar route to Niagara Falls, where he was arrested for vagrancy one night after watching the spectacle of the waterfall by moonlight. Thirty days at hard labor, in the Erie County Penitentiary, was the sentence. Worse yet, he was subjected to various forms of degradation which the authorities regarded as a sure cure for those feckless enough not to have a legal residence, a job, and money in their pockets.

His head was shaved, he was clad in prison stripes and forced to march in lockstep from cell to work detail. The diet was bread and water, with meat rationed out once a week. After a few days of manual labor he was appointed a trusty, assigned to serving the bread and water to the men in the cells. If there was any bread left over, and he usually saw to it that there was, he bartered it for suspenders and safety pins, which he in turn traded for bits of the weekly meat ration. His continuing hunger for meat — the symbol of boyhood privation — made him as ruthless as the next man.

As a trusty with the freedom of the cell blocks he witnessed horrors that would never leave his mind, men going mad in their cells, others beaten and thrown down flights of stone steps. He listened to their stories and realized how brutally society shook out its clinkers and consigned them to slag heaps like the Erie County Penitentiary. As he looked and listened, some of his "plethoric national patriotism simmered down and leaked out of the bottom" of his soul.[11]

He also decided that he would not be caught in that same trap of shiftlessness and petty crime which had landed most of his fellows in jail. Released along with him was the man, a burglar by trade, who had obtained the trusty's appointment for him. To keep on the burglar's good side and hang on to his privileges, he had spent hours with him plotting future crimes. They traveled as far as Buffalo together, then Jack bought him a beer in a saloon and ducked out the rear door.

He kept going until he reached the freight yards, hopped a train and made his way across Pennsylvania. For the next several weeks he was on the move, visiting Washington, Baltimore, and Boston before heading north to Montreal. He had decided to return to the Pacific Coast via the Canadian Pacific. From Montreal he rode the freights across Canada, begging for food at various stops, until he reached Vancouver. He worked his way back to San Francisco as a deckhand on the *Umatilla,* the same ship which, two years hence, would take him to the Klondike.

As he looked back on the experience in later years, the life of a hobo, with all its hardships and brutalities, still exercised a strong appeal. In the world of the hobo, all but vanished now, man seemed to have recovered a bit of his freedom. He lived outside the increasingly restricted, increasingly stifling atmosphere of an industrial society. Instead of carrying a lunch pail, being harassed by mortgages and trapped in domesticity, keeping even with his creditors and living in fear of what the neighbors might think, he wandered free of responsibility. Above all, it was strictly a man's world. Jack's experiences with women, beginning with his mother, continuing through two marriages and a number of catch-as-catch-can romances, were never happy enough to compensate entirely for the freedom he knew as a sailor, oyster pirate and hobo. He delighted in the haphazardness, the variety, the comradeship, the romantic squalor of life on The Road.

Yet there was also the counter-attraction of hopes and fears even stronger than the delights of irresponsibility. He was frightened by what he had witnessed in the Erie County Penitentiary, and knew that The Road could lead into dark and degrading places. He wanted to be a writer and you couldn't write in hobo jungles and boxcars. He had also acquired in his travels a copy of the *Communist Manifesto,* glimmerings of what would later be called a social conscience and a burning determination to help make a better world.

He had left Oakland a skylarking boy and returned a man of purpose.

III

A Girl with Golden Hair

1. *A New Faith*

IN LATER YEARS Jack London would credit his reading of the *Communist Manifesto* while at the bottom of what he called the "Social Pit" with his conversion to Marxist Socialism. Undoubtedly it provided force and direction. Like many writers, however, he tended to dramatize himself and particularly the formative events of his youth. No mere tract, even one so catalytic in its doctrine as the *Manifesto,* could have changed the road kid into a political animal. He had to learn through experience, contact with reality, to be convinced of anything and stay convinced. The Marx-Engels proclamation lighted the way for his new convictions.

They grew out of what he had seen on The Road, and before that in the jute mill, the power plant, the forecastle of the *Sophie Sutherland,* the cannery, and on the Oakland waterfront; not least of all by watching his well-meaning stepfather's efforts to make a living where his particular skills were useless. As a hobo he found himself looking at life from a new and more acute angle. Many of those on The Road, he had learned, were working men, no longer useful to the industrial machine, too old or disabled to be of any further value to employers. They were adrift, not out of shiftlessness, but because they had been rejected by society as it now operated.

"I had dropped down from the proletariat," he wrote many years later, "into what sociologists love to call the 'submerged tenth,' and I was startled to discover the way in which that submerged tenth was recruited . . .

"The woman on the streets and the man of the gutter drew very close to me. I saw the picture of the Social Pit as vividly as though it were a concrete thing, and at the bottom of the Pit I saw them, and myself above them, not far, and hanging on to the slippery wall by main strength and sweat. And I confess a terror seized me. What when my strength failed me? when I should be unable to work shoulder to shoulder with men who were as yet babes unborn?" [1]

What he saw as a hobo and as an inmate of the Erie County jail "hammered" the individualism out of him, he said, and "I was now a Socialist without knowing it, withal, an unscientific one. I had been reborn . . . and I was running around to find out what manner of thing I was."

Thus the resounding call to arms of the *Manifesto,* one day to be echoed endlessly through the loudspeakers of totalitarian dictatorships from the center of Berlin to the boulevards of Shanghai, fell upon a receptive mind. Read in the context of London's time rather than against the background of all that has happened since 1917, its appeal must have been overwhelming: "Let the ruling classes tremble at the socialistic revolution. The proletarians have nothing to lose but their chains. They have a world to gain. Working men of all countries, unite!" All his native traits, especially his sympathy for the underdog and his resentment of authority, combined to urge the logic and justice of the Socialist cause.

To become a more "scientific" Socialist he read the works of Proudhon, Saint-Simon and Fourier, which expounded the doctrine that the real basis of private property is labor, not things. On his return to Oakland he discussed what he read with George Speed, an austere man with chill blue eyes, something of a self-made intellectual, with a force of will that suggested to one newspaperman who knew him that he "might well have liquidated all bourgeois opposition, if revolution had come in his time." Speed had been one of the leaders of Kelly's Western detachment on the march to Washington. Unlike many Socialists of the time, who believed the conflict between the classes would be resolved without violence, Speed was an activist. Given his temperament, London, of course, agreed that action was the only remedy—none of your inch-by-inch Fabianism. Soon he would be signing himself "Yours for the Revolution."

Critics of London's polemical writings have observed that though he regarded himself as a Socialist revolutionary of total Marxist purity his actual beliefs were tinged with a certain unorthodox sentimentality. They find it hard to visualize him, in a showdown, choosing a proletariat dictatorship over the system of individual enterprise under which he hoped to prosper. One of his more perceptive critics, Kenneth S. Lynn, has observed that his Socialism "clearly reflects the success aspirations of an ex-newsboy . . . reveals impingement of the life outlook of Horatio Alger on that of Karl Marx." The Marxist theory that the masses would overthrow the bourgeoise, Lynn adds, "bears no relation to London's prophecy that the revolution would be conducted by a picked group of frustrated Alger heroes." [2] It is just possible that Professor Lynn and others have been overly impressed by the sticking powers of Alger's boy-success stories. Most men subjected to their influence at a helpless age managed to throw off their effects once they encountered the realities of life. It was his own success more than any lingering Algerian influence that nudged London away from the revolution and into the middle class.

Speed, as a recruiting agent for the revolution, not only encouraged Jack's ambitions to become a writer but impressed on the youth the need for more education. He had passed his nineteenth birthday by the time he returned to Oakland, but only in that painful process, Speed insisted, could he gain the footing required to write well and help fight the class war intelligently.

2. *A Tobacco-Chewing Freshman*

In the fall of 1895 Jack obediently entered the freshman class at Oakland High School. It would take three years of preparation before he could be admitted to the University of California, an irksome preliminary for an impatient young man six years older than most of his fellow freshmen. But education was the only sure path leading up from the "Social Pit," and he had sworn an oath that he would never again sell his muscles on the slave-labor market.

His parents had managed to cling to their home on Twenty-second Avenue, and John London was working as a railroad depot guard. Jack would have to contribute what he could, working Saturdays at mowing lawns, beating carpets, picking up whatever odd jobs were available. A little later he got the job of assistant janitor at the high school, working after school at sweeping floors and cleaning the lavatories.

He made an incongruous picture slouching into a classroom, towering over the children who were his classmates. They held him in a mixture of awe and contempt. Obviously he was a roughneck; what was he doing here, a wolf among the lambs? Georgia Loring, who later married Frederick I. Bamford, a friend and mentor of London's, remembered the rather defiant, forbidding appearance he made as a nineteen-year-old high-school freshman. His husky shoulders threatened to burst the seams of a worn and ill-pressed dark blue suit. His face was deeply sunburned from his travels, making his light blue eyes all the more vivid. To the dainty girls in his class, Georgia Loring recalled, he looked "shabby" and "unclean." [3] No doubt aware of their opinion of his appearance he assumed a pose of careless indifference, and was gruffly unapproachable at first when several students made friendly overtures. Eager as he was to get an education, he adopted a bored expression in class, smiling sardonically to himself from time to time, speaking curtly when a teacher called upon him to answer questions. He sprawled negligently at a desk too small for his muscular frame. It didn't help with the little conformists all around him that he chewed tobacco, having picked up the habit as a road kid. He had found that it killed the pain in his cavity-riddled teeth.

One day, Georgia Loring recalled, a couple of girls saw him saunter into a saloon on Broadway with two tramps with whom he had struck up a conversation. His classmates could hardly be blamed for looking upon him as an elderly reprobate. To Georgia Loring, at least, his loutish appearance became more understandable when a boy who carried an Oakland *Times* route at the same time as Jack told her that he "pitied the poor kid . . . he had to bring home every cent of his earnings, and his home was the worst yet."

Jack began to warm up to Oakland High School, and some of the students to him, when he started writing for the *Aegis*, the school magazine. On December 2, 1895 it published a short descriptive piece of his on the sea voyage from San Francisco to Japan. Titled "The Run Across," it was a lyrical recollection of the passage through summer seas, a poetic evocation of tropical nights on deck, "the stars, bejewelling the heavens; the sea, each wave crested with a glittering coronet of fire." Later that month the *Aegis* published "Bonin Islands," an astonishingly frank description of what happened when the sealing fleet sailed into the port on St. John Island and the "white pirates" and "foreign devils" held wassail through the night. The faculty advisors of the *Aegis* must have been very liberal-minded to accept such a lusty piece of writing for a school magazine; either that or they couldn't resist his vivid style. Later the magazine even published two stories about road kids and the experiences of the "Frisco Kid," a young hobo who bore an unmistakable resemblance to London.

Even more than his tobacco-chewing, his frequenting of saloons, his janitoring and his uninhibited literary ventures, his activities as a Socialist agitator made him a notorious and somewhat menacing figure to his schoolmates, particularly those from lace-curtain, middle-class homes. Even their parents became aware of the dangerous youth in their midst when, on February 16, 1896, the San Francisco *Chronicle* published a story about his impromptu missionary work for Socialism:

> Jack London, who is known as the boy socialist of Oakland, is holding forth nightly to the crowds that throng City Hall Park. There are other speakers in plenty, but London always get the biggest crowd and the most respectful attention.
>
> London is young, scarcely 20, but he has seen many sides of the world and has traveled extensively. He was born in San Francisco in the Centennial year, and went through the California grammar schools before he started out in the world . . . He is a High School boy, and supports himself as a janitor in the institution. At present he is fitting himself for a course at the University of California, where he will make a specialty of social questions.
>
> The young man is a pleasant speaker, more earnest than eloquent, and while he is a broad socialist in every way, he is not an anarchist. He says on the subject when asked for his definition of socialism, "It is an all-embracing term — communists, nationalists, collectionists, idealists, utopians, altrurians, are all socialists, but it cannot be said that socialism is any of these — it is all."
>
> Any man, in the opinion of London, is a socialist who strives for a better form of government than the one he is living under.

That first press notice, in which he was tenderly treated for a young man who proposed to topple the social order and denounced everything the conservative *Chronicle* stood for, must have pleased him mightily, even if his view of Socialism as a catchall for the reform-minded dismayed some of his more doctrinaire comrades. It made him a public figure, singled him out among all the propagandists who labored unsung in the same cause. It also taught him how sweet are the uses of publicity, for which he acquired a lifelong taste.

Unfortunately, the *Chronicle* story spurred the authorities into taking action. The people who ran Oakland were not at all amused by the spectacle of a young firebrand who advocated public ownership of the utility companies and called for the workingmen to rise up and overthrow the capitalistic system. Might not another rabble-rousing Kearney be springing up in their midst?

One night the police descended on City Hall Park, snatched Jack from his rostrum and charged him with being a menace to public order. Fortunately he came up before a tolerant sort of judge, who let him off with a suspended sentence and a warning against continued agitation.

At this time Jack also attended meetings of the Henry Clay Society, a debating group formed of young people with a wide range of political beliefs. He was invited to some of the better homes, where the meetings were held. The improvement in social status did not, however, prevent him from participation in all activities of the Oakland local of the Socialist Labor Party.

Now for the first time he was meeting "nice" girls, he noted, "whose skirts reached the ground." He professed not to be at all affected by their "niceness," nor impressed by their polite upbringing, their dainty smells, their delicate manners or their fine clothes. They were the same creatures, except corrupted by unearned privileges and given an overlay of snobbery by their fathers' money, as the shopgirls he had taken on the trolley to Blair's Park. In the pamphlet *What Life Means to Me,* he later described his bitter disillusionment when he learned that the girls on "the parlor floor of society" were "merely the unburied dead." They were molded of the same clay, he said with an air of discovery, as the girls he had known on the "cellar" level of society. They prattled of morality but were "so sentimentally selfish" that he was repelled by their false sense of values. It seemed to him that "the dominant key of the life they lived was materialistic." It did not seem to occur to him that the girls of the working class were equally materialistic, though on a different and humbler scale; that if they wore gingham instead of silk and smelled more of laundry soap than of lavender sachet, it was more a matter of necessity than virtue.

For all his contempt for girls reared on the "parlor floor of society," it was not one of the Lizzies or Mollies of the steam laundries and fish canneries with whom he first fell in love, but a girl of the utmost respectability. Without as yet realizing it, his attachment for the social basement was more defensive and emotional than real. The middle-class parlor was, as yet unconsciously, his goal.

3. *"A Pale Gold Flower"*

In *Martin Eden* the character named Ruth Morse was described as "a pale, ethereal creature, with wide, spiritual blue eyes and a wealth of gold hair . . . a pale gold flower upon a slender stem . . . a spirit, a divinity, a goddess." To the struggling writer, Martin Eden, she was a creature of incredible delicacy and refinement compared with the women he had known, "swarthy, cigaret-smoking women of Old Mexico . . . Eurasians, stamped with degeneracy . . . full-bodied South-Sea-Island women . . . frowsy, shuffling creatures from the pavements of Whitechapel, gin-bloated hags of the stews."

In the flesh, Mabel Applegarth, who unwittingly sat for the portrait of Ruth Morse and could hardly have been pleased with the final result, glowingly though she was depicted in the early pages of the novel, was Jack London's first love. She was a lady, to whom physical love would have seemed a shocking affront. She was the unattainable princess living in an ivory tower of London's own construction, but even on this high pedestal she was not safe from the discerning eye of the embryonic writer. The young man saw her as a creature of such unearthly purity and virtue, at first, that she could hardly be blamed when a few minor flaws — such as her middle-class scale of values — became gaping crevasses to her admirer. They were both victims of his overwhelming consciousness, if not exaggeration, of the difference between the social classes.

Jack met her through her brother Frank, a fellow member of the Henry Clay Society of his own age and inclinations. Jack and Frank began meeting outside the debating society meetings to discuss books and other mutual interests. Although Frank came of a prosperous English family which had migrated to Oakland, he saw in Jack an intelligent young man, well-read and quick-witted, who was obviously cut out for better things even if he had lagged in getting an education. Unlike most others who knew him in that shabby period when he was working his way through high school, Frank did not consider him a social inferior or a tobacco-chewing hoodlum, perhaps because Jack had cultivated a shrewd adaptability of manner. Afterward, while others who knew Jack in his youth spoke of the scabrous poverty in which he was raised, Frank would deprecate the more harrowing accounts, saying, "While Jack London was poor, his poverty has been exaggerated."

Frank, at any rate, considered his new friend quite presentable enough to bring to the Applegarth home and introduce to his sister Mabel. She was three years older than Jack, was taking special courses in English at the University of California, and openly worshipped art, music and literature. Her fragility, her cultivated voice and delicate manner made her seem like a goddess to Jack.

He fell in love with her immediately, with the headlong impetuosity of (to use a favorite phrase of his) "God's own mad lover."

Mabel, despite his feelings of social inferiority, looked upon him with favor. Soon she was as smitten as he was. Perhaps there was something a little crude about his enthusiasms, something outlandish about his experiences, something a little dangerous about his zeal for a Socialist revolution, but he was also electrifyingly vital, with an exuberant smile and a forthright masculinity. If he was not a gentleman by conventional standards, he was capable of taking on a polish.

His first real look at the parlor floor of society and those who lived on it did not repel him so much, after all. It encouraged in him an ambition to come up out of the cellar himself. The other cellar-dwellers could come up later, when the revolution had rearranged the scheme of things.

He was almost as much enamored of Mabel's gracious surroundings as of the young woman herself. The Applegarth home was large and comfortable, with books and paintings in almost every room. People spoke softly to each other, without the empty raging and bickering of the slum districts. Here the human spirit could expand. In surroundings like these, a man of talent could find himself. The Applegarth home was almost as much a revelation to him as his first visit to the Oakland Public Library.

Within a few weeks he found himself accepted in the Applegarth home. His status with Mabel was something between a recognized suitor and a welcomed admirer. They took long bicycle rides together Sundays and picnicked in the poppy fields on the slopes above Berkeley and went sailing on the Bay. A clue to the growing intensity of the relationship may be found in *Martin Eden*. Martin, he wrote, had been "starved for love all his life," and Ruth gave him "the message of immortality." Her slender body was "an emanation of her spirit . . . Her penetrative virginity exalted and disguised his own emotions, elevating his thoughts to a star-cooled chastity . . ." In a man as vigorous as Martin, or Jack, such chivalrous feelings obviously could not endure forever, star-cooled or not. There must be some more substantial reward than merely worshipping the girl. Almost from the first, it was evident, he hoped for marriage.

The girl's intentions were not so apparent, complicated as they were by a feminine concern for what happened when the infatuation wore off. Could she marry outside her class, even with a young man as promising as Jack? What did he have to offer outside his physical magnetism and receptive mind? Wasn't he a bit too much the starry-eyed idealist, the fighter for humanity, the mercurial poet, to make good in the real world, where men went to their businesses every morning and accumulated the money that allowed their wives to live graciously?

As Martin, or the man whose mouthpiece he was, saw it he was a "whiff of ozone" to the girl. She had just enough courage and spiritual enterprise to sense the middle-class stuffiness of her existence. Her admirer had "the primordial vigor of life . . . He was marred and scarred by that mysterious world of rough men and rough deeds . . ." She could not help being stirred by his strangeness, his virility, his challenge to step outside the sometimes stifling coziness on which she had been nurtured. Every venturesome fiber in her delicate body tempted her to take the risk. Perhaps he could be tamed down and persuaded to value the same things she did — the eternal feminine yearning to split a man down the middle. To try him out, she cited as an admirable example her father's partner, a man who rose from a $3-a-week clerk to a $30,000-a-year lawyer. His reply was almost indignant in rejecting the worthy lawyer as a model for himself: "God's own mad lover should do anything for a kiss, but not for thirty thousand a year."

Whatever else it did, the romance with Mabel Applegarth spurred his ambitions almost to the point of frenzy. Instead of completing his three-year course at Oakland High School he decided to drop out at the end of his first year and spend the summer cramming so he could enter the University of California that fall. In four months he would have to absorb two years of high-school studies in order to pass the college entrance examinations. That summer of 1896 he siphoned knowledge into himself relentlessly. For five weeks he attended a cramming school in Alameda, until the headmaster asked him to leave.[4] Word was getting around about Jack's overly ambitious program, and the university might crack down on the cramming school if it learned a man could be prepared for college so quickly.

So Jack went to work on his own, later claiming that he studied nineteen hours a day all that summer. He was close to cracking up by the time the examination approached. His brain was numb with exhaustion. Sensibly enough, having diagnosed himself as suffering from "brain-fag," he closed the books firmly and determined not to look at them again before the examination. Instead he borrowed a salmon boat, stocked it with food and sailed around the Bay for a week, letting himself soak in the sea breeze, the salt air and the hot sun.

By the time he sailed back up the Oakland estuary his mental powers were restored and his spirits revived. He passed the entrance examination without difficulty.

James Hopper, who had attended grade school with Jack and who later became a short-story writer of some renown, described him as he saw him at the opening of the fall term on the steps of North Hall on the Berkeley campus. Jack was "sloppily" dressed, wearing a shirt with a soft collar (in a day when even college students submitted to the possibility of decapitation by high starched collar). Two of his front teeth were missing. He clutched "about sixteen books under his arm," boasted to Hopper that he was going to take all the available courses in English, plus history, philosophy and the natural sciences.

Hopper, a lordly junior and "a bit of a bourgeois prig" in those days, as he later confessed, looked down his nose at the outlandish freshman and spoke condescendingly. Jack, he recalled, was "too bighearted" to resent the condescension — or, more likely, too smart to show his resentment. London owned up to having lost the front teeth "in a fight somewhere" and shrugged his broad shoulders. With his bronzed face and mop of curly light brown hair he looked to Hopper like a cross between a seagoing Swede on the beach and a Greek god.

People who remembered his brief stay on the Berkeley campus said Jack was popular among the few students with whom he associated, though he had little time or money for social life. He was carrying a heavy scholastic load, taking three English courses, two in history, one in philosophy and one in physical culture.

Jack was still doing odd jobs to contribute to the upkeep of Flora's household, and devoted most Sundays to courting Mabel Applegarth. Undoubtedly he wanted to be known as a "college man" largely to win favor in her eyes. In addition he continued his education in Socialist ideology. Often he took the ferry across the Bay at night to attend meetings of the Socialist Labor Party, of which Speed was a leading member, at the Academy of Science on Market Street.

It was during his brief college career that Jack learned for certain that he was illegitimate. Until then, he strongly suspected it, but Flora would never discuss the matter with him. According to his daughter Joan, the information was supplied him gratuitously by "some of his numerous steprelatives," who were jealous of his attempt to obtain an education and rise above them. They "taunted" Jack with a "garbled" account of his birth, Joan London has recounted. Jack asked Flora only for the name of his father, and she told him it was "Professor" Chaney.

With only that name to go on, Jack took up the investigation. In the files of the San Francisco *Chronicle,* he found the story concerning his mother's suicide attempt. At City Hall he found his birth recorded as the son of W. H. Chaney. The "Professor" still had some standing among fellow astrologers, and through a local practitioner Jack managed to trace down Chaney's Chicago address. The brief, unsatisfying exchange of letters with Chaney followed. And at the end of his investigation he knew almost as little as when he started. Either Chaney wasn't his father, as he claimed, or he was a heartless liar; neither reflection was particularly comforting. He was left with an enigma that haunted him to the end of his life. . . .

It was all pleasant enough being a college boy, but various pressures convinced him that he must leave the university at the end of the first semester of his freshman year. The decision, he later affirmed, did not greatly sadden him. It was brought on by several factors. He was running out of money, was convinced that he was't getting enough out of college to warrant the time he was putting into it, and considered that his intensive reading outside the curriculum was giving him more of what he needed than formal study. He was particularly cheered by the improvement in his grammar, which he attributed both to his later schooling and his association with the Applegarths. With some pride he noted that he no longer used the double negative — at least when writing — even though he had not yet been able to drill himself to say, "It is I," which to him was the epitome of refined speech. He quit the campus in late January of 1897 without undue regret.*

For a few weeks after leaving school he made a rather feverish effort to set himself up as a writer, turning out essays, political and sociological tracts, short stories, light verse, epic tragedies in verse, but gave it up when he saw that there would be no quick cash return. And money once again had become an urgent problem. His stepfather, having lost his watchman's job, was peddling pictures from door to door but couldn't make enough to support himself and Flora.

So Jack was back on the labor market, where he had sworn he would never be again, back among the "work brutes." He found a job in the steam laundry attached to Belmont Academy (an experience which provided some vivid scenes for *Martin Eden*). He was given room and board plus thirty dollars a month. The cash had to be sent up to Oakland to help support Flora and his stepfather. He and another man were required to sort, wash and iron all the school's laundry, from the students' white duck trousers to the starched dresses of the faculty wives. Often they had to work far into the night to keep the mountain of incoming soiled laundry from overwhelming them.

Jack was so tired by Sunday, his only day off, that he didn't have the energy to do anything but read the Sunday papers and catch up on his sleep. He had brought a trunk of books along, but never opened it. Stultified by the round of mindless toil, disgusted with slaving away in a steamy hell of wet wash, he wanted nothing more than to get crapulously drunk on his Sundays off. And he would have, he said, if the nearest saloon hadn't been a mile and a half away and he hadn't been too tired to walk there.

He figured that he was making the equivalent of fifty dollars a month now, counting board and wages, and at this rate, if he was lucky, he might some day be earning sixty a month as a watchman or,

* So he maintained in *John Barleycorn*. In his biographical sketch for the Macmillan Company, written some years earlier, he stated that he "hated to give up the hope of a university education." Perhaps he did, but he must have known that a man of his aspirations and his ability to soak up knowledge without formal guidance was not going to suffer greatly by leaving school.

if fortune really favored him, he might get on the force and earn a hundred a month plus graft as a policeman. Of course he never really resigned himself to that; it was just something to brood over as he worked the mangle or pressed some young whippersnapper's white ducks with the crease just so. Somehow he'd release himself from this nightmare, get a decent job, earn enough to marry Mabel Applegarth and start up the hard climb to becoming a writer.

From this humdrum possibility he was saved by reports coming out of Yukon Territory in Canada. They were best summed up by the headline:

GOLD! GOLD! GOLD! GOLD!
Sixty-eight Rich Men
on the *Portland*
STACKS OF THE YELLOW METAL! [5]

The chance for new adventures, the possibility of hitting it rich after a few months' scratching at some faraway creek bottom, the means of escape from the plodding dullness of his days — all were irresistible. Career, marriage, family would all have to wait on satisfaction of his newest urge. Nothing ever stood in the way of Jack London and an opportunity to plunge himself into some new experience, the more hazardous and remote the better.

IV

Self-Discovery in the Klondike

"It was in the Klondike I found myself. There nobody talks. Everybody thinks. You get your true perspective. I got mine."

— JACK LONDON

1. *"A Horde of Fools"*

THE GREAT gold rush to the Yukon, perhaps the last the world will ever see, started almost as simultaneously as though someone had fired a gigantic signal gun. All over America, seemingly, there were thousands of men just waiting to quit job, home and family; take ship from San Francisco or Seattle; climb mountain passes, shoot rapids, make long portages under heavy pack, trudge over hundreds of miles of muskeg; endure starvation and disease, Arctic cold and loneliness . . . all in the faint hope of finding pay dirt in some Canadian creek bed. Perhaps it was a nationwide attack of lunacy, perhaps a symptom of the bursting impatience of American men with the post-frontier restrictions of their lives, or as some social historians have divined (principally Thomas Beer) a last opportunity to get away from the growing domination of the American woman. There had never been anything quite like it; the Forty-Niners' rush to California had been sedate by comparison.

Newspaper writers called the mass compulsion Klondicitis, a fever that induced the victim to abandon everything, sell out, lock up, and take off for a remote and refrigerated corner of the continent — the Yukon River and its tributaries. To the justifiable outrage of Canadian feelings, most people mistakenly believed it was in Alaska and therefore on American soil.

Warnings from the few persons with knowledge of the Yukon country were drowned out in the uproar of the departing gold-seekers. The celebrated naturalist John Muir, who knew the North, declared that the gold rush was composed of a "horde of fools." Louis Sloss, one of the founders of the Alaska Commercial Company, was even firmer in his cautionary bulletin of July 28, 1897: "I regard it as a crime for any transportation company to encourage men to go to the Yukon this fall . . . The Seattle people who are booming the steamship lines may be sincere, but a heavy responsibility will rest on their shoulders should starvation and crime prevail in Dawson City next winter . . . It is a crime to encourage this rush, which can only lead to disaster for three-quarters of the new arrivals." No more attention was paid to them than to the caustic prophecy of Ambrose Bierce in his *Examiner* column: "Will he [the would-be stampeder] clear the way for even a dog-sled civilization and a reindeer religion? Nothing will come of him. He is a word in the wind, a brother to the fog. At the scene of his activity no memory of him will remain. The gravel that he thawed and sifted will freeze again. In the shanty that he builded, the she-wolf will raise her poddy litter, and from its eaves the moose will crop the esculent icicle unafraid. The snows will cover over his trail and all be as before."

All such pessimism was blown away by the hilarious arrival of veteran Klondikers. Prospectors who had been scratching around the wilderness for years before the rush began trudged down the gangplanks of the coastal steamers with their burdens of gold dust and nuggets.

The image of sudden wealth as presented by the returning sourdoughs was irresistible. On July 15, the steamer *Excelsior* docked at San Francisco with thousands of spectators gathered to watch them descend from the stubby, rusty little coastal tramp. Diminutive Tom Lippy, an ex-YMCA secretary, and his wife between them could hardly manage their suitcase containing $85,000 in raw gold. Another group of miners had to hire a four-horse dray to take their gold to the smelting works on Montgomery Street. An ex-laundryman from Seattle was regarded as a poor man because he brought out only $15,000

Two days later, up the coast at Seattle, the steamer *Portland* arrived with even more exciting evidence that the gold fields of the Yukon promised to be the new Golconda. Sixty-eight rich men, ragged, bearded and unprepossessing, disembarked. One man with $100,000 in dust and nuggets wrapped in a blanket had to hire two men to help him carry it off the ship. A Bull Durham sack of gold dust was as heavy as a sashweight. A moosehide bag of nuggets bent a man's back double.

The stories of the returning prospectors, many given to the exaggeration of their calling, contributed greatly to the impression that wealth was waiting up north for anyone willing to bend over and pick it off the ground. "We've got millions," said one. "Richest gold field in the world," said another. The Seattle *Post-Intelligencer* announced that the *Portland* had docked with "a ton of gold" aboard (actually it was more like two tons, worth more than a million dollars). That headline A TON OF GOLD blared across newspapers from coast to coast. "Prosperity is here . . . the depression is at an end," the *Post-Intelligencer* proclaimed.

The Pacific Coast, wrote a New York *Herald* correspondent, had "gone stark, staring mad on gold." In a few days the fever had spread to the Middle West, and a day or two later the supposedly more sophisticated East was as demented as the rest of the nation. Nothing short of war has ever so inflamed the country. People began seeing gold everywhere; a gang of laborers in New York City claimed they found coarse grains of gold in the sandy trench they were digging; a tourist in Victoria, British Columbia, announced that he had spotted an outcropping near the post office and tried to stake out a claim on the main street. Twenty-four hours after the *Portland* docked in Seattle, two thousand New Yorkers tried to buy tickets for the Yukon country. By August 1, at least eight large mining companies, capitalized at a total of $25,000,000, were offering stock on the New York Exchange and did not have to wait long for takers.

One of the first to be dazzled by the golden mirage shimmering over the whole North Country was Jack London, to whom it offered release from predictable years of grubbing, sweating, climbing. The shortcut to all he wanted, he was certain, lay along the sea-road to the Yukon. Why shouldn't he, too, make himself a millionaire in a few months? He was stronger and tougher than most, had roughed it more, had been around more, and was utterly self-confident. Was this the time to be thinking of elevating the masses? Even General Coxey, his late leader, had succumbed to the fever and invented a four-wheel "Klondike Bicycle" designed to convey a prospector and five hundred pounds of freight.

London's enthusiasm for the venture was infectious enough to persuade his stepsister Eliza Shepard to draw her savings of five hundred dollars from the bank and take out a thousand-dollar mortgage on her home to supply Jack and her elderly but similarly bedazzled husband with a grubstake for the journey. It also allowed his mother, whose fondness for any kind of speculation had so far brought the family to the edge of ruin more than once, to part with her chief breadwinner without protest, probably with an enthusiasm that equalled his own. Flora was all for taking a chance; she'd taken one leaving Massillon on her own, another, even wilder, one with Willian Henry Chaney; she was always ready to hazard, to dare. What she couldn't stand — and this was undoubtedly the basis of her occasional differences with her placid husband — was a plodding acceptance of daily bread. Perhaps that was why she kept venturing into the spirit world; you never knew who you might meet at a séance. It was a quality she had passed along to her son in his lifelong combat with the ordinary and the humdrum.

With his stepbrother-in-law Jack London sailed in the first wave for the gold fields outfitted with boots, fur-lined coats and caps, red flannel shirts and underwear, blankets, a tent, a stove, tools to build sleds and boats, and a thousand pounds of non-perishable food. The notice of their departure in the *Examiner* was brief:

SAILED
Stmr. *Umatilla,* Victoria, Port Townsend, Dyea.

It was the same ship on which he had worked his passage down from Canada after his coast-to-coast tour by boxcar and blind baggage. Could that be a bad omen? He was too busy planning for a rich strike in the Yukon, along with newfound shipboard friends, to give the matter much thought.

2. *Over the Chilkoot*

Jack London was not the only literary man who went fortune-hunting in the Klondike. Rex Beach (*The Spoilers, The Barrier, The Silver Horde*), a Chicago law student about London's age, had also joined the first wave of the stampede, outfitted much less practically than London with a rifle, a dogskin suit and a mandolin. The poet Joaquin Miller, "The Sweet Singer of the Sierras," who lived outside Oakland in the Piedmont Hills and would later become a friend of London's, went up with the same midsummer-mad rush with only a knapsack, a ticket back to San Francisco and a commission from the Hearst newspapers to sustain him. So did Wilson Mizner and his equally harum-scarum brothers, members of a prominent northern California family, who took along a Barbary Coast dance-hall girl with them for company. Mizner became a Broadway playwright and a Hollywood screenwriter, more famous for his razor-edged wit than anything he wrote, not the dullest strokes of which he reserved for the "London school" of Klondike fiction with its "supermen and superdogs, its abysmal brutes and exquisite ingenues." None of their trails crossed in the North Country but they shared a common fate. None of them struck pay dirt in the goldminer's sense, and all of them nearly starved to death before they got out.* Robert W. Service, who tapped one of the richest literary veins with his highly romantic verse, arrived in the Klondike several years after the rush was over.

It is clear from everything he wrote on the subject that Jack London joined the rush looking not for literary material, but for a quick fortune in the frozen earth like everyone else. "I had let career go hang," he recalled in *John Barleycorn,* "and was on the adventure path again in quest of fortune."

The *Umatilla* was loaded to the gunwales with fellow optimists from all over the United States, and he quickly teamed up with three of the more congenial, Fred Thompson, Jim Goodman and Merritt Sloper. In addition to the approval and confidence they felt in each other, the particular talents of the four young men seemed to dovetail nicely for the adventure ahead. Jack had handled boats of all sizes since boyhood. Thompson and Goodman claimed some knowledge of mining methods. Sloper was a carpenter, had batted around South America, and also knew something about sailing small boats. The man who got to the Klondike diggings, as they saw it, would have to know how to pack into the untracked wilderness, negotiate portages around impassable stretches of the rivers, sail the lakes up the water chain to Dawson, build sluices, sleds and cabins when he got there.

By the time the *Umatilla* anchored in Dyea Inlet, near the tent towns of Dyea and Skagway and at the foot of the Chilkoot Pass, the gateway to the Yukon Valley, thousands of men, horses and tons of

* The late Alva Johnston, author of *The Legendary Mizners,* summed it up neatly: "The average Yukon literary artist found that the Arctic was God's Country, and then ducked out as quick as he could."

baggage were piled up in mounting confusion on the beaches. Everything that could float and sail was being pressed into service, including garbage scows, sidewheelers and derelicts retrieved from the mud flats of Pacific harbors. Thousands of men were leaving San Francisco, Seattle and Victoria every week, despite warnings from the Canadian government and the U. S. Department of the Interior that they couldn't possibly hope to reach the Klondike region before winter locked in the rivers, lakes and trails. The bottleneck was on the narrow beaches of Dyea Inlet, where the stampeders had to surmount Chilkoot Pass with all their belongings and make a twenty-eight-mile portage to Lake Linderman.

Shepard took one look at the steep pass, another at the mound of supplies which would have to be packed over it, and announced that it was all too much for a man of sixty-plus. He caught the *Umatilla* on its return voyage to San Francisco. The family hopes of fortune were entrusted to Jack. A formidable job loomed before the young man but he was superbly confident that he could make it to the Klondike before the winter closed in. He and Goodman, Thompson and Sloper hauled their possessions to the foot of Chilkoot Pass and prepared to pack inland.

The worst part of the portage was the six steep miles over the Chilkoot in the heat of the Alaskan summer. Hundreds collapsed in exhaustion by the trailside and lay there until they could crawl down and return home in defeat. Indian porters were available but their price had shot up to fifty cents a pound, which meant that Jack alone would have had to pay all he had to get his supplies to Lake Linderman — and the Northwest Mounted Police, on guard at the Canadian boundary, insisted that every man going inland had to have five hundred in cash as well as a thousand pounds of food. Jack, in any case, didn't have any need of help from the Siwash porters. He stripped down to his bright red flannels, loaded a hundred and fifty pounds on his back, and charged up the pass. Each day he made a twenty-four-mile round trip, twelve under pack, until all his supplies were moved in stages to Lake Linderman. It was the proudest boast of his year in the Yukon that he beat the Indian porters in races up to the summit of the pass.

Along the trails to the Yukon Valley the most hideous sight to Jack, who loved animals from earliest childhood, was not the defeated and exhausted men — many of whom died by the wayside — but the dead and dying horses abandoned by their owners. Many of them foundered under the exceptional loads strapped to their backs, others slipped off the trail and lay among the rocks with broken legs, others were disemboweled by corduroy logs sticking up out of sloughs, many collapsed from starvation and ill treatment. Many of their owners could not even spare a bullet to put them out of their misery. "Their hearts turned to stone — those which did not break — and they became beasts, the men on the Dead Horse Trail," as Jack later described it.

Jack and his three companions, once they had cached their supplies, settled down on the shores of Lake Linderman to build two flat-bottomed boats to carry them along the waterways toward Dawson, the center of the Klondike country and the heart of the gold-crusted creeks, which they still hoped to reach before winter. They chopped down trees, sawed them into planks and built the boats according to specifications laid down by Jack, who cut, sewed and rigged the sails for them. He also paused, the day the boats were finished and launched as the *Yukon Belle* and *Belle of the Yukon,* to write a commemorative poem about each of them, a touch of artistry not entirely appreciated by his impatient colleagues.

The boats, with men and supplies aboard, skimmed across the placid waters of Lake Linderman. They also negotiated Lakes Bennett, Tagish and Marsh without difficulty. Lake Marsh, however, emptied into the Sixty-Mile River, which in turn constituted the headwaters of the Yukon. Here the rough roiling white water began, with Box Canyon, Squaw Rapids and White Horse Rapids ahead. The latter was an especially dangerous obstacle, so named because its swirling foam looked like white horses prancing in the sunlight. The river ran swift and deep and from an eighth to a quarter of a mile wide until it reached Box (now known as Miles) Canyon, where it was forced through a passage only eighty feet wide, its waters surging like a mill-race. Then it opened out into a circular court, midway through the canyon, into a whirling, sucking maelstrom in which more than a few boatmen had lost their lives. Several years before two Swedes had been trapped in the whirlpool for six hours before they managed to escape its centripetal currents. Then the river shot through a still narrower passage into the two stretches of rapids.

Before attempting the rough passage Jack consulted the best available guidebook, Miner W. Bruce's *Alaska, Its History and Resources,* written some years before. Regarding this perilous passage, Bruce had written, "If a man is a skilful navigator he can run his boat through the canyon and land on the right hand side. If not, he had better make a portage. From this point he should follow the left hand side two miles to the head of White Horse Rapids. Great precaution should be exercised in reaching the point where the landing is made above the White Horse. Through the White Horse, in a low stage of water, the boat can be dropped with a line; but if the water is high, a portage must be made."

As he told the story later, Jack and his companions put the matter to a vote: whether to portage or to attempt the passage by boat. The first and safest alternative would take two days of back-breaking labor over the trails around the canyon and rapids; the second would take a matter of minutes. "The other boats," Jack told his friends, "tried to fight the currents to keep off the rocks. We'll go *with* the current, and it'll keep us clear." They voted unanimously to try the water passage. Jack was captain, Sloper took the bow with a paddle, and the other two manned oars at either side.

First they took the *Yukon Belle* through, rocking, bouncing, flashing through the wild currents of the canyon. They went so fast the walls of the canyon, Jack said later, looked like two express trains passing them. Sloper broke his paddle in avoiding a crackup. Jagged rocks seemed intent on ripping out their bottom. But they made it safely, with Jack timing the passage at exactly two minutes.

Squaw Rapids was tame enough along its two-mile stretch. Then they paused at head of White Horse Rapids to bail out and batten down before plunging into the most dangerous stretch of the journey.

With Jack again at the steering sweep, the *Yukon Belle* swung out into the swift current and went rocking down the rapids. They narrowly missed a reef on the right. Then they shot into a second, and unexpected whirlpool, which snatched control of the craft away from its struggling captain. "From every quarter the water came aboard, threatening to swamp us. The *Yukon Belle* headed straight for the jagged left bank, and though I was up against the steering sweep, until it cracked, I could not turn her nose downstream." As they later learned they were in the wildest stretch of the river, called "The Mane of the Horse." Jack suddenly realized he was doing the wrong thing, trying to buck the whirlpool. "Like a flash I was bearing against the opposite side of the sweep. The boat answered, at the same time following the bent of the whirlpool, and headed upstream. But the shave was so close that Sloper leaped to the top of a rock. Then, on seeing that we had missed by a couple of inches, he pluckily tumbled aboard, all in a heap, like a man boarding a comet." [1]

Finally they landed in a "friendly eddy" below.

Undaunted, they cached their supplies near the *Yukon Belle,* went upstream and brought the *Belle of the Yukon* down.

By now they were all heroes to the hundreds of men camped or portaging along the rapids, particularly Jack. No one else, they learned, had successfully negotiated the water passage that season. Jack and his crew were immediately swarmed upon with offers to take other men's boats through the canyon and rapids. A price of twenty-five dollars per journey was fixed, and they went into business on the spot. The four men took 120 boats through in the next days, as Jack recounted later, and made three thousand dollars for themselves. His share came to more than he ever pocketed again in the Yukon country.

They could have stayed right there and continued to earn a couple hundred dollars a day, but they were still intent on reaching Dawson before the navigation season closed. They hoped to be among the first to stake claims along its nearby creeks; they wanted wealth, not mere prosperity, and who could resist such place-names up ahead as Gold Bottom Creek, Gold Hill, Orogrande Creek, All-Gold Creek, Too Much Gold Creek, Pure Gold Creek, King Solomon's Dome, not to mention Eldorado, Bonanza and Ready Bullion Creeks?

They pushed on, across Lake Labarge, past the Northwest Mounted Police post, down the swift clear Thirty-Mile River, into the broad terraced valley of the Yukon and onto its mighty channel. The days were steadily growing shorter. Flights of birds were arrowing south. The air had turned crisp, and the wind from the north bore a premonitory chill.

Just as they reached the mouth of the Stewart River with its tangle of channels and islands at the meeting with the upper Yukon, just seventy-five miles short of their destination, the skies darkened and a blizzard blew down from the Arctic. If they hadn't halted to pilot the boats through White Horse, they would have made Dawson with a day or two to spare. Now they were stuck for the winter.

3. *Winter Camp*

All over the Yukon country winterset brought the first wave of the stampede to a frozen halt. From the Arctic Ocean to the Gulf of Alaska, from the Bering Sea to Great Slave Lake, thousands of gold hunters converging on the Klondike were caught short of their goal and forced to hole up for the winter wherever that first blast of Arctic wind and snow struck them. Many unfit or ill-prepared to face a long winter in the Far North would fall victim to frostbite, disease, cabin fever, homesickness and melancholia.

A traveling circus was caught on the Ashcroft Trail in the wilds of British Columbia; on the Kowak River four English gentlemen-stampeders built a cabin, trained an Eskimo to serve as their valet and had coffee and cigars brought to them as they slept until noon; at Minook Creek the future novelist Rex Beach, also stuck for the winter, heard a disgruntled newspaperman tell his companions that "we'll never read any great stories about Alaska and the Klondike. There's no drama up here . . . This country is too drab and dreary." [2]

Perhaps, at the time, Jack London would have agreed with him. He and fifty-odd other stampeders trapped in an old settlement called Upper Island, on the Stewart River, went about making themselves comfortable for the months ahead. He and Thompson, Goodman and Sloper took possession of a former settler's cabin, caulked its seams against the slashing north wind, and chopped firewood by the cord.

Jack was not unduly depressed by their predicament. He had been in worse situations as a road kid and a deckhand; all they had to do was settle down and take it easy. There was no reason to be lonely in a camp like Upper Island, and homesickness was never one of his problems. Being caught in an Arctic winter was something new and strange, with impressions to be taken in and stored away, just as he had automatically — with no exact idea of what value they might be to him — soaked up past experiences. Everyone does that, of course, but Jack like many men of artistic talent had a special facility for it. He had a painter's eye for the countryside, for the way people looked and went about their jobs. Later these images, summoned up by a descriptive power that was one of his strongest points, would illuminate the printed page with brilliance and precision. The reader was plunged into the place London wanted him to be, and transfixed by an awareness of what his guide was trying to show him.

That one winter in the Yukon lasted him for years of writing in novels and short stories, as when he described the immense stillness of the North. Undoubtedly he was recalling those months in the Upper Island camp when he described "a world of silence and immobility. Nothing stirred. The Yukon slept under a coat of ice three feet thick. No breath of wind blew. Nor did the sap move in the hearts of the spruce trees that forested the river banks on either hand. The trees, burdened with the last infinitesimal pennyweight of snow their branches could hold, stood in absolute petrifaction. The slightest tremor would have dislodged the snow, and no snow was dislodged . . . It was a dead world, and furthermore, a gray world. The weather was sharp and clear; there was no moisture in the atmosphere, no fog nor haze; yet the sky was a gray pall. The reason for this was that, though there was no cloud in the sky to dim the bright of the day, there was no sun to give brightness . . ." [3]

In addition, he had time to think in that winter camp; for the first time in his life he was trying to evaluate the past, to know himself, to plumb his capabilities and try to decide what might be done with them. If he got rich out of Klondike gold, of course, many of his problems would be solved; but you still had to know what to do with yourself if you were a wealthy man. Marriage to Mabel Applegarth, would, of course, be made easy. So would a literary career, with the time bought by Klondike gold. He could also become a benefactor of mankind, a promoter of the Socialistic revolution, and a living testimonial to the theory that money could do good in the world as well as evil.

"It was in the Klondike I found myself," he later wrote. "There nobody talks. Everybody thinks. You get your true perspective. I got mine." [4]

From the recollections of men who wintered with him at Upper Island, however, Jack's silence did not exactly match that of the frozen countryside around them. He had always loved to talk, to expound when he had the chance, and here the snowbound men of the winter camps along the mouth of the Stewart provided him with something like a captive audience. There was little entertainment besides conversation.

Jack's cabin evidently was the center of social and intellectual life, with a judge, a doctor, a professor, an engineer and other professional men among those wintering at or near Upper Island. In his baggage he had brought copies of Darwin's *Origin of Species,* Spencer's *Philosophy of Style,* a translation of Marx's *Das Kapital,* Haeckel's *Riddle of the Universe* and Milton's *Paradise Lost.* Once, for lighter reading, Jack walked seven miles to borrow a copy of Kipling's *Seven Seas* from a man camped upriver.

Often there were night-long discussions by the fireside of the cabin Jack shared with his three companions. Jack, of course, argued mightily for the coming Socialist revolution, and evidently found nothing ironic about a group of gold-seekers debating the merits of a system under which the wealth they found would be separated from them for the betterment of their less fortunate fellows . . . a paradox with thorns, as yet invisible to Jack, which would become sharper with the years.

Jack was so busy conducting his fireside forum that, according to Fred Thompson's slightly disgruntled recollection, he could rarely be persuaded to help attend to the camp shores. He hated to leave a lively discussion of Darwin's theories or the scientific approach to making a better world simply to haul water or split firewood. Stanley Searce, another campmate, remembered Jack as lying in his bunk most of the time, smoking cigarets and daydreaming. It was agreed that he spent a notably inactive winter.*

W. B. Hargreaves, another Upper Islander, was grateful for his companionable indolence. "Many a long night Jack and I, outlasting the vigil of the others, sat before the blazing spruce logs and talked the hours away . . . He had a mental craving for truth. He applied one test to religion, to economics, to everything: *What is truth?* He could think great thoughts. One could not meet him without feeling the im-

* Emil Jensen, a fellow resident of Upper Island, said Jack was helpful in other and more imaginative ways. "Jack's companionship was refreshing, stimulating, helpful. He never stopped to count the cost or dream of profits to come. He stood ever ready, were it a foraging trip among the camps for reading matter, to give a helpful hand on a woodsled, or to undertake a two days' hike for a plug of tobacco . . . for the want of a smoke." (Quoted in Irving Stone's *Sailor on Horseback.*)

pact of a superior intellect. He faced life with superb assurance, and faced death serenely imperturbable."

On at least one occasion, however, Thompson was able to lure Jack away from the fireside debates and recall him to the main purpose of their presence in the wilderness. He persuaded Jack that they might be able to do some prospecting even if everything was frozen hard. Off they went with a sled and a dog team Thompson had bought, on an expedition with seriocomic results that must have given both of them an inkling of the shattering disappointments that were part of prospecting for gold. They ventured over the hills that sloped toward the Yukon to a creek that drained into the river below Upper Island.

The swift current of the creek near where they camped kept the ice from freezing over it. They took their shovels and dug into the rock and gravel of the creek bed.

In no time at all — confirming all the glorious reports which had sent them stampeding northward — they came up with shovelfuls of gravel and coarse sand streaked with a magic glitter. Those shiny bits of yellow metal could be nothing but the substance they had trekked, portaged and sailed at great risk to their necks to find.

Gold!

In a few hours they had struck pay dirt. They were rich . . . rich! Thompson, making an impulsive estimate of their find, declared they were each worth a quarter of a million dollars as of now.

They paused only to stake out a claim for each of them, and then hastened back to Upper Island to broadcast the good news. It spoke well for their native generosity that they were eager to share their good fortune with their friends and camp mates. More calculating types would have kept the find to themselves, worked the claims for all they were worth, and possibly wound up trying to murder each other. But that wasn't the way of the Klondike, where men who hit pay dirt generally went whooping to the nearest settlement to lead a pell-mell stampede back to their diggings. So Jack and his partner capered through the settlement shouting the news and then led the whole population of Upper Island back to the creek they had been exploring.

A couple of men with prospecting experience were among the moonstruck stampeders, and the gleaming bits of metal in the creek bed were shown to them for an expert opinion.

A bitter smile rewarded the two amateurs.

What London and Thompson had found was a sprinkling of iron pyrites. It looked like gold to the unknowing eye, but it was worthless. Veteran miners called it "fools' gold." A whole mountain of it wouldn't buy a man a platter of ham and eggs.

There was a certain amount of jeering at London's and Thompson's expense, but their companions took it into account that they'd rushed back to camp to share their supposed strike. It was good-naturedly suggested that Jack return to lecturing and theorizing at his informal University of Upper Island and wait until spring to begin his prospecting career. Jack, as Thompson later recalled the incident, wasn't much disappointed to find their gold panned out as iron pyrites.

And from then on, it seemed, Jack lost interest in the nominal purpose of his trip to the Yukon. He never went looking for gold again.

Subconsciously, perhaps, he had already started digging for something more precious to him: all around was the stuff of which stories were to be made, the characters, the settings, the incidents, the conflict of man against a hostile environment. Here he met the men who, with a blending of imagination, became the Malemute Kid, Elam Harnish, Louis Savard, Del Bishop, Peacock, and all the other Klondikers who paraded through his stories, many of them composites, some of the more heroic types combined with more than a bit of himself.

All that long winter, when his companions thought him notable mainly for his idleness, good nature and garrulity, he was living on a level invisible to them, storing up the images and impressions that one day would be conveyed to millions all over the world, making those men, commonplace to themselves and others, something like immortal. He was weaving a legend, creating a Klondike that never existed except in his imagination, a myth so powerful it was accepted as reality by people who had actually lived it. He was making a fairly ordinary breed of men (the Klondikers, said Wilson Mizner, whose cynicism was unflagging, were "the worst sissies on earth") into a race of heroes, great of heart, mind and body. Without knowing it, he was passing through the most fruitful winter of his life in the camp at Upper Island.

Then the wind began shifting to a more southerly quarter, the skies turned from gray to blue, and the thaw began with thunderclaps of ice breaking up on the Yukon.

He and his three cabinmates split up, apparently on friendly enough terms judging from letters he later exchanged with them, for the continuation of the journey to Dawson. Teaming up with a Dr. Harvey, he fashioned a raft of logs. He and the physician drifted down the river toward the Ophir of the North Country.

4. *Carnival Time in Dawson*

In one month that spring of 1898 Dawson was to become the largest city in the Dominion west of Winnipeg, and only slightly smaller than such American cities as Seattle, Portland and Tacoma. By midsummer its population would reach eighteen thousand. On foot and on rafts, boats and river steamers the gold rushers poured into the town located where the Klondike flows into the Yukon. It was a colorful mob representing the more restless elements of the North American continent, with delegates from western Europe, South Africa and Australia (which also had experienced gold finds), the Hawaiian Islands, even a few strays from the Orient.

They were boomers, fugitives, promoters, pimps, unemployed gunfighters, remittance men, soldiers of fortune, shills, gamblers, con men, lawyers, doctors, cowboys, artists, thieves, thugs, and men who had simply worked for a living; also women by the hundreds — this was a more or less coeducational gold rush — some of them whores, some of them honest widows with children to support, some with virtue, and many more without. All nominally had come in search of gold, power or excitement, but mainly they had left their homes to escape whatever bothered them about American life. The Yukon was a way out. If they had waited a little longer, they could have rushed to the colors (the United States declared war on Spain on April 25, and Dewey's squadron was sailing into Manila Bay about the time the ice was breaking on the Yukon) at less expense and probably less hardship. It was as though the continent had been tilted and all the footloose and the discontented had been jarred free and sent sliding into its northwest corner. And the hell-roaring capital of that feverish mob was Dawson.

Jack London came upon it one mid-May day after a fairly untroubled trip down the Yukon, its broad bosom still churning with chunks of ice. The only misadventure recalled by Dr. Harvey, his raftmate, was when Jack's steering sweep broke and the young man uttered the most all-embracing blasphemy Dr. Harvey ever heard:

"Doctor, I don't know who made this world but I believe I could make a damned sight better one myself."

As they swung around a final bend in the river, past a rocky bluff, they came upon an unforgettable sight, Dawson in the first flush of its boom. On the right, or eastern side, the Klondike poured into the Yukon's spring flood, and on the north bank of the Klondike towered a scar-faced mountain. At the foot of the mountain was Dawson City, mostly a tent town spreading over the surrounding hills and swampy flats and across the Klondike to its south bank, which was a noisome suburb known as Lousetown. In the center of the canvas roofs were a number of false-fronted saloons, stores, warehouses, banks and whorehouses, as well as many other buildings in the process of being built — this was Front Street, a nostalgic reminder for survivors of the good old days in Dodge City, Tombstone, Abilene and Deadwood, as was the presence of Calamity Jane, who soon skipped out, and Wyatt Earp, who later got rich running a gambling joint in Nome.

Here in the middle of the sub-Arctic wilderness, a thousand miles from civilization, a city had sprung up, as the Dawson-born historian Pierre Berton has written, "a little unreal . . . bathed in a halo of sunlight, blurred slightly at the edges by the mists that steamed from the marshes." [5]

Jack wandered through the muddy streets, among the first to arrive of the thousands of stampeders who had been caught upriver, downriver and elsewhere by the onset of winter. In a few days boats and rafts were landing by the hundreds, with a great flotilla from the chain of lakes to the south still on its way. Within six weeks a building lot would be selling for $40,000, a gallon of milk for $30, a pound of tomatoes for $5, and a man-sized breakfast for $3.50.

It took Jack only a few days to learn the depressing truth about a boom town: you had to be well-heeled to live in one. And another truth about a gold rush: there were no prizes for second place. It didn't do much good to get there months after gold had been discovered. All the better claims had been staked. Most of the fortunes made in the Klondike came out of the pockets of the people — their life savings and those of their families, in many cases — who got there too late and had to spend their last dollar just to keep alive. Already the gold rush was feeding on itself.

Jack's earnings as a river pilot soon vanished because of the high cost of living. He was faced with several possibilities, none of them particularly pleasing: he could go to work in a sawmill or construction project, jobs being plentiful; get out of Dawson and look for gold, but that took a grubstake which he didn't have; beat his way out of the Klondike and back home however he could, or hang around and starve.

It looked for a while as though he would accept the last possibility. Fred Thompson said later that London "never done a tap of work" while he was in Dawson. The general wage scale was $17.50 a day, barely enough to cover food and lodging, and Jack wasn't interested in bare subsistence. Nor did he want to clear out, go home and confront his stepsister Eliza with the news that she had mortgaged herself in vain; Jack coming home in defeat was getting to be a much too familiar story. Nor did he have any ambition to chop through the frosty earth on some lonely creek when everyone around Dawson except the most imperishable optimists agreed that all the most promising claims had been staked.

What transfixed and fascinated him, broke as he soon was, was the spectacle of Dawson's boom in full spate, the high life of the saloons, dance halls and gambling joints, Front Street crowded day and night with thousand of men shuffling aimlessly along, as directionless as himself. The local paper, the *Klondyke Nugget,* described that throng as "curious, listless, dazed, dragging its slow lagging step along the main street." Those men had risked everything to pack into Dawson and now they didn't know what to do with themselves. Many would simply go home before the summer ended, as though they recognized that they had been lured northward by some indefinable urge, had used up all their energy on the journey, and had come to realize that it wasn't the gold which they had been seeking, only an opportunity to get away from it all.

With little else to occupy him, Jack spent his days and most of his nights talking to people of all kinds, listening to their stories, questioning old-timers from the pre-stampede days and compiling an unwritten account of how it had been before the gold rush started. By now, undoubtedly, he had acquired a conscious purpose: he'd caught glimmerings of his own Mother Lode. This was the material he would use, once it had been sifted through his mind and colored by his imagination, when he began writing in earnest. In a few months he would start taking notes, but now he stored it all away in his memory.

The best place to listen and observe was a barroom, where men talked more freely; besides Jack always felt in his element among drinking men. He couldn't buy a round himself, but paid his way by spinning tales and entertaining his fellow drinkers. He was, in fact, a high-class barfly.

He watched the Eldorado Kings, the prospectors who had been on the ground when gold was first discovered and had profited accordingly, strutting around and throwing their money away . . . suckers at the Combination dance hall paying two ounces of gold for a pint of champagne . . . barkers with megaphones standing outside the gaudier dives and advertising the charms of the girls within . . . a platoon of Salvation Army lassies banging their tambourines and singing hymns, not quite loud enough to drown out the ragtime music thumping out of the Front Street saloons and dance halls . . . men who had committed some crime against the Canadian law working out their time on the woodpile under Mounted Police guard . . . rudimentary newsreels flashed on bedsheets in the honkytonks showing United States soldiers marching off to war in Cuba and Gentleman Jim Corbett, a fellow San Franciscan, making his comeback for the heavyweight title . . . Gerry the Bum, an alcoholic donkey, sneaking into saloons and begging drinks until the bartender threw him out . . . The spectacle was endless and fascinating.

He also made friends, platonically no doubt, with the girls who danced and sang and whored for a living. His boyish charm and his storytelling ability apparently made up for his lack of money. One friend in particular was a Greek girl, Freda Maloof, who billed herself as "The Turkish Whirlwind Danseuse." Her specialty was the belly dance, or hootchie-kootchie, which Little Egypt had performed to the general astonishment at the Chicago World's Fair. Freda's sinuous hips and artful writhing proved so inflammatory that the Mounted Police stepped in and demanded that she tone down her performance.*

* Years later Jack, famous by that time, ran into Freda Maloof doing her muscle dance at an Oakland street fair. She was fat and forty. Jack gave her a copy of

If a man could have lived on whiskey bought by jovial companions, Jack would probably have survived that summer in good shape. Whiskey, unfortunately, was no safeguard against diet deficiency.

Scurvy became endemic in Dawson with its shortage of fruit, vegetables and other vitamin-bearing foodstuffs. Only those who had staked a lucrative claim or had brought thousands of dollars with them could eat well enough to ward off the deficiency disease.

Jack himself, living off whiskey and a meal here and there, had scurvy after less than a month in Dawson. His teeth loosened in his swollen gums and four upper ones fell out; his face was covered with sores and he was almost bent double with the constant gripping pain that knotted his abdomen and leg muscles. Starvation was not far away. There was nowhere to turn but Father William Judge's hospital, a makeshift affair at the north end of town, far from the high-rolling atmosphere of Front Street, the last hope of thousands of men who were felled by typhoid, malaria, dysentery and the starvation diseases like scurvy and beri-beri. Father Judge, a tall, gaunt man in a tattered cassock who literally gave his life to succor the failures of the gold rush and became rightly known as "The Saint of Dawson," provided a cot, a minimum amount of food and whatever medicines were available to anyone in need of care. A man's religion neither gained him entry nor barred him from the Jesuit's establishment. This was fortunate for Jack, who proclaimed himself an agnostic.

The food and rest supplied by Father Judge, minimal as it was, probably saved Jack's life. In a week or so, he was back on his feet, wobbly, pale-faced, a rack of bones, but able to get around.

What to do next? He had hung around Dawson and seen the sights and worn out his welcome. He had also absorbed enough local color to keep him going for years, provided he ever got started. Dawson could give him nothing more, except possibly another attack of scurvy. It was time to get on with his own job of work which, he was now convinced, was writing. If he waited around too long, he wouldn't be able to leave before the big freezeup.

He didn't want to return the way he had come, from Skagway and over those damned rapids. It was shorter, but he'd seen that bit of

---

The God of His Fathers in memory of her kindness to him when he was down and out in the Klondike. The volume included a story, "The Scorn of Women," in which the leading character was based on Freda Maloof.

scenery. The much longer but easier route, because no portages were required, was down the Yukon to St. Michael on Norton Sound, known as the "millionaires' route" because many traveled it in the comparative ease and safety of a riverboat. From St. Michael, on the Alaskan coast, he might be able to work his passage back to San Francisco.

Late in June Jack and two companions named Taylor and Thorson took a last look at the town which defeated them and so many others, shoved off in a small boat and let the Yukon carry them on the seventeen-hundred-mile journey toward St. Michael and the sea. Jack took charge of the steering.

5. *By Open Boat to the Sea*

From Dawson on, Jack began keeping a notebook in which he recorded his impressions of the sights and sounds of the Yukon country as his boat slid by on the long journey to the sea. The notes were sketchy, impressionistic, rather than a formal journal, but at least the method was more systematic and scientific than relying on his memory to recall the background of the stories he hoped to write. Many of the entries indicated how concerned he was now with possible literary material. Not that he was setting his sights very high; his mistake on leaving the University of California was trying to turn out ponderous essays and tragic verse for highbrow magazines which wouldn't conceivably be interested in him or his work, and he wasn't going to repeat it. His aim now was to write something salable for the more popular periodicals, such as *Outing Magazine* and *Youth's Companion*. They wanted vivid, readable stuff such as his journey could supply, and if he couldn't return home with a poke heavy enough to founder a mule, at least he'd have those notes for future reference.

Many of them turned up, considerably recast and with heightened effects, in an article titled "From Dawson to the Sea."* And the whole experience of the outbound voyage, particularly his meetings with odd characters settled along the Yukon, was rewoven into the fabric of countless stories.

Compared to the rigors of the journey upcountry, drifting down the Yukon and letting the river's current do the work was idyllic.

* Which he sent the Buffalo *Express* after it was turned down by a number of magazines and the San Francisco papers, and was published by that newspaper June 4, 1899.

With hardly a lifted hand from the voyagers, the river carried them along at a steady six miles an hour, 144 miles a day. In a dozen days, unless they spent much time stopping by the way, they would reach St. Michael. Their "home-made," unsheltered boat was just large enough to convey them in comfort. In the bow was the "woodshed," with fuel for fires; amidships was the "bedchamber," fashioned from pine boughs and blankets, and in the stern was "our snug little kitchen." Jack and his two companions swore they were going to make the trip as comfortably as possible, and would halt only to go ashore and replenish their firewood or if something tugged at their curiosity. They passed the days playing cards, telling stories, smoking, and enjoying the scenery.

Along the way they passed mining camps deserted in the mad rush upriver to the Klondike region. Their first stop was on American soil, at Eagle City, Alaska, the population of which had dropped to fifty and was mostly engaged in bucking the tiger at a faro layout. They celebrated their return to American territory with great enthusiasm, he wrote in the newspaper article, because they were fed up with what they regarded as the oppressiveness of Canadian authority. Many Americans, forgetting they were guests of the Dominion, furiously resented the restrictions, most of them eminently sensible, imposed by the government of the Northwest Territory. The Mounted Police, for instance, arrested anyone carrying sidearms, being determined to avoid another Dodge City.*

Three hundred miles downriver from Dawson they came to Circle City, which had been the largest mining camp before gold was discovered in the Klondike. Now it was as deserted as any Western ghost town. Below Circle City they drifted into desolate Yukon Flats, mile after mile of tangled islands and channels, all clouded over with mosquitoes. Here he quickly noted: "Description of Flats — not Thousand Islands of St. Lawrence, not thousands of thousands but thousands of millions — mosquitoes, woods, sloughs, immense piles of drift, all kinds of life what we have been told about, geese and goose eggs . . ." The main problem in getting through the noisome Flats, he noted, was to find the widest channels and swiftest currents. "Men have been known to lose their way and wander for weeks in this perplexing maze."

* There were no gunfights and not a single murder in Dawson during 1898.

Still inside the Flats, near the point where the Yukon crosses the Arctic Circle, they approached Fort Yukon, an old Hudson Bay Company post with an Indian village nearby. "Scattered Indian camps," he wrote in his journal as they drifted toward the old fort, "deserted log cabins, woodyards. Beauty of the night — drifting down the river, midnight & broad daylight, robins and other song birds singing on the islands; partridges, drumming tern, seagulls and loons discordant crys echoing across the glassy river stretches; kildee, plover, ducks, foolish or silly cries of wild geese, Martins, owls, hawks."

The steamer *Bella* was loading at Fort Yukon, causing a holiday in the Indian village. Although it was only four o'clock in the morning, the Arctic sun was out bright and hot, and the Indian bucks were "skylarking" with the maidens, the squaws were gathered in gossiping huddles and their babies were rolling in the mud with tawny beasts half wolf and half dog. The whole scene, he wrote later in the newspaper article, was drifted over with thick clouds of wood smoke and "a mysterious air of unreality."

To Jack's eye there was an enchantment that extended over the whole river journey, "teeming with paradoxes," which no writer, especially a young and impressionable one, can resist. There was a "strange beauty and charm" to drifting down the river at midnight with the sun "poised like a ball of blood on the northern horizon." And there was a haunting beauty to the solitude of the river banks, with no sounds except those from the birds and the roar of a bull moose crashing through the brush.

At the mouth of the Tanana River: "The camp was large and the Indians had arrived from the Tanana and were in full force, waiting the fishing. Dance in progress, white man's dances." He noted with some disapproval that the usual white man, gone native with an Indian bride and half-caste children, was present and treated with great deference by the Indians. The Anglo-Saxon squawman, "always at home in every environment," was regarded as a great catch in those days, though he abhorred work of any sort.

He thought that the halfbreed issue of such unions faced a particularly bitter and pathetic existence, and wrote his impressions of a young halfbreed woman with a baby whom he saw peering at him through tent flaps in a camp a hundred miles below Tanana Station. She had inherited her father's Caucasian features, with a delicate oval face, yet she would have to travel with her tribe, her baby strapped to her back, as it sought hunting and fishing grounds, walking forty miles a day in temperatures that often dropped to fifty degrees below zero and lower. When it came to fathers abandoning their children, he looked no more for "paradoxes" but was overcome by disgust at the irresponsibility of his race; by this time, of course, he had conducted the tragically futile correspondence with his own putative father, "Professor" Chaney.

Jack did not envy the lot of the squawmen he met at the stations along the river. They had escaped the wear and tear of competition in the cities, had no worries about the future so long as they were willing to be content with the "bleak and blank" prospects of life in an Indian village. He was especially touched by the pride of the Indians in claiming an Anglo-Saxon for an in-law. But he didn't see how the white man could endure the essential boredom of Indian life.

The Indians' struggle for existence fascinated him. Here was life stripped down to its barest essentials, the search for daily food ("straight meat and fish diet, washed down with incalculable quantities of vile-smelling seal oil") and shelter. The Malemutes, a part Eskimo tribe living near the Bering Sea coast, lived in holes dug out of the earth and roofed over with driftwood, with an open fire in the center of the burrow for cooking and heating.

The last two days of the journey were spent negotiating the treacherous channels of the Great Delta of the Yukon, before it emptied into the Bering Sea. The danger, he wrote, was that they would blunder into the southern channel and be swept onto the bleak coast far south of St. Michael. If they could follow the northernmost channel they would have an easy enough run up to St. Michael in the lee of the delta's island cluster. Somehow, without guides, they picked the right route and rounded Point Romanoff, where the trip up the coast got rougher and more exciting as they fought their way through the surf. On the way they picked up a Jesuit named Father Robeau, who was having a hard time battling the surf in his three-hole kayak. The priest, whom Jack found to be the most interesting man he'd met in the North, was full of unexpected joviality. To Jack he was an example of the many strange types who had somehow assembled in this remote corner of the continent — "an Italian by blood, a Frenchman by birth, a Spaniard by education and an American by residence." Father Robeau had spent twelve years in Alaska but was a happy man, who had lost himself in the joys of scholarship, which in his case was the job of reducing the Innuit dialect to a grammar. "Possessed of fatal faculty of getting lost," Jack noted in his journal.

He and his companions reached the harbor of St. Michael just twenty-one days after shoving off from Dawson.

At St. Michael Jack signed on as a stoker on a steamer running down to Vancouver, from which he took passage in steerage on another ship bound for Seattle. Completely broke, he beat his way down the coast to San Francisco on the freights, just one of thousands in the backwash of the gold rush returning home with little but memories to show for the experience.

Jack, however, knew how to put those memories to work for him.

BOOK TWO

The Sea

V

"Clubbed into Fortune"

1. A Return to Responsibility

APPARENTLY London in later years was rather inconsistent in his attitude toward his experiences in the Yukon. He could never quite make up his mind whether to be grateful for them or decry the hardships and suffering they entailed. Publicly, as the chief literary celebrant of the gold rush, he was inclined to praise the primitive splendors of life under the midnight sun. The sour grapes he preferred to squeeze and distill in more private conversation. A fellow writer from Oakland, Thames Williamson,[1] said that "he was very bitter about the country when I knew him in Oakland. I was a kid, a hero-worshipper; and I asked him a lot of questions about his life up there. Mention of Alaska made London scowl and curse. It was a hell of a place; it had ruined his health. He went up there to get rich and all he brought back was the scurvy."

It was indeed a bitter homecoming for Jack in the summer of 1898 when the migration to the Klondike was reaching its height and people still believed that only a dunderhead could fail to make his fortune up there, what with the gold lying around waiting to be picked up. The returning failures, who had left promising to buy everyone in the neighborhood a diamond ring, could only look sheepish and try to explain that finding gold was not as simple as it sounded in the newspapers.

Jack, no less brave in his promises than anyone else, came back penniless, soot-stained from riding the freights, gaunt and ailing from his bout with the scurvy. He had tossed away his stepsister's money in a futile continuation of his career as a wandervogel. All he had to show for a year of his life, the first official year of manhood, was a notebook full of random impressions of the lower Yukon. Not even a nugget to flash around as proof he'd been up north.

And as usual he returned to find that his family was in even worse straits than when he left them. John London, his stepfather, had died while he was away, fading out of life as unobtrusively as he had lived it. There was no doubt that Jack mourned him as much as John London could be mourned. The man had given him his name, had always treated him kindly and tried to be a father to him. The fact that Flora dominated the household with her stronger and more perverse will, and that her husband could not offer his charges much protection against it, made John London always an insubstantial, if not inconsequential, figure; one to be loved and mourned as much for his good intentions as anything else.

To keep her company after her husband's death, Flora had adopted Johnny Miller, whom her stepdaughter Ida had brought home to her, and that meant another mouth to feed. Johnny may or may not have been Ida's son, though she was unmarried at the time. Joan London recalls that Mammy Prentiss, who was perhaps more jealous of the Londons' good name than they were themselves, and certainly was more zealous in preserving it, always "stoutly maintained" that Johnny was a foundling whom Ida had unofficially adopted. Most people, however, assumed that the child was Ida's son. He also became Jack's charge until he grew up.

Jack had come back from the Yukon determined to exert himself as what he called a "brain merchant," specifically a writer, but it looked as though he had no alternative but to find any kind of work that would support the family. The only proviso was that it had to be on land because, for all his love of the sea, he felt that long voyages took too much time out of a man's life and like most ambitious young men he was very time-conscious. Besides, a weekly paycheck was needed at home, and a seaman didn't get paid off until the end of a voyage.

The only semi-skilled job he could handle was that of a laundry worker, but there were no openings around Oakland. He signed on with five employment agencies, advertised in the three local papers, answered ads for a sewing-machine agent working house to house and for a companion to an invalid, even trotted around artists' studios offering himself as a model. There were no takers. Everyone said that the depression that began in 1893 was over; a sizable portion of the labor market had been tapped by the gold rush and the armed forces then engaged in detaching Spain from its colonial empire, but around Oakland jobs were as scarce as when he left. Finally he took a Civil Service examination for postmen, though there was no immediate openings.

Meanwhile, he was ridding himself of the last traces of the scurvy by eating raw potatoes; not the finest specific known to medicine, which recommended green vegetables and fruit, but the cheapest and ultimately effective. He was still chewing tobacco to kill the pain of the infection in his remaining teeth, but stopped when his stepsister Eliza Shepard struck a bargain with him. She would have him fitted with a partial upper plate if he would give up the habit. The plate was ill-fitting and soon broke, but he gave up tobacco-chewing for good.

He kept his mother and young stepnephew and himself going by frequent and increasingly desperate trips to the pawnbroker. Flora had become expert at stretching a few dollars' worth of food to last a week or more, but there was also the landlord to be paid for the small frame house they rented at 962 East Sixteenth Street. He hocked his watch and his bicycle, then a mackintosh (for two dollars) which was his stepfather's sole legacy. He also made a deal with a waterfront friend who had somehow — Jack didn't look into the matter too closely — acquired a dress suit. Jack traded a number of all but worthless items he found around the house for the dress suit, then pawned the suit for five dollars.

Daytimes he looked for work as a longshoreman, a swamper, a coal-heaver, a roustabout, a drayman's helper — anything that might pay a living wage — and tramped the streets locating odd jobs, cutting lawns, trimming hedges, beating carpets.

At night, weary or disheartened or sick or hungry as he might be, he began trying to write something that would sell, first of all newspaper articles on his experiences getting into the "Clondyke," as he then spelled it, and his trip down the Yukon in an open boat. First he queried the San Francisco *Examiner* on whether it would be interested in a four-thousand-word story, to which an anonymous editor replied:

"Interest in Alaska has subsided to an amazing degree. Then again so much has been written that I do not think it would pay us to buy your story."

A month later, November 22, 1898, he wrote M. H. de Young, the editor and publisher of the *Chronicle,* making the same offer. De Young replied that he simply didn't have room for such a story.

Undeterred by the obtuseness of newspaper editors across the Bay, he refused to give up hope that what he saw and endured in the Yukon had some merchandisable value. People were still flocking up to the Klondike in droves, weren't they? And all that people in the States were learning about the gold rush came from the sketchy accounts of a few newspaper correspondents, who naturally emphasized the more sensational aspects, the stampedes to newly prospected creeks, the occasional rich finds, the uproarious life in Skagway, Dawson and other towns on the bonanza trail.

In seven nights he wrote a 21,000-word serial for *Youth's Companion,* a periodical that demanded clean-cut, clean-living young heroes (or prigs) captured against backgrounds not too disturbingly realistic. Jack's serial was rejected almost as swiftly as he had turned it out. From that abortive attempt at entering the serial market, he turned to writing short stories.

The situation of the Londons, meanwhile, was getting no better. They barely existed on what Jack made at odd jobs. With winter coming on, he had to continue wearing his light summer suit, and his mackintosh was still in hock.

Jack was never quite able to explain later why he kept turning out stories in his large, sprawling hand, which he later typed, when no one gave him any encouragement. His only confidence at the moment lay in the strength of his body; certainly he was not carried along by any intuition that he would someday be the most sought-after writer in America, or any intimation that a great narrative power was humming inside him like a dynamo, waiting only for its moment of recognition. During those lonely nights at his desk, in the quiet house on East Sixteenth Street, he had nothing to sustain him but his urge to transmit his stories from his imagination to sheets of white paper, the compelling urge of the born storyteller. He told himself that he was simply writing for money, which was superficially true, but beneath that was the stronger compulsion to tell his tale; it was as though his imagination had been damned to the bursting point with the characters and stories that pleaded and demanded to be poured into the release of narration. It was a process that began, unknowingly, when he started telling his stories in the barrooms of Dawson, only partly to share in the conviviality.

He no longer hoped to make writing a career, he recalled in *John Barleycorn,* just wanted to make a few dollars to keep the landlord at bay; thus, he said, he was "clubbed into fortune" by the necessity of keeping on with the writing for lack of something better to do. Yet he would not have trimmed a hedge, for instance, in the vague hope that a householder would pay him fifty cents if he was pleased with the job.

As he looked back upon it, this struggle during the winter of 1898-1899 to write something the magazines and newspapers would buy could have been mitigated if he had known someone who could have told him the shortcuts. He knew no one who made a living at writing, not even so marginal a professional writer as a newspaperman. There was no other person to read his manuscript and tell him where he violated the rules. It also irked him that he had to forget most of what he had learned about literature in high school and college, though he had wasted little time at either. His professors, he said, simply didn't know anything about the practical problems of writing and selling what you had written in the year 1899, learned as they were about the subtleties and refinements of English prose. If they'd known the trick, he said, they would have quit their classrooms and started pounding their typewriters. Nor could he learn anything from the rejection of his manuscripts. The notices he received with them were almost invariably form letters giving him no clue as to where he had failed, or how he could make his stories more acceptable.

From the beginning his approach was strictly professional. Writing for anything but money seemed ridiculous to him. It was hard work for him even then, and got harder with every passing year. The joys of creation, by his own account, escaped him completely. The only thing about writing he would ever enjoy, he insisted, was ripping open the publisher's envelopes with checks enclosed. From the start he was convinced that the joyous fevers of "creative writing" were strictly for amateurs.

His aim wasn't to storm the heights of literature but, as he told his

Socialist friends, to produce a thousand words a day and sell them at a cent a word. It was all "brain merchandise." Nothing was worth doing if it didn't succeed on its merits in the marketplace.

About all this, of course, there was a little too much protestation. Certainly at the end of his career writing became an exhausting task. In his early years, however, the very quality of his prose — its vehemence, its vitality, its surging rhythm — indicated that he must have found at least a momentary delight in his work. Perhaps it was the craftsman's satisfaction rather than the poet's rapture, but the most mercenary of writers can hardly turn out a gemlike phrase without a feeling of self-congratulation.

2. *Flora Comes Through*

One of the more critical turning points in his budding career came on January 16, 1899, when he received a letter from the postmaster of Oakland notifying him that a postman's job was available to him. He had stood near the top in the Civil Service examination and was entitled to one of the first openings.

At the moment his prospects otherwise were dismal. Not a line of his writing had been sold, nor had he received the slightest encouragement from any of the editors who read the manuscripts he had submitted. He was behind in the rent and in the grocery bills. His own health and that of his dependents was suffering from the privations they had been undergoing, which had hardly been reduced by his return to the role of breadwinner.

Clearly his duty — and he was now in one of his intermittently dutiful, responsible phases — pointed sternly toward taking the postman's job. Once in the Civil Service, he was safe and secure for life; the work wasn't too hard; he could sink effortlessly into what would be, to him, a vegetable-like existence. Every month he would be paid sixty-five dollars, a pretty good salary in 1899. It was, he wrote years later, an all but irresistible temptation to give up the lonely struggle, and on honorable enough terms.

Before deciding, he took the problem to Flora. He pointed out that he would be able to support her and Johnny Miller — whom she loved and was devoted to far more than her own son — and possibly even get married, if Mabel fancied a postman.

In that moment Flora London was superb, all but making up for years of neglecting her duties as a mother. This was her chance, possibly her last chance of security; more than that she could hardly expect, unless one of her lottery tickets finally proved to be a winner.

Flora told him to forget about settling for a mail carrier's life and continue with his writing. John London's Civil War pension would pay the rent and they'd find money for food somehow. The odd thing was that, indifferent as she was to him in most respects, she was the one person who believed in his ability to make his way as a writer. He had failed at many things and shown little ability to cling to any occupation. It may have been instinct, or it may have been her willingness to take a gamble, which previously had caused the family so much distress, rather than face the drabness of life on a subsistence level, or it may even have been an unfamiliar essay in self-sacrifice — but she told Jack to stick it out with his writing.

Jack himself still wasn't convinced; he had less faith in himself at the moment, though self-assurance was to be the hallmark of his literary personality, than his mother had. He called the postmaster on the telephone and told that functionary his situation. He'd like to try writing a little longer. Couldn't the vacancy go to the man just below him on the eligibility list, and could he be given a crack at the next opening that occurred?

The bureaucrat at the other end of the line was affronted at the suggestion that any man could possibly pass up a sixty-five-dollar-a-month job.

"Then you don't want the job?" the postmaster icily inquired.

"But I do," Jack replied anxiously.[2] "Don't you see, if you will pass me over this time —"

"If you want it," the postmaster snapped, "you will take it."

Angered by the man's blunt refusal to understand, Jack snapped back, "Very well. I won't take it."

He felt himself finally committed now to earning his living as a writer. A hack, if need be, but a writer. In addition to short stories, he began producing a flood of shorter stuff, light verse, anecdotes, jokes, sonnets, triolets, ballads, jokes, short essays.

Every cent he could spare from rent and food went toward postage stamps to keep this stream of filler stuff circulating through the magazine offices. Everything came back. It must have seemed to him that some sort of gigantic rejection machine was swallowing up his work and mechanically regurgitating it. No one, he was convinced, could be reading any of it. Otherwise the laws of chance would dictate that at least one little scrap of hackwork would be accepted.

He worked so hard and so futilely that once again he considered suicide as the only way out. Half starved and sick at heart, he went so far as to write farewell notes to his family and friends; the only question was how to do it with the least distress to his family. While he was pondering this, something brought him back from the brink. Perhaps it was a square meal or a good night's sleep.*

He was still "at the end of my tether . . . ready to go back to coal shovelling or ahead to suicide," when his luck began to change. Two of the many magazine offices he was sending material announced they saw merit in his work.

First by a few hours, the *Overland Monthly* of San Francisco notified him by letter it was accepting one of his short stories, "To the Man on Trail."

For a few minutes he was jubilant. The *Overland Monthly* had published Twain and Harte, it was still laden with literary prestige.

Then he reread the acceptance letter. Obviously the magazine didn't believe in spoiling its contributors. The *Overland*, Jack was informed in a take-it-or-leave-it tone, paid only on publication, which might be months in the future, and the price would be five dollars. Jack was sick with disappointment. His story ran about four thousand words and represented four days' work, which meant that he was still working at a jute-mill wage scale.

Damn the prestige! What he wanted was cash — a cent a word, which he understood was the minimum rate for magazine work. Just as he was about to reconsider ending it all, the afternoon mail arrived, including a letter from the editor of the *Black Cat Magazine*, to which he had sent a horror story. The *Black Cat* was pleased to accept his four-thousand-word story provided it was granted permission to cut it by half. Furthermore it would pay him forty dollars, not on publication but on acceptance of its offer. Jack immediately replied that he accepted, and they could cut it any way they wanted if they

* His longtime friend Frank Atherton, according to Irving Stone in *Sailor on Horseback*, related that Jack decided against suicide when an acquaintance came to him with the same idea. Jack, though meditating suicide himself, took the opposite side of the argument. In the end he convinced himself as well as the other man that life was worth living.

would send him the money at once. The *Black Cat*'s check came by return mail, and he bailed himself out with the landlord, the grocer and the pawnbroker.[3]

In his mood of temporary affluence, he allowed the *Overland Monthly* to publish "To the Man on Trail." The story brought him a certain amount of local attention and awakened the interest of the Eastern editors. It may not have been his most polished effort, but from the moment the Malemute Kid and his friends, stirring up a Christmas punch of whiskey, brandy and pepper sauce, admit Jack Westondale to their cabin, the reader is carried along by the brisk narrative. Among those present is one Father Robeau, the Jesuit priest whom Jack had met on his way to St. Michael. Westondale, who had just robbed a Dawson merchant of forty thousand dollars, apparently was modeled after the author: ". . . the blue eyes gave promise of the hard-steel glitter which comes when called into action. . . . the heavy jaw and square-cut chin demonstrated rugged pertinacity and indomitability. Nor, though the attributes of the lion were there, was there wanting the certain softness, the hint of womanliness, which bespoke the feminine nature." *

From first to last, Jack's ego would rarely allow him to create a dramatis persona without a character closely modeled on himself being not only present but usually cast in one of the more heroic roles.

Flattered by the response to his first story, though depressed by the slenderness of its financial rewards and the fact that he was not paid even after it had been published, Jack consented to give the *Overland Monthly* another, "The White Silence." For this he was promised $7.50, a fee which in no way diminished its qualities as an American short-story classic. The editors thought well enough of it to publish it the following month. It was a simple, brutal tale, with the Malemute Kid, the rough-hewn and seasoned Klondiker, again a central figure, and also involving a Southerner named Mason and his Indian wife.

* The intermingling of the feminine in London and his work has often been remarked upon, strangely at variance though it may have been with his self-propelled legend of rugged masculinity. The celebrated photographer Arnold Genthe observed "an almost feminine wistfulness about him." The perceptive English critic Stephen Graham was more precise in *The Death of Yesterday*. "Jack London was a feminine man . . . He became exalted in his writing, at times nearing an hysteria more natural to the female than to the male. The women characters in his books voice his own thoughts about himself . . ."

The three are on the trail, struggling to reach their destination with their food and the strength of their dogs fast giving out, when a towering, snow-burdened pine falls and all but crushes the life out of Mason. The Southerner insists that the Malemute Kid and his wife leave him to die alone and save themselves, leaving him to the "White Silence."

Jack's talent for vivid description of the country again was in evidence: "Nature has many tricks wherewith she convinces man of his finity — the ceaseless flow of the tides, the fury of the storm, the shock of the earthquake, the long roll of heaven's artillery — but the most tremendous, the most stupefying of all, is the passive phase of the White Silence. All movement ceases, the sky clears, the heavens are as brass; the slightest whisper seems sacrilege, and man becomes timid, affrighted at the sound of his own voice. Sole speck of life journeying across the ghostly wastes of a dead world, he trembles at his audacity, realizes that his is a maggot's life, nothing more. Strange thoughts arise unsummoned, and the mystery of all things strives for utterance. . . . then, if ever, man walks alone with God."

In one passage, as the Malemute Kid comes to realize that they must abandon Mason as he insists, there is an old twist of characterization which anyone overly influenced by Freudian doctrine might interpret as latently homosexual. "So close was the tie that he [the Malemute Kid] had often been conscious of a vague jealousy of Ruth [the Indian wife], from the first time she had come between [him and Mason]." For the year 1899 it was an unconventional view indeed, that one man should be jealous of a woman rather than of his friend for having the woman.

While turning out work that was really first-rate and would soon be recognized as such, Jack continued to hack out the shorter stuff in hopes of bringing in a few dollars. Quite as he suspected, you couldn't live on praise or even the heady satisfaction of seeing your stories in print. There were five weeklies being published in San Francisco, which considered itself a literary fountainhead second only to New York. The *Argonaut*, long established, was somewhat pretentious in its claims to being an intellectual generator for the whole Pacific Coast. The *News Letter* and the *Wasp* also had their coterie of followers among the more sophisticated readers. *Town Talk* was a soufflé of gossip, criticism, light verse and comment published in hopeful emulation of New York's *Town Topics,* Colonel William d'Alton Mann's successful combination of journalism and extortion. The *Wave,* the best of the San Francisco weeklies at the time, was edited by John O'Hara Cosgrave with evident ambitions to become the *Collier's Weekly* of the West Coast. Before beginning his own writing career, Frank Norris was Cosgrave's assistant and together they managed to raise the level of weekly-magazine standards in the Bay area.

Jack was directing much of his literary chaff at this convenient market, and soon began to sell triolets and other verse to *Town Talk,* and subsequently longer prose pieces to the *Wave.* He sold articles on language to the scholarly *American Journal of Education,* a story to something called the *Orange Judd Farmer,* and travel pieces to the Buffalo *Express* and *Home Magazine* (previously quoted). That fall he sold stories to *Youth's Companion* and the *Editor.* It was encouraging, but hardly a windfall at current space rates, since he was averaging less than twenty dollars a month.

Two more stories went to the *Overland Monthly,* whose readership was highly pleased with Jack London, although he had yet to be paid for the first they had published. Finally, his amiability vanished in a thunderclap of rage at the possibility he was being gulled; he stormed across the Bay and confronted two of the *Overland Monthly* executives, Roscoe Eames and Edward Payne, in their shabby offices. Later he would get to know both gentlemen much better — to his eventual sorrow.

Eames was a dignified-looking man with a full white beard who closely resembled Charles Evans Hughes in everything but mental competence. He was one of the *Overland*'s two editors. Payne was the business manager, a suave article expert at fending off creditors.

Both men chortled with delight over meeting their young star contributor from Oakland. They were flattered at his call. They were thrilled at standing in the presence of such a magnificent talent.

He didn't want a lot of guff, Jack growled, just five dollars for the first story they'd published, cash on the barrelhead.

They'd send him a check next day, Eames and Payne promised. Meanwhile, perhaps he'd have a cup of tea with them and discuss plans for the future. Did he know people were beginning to compare him to Kipling?

To hell with literary small talk, Jack said firmly; he wanted five dollars now or he'd have to consider knocking their heads together. There was no food in Flora's kitchen, and he didn't even have the price of a ferry ride back to Oakland.

Between them, emptying their pockets, Eames and Payne managed to come up with five dollars in paper and silver.

Jack left hoping that he wouldn't have to combine bill-collecting with all the other vexations of a writing career.

His confidence, however, was growing that summer. Obviously his tales of the Yukon country were beginning to catch on, only around San Francisco at present, in the main circulation area of the *Overland Monthly,* but their local success raised his hopes of cracking the national magazines. Conceivably, considering the state of magazine fiction, that might take some doing. The big guns of popular fiction were Robert W. Chambers with his frothy historical romances; Richard Harding Davis, hardly a hard-bitten realist, and George Barr McCutcheon with his improbable tales of adventure in Central European courts. Jack's stories possessed a gripping narrative power and were laid in a corner of the world currently fascinating to the public, but his characters wore mukluks instead of silver-buckled shoes, drank hooch instead of champagne, and were definitely not refined ladies and gentlemen. Editors like Edward Bok of the *Ladies Home Journal* and George Horace Lorimer of the *Saturday Evening Post* required dainty and deodorized people in their fiction, and as little contact with reality as possible. They held that readers had enough grimness in their daily lives, and preferred to escape to Graustarkian realms in their magazine fiction. Fictional characters, even the villains, had to be polished and immaculate. The hero not only had to win out but do so with a gentlemanly grace. The stories in which they figured had to contain a certain quantity of uplift.

Subsequently, when Jack submitted one of his lusty Klondike stories to the *Saturday Evening Post,* an anonymous editor wrote back that he liked it but his magazine never published anything with a "tragic" theme.

There were, of course, magazines with a more realistic outlook. Somehow, through them and through republication of his stories in book form, Jack was confident that he would find his audience.

As early as July 10, 1899, when he had published only the several short stories in the *Overland Monthly,* he began casting around for a book publisher. That day he wrote the first of hundreds of letters to George P. Brett, the courtly head of the Macmillan Company, suggesting he might like to publish a collection of nine of his Yukon stories. He emphasized that he had been to the Klondike himself, and not as a mere sightseer. Brett, however, passed up the opportunity to become his first book publisher.

3. *A Part-time Intellectual*

Of the several things in which Jack took an almost belligerent pride, it was his hard-won self-education that pleased him the most. Nothing would dismay him more than the knowledge that modern critics dismiss him, for the most part, as an able producer of action-adventure yarns, a superior example of the blood-and-brawn school. The books to which he devoted his weightiest and most profound thinking were not outstandingly successful in their time, nor have they since been given any great amount of serious or favorable attention.[4] He wanted to be known as a thinker, a reformer, and a practical philosopher because he regarded it as his due. Even his popular fiction, he would point out, was solidly grounded on concepts borrowed from the nineteenth century's greatest minds.

One of the few occasions on which he was visibly aroused by criticism in the public prints and allowed his tormenters to see that they had drawn blood was after publication of his intensely autobiographical *Martin Eden*. There was carping comment that it would have been impossible for his hero to have converted himself in three years from a sailor with a grade-school education to a novelist of the first rank. A writer's only defense in a situation like that is to claim that the improbable is possible, that it happened in real life, which of course is regarded as a paltry argument because credibility in fictional terms is the writer's responsibility and no "proof" is substantial enough to win his case once his novel is committed to cold type.

With some heat, Jack pointed out that he himself had accomplished what he claimed for Martin Eden, had started publishing in the better magazines and was preparing his first book for publication after less than two years in high school and college and one year as a working writer. Not only that but he was being offered, and was declining, the post of associate editor on a New York magazine (*Cosmopolitan*), all by the time he was in his twenty-third year.

In that year, with a foretaste of success already in his mouth, he exhibited a swagger and a cockiness that some of his elders and perhaps some of his betters found a little hard to take. A young fellow was entitled to a certain amount of bumptiousness, especially one who'd cut as wide a swath through the world as young London, but did he really imagine that he knew all about everything?

It seemed so, for instance, when he attended a meeting in Oakland addressed by David Starr Jordan, the president of Stanford University. Dr. Jordan had gained world renown as an authority on marine life. After his lecture on piscatology, during a discussion period, Jack was not at all overawed by Dr. Jordan's reputation nor inhibited by the fact that his own knowledge of the subject came from his forays as an oyster-bed looter and a voyage on a sealing ship. He not only disputed Dr. Jordan on a number of points but, as one present recalled, he launched on an hour-long discourse of his own and "proceeded to tell the Doctor all about fishes." [5]

A good deal of his intellectual pride undoubtedly stemmed from the fact that his knowledge was largely self-acquired. His grounding, certainly, was based on the authorities most admired by his generation. He read and reread Darwin and Huxley. He absorbed the works of Herbert Spencer, whose doctrine of the survival of the fittest and theory of atavism were the philosophical foundation of most of his stories about men contending against nature and each other. It was Spencer's work which persuaded him to adopt as his principal theme the struggle between his rugged heroes and almost equally stanch heroines — who atavistically had inherited their genes from remote ancestors and were in a sense throwbacks to a worthier time — and his weakling-villains, who were supposed to be the best products of civilization but actually were less noble and generous than the primitives to whom they were opposed. He also delved into the Greek philosophers, Gibbon's *Decline and Fall of the Roman Empire,* and the history of Europe during the Middle Ages and the Protestant Reformation. He read his way through the later philosophers from Kant to Spinoza, Hegel to Leibnitz; studied biology and anthropology, and gorged himself on everything written on the budding science of sociology, particularly as it affected the class struggle and the conditions under which the poor lived.

Karl Marx, of course, was his political lodestar, and he also sought guidance from the works of the Marxian disciples and camp-followers. He pored over the works of Eugene V. Debs, the American Socialist leader, and studied the writings of the anarchist intellectuals, C. L. James's *A History of the French Revolution,* Benjamin Tucker's *Instead of a Book,* and the calefactory prose of Emma Goldman, who was to be charged with encouraging the assassination of President McKinley, and Alexander "The Hammer" Berkman. The latter, putting his theories into action, tried to kill Henry C. Frick for his role in suppressing the Homestead strikers.

But it was Friedrich Wilhelm Nietzsche's deep dark well of pessimism at which he drank the most copiously. The embittered German philosopher, who died in 1900, seemed to confirm and enlarge upon so much of what he had learned from experience. "I teach you Superman. Man is something to be surpassed . . . Man is a rope stretched between the animal and the Superman — a rope over an abyss." From his early teens Jack had secretly regarded himself as a superior creature, one born to dominate his fellows because he was stronger and wiser. This belief existed side by side, uneasily and incongruously, with a fervent dedication to Socialism, which was supposed to protect the weaker and more ignorant.

His own antireligious beliefs, directed as much against his mother's Spiritualism and the recollection of being dragooned into serving as a medium at her séances when he was a child as against his stepfather's more conventional career as a Methodist deacon, were given sustenance by Nietzsche's tirade against Christianity: "I call Christianity the one great curse, the one enormous and innermost perversion, the one great instinct of revenge, for which no means are too venomous, too underhand, too underground and too petty. — I call it the one immortal blemish of mankind." Or, "After coming in contact with a religious man, I always feel that I must wash my hands." Or, "All prejudices may be traced back to the intestines. A sedentary life is the real sin against the Holy Ghost." Even his flirtation with suicide found a certain amount of confirmation in the German: "The thought of suicide is a great consolation; by means of it one gets through many a bad night." Throughout his life Jack held that death was final and man was obliterated by it as completely as a casually swatted mosquito.

If his own credo in regard to the supernatural had to be reduced to two words, he said, he would identify himself as a "materialistic monist," one who believed that all matter was composed of the same fabric. Yet he would also say that of all men who ever lived, Jesus Christ was one of the two whom he admired the most; Abraham Lincoln was the other. The mutually exclusive held no terrors for Jack London. He could be an atheist who valued the example of Christ, a Socialist who believed in the leveling process of revolution at the same time he raised up the image of a Superman who would rightfully dominate the stupid herd. Even in his worst nightmares, however, he could hardly have conceived that the self-appointed Superman who finally arose from the Nietzschean compost-pile would be an Adolf Hitler.

No matter how contradictory some of his beliefs, Jack was prepared to defend them to the utmost in debate and discussion. In disputing with others, he was likely to be more passionate than logical, more emotional than rational. Above all, both as a writer and a political animal, he was inclined more to the romantic than the realistic, though his contemporaries mostly believed the opposite. One who was not deceived was Will Irwin, a young San Francisco journalist who succeeded Frank Norris as assistant editor of the *Wave,* who believed that even Jack's Socialism was essentially a romantic attitude. A Socialist was then regarded by the middle classes — whom Jack was constantly seeking to shock and impress — as something between a dangerous renegade and a slightly mad idealist, happily unaware that by 1939 most of what Jack and his co-believers advocated would come to pass without any revolutionary mobs storming the Capital. London, wrote Irwin, held Socialism "identical with democracy, not realizing that in its pure form it could be administered only by a dictatorship." [6]

Jack was willing to concede that under Socialism there was likely to be a cessation of industrial progress; that it would not be as efficient in the productive sense as capitalism, with much of the incentive to work removed; that as a consequence of greater solidarity in their unions the English workingmen were producing less than half as much as their American counterparts. Very well, productivity would be sacrificed to the cause of humanity. He had an ingrained respect for hard work and efficiency, which certainly ruled his own methodical habits as a writer, but he was still, as he always signed himself, "Yours for the Revolution."

The principal proving grounds of his beliefs were the Socialist locals of Oakland and San Francisco. At the former, during 1899, he delivered several lectures as part of an educational program the local was presenting, and argued his views lustily with debaters from the floor afterward. He also expounded on the evils of American policy in regard to the remnants of the Spanish Empire. Cuba had been occupied by American troops following the rout of the Spanish land and naval forces the previous year, and Washington was showing a more than big-brotherly interest in the island's sugar and tobacco crops; meanwhile in the Philippines the natives were objecting strenuously to the increasing number of American troops being deployed throughout the archipelago. Jack was an admirer of Rudyard Kipling as a magnificent storyteller but didn't agree that the United States should be called upon to help share the white man's burden. At this stage there was another striking contradiction in his thinking. He was all for liberating the Filipino but was violently anti-Oriental, inheriting the racial views of most Californians on Chinese and Japanese immigration and holding, quite as violently as his fellow Native Son, William Randolph Hearst, that the Yellow Peril must be stamped out.

A polite atmosphere in which to hammer out his social and political beliefs was the vaguely left-wing Ruskin Club. Here the atmosphere, in contrast to that of the Socialist Locals, was more intellectual than working-class. Many of its members were instructors and professors at the University of California, doctors and lawyers. The Ruskin Club, which frequently gave rather sumptuous dinners and discussed the class war through a rich cloud of cigar smoke, was organized by Frederick Irons Bamford, the reference librarian at the Oakland Public Library. Jack first met him as a boy. Bamford had guided his reading along Socialistic lines at an age when his contemporaries were following the exploits of Frank Merriwell with breathless interest. Bamford, a rather self-conscious intellectual, wore a goatee and adopted a manner as benevolently aloof as a churchwarden. Obviously there was something about him that conjured up the image of a religious servitor rather than a radical prophet. Upton Sinclair, who attended Ruskin Club meetings occasionally, said Bamford ran it "with a firm hand" and observed that "he must have been a Sunday School superintendent before he came to the Socialist movement," judging from his authoritarian manner.

At the Ruskin Club meetings and those of the Socialist Locals he met several men who influenced him in both a political and literary way, particularly Austin Lewis and Herman "Jim" Whitaker, both of whom had migrated from England. Lewis, a former member of the British Socialist Party, an instructor at the Marin County Academy and a law student, often attracted Jack to the Turk Street Temple with his lectures. Whitaker was a well-born and well-educated Englishman, nine years older than Jack, who had operated a Canadian ranch and was now determined to become a writer.

Lewis and Whitaker both tried to convince him that he needed a firmer grounding in certain subjects, particularly economics, to make up for his lack of formal education. With Whitaker especially, Jack was on close terms for several years. The intimacy came to an end, according to Joseph Noel, who knew them both well, because there was an antagonism between the two men that "went deeper than disagreement over moot points in socialist technique or philosophy. This may have been racial. It may have been a question of morals . . . Jim was staunch for what he called the eternal decencies." [7] The strongest bond between the two young men was their fierce determination to make their living as writers.*

Whitaker insisted that Jack must pay more attention to what he called "the drudgery of art," grammar and sentence structure. He also taught Jack, according to Noel, "how to put his narrative style under control of what he called the inevitable rhythm," and insisted that Jack study Chapter 25 of Dickens's *Dombey and Son* to acquire his own narrative rhythm. Jack began selling more of his output after meeting Whitaker, and it may well be that he learned certain bits of technique from the Englishman, but the typhoon story he wrote when he was seventeen and without guidance suggests that he had the instinctive, swinging pace of the born storyteller.

Noel recalled that Whitaker also urged Jack to gain a firmer control over his emotions, that he rein in his impulses, and warned that one day "his appetites would destroy him." But no one could tell Jack London that life wasn't meant to be gulped down like shots of barrelhouse whiskey; he was not the man for nuances, tame pleasures or the joys of meditation.

Another glancingly influential force in Jack's life at the time he

* Whitaker later published a novel, *Cross Trails,* and a number of short stories, but never achieved anything outstanding.

was struggling to become a professional writer was Nathan L. Greist, a newspaperman who had once worked for the hardest taskmaster in journalism, Charles A. Dana of the New York *Sun*. Greist was a tall, lean, handsome man with an eloquence that gathered around him a number of impressionable people interested in making a better world according to their own prescription, some of them anarchists, others partisans of free love or the single tax or other exotic remedies — not too different a set, actually, from the one Flora Wellman and "Professor" Chaney had traveled in a quarter of a century before. One fellow who frequented Greist's "clearing house of ideas" in his Market Street apartment was Ben Reitman, who argued that society should adopt a more sensible and liberal attitude toward rape and offered historical precedents. "The rape of the Sabine women by the old Romans," Reitman would argue, "was the real beginning of the Roman Empire." Reitman never quite spelled out what sort of wholesale rutting he advocated for the present male population, but Jack said that he read Roman history with new interest after listening to Reitman.

Others who attended the Greist forum included the editors of *Mother Earth*, an anarchist magazine which proclaimed that a man's ego was supreme and should not be circumscribed by artificial laws or religious commandments. A man should be free to do whatever he pleased, uninhibited by conventional morality.

Undoubtedly Jack drank in all this philosophical anarchism with an eager thirst because it confirmed his own views. He had been something of a nihilist and egoist for years, had dropped family responsibilities without any apparent flicker of guilt, had no overwhelming respect for the sanctity of laws he believed were made by the rich and powerful to protect their own interests. Already the people who knew him were learning that they had to make room for what Charmian London was to call his "princely" ego if they wanted to remain close to him. Later, in *The Cruise of the Snark*, he was to express his feelings about the supreme importance of the first person singular in the bluntest possible fashion: "The ultimate word is I LIKE."

Another member of the Greist circle was Frank Strawn-Hamilton, who was to be a lifelong associate of Jack's and who was regarded by many as "one of the finest intellects of his time." Strawn-Hamilton devoted his life to contemplation and the study of the classic philosophers. Essentially he was a teacher, a free-lance educator without tenure, classroom or degrees. Those who knew him always expected him to produce a masterwork that would explain Western civilization to itself, or relate the modern world to that of the ancients in whose company he dwelled, but it was never forthcoming. He was a man of meditation with the fatal flaw of procrastination; he had none of the Western "push" and need to make something practical out of his endowments, and his genius lay in talk, discussion and propagation. Noel said he "accepted nothing, questioned everything . . . he could re-create what he had just finished reading and make it sound like a masterpiece . . ."

Austin Lewis said that Strawn-Hamilton gave Jack "far more than he could have obtained with tremendous effort from a complete course of philosophy in any university." Almost to the end of his life Jack was willing to listen to Strawn-Hamilton when, in his years of success, he cut himself off from other of his old mentors. Whether Strawn-Hamilton, as a leading Socialist intellectual, contributed anything helpful to Jack as a writer is more doubtful. The best of his work, the pure storytelling, was uncluttered by the intellectual baggage he acquired too hastily to make proper use of. His attempts to impose intricate theories on the basically simple design of his stories tended to blur their clean, muscular line.*

Not the least of the Greist apartment's attractions for Jack in his lean and hungry period was Mrs. Greist's talent for cooking. Both Greists are mentioned in *Martin Eden* under the name of "Kreis." Later there was a certain amount of resentment on Greist's part over a passage in *Martin Eden* in which Martin gives Kreis money.

"Jack had a mind that might have been of first rank," Greist said in later years, "if it had not been hampered by bourgeois ideology. When beaten on the intellectual field, he always recovered his equilibrium by saying he earned more money than his opponent anyhow.

"A case in point is his using my name in *Martin Eden* thinly disguised as Kreis. By saying that he had given me money when the reverse is true, he evened up in public print for his many defeats in

* H. L. Mencken (*Prejudices: First Series*) held that the "materialistic conception of history was too heavy a load for him to carry." In creating his best books, Mencken believed, Jack had to cast off his political dogma just as Wagner "threw overboard" his intellectual baggage in composing some of his greater works. "A sort of temporary Christian created 'Parsifal.' A sort of temporary aristocrat created 'The Call of the Wild' "

private argument. . . . He had a mentality of that sort. There's no question of it. He could not endure the agony of playing second fiddle. Even when we were discussing subjects about which he knew nothing, he wanted to hold the center of the stage." [8]

Jack's bumptiousness in argument, his vehemence and volubility unchecked by any reluctance to offer dogmatic opinions on any subject, even when his opponents were far better informed, irritated many and dismayed those who liked him. Perhaps it was the inevitable result of all the information he had crammed into himself without allowing time for mental digestion — an eager regurgitation that should have been regarded with understanding, at least by people who claimed they were his betters in education and breeding. How it must have galled them that, of all that vigorously fermenting group, Jack was the only one who gained renown.

4. *The Lily Maid*

On his return from the Klondike, Jack resumed courting Mabel Applegarth. He was still determined to marry her as soon as his income was sufficient to support a wife as well as his mother and Johnny Miller. Both must have had their doubts about marriage. Her frailty and timidity, her abhorrence of the harsher realities of life, would have hardly made her the ideal Mrs. London. Any woman who married Jack, no matter how much he loved her, as Mabel must have sensed, would have to be prepared to withstand many shocks and endure many domestic upsets. He would always live near the eye of the hurricane. A certain amount of quiet was necessary during working hours but after them he was ready for a spell of riot. He may have yearned for peace and domesticity and was in a marrying mood earlier than most males, partly to make up for the lovelessness of his upbringing, but his nature was tempestuous.

In her long and curiously unrevealing biography of Jack, his second wife Charmian, with a rare glint of animus, never referred to his first love by name, only as "The Lily Maid." This scathing reference undoubtedly was a reflection not only of Charmian's jealousy of a predecessor but Jack's own attitude toward Mabel.

If he was initially attracted by her delicacy and flattered that such a refined creature should take an interest in him, he eventually grew bitter over the fact that she was not strong enough to break with her family, risk all and marry him. In *Martin Eden* she was re-created in terms that must have been painful to her when she read the book. The conflict between Ruth and Martin in the novel was pictured as the natural misunderstanding between an "ignorant sage" (Jack) and an "educated fool" (Mabel). In one passage, when Martin reads the girl a brutally realistic story which has just been rejected by the over-refined editors back East, she cries out, "It is not nice! It is nasty! . . . Why didn't you select a nice subject?"

As he saw it, through the created prism of *Martin Eden,* his was essentially a "love nature," passionate and demanding a passionate response, while her attitude was "largely tactful and sentimental." Opposites, in their case, had indeed attracted but the attraction wasn't strong enough to overcome all obstacles.

The major obstacle was Mabel's mother, who had been left widowed and did not propose to be deprived of her daughter's companionship. Her son Frank once observed that "Mother was always a selfish woman; Mabel spent her life taking care of her."

It was Mrs. Applegarth's ambition, as Jack believed, to marry Mabel off to a man of substance, generous or foolish enough to accept his mother-in-law as a member of the household.

Mrs. Applegarth and her devoted daughter subsequently moved to a new home in San Jose, possibly because Mother Applegarth hoped that placing themselves at a distance from Jack would cool off the romance. Jack, however, was persistent. He cycled down to San Jose as frequently as possible to press his campaign for Mabel.

Then, late in the fall of 1899, came the break he had been working and waiting for. The *Atlantic Monthly,* the most prestige-laden of American magazines, was willing to publish a lengthy short story of his titled "An Odyssey of the North," if he would accept $120 as payment. He had sent the manuscript to the *Atlantic* with little hope of acceptance, and now they were offering him three times what he had ever got for a story before. He accepted with haste.

The story would be published in the periodical's January, 1900, issue. It was the best as well as the longest of the Yukon tales he had turned out that year, once again with the Malemute Kid as a leading character. As the Kid listens to the story of Naass, an Eskimo seal hunter, "a chief and the son of a chief," and his ill-fated love for Nunga, the whole way of life of a primitive people is unfolded as in a stark and somber tapestry. Its tragic climax is entirely in keeping with the background. The Malemute Kid refuses to judge Naass by the rules of a softer civilization, and concludes, "There be things greater than our wisdom, beyond our justice. The right and wrong of this we cannot say, and it is not for us to judge." The story and its implications were strong medicine for the *Atlantic*'s polite readership, contrary to all the black-and-white, crime-and-punishment formulas of contemporary fiction, but its vitality and compelling style persuaded the editors to take a chance on it.

Nor was that the best part of his breakthrough to the pages of the *Atlantic*. Houghton Mifflin, the book publishers, were also located in Boston and got wind of the *Atlantic*'s find. The Houghton Mifflin editors collected his *Overland Monthly* stories along with proofs of "An Odyssey of the North" and were considering publication of a volume of his short stories. The first reader's report observed that London's style was slangy and lacked elegance, but its vigor and narrative sweep were undeniable. "He draws a vivid picture of the terrors of cold, darkness and starvation, the pleasures of human companionship in adverse circumstances, and the sterling qualities which the rough battle with nature brings out. The reader is convinced that the author has lived the life himself."

In December of 1899 Houghton Mifflin offered Jack a contract for the volume to be published in the spring as *The Son of the Wolf*.

Surely now, with the most respectable magazine in America and a leading Boston publishing house acclaiming his work, he was worthy of the hand of Mrs. Applegarth's only daughter. Soon he would be able to make a good living at writing. With his energy, his youth (he was just about to turn twenty-four) and his now confirmed talent, he considered that his prospects were promising enough even for the son-in-law of Mrs. Applegarth.

Bearing galley proofs of the *Atlantic* story, he appeared at the Applegarth cottage in San Jose prepared to argue his case all night if necessary.

He outlined his prospects before Mrs. Applegarth and her daughter and demanded to know whether the long, informal engagement might not terminate in marriage immediately.

Mabel was willing. For almost four years she had been prepared to marry Jack as soon as it was clear that he would be able to provide for her. Perhaps, too, she saw that this was her last chance to break away from her mother, who claimed to be in poor health and often insisted on having her meals served in bed. Stretched before her was the genteel drudgery of many another only daughter bound to an iron-willed and self-centered martinet determined to be pampered through a lengthy and complaining old age.

Mrs. Applegarth surprised both Jack and her daughter by saying yes to his plea for an early marriage.

Yes, but . . . there was a codicil.

Jack would either have to move into the San Jose cottage — another hand around the house wouldn't be amiss — or if he insisted on living in Oakland he would have to establish a home there in which Mrs. Applegarth would have her preferred place.

He was stunned at the hopelessness of the choice she gave him. If he moved to San Jose, he would still have to support Flora and Johnny Miller in Oakland. If, on the other hand, he took Mabel and her mother to Oakland and rented a larger house in which there would also be room for Flora and the boy, the result would be nightmarish. The idea of two quarrelsome and headstrong women like his mother and Mrs. Applegarth living under the same roof was unthinkable. They'd be at it hammer and tong, night and day; Flora would start having her heart attacks again while Mrs. A. lay abed upstairs and clamored for her breakfast. Each day would bring a new crisis. He and Mabel would spend most of their time keeping the two women from clawing each other. How could he possibly work in such an atmosphere?

Jack argued mightily that Mrs. Applegarth should let Mabel live her own life, but the older woman was adamant. Mabel herself could only sit there silently, white-faced and helpless, while her mother and her fiancé battled for possession of her.

What Mother Applegarth's dictum amounted to was that either Jack would have to desert his own mother, or Mabel would have to abandon hers. And Mrs. Applegarth was confident of the hold she exercised over her daughter.

Jack went back to Oakland sick with frustration. He was sure of a moderate income in the months ahead, but it might be years before he earned enough to support two households. Even when that day arrived, he would have to face the necessity of living in the same house as Mrs. Applegarth; she made it clear that she would not live alone, no matter how large an allowance was made for her.

It was hopeless. Much as he loved Mabel, constant as his feelings had been for her since he was nineteen years old, he could not see a happy marriage evolving from such a situation. He did not propose to have a she-dragon poised on his hearth. If Mabel couldn't stand up to the old lady, couldn't fight for her own happiness, there was nothing he could do about it.

He and Mabel still considered themselves engaged but he saw less and less of her.

It wasn't too long before he was beginning to notice that there were other females in the world without the encumbrance of possessive mothers. As he indicated in letters to friends, he was still in a marrying mood.

VI

"Seven Sturdy Saxon Sons . . ."

1. *Anna and Bess*

WITH THE publication of his story in the *Atlantic Monthly* and the announcement that one of the major book publishers would bring out a volume of his short stories, Jack achieved a gratifying amount of attention both from the Bay area newspapers and literary circles in San Francisco and Oakland.

He basked in the first ego-warming glow of celebrity. As with most authors, recognition was what he thirsted most for, crasser considerations aside. A newspaper clipping was visible proof of his importance, and Jack was beginning to acquire a sizable collection.

From the first he placed a realistic value on publicity. He would even interrupt his work, the ultimate sacrifice for any writer, to talk at length to a reporter. It wasn't enough to be admired by those who knew you, by literary camp-followers and taste-makers. You had to get out in the marketplace, where storytellers in ancient times held forth among the other merchants. You had to get yourself written about and talked about outside literary circles to acquire a general readership, and Jack courted popularity.

With the gradual disintegration of his relationship with Mabel Applegarth, he began spending some of the energy and time which had gone into forty-mile bicycle trips to San Jose on a livelier social life in Oakland and across the Bay. Perhaps already he had begun looking for someone to take Mabel's place, though he still considered himself in love with her and wasn't sure he would ever get over it.

Will Irwin told of meeting London for the first time at a party in the San Francisco studio of Leslie Hunter, a Scottish-born painter, during this period of emotional drift and doubt. London was flaunting a flannel shirt in that more conventionally dressed group and "sat in a corner with a pair of remarkably bright eyes fixed on vacancy. He had strong shoulders, a fine head, features of chiseled type." Irwin couldn't help wondering why such a handsome, hearty-looking fellow skulked in a corner away from the merriment and looked morosely unapproachable.

Irwin went over to him and said, "Having a good time, old man?"

London glowered at the banality of the question, and curtly replied, "I can't enjoy this kind of thing. I was never young," and went back to his brooding.[1]

As it turned out, Jack wouldn't have had enough money to marry Mabel immediately, despite the first flush of optimism over his *Atlantic Monthly* sale and Houghton Mifflin's plans for him. He had paid off his debts and retrieved a number of articles from the pawnshop, but a month later, in February, he was sinking into the morass again. Back into pawn went his best suit, his watch, his books and everything else that would bring a few dollars for food. Being plunged back into poverty just at the point he was being taken seriously as a writer made him more certain than ever that art for art's sake was hogwash, and that a writer who didn't write for money was an idiot. On March 1, 1900, he wrote Cloudesley Johns, a young Southern California writer who praised "To the Man on Trail" in a letter, that he was bending all his efforts toward writing anything that would bring in money. He wanted fame, but only if it increased his income. The job of earning money, he wrote Johns, was detestable and would never become one of his vices. Furthermore — and this was to grow in him like a cancer, corrupting his life and his work — he was filled with disgust and resentment when he sat down to write something for money. His career had only just begun, yet he already viewed the necessities of his profession with repugnance. By his own account he never wrote anything, except Socialist tracts and essays from which there could be little or no reward, without a dollar sign dancing on every page of manuscript; even the typhoon story he wrote as a seventeen-year-old was produced in the hope of winning a twenty-five-dollar prize.

Although he had barely started working his Klondike vein, there is evidence that even then he was having trouble finding durable plots and ideas. Literary historians have asserted that that was a malady of the latter phase of his career, when he was a sort of literary sausage-maker turning out stories under contract to the slick magazines. Yet on May 5, 1900, he wrote Cornelius Gepfert, whom he had met in the Klondike and corresponded with since, asking him to send along any idea which might be turned into a short story. He added that he needed a situation rather than a plot.* When Gepfert asked him if he would join another rush to the Klondike, there being rumors of startling new finds, Jack replied that he might consider it, but only as a newspaper correspondent — and the next time he would take along a camera instead of a pick and shovel.

Of great consolation to him during the early months of 1900, while he was struggling to keep himself afloat emotionally and to make the most of what seemed to be a growing vogue for his rugged tales of the North Country, his friendship with Anna Strunsky, whom he met in the Socialist-Bohemian circles of San Francisco, was growing in warmth and depth. It would never be more than friendship, but it had undercurrents and potentialities unusual for a platonic affair: they always seemed on the verge of falling in love.

Almost from their first meeting, which occurred after attending a lecture by Austin Lewis at the Turk Street Temple, they were obviously delighted with each other. Jack described her as "a Russian Jewess who happens to be a genius." To Miss Strunsky, Jack had the magnetism of a Byron and an enthusiasm for ideas the equal of which she had never encountered. It was the beginning of an affair of intellectual passion which culminated in a curious offspring, a book called *The Kempton-Wace Letters,* the only collaboration Jack ever undertook. It endured long after Miss Strunsky became the wife of William Walling English, a millionaire Socialist.

Anna Strunsky, an intense, dark-eyed, black-haired girl a year or two younger than Jack, was a sterling example of the vigorously independent New Woman whom Jack would soon be casting as the heroine of his stories and novels. The revolutionary tradition being strong in her family, she reacted adversely to academic discipline and the

* The letter may be found in the Jack London collection at the University of California's Bancroft Library. It also related that Fred Thompson, who had joined Jack in the fool's-gold stampede, was still in the Klondike full of wild schemes and smoking good cigars. Then and later Jack and Thompson, each a little antagonistic, accused each other of "never having done a tap of work" in the Klondike.

conventions alike. While a student at Stanford, she had been suspended for defying the rules by "receiving a male visitor in her room instead of the parlour." [2] She and her younger sister Rose (with whom Sinclair Lewis later fancied himself in love) were brought up in a permissive style as yet rare in the United States. Her well-to-do parents allowed the girls to invite whomever they pleased to the family dinner table. Jack London first met Emma Goldman, the flaming anarchist whom the more conventional people regarded as "the most dangerous woman in America," in the Strunsky parlor. Will Irwin remembered Anna at studio parties, "all Russian temperament and imagination, sitting on the floor and arguing out the theory of revolution or reciting 'Porphyria's Lover.' "

She and Jack argued vociferously on all topics, from the course of the coming Socialist revolution to the changing nature of relations between the sexes. Jack argued against the concept of romantic love, regarding it as a delusion. Anna's attitude on the subject was exactly the reverse; as she expressed it in her section of *The Kempton-Wace Letters,*[3] "the touch of a hand . . . the tears that come for unnamed sorrows are more significant than all the building and inventing done since the first social compact. You cannot explain the bloom, the charm, the smile of life, that which rains sunshine into our hearts, which tells us we are wise to hope."

They also differed violently on his position as a Socialist writer. Born into comfortable circumstances herself, Anna was shocked at his materialist outlook, his brash statements that he would write for money and show the capitalists a thing or two. He'd demonstrate through his own financial success that a Socialist wasn't necessarily a failure in life whose philosophy was a distillation of sour grapes. What better way, Jack demanded, to show up the capitalists than having a Socialist beat them at money-making? Anna argued that he couldn't have it both ways, that he'd ruin himself as a Socialist, a writer and a human being, that no real Socialist could hoard up his money until he had a fortune because his compassion for the less fortunate would force him to give it away.

Though she may have been repelled by what she regarded as an unworthy ambition, Anna valued Jack especially for his gusto, his appetite for living, his vitality and customary high humor, which charged the atmosphere around him with a sort of intellectual electricity. His high spirits, she observed, somehow made everyone around him more lively and interesting. "To know him," she said, "was immediately to receive an accelerated enthusiasm about everybody."

To watch Jack strike into a room — usually in a black turtleneck sweater, then more the costume of the gashouse district than artistic circles, and with bicycle clips still fastened around his trouser cuffs, his hair tousled, his blue eyes glittering with mischief or excitement — was like having a window thrown open on a room thick with tobacco smoke and stale scent. He provided a vivid contrast to the pale posturing men who fancied themselves artists, intellectuals and revolutionaries, and who winced or cringed when he slapped them on the back.

Between the two of them ran a current of understanding and mutual encouragement. Jack thought so highly of her critical faculties that he allowed her to read and correct his manuscripts, an honor he did not bestow lightly. Anna, in turn, submitted her own writings for his criticism, each valuing the other enough to be outspokenly tough-minded. But it remained an affair of the head rather than the heart, probably at Anna's insistence.

In those early months of 1900 Jack was getting to know another young woman who resembled neither Mabel nor Anna in the slightest. She was Bess Maddern, and like the other two young ladies she came of a family socially and economically several levels above the Londons. She was a first cousin of Minnie Maddern Fiske, whom many historians of the stage consider the greatest actress this country has produced. Another cousin was Emily Stevens, who also became a star on Broadway. In Bess herself, however, there was no inherited yearning for make-believe or the superficial glamour of the theater. Mrs. Fiske wanted Bess to accompany her on tour and possibly train her for an acting career; Bess was her favorite cousin and she often visited the Madderns when appearing in California. Bess's parents, Henry and Melissa Maddern, considered the theater — even under the chaperonage of the utterly respectable Cousin Minnie — an improper place for a proper young lady, however, and Bess quite willingly stayed home.

Bess was a good friend of Mabel Applegarth's and the two girls, with Jack and Bess's suitor, a young man named Fred Jacobs, sometimes made a foursome. Thus Jack was a familiar in the Maddern home long before he became seriously interested in Bess. On a number of occasions the two girls tried to teach him how to dance in the Maddern home, with Mabel at the piano and Bess bravely trying to guide him through the proper steps, but they finally agreed he would be hopeless, if not an active menace, on the dance floor.

Bess's interests, outside the primary ones of becoming a wife and mother, lay in the direction of mathematics and schoolteaching. She had attended business college for two years and had mastered algebra by herself. Mathematics was almost a passion with her and she would have liked to pursue the subject at the University of California, but her father believed that higher education wasn't at all essential for young women. Rather than take a bookkeeper's job in an office, she tutored pupils unable to attend school, in their homes. In later years, according to her daughter Joan, she absorbed calculus and trigonometry, studying by herself, and was able to coach University of California students having difficulty in those subjects.

Bess was a handsome girl with strong, regular features, blue-black hair and hazel eyes, a serene brow, a firm, well-shaped mouth. There was a steadfast quality stamped on every feature; even as a girl she gave every evidence of a firm, sensible and practical character. Her calmness, almost stolidity, was the first thing people noticed about her. She was almost as tall as Jack* and had a trim athletic figure, kept slim and vigorous by cycling from her Oakland home to her pupils scattered through Alameda and other Bay communities.

If the golden-haired Mabel was the essence of frail protected femininity and Anna the volatile intellectual temptress, the dark-haired Bess was the eternal homemaker. She had little overt interest in the arts, politics, faraway places or the self-indulgent turmoil of Bohemia. Jack could be at ease with her. He did not have to guard against a slip in grammar or a minor breach of etiquette as with Mabel because Bess was too tactful to take notice of them, or strive constantly for brilliance as with Anna.

Bess had her own kind of intelligence as was indicated by her unusual aptitude in mathematics, but it was not constantly on display. Jack found a quiet, restorative pleasure in her company. Her serenity balanced and soothed his own excitable, often overenthusiastic or intermittently melancholy nature.

Soon he was spending more time with her, either at the Maddern

* He was about five feet seven.

home, on picnics in the countryside or excursions into the foothills behind Oakland, crossing the Bay to attend the theater or the opera in San Francisco, than with any other girl. And Bess had taken over the chore of correcting his manuscripts. That was a sure sign of esteem.

If he had to have a wife, and he believed he did, why not a young woman like Bess with her calm strength and her stanch belief in the domestic virtues?

Love? That could come later. It might be all the more enduring if it grew slowly, from a firm base of affection and mutual respect.

Bess, too, had experienced a tragic ending to her first love. Her fiancé, Fred Jacobs, had enlisted in the army at the start of the Spanish-American War, and was shipped out to the Philippines on a troop transport. In mid-ocean he contracted a fever and died before the transport docked at Manila, one of the unsung victims of that "brisk little war." Bess still mourned him but was too sensible a girl to waste her life on the futility of grief.

Jack seldom cycled down to San Jose and the Applegarth cottage any more. The old love was dying on the vine. He began to wonder just how strong it was if a prospective mother-in-law could appear to be a fatal obstacle.

Just as *The Son of the Wolf* was coming off the presses in Boston, he made up his mind to marry Bess. He expected that royalties from the book and continued sales to the magazines would allow him to support a slightly enlarged household in comfort if not in style. He wrote in a notebook that he was keeping at the time that he still feared being tied down, but "I'm already tied. Though single, I have had to support a household just the same. Should I wish to go to China, the household would have to be provided for whether I had a wife or not."

Two weeks before he proposed to Bess, he and Jim Whitaker discussed the economic aspects of combining marriage with a writing career. Whitaker was supporting a large family on the eight dollars a week he earned clerking in a grocery and selling occasional pieces on the side.

Whitaker asked Jack if he would "advise" him to throw over the clerking job and take up writing as a full-time career.

"No," Jack replied.

"Well," said Whitaker, "I think I will anyway."

"So would I!" Jack said with a shout of laughter.

During the same conversation Whitaker advised the younger man to wait a few years before considering marriage, and Jack solemnly agreed. Two weeks later, no more willing to take advice than Whitaker, he decided marriage would steady him and allow him to concentrate harder on his work. "God's own mad lover" firmly in control for the time being, he proposed to Bess.

On brief consideration she accepted the proposal. They would be married on the basis of "affectionate companionship" — no nonsense about romantic love — and hope for the best. Free of illusion, they would have children and devote themselves to their home and Jack's career. Perhaps they were luckier than they knew; at least they wouldn't be starting out with the high expectations, quickly dashed in most cases, which blighted other marriages.

With typical exuberance Jack announced that the marriage would produce "seven sturdy Saxon sons and seven beautiful daughters." *

2. *Settling Down*

Simplicity was the keynote of their wedding as befitted a match based on common sense and practical objectives. They were married at the Maddern home on April 7, 1900, with only members of her family and a few friends attending. Flora did not approve of the marriage and stayed away from the ceremony, in itself an ill omen since she and Bess would have to share the responsibility of keeping house. If there was a shadow across the scene, it was that of the unseen Flora, whom Bess was expected to get along with in spite of all Jack knew about his mother.

A photograph taken of the couple in the garden of the Maddern home before they climbed on their bicycles and pedaled off for a three-day honeymoon in the flowering hillsides above the Bay showed Jack in a carefree mood, smiling widely, with a cigaret dangling from his lips. He wore knickerbockers and a cap pushed back from his tousled hair, and looked more like a kid on holiday than a newly married man.

* As Rose Wilder Lane quoted him in her serialized biography, "Life and Jack London," the first to appear, which ran in the *Sunset Magazine,* October, 1917, to May, 1918, but was never published between hard covers. Just where all the "Saxon" blood was coming from, he didn't make clear. Jack himself was at least half Welsh while Bess was of Cornish (also Celtic) extraction.

Bess was prim in a starched shirtwaist and long skirts, and smiled more cautiously.

On returning from their honeymoon, they settled down in a fairly large house at 1130 East Fifteenth Street, which had plenty of room for the newlyweds as well as Flora and Johnny Miller. A bedroom was converted into an office for Jack. Comparative harmony reigned in those first weeks with Bess continuing her tutoring and contributing to the support of the household. She also corrected and typed his manuscripts. On Sundays they went to the beach or on picnics in the foothills. They got along well and considered that the marriage had been a wonderful idea.

In later years Bess said that she fell in love with her husband "very soon" after they were married.

If there was a shadow on the early months of their life together, it was Flora's open resentment of the bride. Mrs. London didn't want her son to be married, in the first place, and she was further angered by the fact that Jack didn't ask her approval, didn't even give her time to know the girl before a daughter-in-law was thrust upon her. In addition, there was little sympathy between the women, Bess always the earthbound, Flora with her consuming interest in the supernatural. Flora had always been an indifferent housekeeper at best — the one domestic talent for which she was remembered by her granddaughter Joan was a special way of frying steaks — but now she resented the intruder. Bess insisted on taking over the work and responsibility of keeping house even though she was busy enough with her tutoring and her labors over Jack's manuscripts. The result was, first, much muttering and glowering from the supplanted Flora, and then open clashes. Bess, after all, had a temper beneath her placid exterior and she did not intend to have her home ruled by a domineering mother-in-law. Soon Jack was having his work interrupted by the quarrels in the kitchen, and would have to come downstairs and play the peacemaker, a role for which he was ill fitted by his own impatient temperament.

Finally the problem was solved, for Jack and Bess at least, when enough money began coming in to allow him to establish his mother and Johnny Miller in a smaller house a few blocks away. But Flora was outraged, considered herself abandoned by an ungrateful son and a scheming daughter-in-law. This displacement did not, however, prevent the older woman from coming over to the young couple's home and renewing her feud with Bess, who later admitted that she could have been more tactful and forbearing with the senior Mrs. London.

What Flora especially resented about being packed off to her own house was that she could no longer preside over the Wednesday night parties Jack began giving as soon as his income was large enough to provide a batch of spaghetti and straw-covered flagons of Chianti for his guests.

Flora, according to Joseph Noel's wincing recollection, loved to hold stage-center at these parties as long as possible, reciting various set-pieces with the opulent gestures she had learned as a girl studying elocution. She would get into something vaguely resembling Egyptian costume, have the lights placed so that they were focused on her, and deliver the "I am dying, Egypt, dying" speech as a middle-aged Cleopatra.

Painfully aware of the ridiculous figure his mother presented as a thwarted ingénue, Jack finally put his foot down and forbade Flora to give any more performances in his parlor.

Flora, of course, blamed Bess for this brutal termination of her career as a parlor entertainer, and began telling everyone who would listen that Bess wasn't worthy of the honor of being Jack London's wife.

Aside from mother-in-law trouble, the marriage prospered almost from the beginning. Publication of *An Odyssey of the North,* followed by the book *The Son of the Wolf,* was attracting considerable attention in the East as well as Jack's home territory. Even the more conservative critics, accustomed to tamer fare in a day when William Dean Howells was regarded as a sometimes shocking realist, praised the collection for its virility, its narrative qualities and masterful descriptions of the North Country. He was being compared to Kipling as an apostle of the heroic and a minstrel of brave men contending with a savage environment. An admirer of Kipling himself, he was not at all displeased at being called the "Kipling of the North."

He could see that there was a receptive market for what he had to offer at the time; his generation needed reassurance that America could produce a vigorous breed of men even though the frontier had been steamrollered into oblivion. "He had only to tell his life over again — to make a story of it in the newspaper sense — to feed the romanticism of the big urban populations which now began to swallow the five, ten and fifteen cent magazines," Lewis Mumford has written.[4] Thus he would become "a sort of traveling salesman of literature, writing to his market, offering 'red blood' and adventure to people who were confined to ledgers, ticker tapes and Sunday picnics." It is doubtful whether London ever saw himself in such a mundane role as a traveling salesman, though he came close enough to it in his frequent references to himself as a "brain merchant."

His merchandise, at any rate, attracted the approving eye of S. S. McClure, a flamboyant and venturesome book and magazine publisher who subsequently achieved a great deal of prominence as a pioneer of the muckraking movement. He considered Jack's forthright style just right for his magazine. *McClure's,* designed largely for a male audience, particularly the stay-at-homes who had resisted the call to arms and the Klondike stampede, used a lot of outdoor adventure stories.

McClure believed that the day of the genteel romancers was done, and new voices, disdaining the sentimentality and insipidity of the previous generation, must be given a hearing. He bought two stories from Jack, and wrote him, "I wish you would look upon us as your literary sponsors hereafter." McClure said his publishing house would use anything it could of Jack's and "what we cannot we will endeavor to dispose of to the best possible advantage." As evidence of good faith McClure paid him three hundred dollars for the two stories, "The Grit of Women" and "The Law of Life," plus an article titled "The Question of the Maximum."

That summer of 1900 Jack had been thinking of attempting a novel. Like all his short stories thus far, except the horror piece sold to the *Black Cat,* it would have a Yukon background. In a novel he would be able to convey more of the expansive spirit of the country he was writing about, develop his characters more fully and give his narrative the epic sweep it should have.

Since McClure was a partner in the book-publishing firm of McClure, Phillips, Jack wrote him about the projected novel, remarking that the only obstacle in the way was the lack of an assured income to support his family while he worked on it. McClure was both understanding and generous — and a lot more willing to risk his money than most publishers would have been, since it was not yet customary to pay advances against possible earnings on unwritten novels by neophytes — and replied that he was willing to gamble on London's talent: "We will back your novel on your own terms. We will send you a check each month for five months for $100, and if you find that you need $125, why we will do that. I am confident that you can make a strong novel. At any time when you feel in need of any sort of help, please let us know."

With McClure's $125 plus other income from newspaper and magazine pieces — including a cozy article on "Housekeeping in the Klondike" published by *Harper's Bazaar* — Jack was enabled to move into more comfortable and roomy quarters. It wasn't really necessary, but Jack had already acquired a taste for living above his means. Already there was a picture in the back of his mind of himself as a northern California grandee surrounded by dependents, friends, admirers and perhaps a few servants. Extravagance could be a spur to drive a man on toward better things. You had to keep overreaching yourself or you shriveled in spirit and settled for less and less.

Furthermore Bess had just announced that she was pregnant; the child would be born, happy omen, just about the time he was scheduled to finish his Yukon novel, *A Daughter of the Snows*. Jack was overwhelmed by the news. Most men, at twenty-four, might have had divided feelings about becoming a father and the increased responsibility it entailed, but he was eager for fatherhood; he saw himself as the founder of a distinguished line. It was unthinkable that his first child would be a girl, because a girl would marry and assume her husband's name.

In *The Kempton-Wace Letters,* his collaboration with Anna Strunsky, Jack was to make it clear that his principal reason for marrying Bess was that she would make an excellent mother. His alter-ego, Herbert Wace, wrote Dane Kempton (Anna) that he didn't regard romantic love as a necessary ingredient of marriage and that he was going to marry Hester (Bess) because she would bear him splendid children. "What a comely young woman, is what I thought as I pressed Hester's hands; and none of the ordinary sort either. She has health and strength and beauty and youth, and she will certainly make a most charming wife and excellent mother . . . Believe me, I am very fond of Hester. I respect and admire her. I am proud of her, too, and proud of myself that so fine a creature should find enough in me to be willing to mate with me. There is nothing cramped or narrow or incompatible about it . . . We know each other well . . . a wisdom that is acquired by lovers only after marriage, and even then with the likelihood of its being a painful wisdom." Without any great originality, he also wrote that "Considered biologically, love is an institution necessary for the perpetuation of the species."

Now his marriage was justified on biological grounds, and they moved into an odd-looking villa called Capricciosa not far from the swampy shore of Lake Merritt.

The villa was a masterpiece of the rococo, built by an Italian sculptor named Felix Piano. It was decorated with an excess of tiny balconies and miniature towers like dunce caps. Its grounds looked like the workyard of a bankrupt dealer in cemetery ornaments, full of Mr. Piano's creations, including cement cherubs and angels, plaster fawns and fluted urns. In the grape arbor a nude female in plaster of paris reclined voluptuously, a sight which gave some of Jack's tipsy guests quite a turn when they stumbled upon her in the darkness. Inside, the decor also verged on the eccentric with tiny doorways, corridors at odd angles and narrow winding stairs. Bess once fell down one of the tricky stairways with her first child in her arms. But the place was spacious, pseudo-artistic, and pleased the suppressed romantic in its new tenant.

Joseph Noel came out to Villa Capricciosa to interview him for the San Francisco *Advance* and found him smoking expensive Russian cigarets (Imperiales) while brooding over his unpaid bills. He explained that he had worked out an arrangement with Mr. Piano whereby the sculptor occupied a suite of rooms in the house and took his meals with the Londons, in exchange for which they lived there rent-free for the time being.

"Lucky I don't have to pay him cash," Jack told his interviewer, though he gave the impression of being highly skilled at fending off creditors, which he was. "He'd have to wait. I haven't been selling any stories lately."

Apparently he meant that he had been concentrating on the novel, *A Daughter of the Snows.*

Noel was charmed by his frankness about his financial condition. "I have half a dozen of those tradesmen on my trail," Jack continued. "But will any one among them stop and say: 'Well, I'm glad that unpaid bill is due from a fellow that can write?' No, they want cash, not fine words."

Jack showed his caller how he had rigged the notes for his book on two lengths of twine fastened to the tops of two chairs near a couch on which he wrote in longhand while lying down. His daily stint, he said, was one thousand words. "Sometimes I write more, but they seldom are what I want when I read them over. The thousand words must be the best I can do each time." That became the work habit of his career, turning out his thousand words of finished prose daily; once they were done, he rarely rewrote; the only revisions came when Bess, or her successors as monitors of his grammar and syntax, went over the manuscript.

Noel was impressed by Bess's attractive face, figure and demeanor. "She was slender and, no doubt because she had her hair in the Pompadour mode, looked nearly as tall as Jack. Her face, strong, well-modelled, was enhanced by gray [sic] eyes fringed by chorus-girl lashes. When she smiled she was at her best. The surroundings were brightened."

On leaving the villa, Noel was introduced to Mr. Piano, the landlord-boarder, and remarked that "his really beautiful eyes suggested the perplexities of the poet."

"No, it's the perplexities of the grub," Jack said with a grin. "It hasn't been coming in regularly."

Three days after his twenty-fifth birthday, on January 15, 1901, his first child was born. To his unconcealed disappointment it was a nine-pound daughter, whom they named Joan. He was absolutely certain that his firstborn would be a son, and his attitude, then and later, suggested that Bess had let him down by producing a daughter.

Joan London — whose resemblance to her father is striking, with the same eyes, the squarish jaw and vividly expressive features, the same vitality and quick intelligence — remembers that her mother told her that Jack's paternal pride welled up quickly enough after his initial disappointment. With Bess as his instructor he had taken up photography, both as a hobby and an adjunct to his writing, and spent hours photographing the infant soon after she was born. That was the beginning of one of his few unpublished works, a photo album titled "Joan, Her Book." The baby was given over to the care of Mammy Jenny Prentiss, who promptly moved in when Bess was slow to recover from childbirth and cared for Joan as she had for her father (though not as a wet nurse).

Despite the deplorable fact that she was of the wrong gender, Jack would undoubtedly have taken pride in the course of his elder daughter's life. She inherited not only his best qualities but also a greater staying power where her ideals were concerned. A lifelong Socialist, she served the California Federation of Labor for years until her recent retirement. Possibly having profited from her father's tragic experience, she holds money and possessions in a wry, half-contemptuous perspective. In her 1939 biography of Jack, written before she adopted a mellower attitude toward childhood memories, she dealt unsparingly with his abandonment of ideals for material profit. Of all the things he would admire about the adult Joan, perhaps that unfilial excoriation would please him the most.

3. *Mr. McClure Regrets*

In S. S. McClure, Jack was dealing with a publisher almost as mercurial himself, a man of quick enthusiasms and equally hasty retreats. For a time McClure was convinced that he had discovered a writer who would put Richard Harding Davis in the shade, and he faithfully sent Jack his $125 check each month. His faith seemed to be sustained — in everything but sales figures — when McClure, Phillips published a collection of Jack's short stories, *The God of His Fathers,* in May of 1901. The volume included "Jan, The Unrepentant,"* "The Man With the Cash" and other adventure yarns told against a Yukon background. Generally the reviews were excellent, with the much-respected *Nation* delivering something close to a rave notice. "The stories in *The God of His Fathers* are vivid, concise, dramatic. They are sometimes coarse, generally disagreeable, always cynical and reckless. But if any one wants to be interested, amused, and thoroughly stirred, he cannot do better than read this volume." Other reviewers compared him to Bret Harte, pointing out that he was doing for Alaska what Harte did for California, and praised his exaltation of the masculine virtues.

Jack could expect no cash from this book, since its royalties were charged off against the $125 a month he was receiving and its sales were not large enough to create a surplus.

To compound his difficulties, *A Daughter of the Snows* was turning out to be a disappointment. McClure, on reading it, decided against publishing it serially in his magazine. His book-publishing subsidiary also turned it down. Finally McClure sold it to J. B. Lippincott of

* In which a dog named Buck made his first appearance.

Philadelphia, which paid an advance of $750, most of it kept by McClure to replenish Jack's drawing account.

A Daughter of the Snows, published in 1902, suffered partly from a first novelist's attempt to cram in too much plot, incident and picturesque action. Also its central character was a woman, Frona Welse, and Jack, to put it gently, was not at his best in the creation of fictional women, any more than he was expert at dealing with women in the flesh. He had only the sketchiest conception of what went on in a woman's mind. His heroines often tended to be smaller, softer and more rounded versions of his men. Neither his colorful reputation as a womanizer nor his experience in coping with that difficult and complex woman who was his mother seemed to have provided him with an understanding of the feminine mind. It has been observed that few American novelists have been capable of creating mature, realistic women, possibly because of an insufficiency of living models.

Yet Jack did manage to create, first in Frona Welse and then in other heroines, a new conception of the American woman. Until then she had been either a delicate, unearthly creature serving only as a dutiful satellite to the male characters, or much less often as a "bad" woman defined even less explicitly. Stephen Crane's *Maggie,* the girl of the New York streets, was the first honest, compassionate look at what was supposed to be a "bad" girl.

It was London who brought forth the Natural Woman for the first time, the girl who fought for and won equality with men, who would riot in the streets to acquire the right to vote and abolish the "double standard," who wanted to be man's co-worker, partner and comrade — and who wound up half a century later in the greater servitude of suburban life. She was the girl who insisted on working for a living, on being independent, on thinking and saying what she pleased, to the ultimate disfranchisement of the heavyhanded Victorian father as the head of the family. Displacing the "ailing, drooping Victorian Lady," as Maxwell Geismar has commented,[5] she became "the good sport, the pal of American letters" — the literary antecedent of many of Sinclair Lewis's heroines from Carol Kennicott to Leora Arrowsmith.

Frona Welse was the first of that durable breed, the daughter of a trader in a Yukon society "as primitive as that of the Mediterannean Vandals." Somewhat like her creator, she could box, wield the fencing foils and walk on her hands. She was not so much a character in her own right as a figment of Jack's dream of the perfect woman, the mate worthy of modern man. From her he stripped all that he disliked and distrusted about women in the flesh — their dependence, their intellectual dishonesty, their aversion to (male) logic — almost everything that characterized the Victorian woman, who of necessity had to be a bit tricky in dealing with the lordly and dominant male. The new woman was frank and open, non-sentimental and tough-minded, possessed none of the traditional feminine wiles. She was Jack's standard-bearer, and in later development would wield more influence than most literary heroines of her transitional time. And he would continue to exalt her — Frona and all her literary sisters — long after Jack himself, as Upton Sinclair[6] has pointed out, ceased to believe in her reality.

She was unreal because she was unbelievable, not so much a woman as Jack London recasting himself as a woman. She was a mouthpiece. Much of her thought and speech sounded like a sociological or political tract.

Frona Welse mouthed Jack's own pet theories about Nordic supremacy, a theme which was first presented in *A Daughter of the Snows* and was to be repeated in more virulent terms in later novels. She keeps priding herself on her Anglo-Saxon ancestry, so much tougher and smarter than the lesser mongrel races. No *Waffen-SS* recruiting poster could have been more lyrical about the virtues of the yellow-haired, blue-eyed descendant of the Vikings, though in fact the Anglo-Saxon is a mixture of Celt, Teuton, Latin and an aboriginal fellow who painted his face blue and lived in a tree. To Jack's mind "the dominant races come down out of the North." The Nordic was "a great race, half the earth its heritage and all the sea! In three score generations it rules the world!" In his enthusiasm for the blond Superman, Jack apparently forgot that he was at least half-Celtic himself, being Welsh on his mother's side, and therefore only a half member of what he deemed the master race.

After finishing *A Daughter of the Snows,* he continued writing short stories, several of which McClure also rejected. So far his deal with London had produced only the volume titled *The God of His Fathers;* he had peddled *A Daughter of the Snows* elsewhere, and now his new stuff wasn't what he fancied the readers of *McClure's* would be enthralled by. "Your work seems to have taken a turn which makes it impractical for this magazine," he wrote Jack in the summer of 1901, announcing that in a few months he would have to drop the $125 monthly allowance.

Jack, deep in debt and with five people to feed now, was in a state that would have been thought desperate by any but a longtime resident of Grub Street. Now that he had a reputation and was something of a local celebrity, he could overawe creditors into waiting awhile longer. It was even easier to live above your means in a large house than in a few tenement rooms. He kept turning out stories, plotting larger ventures, and for ready cash agreed to write a series of articles for the San Francisco *Examiner's* Sunday supplement on topics that ranged from prizefighters to a German beer bust. He had absorbed the free-lancer's credo that if you keep producing and circulating your stuff, in quantity, some of it is bound to find a home.

He had even found time earlier that year to run for mayor as the candidate of the Socialist Labor Party, stumping Oakland vigorously in the weeks before the final election and demanding, first of all, that the city assume ownership of the public utilities. 1901, however, was not a vintage year for radicalism, the privations of the previous decade were forgotten, and Jack persuaded only 245 voters to mark their ballots for him. It appeared that even his fellow Socialists could not take him seriously as a political candidate.

4. *Across the Bay and on the Heights*

Jack was not yet a literary lion with full mane, but already he was in demand socially both in Oakland and across the Bay. As a guest at a dinner party or a less formal studio affair he was a variable and unpredictable quality. He couldn't abide dullness, and in a fit of boredom was likely to blurt out anything that came into his mind, no matter how stuffy or shockable the company.

At one ultra-proper dinner party, with both sexes at table, Jack began yawning loudly as the others droned on. Will Irwin, who was present, said that Jack threw himself back in his chair and loudly proclaimed:

"Science has proved that every embryo at the moment of conception —" [7]

Whatever else he was going to say was drowned out by gasps from the ladies and indignant protests from the men. One didn't discuss such subjects in mixed company, certainly not at the dinner table; but

Jack, smiling to himself, had achieved his purpose in shaking up the dullards.

Perhaps the most famous of Jack's photographic portraits, showing him jacketless in a soft-collared shirt and dark tie and catching the odd combination of ruggedness and sensitivity in his face, was taken at this time by Arnold Genthe, who became one of his friends. A proper Prussian, Genthe had come over to the United States as tutor to the son of Baron von Schroeder, who had married a daughter of Peter Donahue, the wealthy railroader. Genthe got interested in photography, established a studio in San Francisco and soon was in great demand as court photographer to the beldames of Nob Hill and their sightlier descendants. Away from his studio Genthe haunted Chinatown and the sordid alleys south of the Slot to document with his camera the amazing variety of life in San Francisco's streets, a body of work which subsequently made him much more famous than his studio portraits of society ladies encrusted with precious stones. Genthe cornered Jack as a subject after receiving a note from John O'Hara Cosgrave, who had just published some of Jack's pieces in the *Wave,* asking him to take a picture of the writer because "He has written a rattling good story for *The Wave* and I feel sure he will be heard from in the future."

Genthe was equally impressed.[8] "Jack London had a poignantly sensitive face. His eyes were those of a dreamer . . . Yet at the same time he gave the feeling of a terrific and unconquerable physical force."

Through Genthe and other new friends who traveled in the better circles Jack began making the Bohemian Club one of his regular stops in San Francisco, at first on a guest-card basis but later as a member. The club was and is a unique institution which could only have sprung up in that city, an amiable meeting ground where poets and professional men, painters and stockbrokers have rubbed and lifted elbows since the club was founded in the Seventies by Mark Twain, Henry George and others. Every year the membership adjourned to a large tract on the Russian River on a non-religious retreat, the main feature of which was the presentation of a poetical play, or masque, with the words and music written by members and performed by members. It was the only social club Jack ever joined, a place where he could drink, play cards and be safe from his womenfolk.

He also attended its stag dinners, usually with a visiting celebrity as the centerpiece. The free-swinging mood of those occasions was typified by the appearance of William Butler Yeats as an honored guest. The Irish poet detested long-winded after-dinner speeches. He was introduced by Dr. Henry Morse Stephens of the University of California who took considerable pride in his graceful tributes to the visiting great. Dr. Stephens composed a masterpiece of felicity to introduce Yeats, but it was delivered at a length almost as irksome to the poet as the professor's Oxford accent. Yeats's reply was brief and painful: "A Dutch traveler of the Seventeenth Century described the English as witty, boastful and corrupt. How the English have changed! They are no longer witty."

Apparently there was some slight opposition to Jack's membership, partly because of fear that his radical views might disturb some of the more conservative Bohemians and partly because of his style of dress, which now featured white silk shirts and flowing ties and brought with him a specious whiff of Montmartre. There was such a thing as being too Bohemian. However, all objections were stifled. The local weekly *Wasp* reserved one of its best stingers for the occasion under the paragraph heading JACK LONDON'S SHIRT VINDICATED: "The Bohemian Club has relented against Jack London's negligee shirt and taken the novelist into membership — honorary membership at that. Why honorary, I cannot say . . . *The Wasp* would be only too glad to help in placing laurels on the brow of Mr. London if he deserved them, but he must furnish better evidence of his literary quality before this journal will assist in decorating him. *The Wasp* decorates as masters no apprentices whose work is more conspicuous for its blemishes than its finish." His works, the paragrapher declared, were better suited to the waterfront saloons than "the shelves of libraries or the tables of reading rooms frequented by people of even superficial culture." The best that could be said for his work was that "it is a poor and clumsy imitation of the new Russian school of tramp literature, which has given to the world a series of novels dealing with the scum of humanity," and for London himself that he "shows more fitness for the post of second mate of a whaler than a leader of the great army of imaginative scribblers."

Jack must have known that he was on the threshold of success, if only because of the barbed comment he was beginning to attract from his colleagues. One of these envious observers was a columnist who signed himself Yorick, who recommended one of Jack's Sunday supplement pieces in the *Examiner* "as a model of style and finish to all aspiring young magazine writers and yellow journalists serving their apprenticeship." When he covered the Ruhling-Jeffries fight for the *Examiner,* Yorick expressed fears that "even Mr. John London is on the broad highway that leads down to wealth and destruction. He is reporting prize fights for the *Examiner,* and that is proof that he is either starving in a garret on the husks and crusts of magazine literature, or that he has resolved to wear the purple and fine linen of yellow journalism and dine daily on mock turtle and the fatted calf a la prodigal." Jack laughed it off. He had long ago discovered that he was not a poet writing to express himself but a professional writer — a hack, if need be, at times — who labored strictly for financial reward, for "belly needs." The whole keynote to his striving, he said frankly, was to attain popularity, because popularity paid off.

Socially Jack shone best on his own grounds, even when Bess was hard put to collect the ingredients for an Irish stew to serve their guests on one of their Wednesday night parties. He needed the stimulation and flattery of his friends, neither of which Bess could supply. She was one of those women — not phlegmatic but appearing to be so — who let their feelings show only under great stress or provocation. She viewed everything and everyone, including her volatile young husband, matter-of-factly and with a firm sense of proportion. "Bess neither praised nor flattered," as her daughter Joan has written.[9] "Lifelong she retained her belief that if someone did something well there was no reason why he could not then do it better. Jack's success pleased but did not surprise her. But Jack, with good work performed, needed congratulations."

Among those who gathered at the Villa Capricciosa were Jim Whitaker, who, with seven children to support, was now a full-time writer; Frank Strawn-Hamilton, the philosopher, who often was forced by Jack to take a bath before he was permitted to join the party; Xavier Martinez, a jovial Mexican-Indian painter; James Hopper, who had graduated from the playing fields of Berkeley, where he was a U. C. football star, and was showing considerable promise as a short-story writer; and such old friends and mentors as Frederick Bamford, Anna Strunsky, Austin Lewis, and Ninetta Eames, wife of the *Overland Monthly* editor, who sometimes brought her niece Charmian. The

Wednesday evenings were largely occupied by a reading of manuscripts, followed by a long session at the poker table for the men present.

Jack continued to be the center of "The Crowd," as they called themselves, when he left the Villa Capricciosa early in 1902. The year had started badly, with McClure's subsidy now cut off. When Cloudesley Johns visited him, Jack said he was able to keep food on the table only because "I'm doing credit on a larger and Napoleonic scale." If he died suddenly, he said laughing uproariously at the thought of his discomfited creditors, he'd be "ahead of the game." He was determined not to lower his standard of living, but to raise his income; he would submit to the classic spur of so many great writers, Balzac, Dickens, Scott among them, and be roweled into fame and fortune by the importunities of his creditors. Instead of moving back into the low-rent district of Oakland as practicality dictated, he took a large and comfortable house at 56 Bayo Vista Avenue on the lower slopes of the suburban Piedmont Hills, though he had always sworn he would never leave the city and had been certain that country air would ruin him.

The Londons moved to their hillside bungalow early in February, and Jack found that country air could be positively exhilarating. His new house, rented for thirty-five dollars a month, was spacious and rambling, with a large redwood-paneled living room for entertaining his guests and a long breeze-swept porch which commanded a magnificent view of San Francisco Bay, the Golden Gate, Mount Tamalpais, the Marin County shore and the ocean itself. It was surrounded by fields of golden poppies, a clump of pine near the house and several acres of orchard. Also on the five-acre property was a tiny cottage into which he moved Flora and Johnny Miller. There were spare beds for guests who came from other cities or who simply were too exhausted or tipsy after a long evening at Jack's hearth to make their way home.

The Piedmont Hills were beginning to attract those young Bohemians who favored fresh air over the more strident atmosphere of San Francisco's artistic world. "The Crowd," which now made London's hillside house the center of its frolics, particularly on Sundays, included most of those who had attended his "Wednesday evenings," and additionally a couple of Ambrose Bierce protégés, Herman Scheffauer and George Sterling; another poet, Edwin Markham, and Blanche

Partington, the member of an intellectually distinguished San Francisco family. Jim Whitaker and his wife and seven children occupied a cottage nearby. Xavier Martinez, who married one of Whitaker's daughters, established his studio a short distance away.

Sterling, Martinez and Miss Partington were to be his lifelong friends — Sterling above all.

Martinez was almost as colorful a fellow as London himself, with his shock of black hair and "eyes like great beads of jet" [10] and a style of painting almost as vivid as his taste in clothing. He wore outsize corduroy trousers, a crimson sash around his protruding stomach, robin's-egg-blue shirts and flowing red ties, a costume that affronted neighbors who were increasingly disturbed by the Latin Quarter atmosphere being imported to the foothill suburb. He held open house every week with a huge pot of chili and plenty of red wine. Extremely jealous of his beautiful young wife, he often terminated his own parties by threatening, quite sincerely, to kill one or the other of his guests who had been too admiring of Mrs. Martinez.

Scheffauer was a darkly handsome Bavarian, but without the carefree spirit of many Bavarians. Will Irwin said he was so stiffly dignified and humorless that he seemed more Prussian than South German. His chief claim to distinction was Ambrose Bierce's sponsorship when Bierce was conducting the *Examiner*'s "Prattle" column and Scheffauer was a poet-contributor. Scheffauer, Bierce proclaimed in one of his quick but not too durable enthusiasms, was *the* greatest California poet, an accolade he also bestowed on Ina Coolbrith, George Sterling and others. Several years before he attached himself to London, Scheffauer and Bierce had participated in one of those journalistic hoaxes which so delighted nineteenth-century newspapers, and to a much lesser extent their readers. In his column Bierce published a long poem of Scheffauer's titled "The Sea of Serenity" which resembled Edgar Allen Poe in style and context if not talent. Bierce, in a foreword, claimed that the poem was a long-lost fragment of Poe, which had been given to Bierce by a relative in Southern California. The hoax collapsed in sickly fashion when Bierce's readers, instead of stirring up a controversy at his pleasure, exhibited complete indifference to who wrote the poem. Bierce, a few days later, confessed that the poem's author was Scheffauer, whose "modesty alone was responsible" for the attempt to palm off the work on the late Mr. Poe.

Scheffauer, who was an architect in his more prosaic hours, was drawn to London by their mutual fascination with Nietzsche. Joseph Noel recalled a dinner at which London, Scheffauer and Jim Whitaker discussed the German philosopher. Whitaker was repelled by the Superman doctrine. He held that if Ehrlich had discovered salvarsan (the specific for syphilis) sooner, the world "might not have been spared Nietzsche but it would have saved us from Nietzschism."

"Do you mean to say," Scheffauer demanded, "that a social disease had anything to do with Nietzsche's philosophy?"

Whitaker held firm. "You can trace its growth from *Ecce Homo* to *Thus Spake Zarathustra.* As the pallid spirochete multiplied and developed intensity, the philosopher's megalomania grew. Nietzsche knew he was doomed and spoke loudly that his voice might ring in our ears when he was gone, which it evidently does. Some of us can't hear anything else." [11]

Both London and Scheffauer took this as a personal affront, Noel said. Whitaker, a former British army training instructor, had been teaching Jack how to handle himself with boxing gloves and fencing foils, but for this dinner-table attack on Nietzsche and other long-festering resentments Jack began excluding the Englishman from "The Crowd," whose social arbiter he was, when they went on Sunday picnics.

On those Sunday excursions Jack and his friends sallied into the foothills in carryalls laden with hampers of food and various more or less potent liquids. One of the games they played was one in which the loser had to drink everything offered him, a contest which usually ended disastrously for at least several participants — but never Jack, with his waterfront saloon training.

On other occasions they would journey to the crest of the hills to pay a ceremonial call on Joaquin Miller, the white-bearded "Sweet Singer of the Sierras" and patriarch of northern California literature. The Indiana-born Miller had come West before the Civil War and distinguished himself as a crusader for justice toward the Indians, about the most unpopular cause he could have found; as a follower of "Mountain Joe" DeBloney's short-lived Indian Republic who was saved from summary justice by a friend who sawed out the bars of Miller's jail cell; as editor of an Oregon newspaper so pro-Democratic it was suppressed by the federal authorities when the Civil War began, and as author of *Songs of the Sierras,* poetic chromos of the primeval California mountains. Clad in buckskins he had journeyed to England, where the American West had always been endlessly fascinating, and was made the darling of Rossetti and his ultra-aesthetic circle. Bret Harte, rather jealous of his own standing as an authentic frontiersman in London drawing rooms, said of his rival, "Joaquin Miller is the greatest liar the world has ever known," a statement which started one of the livelier feuds of the day.

Since returning from his tour of duty as a Hearst correspondent in the Klondike, Miller rarely stirred from his hilltop home, The Hights, as he spelled it.* Adding mukluks and mittens to his costume, and Arctic odes to his repertoire, he had toured the vaudeville circuits on his return from the North and made a small fortune. At The Hights he was hospitable to pilgrims and served 110-proof whiskey from a two-gallon jug.

London and his friends often stopped by to have a few drinks with the old man, flatter him, listen to his stories ("I am not a liar. I merely exaggerate the truth.") and admire the ten-foot-high stone pyre on which his remains were to be cremated and the ashes scattered by the wind.

Recently the gorgeous old ham had attended a banquet at the Bohemian Club and had a fine time until the speaker of the evening, unaware of the old feud, expressed his high opinion of Bret Harte's tales of early California. Miller, full of wrath and whiskey, stalked out of the banquet hall, his long white beard bristling and his buckskins flapping with indignation. During the question period a few moments later, someone asked the speaker, "What has become of the old, picturesque Wild West?" The speaker replied, "Didn't you notice? He just walked out."

Both as an inheritor of the California literary tradition and as a writer who already understood the uses of showmanship, Jack admired old Joaquin and was outwardly respectful in his presence, but it was a different kind of Western frontier which he would write about, deplore and interpret, in love and despair, for the rest of the world. Instead of buckskins he would flaunt the red sweater of the revolutionary. Instead of an Indian Republic he would crusade for a Socialist government. He would sing of supermen instead of super-mountains.

* Miller once rhymed Goethe with teeth.

His saga was of industrial cities springing up over the old mining camps, of "a civilization victimized by its own success." But his methods of bringing that work to the attention of the public, while more refined and less redolent of vaudeville dressing rooms, were not much different than those of the old showman who lived at The Hights and whom, as it turned out, he outlived by only three years.

Despite such distractions as "The Crowd" offered, 1902 was a productive and growingly successful year for Jack, the beginning of his several confident years when his creative processes were working at their best and he wrote *The Call of the Wild, The People of the Abyss* and *The Sea Wolf*, among other books.

As a man, he was heartened by Bess's announcement that she would become a mother again in the autumn. This time, he was absolutely certain, the child would be a boy. It had to be; no Chinese peasant could have yearned more for one. His disapppontment with Bess if she failed to produce a male heir would be overwhelming.

As a writer, he was greatly encouraged by the fact that the Macmillan Company's astute George P. Brett had undertaken to become Jack's publisher. First off, that fall, Macmillan would publish *Children of the Frost,* another collection of Klondike stories, for which Brett paid Jack a two-hundred-dollar advance on royalties. In September and October of that year, in addition to *Children of the Frost,* his first novel, *A Daughter of the Snows,* would be published by Lippincott and a juvenile titled *The Cruise of the Dazzler* by the Century Company — three books in the space of not much more than a month. On top of that he and Anna Strunsky would be collaborating on *The Kempton-Wace Letters,* and he would write *The People of the Abyss,* both of which were published the following year along with *The Call of the Wild.* Nothing was allowed to interfere with the thousand-word stint he assigned himself each day. He was conscious of a surge of power, and on April 28, 1902, wrote Brett that he knew that there were books of more heroic size already fermenting in him and that it was only a question of time before they would be written. Less time, as it developed, than he imagined even in his presently confident mood.

VII

A Dog Named Buck

Of all the enemies of literature, success is the most insidious.

— Cyril Connolly

1. *Discovery of a Playmate*

THE IMAGE that Jack London contrived for his public was one of the more expert and imaginative creations of his career, a project that he began working on long before there was any necessity for a salable personality. To all but his most intimate friends, he presented himself as a carefree, venturesome, uncomplicated man of action, though underneath the picaroon was a man tormented by the act of his illegitimate birth, the lovelessness of his upbringing, his need to gain recognition, his almost desperate longing for a son, his conviction that he had been deprived of the joys of boyhood. In the last instance, he was determined to make up for lost time and thwarted opportunities.

If he had "never been young," as he often said, it was also true that he never quite grew up. By way of self-compensation, he cultivated a boyishness, marked by frequent abdications of responsibility, that he maintained until almost the last year of his life. His insistence that what "I LIKE" was the ultimate thing with him, that his own whims and desires had to be paramount to all other considerations were part of his willful immaturity.

What he needed in this pursuit of boyhood was a playmate. Never in his boyhood or his youth had he acquired a friend to grow up with, to fight and make up with and to share in the discovery of the wonders of the world around him. His family had moved around too much, for one thing, and his time outside school was largely taken up by chores and odd jobs. Thus, as he said later, he had always longed for "the great Man-Comrade," just as he was always searching for the perfect "Mate-Woman"; and the fact that these are two of the most nauseatingly romantic phrases he ever uttered in no way diminishes the pathos of his search.

Eventually, however, he found his playmate, his grown-up chum, Tom Sawyer to his Huck Finn.

He was George Sterling, a man of great charm, a poet of minor talent, a handsome fellow whose resemblance to Dante was noted by all and commented on until it became one of the more tiresome clichés of the Western literary world. Unlike Jack, he came of a very respectable and prosperous middle-class family, had a classical education and clung to an office job while writing in his spare time. He was seven years older than Jack, born and brought up in the East. Like Jack, he had a fondness for strong drink, long conversations about art and life and philosophy, an aversion to bourgeois values, and a similar tendency toward play-acting. Fortunately their chosen roles — George as a medieval poet unaccountably cast up on the shores of California, Jack as a rough and ready, swashbuckling revolutionary — though incongruous, did not conflict. There was no necessity for attempts at stealing scenes from each other. And besides George lacked Jack's grinding determination to get ahead, to be the leader of any circle in which he happened to be traveling, to stand out in the crowd, to produce more and ever more popular books.

His was a gentler and more generous spirit. Everyone who knew him spoke or wrote of him with an indulgent affection. "A charming companion," Upton Sinclair has described him, "tenderhearted as a child, bitter only against cruelty and greed; incidentally a fastidious poet, aloof and dedicated." [1] Jack could and would make enemies in his crunching advance on success — though fewer than most men as throughly committed as he was — but George made an enemy of only one man, himself, and ruined only one other life, that of his wife.

Boys love nicknames, and those of Jack and George were touchingly revealing. Jack always addressed George as "Greek," because of his classic profile, a sobriquet which greatly flattered and pleased the poet, who made a habit of displaying his profile as shamelessly as any stock-company matinee idol. George always called Jack "Wolf" — which was equally pleasing to his friend. Jack's fancy for being called

"Wolf"— he once complained in a letter to his second wife that she did not call him "Wolf" often enough but forgot herself and addressed him more endearingly — probably had psychological roots fascinating to anyone adept at this kind of speculation. Whatever the reason for it, he stamped his "Wolf" image as frequently and indelibly as possible on everything his life touched, at the bottom of his letters to friends, on his dream castle, on his book titles. Contrary as this lupine fetish was to his innately gregarious nature, he evidently liked to think of himself as a wolf, running free, proudly alone as he loped through the wilderness, a throwback to the animal state for which he atavistically yearned. The conception, ridiculous as it sounds, was very real and deeply significant to him, as may be realized by reading the most lyrical passage he ever wrote, the last sentence of *The Call of the Wild.*

Sterling was born in Sag Harbor, Long Island, the son of the senior warden of the local Episcopal church. On both sides of his family he was descended from Puritans of the stanchest stock. When George was seventeen, however, the Puritan link was broken when his father was converted to Roman Catholicism and persuaded George to follow him. George attended a Catholic academy in Maryland in obedience to his father's fervent hope that he would become a priest. Instead, however, one of his reverend preceptors instilled in him a love of poetry, and thereby spared the Church what might have been a beautiful but frolicsome priest.

On deciding against the priesthood, George was dispatched to California, where his mother's brother, Frank C. Havens, an Oakland real estate magnate, would provide a job in his office, though George obviously was no more cut out to be a businessman than a bishop.

About all he found in Uncle Frank's office, besides a regular paycheck, was a handsome, Junoesque blonde stenographer named Caroline Rand whom he married and made intermittently unhappy with his conviction that even a part-time poet needed other women in his life. As a fellow writer, Mary Austin, wrote, he believed that he "required the stimulus of sex to have a releasing effect on him," when he was on the verge of composition.[2] Caroline, as it developed, was ill-suited to the role of consort to poetic genius. She wanted George to concentrate on business and provide a secure, unfrivolous future for both of them. His uncle was attaining wealth and power as head of a realty syndicate which controlled much of the desirable property in the

East Bay area, and George could have advanced with him, perhaps become a partner in the firm, if only he would divert his attention from sonnets to commerical frontage, and place his ambitions in escrow until he had made his fortune. The best George could do, in that line, was show up for work punctually each morning, often with a colossal hangover; he never rose higher in the Havens firm than personal secretary to Uncle Frank. Caroline's unwillingness to accept the fact that George would never be anything more than a time-server in business undoubtedly contributed greatly to her husband's need to find other women who would be impressed by the poet in him, flowing black tie, long dark mane, and all.

Just as Jack was trying to escape from his past, George was bent on fleeing from the prosaic present and humdrum future which his wife and uncle had in mind for him; and both would find escape in such essentially boyish pursuits as drinking, wenching, hanging around bordellos and defying poor old Mother Grundy.

Sterling's first ventures outside Uncle Frank's counting-house world were abetted by Ambrose Bierce, who rejoiced in the purplish title of the "Rhadamanthus of Pacific Coast Letters" and pampered his ego by acquiring protégés as other men might collect stamps. Bierce was a Civil War veteran, born in Indiana, who drifted out to San Francisco and into the city's lively journalism before London and Sterling were out of rompers. His marriage to a San Francisco girl ended so disastrously that his favorite toast was, "Here's to woman! Would that man could fall into her arms without falling into her hands." He was a critic, a poet, a social and literary commentator whose satiric bent raised up enemies for him by the regiment, and a storyteller whose best work, which cast a spectral light on the Civil War, ranks with Edgar Allan Poe's.

Sterling knew he had to meet Bierce after Joaquin Miller described him as "an old soldier, a damn cynic and the former friend of Empress Eugénie." (Bierce had served as a sort of public relations counsel to Eugénie when she went into English exile after the collapse of the Second Empire.) He was then conducting his anti-bromidic "Prattle" column for Hearst's *Examiner* and lashing out at Hamlin Garland and "other curled darlings of the circulating library set."

Sterling persuaded Bierce's brother Albert to arrange an introduction, which took place at the latter's camp on the shore of Lake

Temescal. That evening both Ambrose Bierce and his awestruck young admirer — Sterling was then twenty-two — slept out in the open, wrapped only in a blanket apiece. Sterling said later that "throughout the night the cynic's eyes under shaggy yellow eyebrows were fixed on the fainter blue of the star Lyra." Bierce detested poseurs but did not hesitate to cultivate the picturesque in his own personality.

From then on Sterling always called Bierce "The Master." Everything he wrote was submitted to Bierce and much of it was published in the "Prattle" column. "The Master" began proclaiming that young Sterling was the equal of any of the century's poets and superior to most. If only he would continue producing his exquisite verse, with its jeweled images, its celebration of the beauty in all things, if he would hold to the Biercean philosophy that art must be created for its own sake, his future would be glorious. To hell with Uncle Frank's paltry business world. And to hell also with the Bohemian world, which Bierce defined as "A taproom of a wayside inn on the road from Boeotia to Philistia," and which he believed had ruined more promising careers than bad liquor or cruel landlords. He must avoid "posturing in cafes," taking up lost causes, which would only sap his creative energy, and preserve himself from the distractions of literary cliques, which kept a man from his work.

In particular Bierce warned his protégé against succumbing to the intellectual snares of Socialism with its easy promises of a better world. Both Sterling and Upton Sinclair claimed there was more of a personal than an ideological slant to his hatred of Socialism, which Sinclair said was "pathological." Bierce had once lost a girl to a Socialist writer named Lawrence Gronlund. There was no doubt of the depth of his resentment of anyone tarred with the Marxian brush. Once he was involved in a public debate with Morris Hillquit, the Socialist leader, and afterward told him, "You have a lovely long neck, Mr. Hillquit, and some day I hope to be one of those who will put a rope around it." Social reformers, he held, "are 'missionaries,' who, in their zeal to lay about them, do not scruple to seize any weapon that they can lay their hands on; they would grab a crucifix to beat a dog. The dog is well beaten, no doubt . . . but note the condition of the crucifix."

In manner if not in birth, "Bitter" Bierce considered himself an aristocrat and demanded a similar loftiness in anyone he stamped with his approval. His protégé must cultivate an unassailable independence, such as "The Master" flaunted when he wrote of the war promoted by his employer, "We can conquer these people [the Spanish] without half trying, for we belong to a nation of gluttons and drunkards to whom dominion is given over the abstemious."

Sterling was faithful to these commandments as long as Bierce was around to enforce them. Then Bierce was transferred to Washington by the Hearst papers, and George strayed. It was inevitable: he was a born satellite who had to revolve around the sun of a stronger personality. Within a few years he had forgotten all about "The Master's" strictures and had taken up cafe-posturing, associating with Bohemians, drinking in the arguments of Socialists and anarchists, and all manner of loose conduct.*

Worst of all, he had fallen under the influence of Jack London, who stood for all that Bierce abominated in life and letters. Sterling read Jack's first stories in the *Overland Monthly* even before meeting the younger man, and probably was his first and most enthusiastic fan. When they met, George was even more impressed. Jack's magnetism was overwhelming, his arguments that life must be lived to the hilt and that art should serve some nobler purpose than existing for its own sake were as forceful as Bierce's to the contrary. Soon the two young men were dining out together, with Bess and Caroline left at home while their husbands toured the nautch joints, burlesque houses and deadfalls of the Barbary Coast. Still something of a prude by Jack's standards, a Puritan with a Catholic overlay, George was rather horrified by the Hogarthian wickedness on display. Nor could he take the enjoyment Jack did in watching the prizefights. While Jack was yelling for blood, George watched the brutal exhibitions in silence, sickened by their savagery. Afterward Jack would wolf down a "cannibal sandwich" — chopped raw beef and onions — while George struggled to keep his own dinner from coming up. He understood that Jack was trying to show him how life looked at the street level rather than from the ivory tower in which Bierce had commanded him to stay.

Joseph Noel heard Jack arguing on one occasion against "the genteel tradition" ordained for George by "The Master," and quoted him as saying withdrawal from life was "just someone else's way of thinking

* In an acidulous portrait of his old mentor ("The Shadow Maker," *American Mercury*, October, 1925) Sterling wrote that Bierce's pessimism was "of the sophomoric order" and he "gave too much time to breaking of butterflies on the wheel."

and living you've taken over, and it's not what you want. If it was satisfactory, you would stay close to Piedmont over the weekend [by this time George was also living in Piedmont Hills] and make money the rest of the time. You have everything to make you a financier and you want to be poet." [3]

Soon Jack was the dominant influence in George's life. To Caroline's distress, George made no effort to obtain the presidency of a bank, control of which had just been taken over by his Uncle Frank; nor did George protest when the managing editorship of the Oakland *Herald* was not forthcoming, even though his uncle acquired a majority interest. He was content to draw his weekly paycheck as a glorified secretary, polish his gemlike verse for *The Wine of Wizardry*, which was to be privately published like all his works, and let himself be guided down the primrose path by Jack London. And to Ambrose Bierce's distress, when gossip drifted back to him, George was being indoctrinated with Socialism and echoing the beliefs of the upstart London. Bierce was upset by this news but held his peace for the time being. Sooner or later there would have to be a showdown over possession of the hapless poet.

Instead of being embarrassed at being caught in the middle of this contest, Sterling was secretly enjoying himself, as became evident later. He couldn't help feeling important with the old champion of West Coast letters, so long the man who made or wrecked reputations with his waspish comment, and the young challenger, whom many believed to be a genius who would eventually put Mark Twain in the shade, both struggling to influence him.* Everyone knew, of course, that Bierce couldn't abide London because that young man had risen to prominence without Bierce's counsel and approval. It was also known that Jack considered Bierce had outlived his usefulness, that his mental processes had coagulated before he and Sterling were born, that he would be remembered only as the author of a few, admittedly first-class tales of horror and the supernatural.

Eventually, of course, Jack won the contest over Bierce — and over Sterling's wife and mother as well. The two ladies were dismayed by London's influence over George, who began staying out all night and acting as Jack's drinking companion. Sterling's mother, who had

* Years later Sterling wrote that "London seemed vastly to interest Bierce . . . London was even more fascinated by Bierce." (*American Mercury*, October, 1925.)

moved to Oakland with the rest of the family several years before, warned that his conduct would reflect upon his sisters, that he was becoming the black sheep of a family noted for its rectitude. George, according to his friends, paid no more attention to his mother than to the angrier attitude of his wife.

Yet Jack was not completely satisfied that he had weaned his friend away from the bourgeois respectability of his wife, mother and prosperous Uncle Frank as well as the intellectual domination of Ambrose Bierce. The latter was already threatening to remove his patronage from George for his "irresponsibility" just as he washed his hands of Herman Scheffauer because of his "insufferable conceit." Jack wrote Sterling a curious letter complaining that they had never achieved a true intimacy, that the poet seemed to be keeping some part of himself aloof.[4] The thought that anyone whom he liked could keep some corner of his mind private was disturbing.

Despite such irksome doubts, Jack also wrote that he considered "Greek" the best friend he ever had. The friendship was so intense that his daughter Joan believed that the "emotional interplay" between the two men over the years indicated a "latent homosexuality of which neither was aware."

The friendship of "Greek" and "Wolf," while it was of great consolation to Jack, especially, was probably as harmful to both men as it was touching. Each, in his immaturity, encouraged the profligate, the self-destructive boyishness in the other.

2. *At the Abyss*

In common with other hedonists, Jack believed that resisting temptation was a ridiculous waste of willpower. He preached the doctrine of succumbing to sexual impulses with such success, according to Joseph Noel,[5] that Sterling rented a hideaway apartment in San Francisco where he could entertain young ladies impressed by his Dantesque profile without affronting the middle-class morality of his wife and family. And Jack practiced what he preached.

As an example of his own lusty, unrestrained attitude toward sex, he cited his experiences aboard a train bound for Chicago in July of 1902, en route to New York and further adventures abroad. He met a woman on the train who was traveling with her child and a maid. It was lust at first sight. They retired to his compartment and spent the whole three-day journey, Jack claimed, in sexual riot. Presumably the child was left in the care of the woman's maid. When the train reached Chicago, they parted and never saw each other again. The affair was meaningless except for the momentary pleasures involved; Jack felt nothing for the woman, nor she for him, except as an object of passion; it was a simple sexual transaction as uncomplicated and emotionless as a handshake.

Jack remembered the encounter with a delight untinged by guilt. That, he believed, was how relations between the sexes should be managed, hit and run, slam-bang, thank-you-ma'am. The art of seduction, which would have taken too much time from his work, was not for him. If a woman wasn't overwhelmed by his magnetism, ready to fall without too much preliminary, he couldn't be bothered. Few, it seems, exhibited much resistance when Jack was on the prowl. His friends were soon calling him "The Stallion," though they had to take his word — readily given — for many of his conquests. The better known he became as a novelist and public figure, the easier it was to have his way with women, and not from the cellar floor of society. The mere fact of celebrity, he found, was more impressive to women than good looks, money, flattery or a generous heart.

Fortunately for him in his extramarital forays Bess was willing to stay at home and neither question nor interfere in his activities. So long as he was reasonably discreet there was no reason he couldn't have his marital cake and his illicit frosting without domestic discord.

On the occasion of his sexual conquest under the auspices of the Pullman Company, Jack was heading for South Africa, having received an offer from the American Press Association to write a series of articles on the aftermath of the Boer War and how it affected the conquered colonists. He was at loose ends, having just completed *The Kempton-Wace Letters* with Anna Strunsky, and was in the mood for adventure when the press association's telegram arrived. He accepted at once, and left immediately for New York. An occasional dip into journalism, he believed, wouldn't permanently blight the creative processes, and besides he had conceived an idea for a book which would fit in perfectly with the American Press assignment. While stopping off in London on his way to Capetown, or perhaps on his return from South Africa, he might be able to gather material for a book about the slums of the East End of London and contrasting the lower depths of English life with those of America.

During his stopoff in New York, late in July, he met George P. Brett, head of the American branch of Macmillan and his new publisher, for the first time. Brett, judging from the Macmillan correspondence files, was as impressed by Jack as Jack was taken with the publisher, who was a gentleman and a scholar but did not make a show of it. Brett agreed to publish *The Kempton-Wace Letters,* though both believed it was a risky proposition from the commerical standpoint. Brett thought its sales appeal would be limited, Jack that it would be a big success or a complete disaster. They also discussed his projected survey of conditions in the London slums, with Brett giving his tentative approval to the idea.

When Jack arrived in England early in August, he found a cable from the American Press Association awaiting him, notifying him that it was canceling plans for the South African series. All that Jack possessed was his round-trip ticket and a few hundred dollars which the press association had advanced him. But he was undismayed: the cancellation would allow him to proceed at once with his plans for *The People of the Abyss,* as the book about the East End was to be titled.

He bought some old clothes, worn brogans and a greasy cloth cap from a dealer in Petticoat Lane and prepared to plunge into "this human hell-hole called the East End," where almost half a million people lived in the utmost squalor and hopelessness. He applied for guidance at Thomas Cook & Son, which was able to send a traveler to the Congo or Tibet with routine ease but couldn't direct him to the recesses of the East End, "barely a stone's throw from Ludgate Circus." Nor could the American embassy offer any advice or assistance. English acquaintances advised him to apply for a police escort, but he protested that he wanted to "see things for myself." He was warned that his life wouldn't be "worth a tuppence" in the rookeries of Whitechapel — "the very places I wish to see," as he replied.

No doubt there were those who thought him a bit off-center mentally: he proposed to explore and learn all that was essential about the East End within six weeks, and do most of the writing besides. On September 3, he wrote Brett that he was imposing a schedule on himself that would necessitate writing half the book in three weeks at the same time he was collecting material for the balance of the book, which, he admitted, didn't give him much time for reflection.

From the start of his explorations, he was impressed by the fact that, as in the "submerged tenth" of American life, the people of the London slums were victims of the economic system, for the most part, rather than born idlers or congenital loafers. Many had outlived their usefulness to an industrial society, others were too old or sick to be of value to employers. As he was to explain in his book, ". . . the Abyss exudes a stupefying atmosphere of torpor which wraps about the people and deadens them. Year by year rural England pours in a flood of vigorous young life that perishes by the third generation. At all times four hundred and fifty thousand human creatures are dying miserably at the bottom of the social pit called London."

Day after day he ventured into the mean streets, drifting along with the shambling men and women and the starveling children and feeling the hopelessness of their situation, absorbing the desperation of their condition through his pores, until (he wrote Cloudesley Johns) he feared that the book itself would reflect the hysterical edge of his mood. Yet he would not simply make observations, take notes and return home to write his impressions; as in everything else he attempted, he wanted *The People of the Abyss* to be charged with immediacy. The method was unscientific, the approach was more journalistic than literary, but he did not want to risk losing the sharpness, the raw surface of his perceptions. The tactile quality of what he wrote would make up for what it might lack in balance and reflection.

On August 9, Coronation Day for Edward VII, he stood in Trafalgar Square watching the panoplied majesty of empire display itself in gilt coaches and mounted Guards regiments in scarlet and gold, with two new friends from the lower depths at his side. One was an unemployed carter, fifty-eight years old, who hadn't slept in a bed for three nights; the other a sixty-five-year-old carpenter who hadn't slept under cover for five nights.

If the prosperous people of London, "full of meat and blood," had endured what his friends had, they would "think a thousand centuries had come and gone before the east paled into dawn . . . would shiver till they were ready to cry aloud with the pain of each aching muscle . . . would marvel they could endure so much and live." Both men had lost their wives and children to smallpox and scarlet fever. They were so emaciated their ribs stood out like washboards. If they were lucky enough to be admitted to the Popular Workhouse, a survival of Dickens's time and before, they would be given six ounces of bread and "three parts of skilly"* before they were shown to their cots for a night's sleep. In the morning they would have to "pick four pounds of oakum," as the carter told Jack, "or clean an' scrub, or break ten to eleven hundredweight o' stones," in payment for their board and lodging.

As he walked along the Mile End Road through the heart of East London, Jack said, he noticed that his companions frequently paused, bent down and picked something up from the "slimy, spittle-drenched" sidewalk. At first he thought they were scavenging for cigaret and cigar butts, then he saw that they were snatching up orange peels, grape stems, apple cores and plum pits which they cracked between their teeth for the kernels inside — all this in "the heart of the greatest, wealthiest and most powerful empire the world has ever seen."

Jack was so sorry for them that he dropped his pose of being a seaman who'd spent all his money on a drunk, extracted a gold guinea which he had sewn into the lining of his coat, bought the carter and the carpenter a supper of bacon and eggs and gave them several shillings each to sleep in a decent bed that night.

For six weeks he wandered the streets off Mile End Road, frequented workhouses, pubs, dives, doss houses, Salvation Army hostels and the grubby parks where the homeless spent their nights if they couldn't obtain shelter elsewhere. He also studied sociological works, government reports and pamphlets, searching for statistics to back up his argument that "the present management is incapable." To him the "riotous and rotten" West End and the "sickly and underfed" East End were opposite sides of a coin without value. "A vast empire is foundering," he declared; ". . . the political machine known as the British Empire is running down."

Another week, and he had the manuscript finished. Like much of his best work — regardless of what the literary sages said about the necessity of rewriting, polishing, revising, cutting and reorganizing — it was written at white heat. Years later he would say that of all his books he liked *The People of the Abyss* best, that he put more heart

* A thin gruel.

into it than any other; and despite all his proclamations that he wrote strictly for money, it could not have been conceived as just another commercial venture. He wrote it because he wanted to. It has often been written that London was ruined by his drive for the big money; that America and its materialistic values "got" Jack as it got Mark Twain;[6] yet he would often interrupt his more lucrative activities to work on something like *The People of the Abyss* which was unlikely to turn a profit. (Unlikely as its prospects were, that book eventually sold 21,550 copies, according to Macmillan's records — more than anyone could have anticipated.) By turn, Jack tended to be a furiously scribbling hack one day, a dedicated artist the next, a prophet and pamphleteer the next, his multiple talents revolving like a Gatling gun with each new inspiration. Had he been less versatile, he would have found it difficult to survive as a professional writer.

Packing his completed manuscript in a suitcase, Jack took off on a three-week tour of France, Germany and Italy in October before returning to the United States. He came home several thousand dollars in debt. Brett read *The People of the Abyss* immediately and decided to accept it for publication to follow *Children of the Frost,* which had just come out. First, however, he sent the manuscript to Professor G. R. Carpenter of Columbia University's Department of English for an outside reading. Professor Carpenter, as his reports in Macmillan's London file show, was not greatly enthused over Jack's talent, an opinion shared by many academic critics during the beginning of Jack's career, for he had too much vulgar creative energy, too little sense of the literary niceties and regard for "fine" writing to endear himself to the pedants. Carpenter had advised against publishing *The Kempton-Wace Letters,* which he regarded, with justice, as a somewhat callow and overly feverish exchange. As for *The People of the Abyss,* the professor wrote Brett on December 2, it "reveals nothing that has not been published." He conceded that London had "a certain Victor Hugo-like union of ferocity and tenderness," but reminded Brett that this was "scarcely the thing for your London house to issue." It was his considered opinion that Macmillan should "let this manuscript go by," though rejection of the book might lose the author to another publisher. Brett, however, ignored Carpenter's advice, and four weeks later obtained Jack's agreement to write a more "hopeful" final chapter, otherwise allowing the manuscript to stand as it was.

3. *Super Dog*

On his return from England early in November, Jack seemed a happier man, more confident of himself and of attaining his goal. The trust he felt in his new publisher, and Brett's apparent faith in him, were probably the principal reasons. His experience in the East End slums, too, seemed to have made him realize how well off he was by comparison — the waterfront streets of Oakland were paradisiac compared to those of Whitechapel and the East India docks. And he had the feeling — the secret joy known only to the writer, architect, painter, sculptor, composer — that he was on the point of conceiving something splendid. It hadn't taken shape, but it would in due time.

His assurance was so great that he was not dismayed by the fact that Bess once again, on October 20, 1902, had presented him with a daughter. The new baby was also named Bess. Instead of brooding over another failure to produce a son, he reminded himself that he and his wife were only twenty-six and there was plenty of time for other children. The law of averages dictated that sooner or later they would have a boy.

On November 21, he wrote Brett concerning his plans for future books. It was a lengthy and revealing letter. One point he wanted to make clear — perhaps to himself as much as Brett — was that though his responsibilities had increased, he did not regret them; on the contrary he was using them in making his life steadier and more balanced; his dependents were not a millstone around his neck but an anchor to keep him from drifting. He wanted Macmillan to advance him a hundred and fifty dollars a month for the next year, in return for which he would guarantee them a minimum of six books to be written at a pace best suited to good work. At the moment he believed it would be best if he confined himself to writing one book a year (a noble thought which vanished almost as quickly as the ink dried on his letter). Until now, he told Brett, he had been floundering around, working too hard and too aimlessly, but now he had found himself. He saw his way clear to achieving the promise other men saw in him.

First of all, he wanted to get away from writing about the Klondike. That field, he felt, had been exhausted as far as he was concerned. He wanted to write about something — in fictional terms — with a larger scope and more general interest.

Right then, he said, he was blocking out a novel tentatively titled *The Mercy of the Sea.* It would be a tragedy of the seafaring life, based on his own seven months as a deckhand aboard the *Sophie Sutherland.* This, of course, was the inception of *The Sea Wolf,* the first glimmering of his plans for one of the three books on which his fame is based, but it was to be laid aside to gestate awhile longer. In the meantime he would be writing *The Call of the Wild.* Thus within a few months of late 1902 he conceived two of the great books of his career. The feeling that he was on the verge of producing great work was strikingly justified by the event.

Brett readily agreed to have his company send Jack a hundred and fifty dollars a month for running expenses, and his faith in Jack, though it was to undergo many vicissitudes, was maintained to the end of his career. Few publishers have extended so much understanding and sympathy — backed by frequent remissions of solid cash — to an author of London's ups and downs, artistic and temperamental. He never lectured Jack, never scolded him, but was tactful and restrained even when the author was least reasonable. He and Jack never became intimate friends, partly because Brett was a convinced New Yorker and Jack was an equally fervent anti–New Yorker, partly because there was a sizable gap in their backgrounds, and partly, perhaps, because Brett, as a man of great discretion, knew it wasn't wise for a publisher to embrace *any* author too closely.

While he was thinking about his sea tragedy, Jack went to work on a short story, which he planned to tell in four or five thousand words. It would concern a "civilized" dog suddenly thrust into the sub-Arctic wilderness and made to fight for survival. He had no intention of writing another novel about the Klondike, as he had informed Brett, particularly since *A Daughter of the Snows* had sold only a few thousand copies.

He first planned the new story as a companion piece to "Batard," which told of a dog and his feud with his equally savage owner which resulted in the death of both of them.[7] The dog in that story was a vicious brute, and Jack wanted to make amends, he said later, by portraying a much finer specimen of the breed.

Almost from the first pages, the story of Buck, half St. Bernard, half Scotch shepherd, got away from him. In a few days he could see that he had a much longer and more powerful story to tell. On March 13,

1903, after it was finished, he wrote Anna Strunsky that his short story had simply got out of hand, had run away with him and ended up as a 32,000-word novel. It was an amazing instance of a story taking command of its author — and one of the few that turned out so happily. In what was to be titled *The Call of the Wild* all of the finest and purest elements of Jack's talent happened to crystallize. Writing out of his unconscious, not pausing for flourishes and lectures on significance, he told his story with a powerful simplicity.

Just whom Buck was modeled on later caused something of a commotion, though no one sued him for having stolen the personality of his dog. Some critics, mindful of Jack's autobiographical tendencies, even claimed Buck was Jack in dogskin. One of the more vigorous claimants was the wealthy Belinda Mulrooney, who made a fortune operating the Fairview House in Dawson and who believed that her big black Nero was Jack's hero in *The Call of the Wild*. Actually Buck was a dog owned by Judge Marshall Bond, who operated a ranch in the Santa Clara Valley, and was taken to the Klondike by the judge's son, Louis W. Bond. Jack settled the controversy himself by writing the judge on December 17, 1903 that Buck was indeed his dog.* Before that controversy died down, Jack was also forced to acknowledge his indebtedness to a study of *My Dogs of the Northland*, by Egerton R. Young, from which Jack borrowed liberally, particularly in making the traits of the other dogs in the novel authentic.

Jack found that the story almost wrote itself, flowing from his imagination to sheets of white paper at his standard rate of a thousand words a day. He finished it in less than five weeks. There were no revisions. It was a miraculous sort of literary birth, all but free of labor pains.

The story leaped into life and churning action from the moment Buck, genteelly bred and raised, was sold by a larcenous ranch hand for fifty dollars and transported to the Yukon for brutal service in a dog team run by a French Canadian named Perrault. Until he was thrust into the dog-eat-dog environment of the North Country, Buck had been an amiable fellow, but he quickly learned that to survive under these new circumstances he would have to adapt, be

* The letter may be found in the Jack London Collection of the University of California's Bancroft Library, along with a photograph of Bond's two dogs, Buck and Pat, taken in Dawson in the spring of 1898.

stronger, crueler and craftier than his mates on the dog team. His first lesson was snatching a piece of bacon away from the other dogs, which marked the beginning of the disintegration of his canine morality, "a vain thing and a handicap in the ruthless struggle for existence. It was all well enough in the Southland, under the law of love and fellowship, to respect private property and personal feelings; but in the Northland, under the law of the club and fang" it was all but suicidal. (He may have made a bit too much of Buck's formerly civilized tendencies. Most dogs would have stolen that piece of bacon anywhere, having none of the morality Jack attributed to Buck. But this is the sort of quibble that later would cause Jack to cry out in anguish against people who quarreled with him over "dog psychology.")

Buck was hitched to the team for the run to Dawson over the trail Jack himself traversed and soon became as savage as any of the other members of his team. Soon, too, he began to realize that there was an older, deeper atavistic strain in him when his comrades gave voice to their nocturnal song. "With the aurora borealis flaming coldly overhead, or the stars leaping in the frost dance, and the land numb and frozen under its pall of snow, this song of the huskies might have been the defiance of life, only it was pitched in minor key, with long-drawn wailings and half-sobs, and was more the pleading of life, the articulate travail of existence. It was an old song, old as the breed itself — one of the first songs of the younger world in a day when songs were sad." Buck began joining the huskies in their plaint which "harked back through the ages of fire and roof to the raw beginnings of life in the howling ages."

He had so adapted himself to the new conditions of his life that before the drive to Dawson was completed he fought the leader of the team and drove him yowling into the wilderness. After the return trip to Skagway, Buck and his teammates were sold to another owner, who was about to kill Buck in a winter camp at White River when John Thornton, the only decent human in the book, rescued him and took him in charge. Several times Buck, who adored his new master as he had no other human being, saved Thornton's life in camp and on the trail. The gentler influence of Thornton almost, but never quite, retrieved Buck from the primitivism into which the raw Northland was coaxing him. After Buck won a weight-pulling contest in Dawson

— an event London related superbly — Thornton was offered twelve hundred dollars for Buck but refused.

One day Buck left camp to trail a moose, and after four days of pursuit hauled him down and killed him. When he returned, he found that Thornton had been killed by a raiding band of Yeehats. From then on, Buck, known to the Indians as the "Ghost Dog," haunted the valley, robbed their camps and killed hunters who strayed. Most of the time Buck traveled alone, "a great, gloriously coated wolf, like, and yet unlike, all other wolves." He had reverted to the savage state of his ancestors.

The last sentence of *The Call of the Wild* is the most vibrant he ever wrote, and the morning he finished his daily stint and the book itself, the morning he wrote that sentence must have been the most thrilling moment of his inner life, the enclosed and unreachable life in which a writer is most truly himself:

"When the long winter nights come on and the wolves follow their meat into the lower valleys, he may be seen running at the head of the pack through the pale moonlight or glimmering borealis, leaping gigantic above his fellows, his great throat a-bellow as he sings a song of the younger world, which is the song of the pack."

4. *Success in Full Measure*

The rewards for *The Call of the Wild* began showering down almost immediately, like the bursting of a Mexican *piñata,* gifts of money, trinkets of praise, an incessant tinkle of flattery. It was recognized immediately, both as a little masterpiece of storytelling and a commercial property. Jack sent one copy to Macmillan, another to the *Saturday Evening Post.* Both accepted with significant haste. Brett, on behalf of Macmillan, proposed to buy the American book rights for two thousand dollars, a fairly common practice at the time. In return, Macmillan would allot a larger than usual budget for advertising, which would benefit his future works. Jack did not hesitate to accept Brett's offer, since he had no idea that *The Call of the Wild* would be anything more than a mild success; its leading character was a dog, after all, and it was only a third the size of the standard-length novel. Jack, in fact, regarded the offer as downright generous, especially with the additional advertising thrown in. Brett thought another title might prove more salable but allowed Jack's judgment on that to stand. The end result was that Jack got two thousand dollars for a book that has sold 2,019,918 copies in the United States hardcover editions alone, according to the most recent Macmillan sales figures.

The *Saturday Evening Post* bought the serial rights, despite its previous inhibitions about anything with a grim or tragic theme, and published it in installments between June 20 and July 18, 1903. According to other biographers, he received two thousand dollars from the *Post* but in a letter to Brett, Jack stated that he received three cents a word from the magazine, which would have made the *Post*'s payment about $960.[8]

The book was translated into every language under the sun and made its author world-famous. In the United States, its first printing of ten thousand copies was sold out on publication day. Some reviewers paid him the ultimate compliment of the time by saying *The Call of the Wild* was as good as anything Kipling wrote. The New York *Sun,* not easily impressed, declared it "a wonderfully perfect bit of work; a book that will be heard of long." Others nominated it "an American classic," and said that he had only to keep up the good work to attain an equal footing with Stephen Crane in the naturalistic field. By fall it was leading *Mrs. Wiggs of the Cabbage Patch* and *Rebecca of Sunnybrook Farm* on the best-seller list and was topped only by *The Bar Sinister,* also a dog story, and *The Little Shepherd of Kingdom Come* — a fair indication of the current state of American literature.

In full possession of his creative faculties with *The Call of the Wild,* Jack had finally struck the chord that awakened the fullest response in American readers, had discovered for them "the dreamland of heroic opportunity," as Granville Hicks has written.[9] He had found his audience. He had only to remain true to himself to gather in a lifetime of benefits. Yet within a few months in that heady year of 1903, with his sure instinct for tearing down what he built up, he proceeded to rip apart his no longer private life.

5. *Back with "The Crowd"*

When he returned home from the sobering experience of London's East End, during and just after writing *The Call of the Wild,* until in fact that novel was assured of success, Jack was living a sensible, apparently contented and productive life. He seemed devoted to Bess, to whom he inscribed an advance copy of *The Children of the Frost:* " 'The first book of mine, all for your own,' you said. But what matters it? Am I not all your own, your Daddy-boy?" To Bess he was still, mawkishly enough, "Daddy-boy," while he called her "Mother-girl." In the months following his return from Europe he was content to do his work, forego George Sterling's companionship, give up nights on the town across the Bay and do without the frolicsome, time-consuming company of "The Crowd," which was given to understand that Jack was working and did not want to be disturbed. He wrote Anna Strunsky and Cloudesley Johns that he was staying home and seeing no one. To Johns he also wrote, reminding his Southern California friend he had somewhat cynically withheld congratulations on his marriage until he (Johns) was sure it would work out, that it was about time he offered his overdue compliments. If Johns wasn't willing to take his word for it that he was happy with his wife and two young daughters, he could come up and take a look for himself.

For the first time in the marriage, Bess had her husband completely to herself, and was happy and secure. They hadn't married for love, she believed, but they'd found it anyway. And now Jack had his feet so solidly on the ground that he didn't even need "The Crowd" around with their fun and games and gossip — those people who, as the sensible Bess saw them, laughed a little too loud, drank a little too much, and were a little too insistent that they were the brightest-gayest-youngest-cleverest people in the cities of the Bay.

Bess thought she had every reason to believe it would go on this way, Jack happy and hard-working in the bosom of his family, but Jack wasn't made like that.

Jack was always at his best when he was hard-pressed, cornered by creditors, surrounded by obstacles. Then all his thought and energy went into his work. The challenge of battering at an indifferent publishing world brought out the fighter in him, and kept him involved with his work. When his ego needed satisfaction, which only work at his desk could produce, its demands were paramount. So Jack, in his *The Call of the Wild* working period, was content with rustication; he appreciated the domestic harmony provided by Bess not so much for itself but because it allowed him to get on with his job.

When success came, friends, toadies and admirers were once again welcome at his doorstep. He needed their flattery to assure him of the reality of success. He wanted it dinned in his ears. The one thing Bess couldn't give him was a sense of self-importance; she had a hardheaded attitude toward both giving and receiving praise. So he would have to hear it from others, no matter how insincere or worthless. Ten years later, in *John Barleycorn,* he wrote bitterly of the "insipidities and stupidities of the women" and the pomposity of the "little half-baked men" who surrounded him — at his own eager invitation — in the first flush of real success. By then he had wasted much of his substance on people who could only distract him from his main purpose.

Immediately after finishing *The Call of the Wild,* he began work on *The Mercy of the Sea,* later known as *The Sea Wolf,* which, as he wrote Brett on January 20, 1903, would deal with the subject of mastery. Although he later claimed that he wrote *The Sea Wolf* in six months,[10] actually he stopped work on the book a number of times during that period, rather than working straight through as he did on its predecessor. Instead of paying off his debts, which had mounted up despite his assurance to Brett that he could support his family on a hundred and fifty dollars a month, he used the first cash returns on *The Call of the Wild* to buy a sleek little sloop called the *Spray*. A servant was hired to help Bess around the house, since she had not yet entirely recovered from the difficult birth of her second daughter.

Soon enough he was learning to roar like a literary lion. Again he held open house on Wednesday nights, and there were many new faces in "The Crowd." Anna Strunsky was living in New York; Frank Strawn-Hamilton was also in the East, and Jim Whitaker was no longer traveling in the London social orbit, though he still lived nearby. Many of the newcomers, his daughter Joan has written, were "sycophants, well dressed, well mannered and glib," people who flocked around the celebrity of the moment and "made up the Greek chorus at studio teas and literary dinners." Inevitably their cricket-like chorus of praise had its effect on Jack; his ears had been attuned to the sounds of recognition for the past ten years, and a writer, working in isolation as he does, often without encouragement, is a little more desperate than most to catch the first signals of public approval. To him praise is always long overdue, and only an echo of what he has been telling himself all along.

The result naturally enough was a certain chestiness, though it never hardened into arrogance. Jack himself often told of one comeuppance he got in the euphoric period following publication of *The Call of the Wild.*

He was invited to speak at the University of California and accepted, despite his conviction that formal education was largely a waste of time. The semester he had spent on the Berkeley campus, he now believed, had given him nothing of value. He would claim in later years that the only moment of satisfaction he knew during that semester was whaling the tar out of a snooty classmate. (Later he forbade Bess to send their daughters to college, but they defied the paternal injunction even though they had to work their way through.)

When he got up to speak, he decided to let the faculty have it between the eyes. Their methods of instruction, he told the assemblage, were dessicated, unrealistic and rooted in a zombie-like fixation on the cultures of the past.

After the speech a number of listeners gathered around him, among them Professor Charles Mills Gayley, who had taught one of the English classes Jack attended. To Professor Gayley, with more force than tact, he reiterated his belief that universities gave their students an inadequate grounding in literature by insisting that they read the "dead" classics to the neglect of the more vital and meaningful works of contemporary authors. He was not at all abashed to grind his own ax.

"Perhaps you are not aware, Mr. London," Professor Gayley drily replied, "that we are using your own *Call of the Wild* in our classes?"

Jack had the grace to join in the laughter at his own expense.

During the spring of 1903, with the success of *The Call of the Wild* seemingly assured and the process of creating another novel of perhaps greater power under way, Jack was a busy and happy man. When he wasn't writing, he was entertaining or, when he wearied of sycophantic voices, off sailing the wide expanse of the Bay on his sloop.

Bess, however, was no longer so sure of herself or her place in a successful writer's life. She had endured the three years of financial insecurity without complaint, but living in the glass-house style Jack now ordained for them was not pleasing to her. The only reality for her was her husband, children and home. Outsiders who trooped through their rambling bungalow day and night were no more than intruders, whom she must make welcome only because her husband insisted on it. Joan London related that her mother "found herself hostess to numerous people with whom she not only was barely acquainted, but felt acutely ill at ease."

Scores of people "popped in" for a few hours, a few meals or a few days, many of them women who did not hide their adoring glances at her husband.

Bess grew jealous of these bold females who cruised openly under a pirate flag, apparently with good reason. Jack did not require a great deal of allurement. He admitted that he followed his hedonist's code and took what was offered. He insisted, however, that he never seduced a woman — or just as likely was seduced *by* one — with any protestations of love. This he regarded as a point of honor, if he had been capable of using such an outmoded term. It was his theory that a man could and should pile into bed with a woman purely out of lust, because that was the way he was made. He did not extend the same privilege to women. A woman who went to bed with a man, without being in love with him, was either an idiot or a whore. In either case, it was no concern of his. Momentary pleasure was the only consideration with him. That, at any rate, is what he related to friends about his activities that spring when he was on the verge of breaking up the cozy pattern of his life with Bess and the children; he did tend to glory in and embellish his reputation as The Stallion of the Piedmont Hills.

It may have been of equal importance that Bess seemed to be unable to live up to their new position in life. He wanted her to buy new clothes and dress herself in a fashion befitting the wife of a famous author, but she clung to blouses, skirts and sailor hats and refused to wear formal dress even when they were invited to dinner parties or banquets, such as the one honoring Jack at the Bohemian Club at which she appeared to a disadvantage beside the other women in their elegant gowns and hairdos. Jack was no fashion plate himself, affecting soft-collared shirts and flowing ties and scorning evening dress as the uniform of the class enemy; yet it offended his self-esteem that Bess should cling to her middy blouses.

Apparently he also felt that Bess wasn't "keeping up" with him mentally by reading and discussing books with him. Instead she busied herself with the children and the household chores. After all, they had a servant to care for the house and Mammy Prentiss to look after the children.

It was during this period, when Jack was first tasting the fruits of success and wondering whether he hadn't married wisely — too wisely — but not well enough, that a certain young woman became an increasingly frequent visitor at the London home. Bess had no reason to regard her as a possible interloper: she was five years older than Jack and no great beauty, certainly not the man-killer type. Why, she even boxed and fenced like a man . . . or as Bess was to learn to her sorrow, one of those "mate-women" Jack was always talking about.

Her name was Charmian Kittredge.

VIII

Enter Miss Kittredge, Exit Mrs. London

Nothing will ever crush Charmian Kittredge.
— Rose Wilder Lane

1. *"Childie"*

JACK first met Charmian Kittredge a few weeks before he married Bess Maddern, early in the spring of 1900, when he was a shabby young man just beginning to be noticed in the San Francisco literary world. She was the niece of Mrs. Ninetta Eames, who was her guardian and raised her from infancy. Her mother, Dyelle Kittredge, a poetess, died shortly after Charmian was born.

The day Jack and Charmian first met, Mrs. Eames had invited him to lunch before taking him over to the museum in the Ferry Building and posing him in Alaskan furs for publicity photographs to be published in the *Overland Monthly,* of which her husband Roscoe was an editor. Mrs. Eames also asked her niece to join them at Young's Restaurant on Montgomery Street. Charmian later recalled being irked by the idea of her aunt's picking up the check for lunch, which she regarded as a male prerogative.

Nor was she impressed when Jack appeared riding a bicycle with a cloth cap tilted boyishly over his tousled light brown hair. Even to the least discerning eye he was down at heel, not well educated and lacked the polished manners of the men who escorted her to parties and the theater. Mrs. Eames later recalled that Charmian was "snippy" about Jack's shabby appearance. Charmian herself remembered that after talking to him for a while she began to forgive his rough exterior and was conscious of his innate gentleness.

Even if he hadn't suddenly married Bess Maddern a few weeks later, however, she wouldn't have considered him eligible as an escort or suitor. The men who took her out had to be in the flowers and wine and hansom-cab class. Although she was working as a stenographer, she made it plain in her recollection of the youthful Jack, she was earning enough to maintain an apartment, employ a Swedish maid, buy party gowns and pay for stabling her saddle horse. A short time after Jack's marriage she was able to afford a trip to Europe. Whether she managed this on a stenographer's salary, or had some private income, she did not disclose.

In the opinion of Jack's friends there was much that needed explaining about the young woman after she reappeared with fateful effect in his life. Many who knew her believed that she started taking an interest in him only after he seemed sure of prominence as a writer; that once she decided to supplant Bess she set about her program of homewrecking with a ruthless cunning. Her few defenders, on the other hand, would point out that Jack had started roaming long before Charmian made her influence felt.

Undoubtedly Charmian was a young woman on the make, desperately anxious over being unmarried at thirty-two, going on thirty-three. She wasn't reconciled to spinsterhood, she was ten years past the usual marrying age, and the men she had known had proved treacherous and elusive. And Aunt Netta, Mrs. Eames, kept urging her to settle down, pick out the most eligible man she knew and lead him to the altar.

Much of Charmian's character was shaped by Mrs. Eames, it was evident. Her aunt was a sweet-faced, fluttery woman of fifty who managed her elderly husband with an iron hand; she was also ambitious, rather grasping and hardheaded despite her twittery speech and helpless manner. Jack London was the first *Overland Monthly* discovery in its years of faltering under the Eames-Payne management to indicate promise of becoming a big name, and she didn't mean to let him escape her even though Jack had been forced to threaten Eames and Payne with assault if they didn't pay for his first story. It was undoubtedly Mrs. Eames who kept Jack contributing to the *Overland Monthly* although it could pay little or nothing for his stories. And when Jack suddenly married Bess Maddern, a few weeks after she had hopefully introduced him to her niece, the news probably came as a shock.

Admittedly she took an unusual amount of interest in the progress of that marriage while Charmian was flitting around Europe. She would recall in later years that two days after they were married Jack and Bess came to her with the complaint that they were ill-mated and asked her advice. She told them, she recalled, that they could hardly expect to be deliriously happy when they admittedly weren't in love with each other. The recollection, however, is suspect. While it was not impossible that Jack would discuss his marital relations with a third party, given his frankness and lack of inhibition, the picture of Bess, with her rigid sense of propriety, making such a confession to a woman she barely knew is hardly credible. Furthermore, on the second day after their marriage Jack and Bess were still honeymooning.

In her recollections of long afterward, Mrs. Eames, who was estranged from Charmian by then and said she felt nothing but pity for her, insisted that her niece had always been a source of deep concern. She had called her "Childie," a pet name that says something about both women when still applied to a female in her thirties. For years she had worried herself sick over Charmian's failure to find a husband, over her suspicion that "Childie" might be misbehaving with some of her admirers, not all of whom were unmarried.

She might well have been concerned if she ever had a look at the diary Charmian kept as a girl and young woman. It was unabashedly revealing, with Charmian picturing herself as possessing a fatal fascination for men; rather touching too in its shaky conceits, like reading the diary of Booth Tarkington's Alice Adams. She frequently reported that men fell victim to a single smile from her, that other women were terribly jealous of her. Occasionally she would remark that everyone she knew was getting married and she felt left out. More than once she noted that "Auntie" was fretting over whether a certain gentleman caller would get around to asking for her hand. On one occasion she recorded overhearing Aunt Netta telling someone that Charmian never allowed any admirers to take liberties unless they were pledged to marry her — one can almost see Charmian smiling to herself as she listened outside Mrs. Eames's parlor door — and commented slyly that she hoped her aunt never learned the truth.

She grew increasingly desperate over the way her beaux, married or otherwise — it never seemed to occur to her, even in the privacy of her diary, that there might be something wrong about encouraging the attentions of other women's husbands — kept slipping out of their promises and her clutches. In December of 1900 she had reason to complain of one Will, who kept speaking of wanting to marry her in three years. Later Will sent a letter breaking off the relationship, and had it delivered by another girl.

And one Herbert, to whom she frankly was attracted because of the amounts of money he spent when he took her out, also proved tricky. Herbert was married, and Aunt Netta finally stepped in and told him not to trifle with "Childie's" affections. A short time later Herbert's wife divorced him in Chicago, and Charmian, always hopeful, sent him a letter of congratulations. Either caddish or cautious, Herbert did not reply.

Another married admirer of hers, whom she described as handsome and impetuously passionate, took her to his home. He began making love to her and flew into a rage when his young son and a servant happened to enter the room. Charmian's only comment on a scene that would have mortified most women was that the man was astonishingly expert at rousing her passion.

In her diary she also wrote of an admirer named Wemple, who was a "passionate little fellow," and of exchanging thirty-eight-page letters with another man who had gone to New York and was promising to send for her. She could barely wait to "fly to New York and nestle in his arms forever." *This* time she was sure that marriage was in the offing. But once again she was let down. Regarding another man, named Clarence, she exclaimed over the beauty of his figure "— and I know whereof I speak!"

Obviously Aunt Netta's "Childie" was an anxious young woman, her apprehensions of winding up a lonely old maid constantly prodded into life by Mrs. Eames, when she insinuated herself into "The Crowd" and began casting appraising eyes on the restive young Mr. London. She was not at all dismayed by the fact that Jack was twenty-seven to her thirty-two, still secretly convinced that no man could resist her charms.

Just how attractive she was depended on the sex of the observer. She was one of those women who drew more than her share of watchful dislike from other women. Fairer than most in her judgment, surprisingly enough, was Joan London, who wrote that she was "a forerunner of a type of American woman of the middle class who would not fully emerge for nearly a quarter of a century," that "in an era when women's thoughts and actions were still narrowly circumscribed she managed to achieve extraordinary freedom without being socially ostracized." But there were many in the group that congregated at the London home who "found her laughter a little loud, her horsemanship too spectacular, her eagerness to play and sing at the piano distasteful" because they "did not fully appreciate that behind much of this exhibitionism lay a woman's very natural desire to attract a husband before it was too late."

She was a small woman with a slight but shapely figure. Her mouth was too wide and her nose turned up impishly; she had a smile, or grin, that was incandescent with high spirits. Her charm stemmed from her lively personality, her willingness to accept any kind of challenge, rather than a pretty face. She was more soubrette than siren, more hoyden than temptress, and no stage producer in his right mind would have cast her as a homewrecker. Joan London remembers a friend of the family saying that Charmian "has a mug — not a face." If one habit of hers was likely to dismay any man — and it may well have driven off some of those other suitors — it was her endless prattle. She talked at top speed, rattling off her opinions on any and all subjects with a superb recklessness. The single quality Joan London remembers about her, both as a young and an aging woman, was her childishness. Her self-absorption, ruthless as it seemed to people she hurt or offended, was that of a child, innocently excluding all considerations but her own. "Childie" she was then, and always.

Joseph Noel recalled that she had "as neat a pair of hips as one might find anywhere," which were enhanced by the short tailored skirts she wore as part of her fencing costume, and "well-turned ankles." He also noted that there was a quick glint of appraisal in her eyes that left him wondering whether there wasn't something of the "incipient clubwoman" in her instead of an inveterate tomboy.[1]

Jack was entranced by her from the moment she re-entered his life. Perhaps if she had given him any encouragement when they first met in the spring of 1900, he would have made a play for her then and never married Bess; but it seems fair enough to say that she didn't find him interesting until he was established by *The Call of the Wild*. The men who preceded him in her affections were usually well-heeled, sophisticated and accomplished, and the fact that some of them were married only seemed to arouse her competitive spirit.

She was clever in several ways that Bess wasn't, knew how to maneuver men (up to a point), was quite well read, musically adept, an excellent horsewoman. The paradox of her delicate figure and her athletic skill fascinated Jack. She was eager and responsive where Bess was inhibited and matter-of-fact, romantic and imaginative while his wife was the soul of practicality and settled in domestic routine. Or so she appeared in those first dazzling months of reacquaintance.

Above all, Jack had met her before under the most alluring of all possible circumstances — in his own stories. She seemed to be one of his heroines miraculously sprung to life. Nothing could be more enchanting to the author than to find that one of his dream women, who had lived only in his imagination and on paper before, could actually exist in the flesh.

She could have been the model for Frona Welse of *A Daughter of the Snows*. Or Edith Nelson of his short story "The Unexpected,"[2] one of his more striking examples of the New Woman, the Mate-Woman, the all-around pal, concupiscent comrade, spirited and proud of her independence. Edith Nelson, in one of his tautest stories, was having breakfast with her husband and two other men in their Alaskan cabin when a neighbor walked in and killed their two guests with a shotgun. They disarmed the killer, knowing he would kill them too if he had the chance, and held him for the law. Then they realized there wasn't much law around, and that they couldn't hold him under guard indefinitely, so they constituted themselves a court of two and sentenced him to be hanged. Edith, as Jack portrayed her, was cooler and more determined than her husband in the crisis, one of those who "make toward survival, the fit individuals who escape from the rule of the obvious and the expected and adjust their lives to no matter what strange grooves they may stray into . . ."

Soon it was noticeable — though apparently not to Bess — that Jack and Charmian were taking an extraordinary delight in each other's company. He would stand over her at the piano and turn the sheets of music for her. They boxed and fenced and rode and picnicked, always with "The Crowd" around but increasingly not a part of that group. The day Joseph Noel first met Charmian she and Jack had just been fencing. Charmian won the match, and with raised eyebrows all around Jack impulsively embraced and kissed her. "It was soon evident," Noel recalled, "that others were sensitive to those gifts of

Charmian's that menaced the complacency of the smug little group . . . When I suggested that she would be an addition to our Sunday picnics, George [Sterling] opposed it with so much heat that I knew at once he knew as much as I suspected." [3] Sterling, it seemed, was all on the side of sanctity of the home where his friend was concerned, more out of an initial dislike of Charmian, perhaps, than any lingering middle-class morality.

The last time Noel saw him before Jack made his big decision, on a picnic in a nearby cherry orchard, Jack was bleak-faced with melancholy and drank more heavily than usual. He was not long for the poppy-emblazoned hills in which he did the best writing of his life.

2. *"I'm Leaving you . . ."*

Self-justification, even to such an avowed anti-moralist, apparently was necessary to Jack. He had known so little genuine, unquestioning love in his life that he could not give up his wife and daughters lightly. To Sterling and others he began airing his views on the inequities of marriage. It was, he believed, strictly a woman's game. The real man resisted marriage as violently as the real anarchist opposed government, and for much the same reasons. All through the ages man had struggled to be free of the tyrannical rule of the law and the stifling encirclement of domesticity. "Woman with her avid desire for four walls that must be kept strong to protect the young is the enduring grief of the poet, the creator, the dreamer," he said. "She brings her narrow little idea of what's right in the door and every suggestion of beauty and bigness in life flies out the window."

He made his dissatisfaction with Bess more specific one spring night when he was returning from San Francisco with Noel and Sterling.

Bess, it seemed, had become difficult over his habit of occasionally spending a night on the town and was showing concern over his antics while away from home. "When I tell her that morality is only a sign of low blood pressure, she hates me. She'd sell me and the children out for her damned purity. It's terrible. Every time I come back after being away from home for a night she won't let me be in the same room with her if she can help it. I can see the horror in her eyes when I go near the children. She wants to make me a house animal that won't go anywhere without her approval. And worse than anything else, she's converting that bungalow into a prison. I don't want to live in a prison."

Jack apparently was trying to convince himself that he would be justified in breaking out of his "prison." He was twenty-seven years old, and it would be better if he made the break while he and Bess were still young. Bess would find someone else; before him she'd been in love with Fred Jacobs, hadn't she?

As it happened an accident hastened the course of events. In June it was proposed, probably by Jack, that Bess take the children up to the foothills of Sonoma County for the summer. Ninetta Eames and her husband's associate, Edward Payne, had built several cabins near Glen Ellen, in the Valley of the Moon, for rental to summer visitors. Nearby was also a house, Wake Robin, and a rustic tabernacle where Payne, an unctuous ex-preacher, proposed to hold revival meetings. Bess and the children would occupy one of the cabins.

Jack, however, intended to stay on at the bungalow in Piedmont, telling his wife *The Sea Wolf* was almost half done and he wanted to concentrate on finishing it. Besides he wanted to be able to take the *Spray* out for a sail whenever he needed to recapture the moods of the sea and the feeling of a deck beneath him. Undoubtedly there was also the thought at the back of his mind that he might be able to see Charmian without wifely surveillance. Summer is a dangerous time for vacationing wives.

Late that month the accident occurred. He and George Sterling and several other men were traveling in a buggy over the steep roads of the Piedmont Hills. The buggy slipped off the road and tumbled into a ravine. None of the others was hurt but Jack's leg was injured; no bones were broken but there were painful lacerations. This, apparently, was Charmian's cue. What more fetching role than that of nurse to the wounded young genius? She was a frequent visitor at his bedside and obviously made the most of her opportunities.

Later Charmian maintained that Bess herself asked that she look in on Jack, never suspecting any rivalry, and see that he was made comfortable. She also claimed that she never encouraged him to think of her as anything but a friend; that she wasn't, in fact, in love with him at the time.

If so, she was giving Jack the wrong impression in letters fervently exchanged during June and early July between Charmian's office or apartment in San Francisco and Jack's bungalow in the Piedmont Hills across the Bay.

She wrote that at their last meeting she saw his face grow younger under her touch, a little later that she was proud of not having failed him where she feared she might fail him the most, that she lay abed murmuring his name. The language was not that of platonic friendship. In reply, Jack strove manfully to match her ecstatic, exclamatory protestations, but he had not acquired any experience in writing love letters and they sounded a trifle lame. He did manage to convey the idea that he was grateful she hadn't turned coy on him while playing nurse, that she hadn't been a prude while ministering to the invalid.

Charmian was also noticeably anxious to get across the idea that she was not overawed by his success,* and that she had fallen in love with Jack London the man rather than Jack London the writer.

In July both Jack and Charmian, traveling separately, went up to the summer colony in the valley above Glen Ellen. So far as can be determined nothing had been settled at that point. Jack realized he had reached a turning point but didn't know himself which direction he would take. He was sick of the Piedmont Hills setup, of "The Crowd," and probably himself. Perhaps if he could take Bess and the children away somewhere, he'd forget about Charmian. His philosophy about women, after all, dictated a certain ruthlessness; love, or lust or whatever it was, wasn't supposed to turn his life upside down. Perhaps he sensed that in exchanging Bess for Charmian he might deliver himself into the arms of a woman more possessive than his present wife, less willing to stay in the background while the lord and master roved as he pleased. The idea of moving his family to Southern California and settling down on a desert ranch occurred to him; out on the Mojave he'd be safe from distraction, sexual and otherwise; then, when the children were older, they could accompany him and Bess on the travels he planned throughout the world.

Even then he might have carried through this plan, but shortly after he arrived at Wake Robin, Charmian appeared to spend her vacation with Aunt Netta, Uncle Roscoe and the ex-Reverend Mr. Payne (a trio that was also soon to be rearranged).

* *The Call of the Wild* was then running as a serial in the *Saturday Evening Post.*

As Bess later told the story of how her marriage suddenly dissolved, Jack appeared to be as contented as ever when he rejoined his family. In the morning he worked on *The Sea Wolf*, later he played with the children, and early in the evening the whole Wake Robin colony gathered on the bank of the stream that ran through the summer camp, cooked their meal over an open fire and dined together off tables under the trees.

One afternoon late in July Bess and Jack strolled along the river. He wanted to get away from Piedmont Hills, the whole Bay area, in fact, because he knew too many people and they disrupted his work. He asked her if she would mind living on a desert ranch in the southern part of the state. She said she was willing to make the move providing their new home would have modern conveniences for the children's sake. They agreed to plan on leaving the Piedmont Hills bungalow that fall.

Bess recalled that she took her two daughters back to the London cabin for their afternoon nap. On the way she saw Charmian, who evidently had been waiting for him, lead Jack to a hammock slung at the side of the Wake Robin lodge. Bess thought nothing of it because Jack and Charmian often had their heads together; neither then nor a long time afterward could Bess conceive of Charmian as the interloper; if anything she was rather sorry for Charmian and her obvious despair at still being a spinster.

Four hours later, all that time spent in the hammock with Charmian, he walked up to their cabin and without preliminary announced: "Bessie, I'm leaving you."

"You mean you're going back to Piedmont?" Bess asked.

"No, I'm leaving you . . . separating."

Bess was dumfounded. "Why, Daddy," she said, sitting on the edge of a cot and staring at him in disbelief, "what do you mean? You've just been talking about Southern California."

Jack kept saying over and over that he was separating from her, and would not elaborate.

"But I don't understand," Bess insisted again and again. "What has happened to you?"

Jack left without giving her a word of explanation.

Once having made the break, he moved with dispatch to cut the ties that bound him to Bess. The day after he told her he was leaving her, he removed his clothing and other possessions from the bungalow in Piedmont Hills and took a room in Oakland. He hoped for enough peace and privacy to be able to finish *The Sea Wolf*, but the newspapers got hold of the story of his marital breakup and splashed it across the front pages from coast to coast. In the absence of any definitive word on the reason for the separation the newspapers reported that publication of *The Kempton-Wace Letters* was the cause of the split. The book had been published a few months before, in May, and some of Jack's ideas on love and marriage were shocking to a generation still enthralled by Victorianism. While Anna argued for the poetic and romantic side of love, Jack insisted the emotion was based on biology, that there were only two kinds of women — the "Mother Woman . . . highest and holiest in the hierarchy of life" and the "Mate Woman . . . wonderful and unmoral and filled to the brim with life." Among other things Jack had written, in the guise of Herbert Wace, that he had concluded that love was not based on reason. Some of the newspapers said this statement so wounded Bess that she threw him out of the house. Others hinted that Anna Strunsky herself was the cause.

In the absence of proof to the contrary, Bess came to believe that Anna indeed was her rival and eventually named her as co-respondent. Jack refused to say anything at all to the reporters who kept dogging him for a statement. If he had, it might have saved a lot of grief and embarrassment all around; but that would have entailed publicly confessing his love for Charmian, and neither of them was ready for that.

He wrote his publisher from his new quarters at 1216 Telegraph Avenue that there was little he could say about his marital troubles except that *The Kempton-Wace Letters* had nothing to do with them. The causes of the estrangement, he added, began long before he and Bess separated.[4]

Eight days later, indicating that his new novel was uppermost in his mind no matter what emotions were swirling around its perimeter, he telegraphed Brett that "Sea Wolf" or "Sea Wolves" must be part of the novel's title, *The Mercy of the Sea* having been found inadequate. During all the upsets, recriminations and emotional turmoil of the several months ahead, Jack worked steadily away on his sea novel. Any dedicated writer can keep going no matter what storms are raging outside. If this is callousness, it is still an essential part of his equipment; he could never endure without this carapace to shut out the world's confusions.

For the time being his work, the hours aboard the hell ship *Ghost* on the seascape of his imagination, was his sanctuary.

3. *Superman Afloat*

One of the more incisive and scathing critics of Jack London has been Lewis Mumford, to whom the philosophical mishmash underlying London's work, the hastily absorbed and haphazardly ingested works of Darwin and Spencer and Nietzsche, not to mention Marx and the anarchist prophets, indicted him as a parvenu and opportunist of letters.[5] Mumford charged that London even "clung to socialism, it would seem, chiefly to give an additional luster of braggadocio and romanticism to his career; for socialism, to London's middle-class contemporaries, was an adventure more desperate than the rush for gold in the Klondike . . . he betrayed his socialism in all his ingrained beliefs, particularly his belief in success, and in his conception of the Superman."

In *The Sea Wolf,* of course, Jack created the most outwardly exact replica of Nietzsche's ideal human; not, however, as Nietzsche would have conceived him but as Jack believed a superman in real life would have turned out.

To Mumford, London's conception was a perversion rather than a projection. "The career of the Superman in America is an instructive spectacle," Mumford wrote. "He sprang, this overman, out of the pages of Emerson; it was Emerson's way of expressing the inexhaustible evolutionary possibilities of a whole race of Platos, Michelangelos, and Montaignes. Caught up by Nietzsche, and colored by the dark natural theology Darwin had inherited from Malthus, the Superman became the highest possibility of natural selection; he served as a symbol of contrast with the cooperative or 'slave morality' of Christianity. The point to notice is that in both Emerson and Nietzsche the Superman is a higher type: the mark of his genius is the completer development of his human capacities . . . London, however, seized the suggestion of the Superman and attempted to turn it into reality. And what did he become? Nothing less than a preposterous bully . . . like his whole gallery of brutal and brawny men — creatures blessed with nothing more than the gift of a magnificent animality, and the absence of a social code which would prevent them from inflicting this gift upon their neighbors. In short, London's Superman was little more than the infantile dream of the messenger boy or the barroom tough or the nice, respectable clerk whose muscles will never quite stand up under the strain. He was the social platitude of the old West, translated into a literary epigram."

The true significance of *The Sea Wolf,* to its author, was that the Nietzschean hero was doomed by his inevitable imperfections. London was plagued to the end of his life by the way his contemporaries, particularly his fellow Socialists, misconstrued his portrayal of Captain Wolf Larsen. Even the most casual reading of *The Sea Wolf* would seem to bear him out. Wolf Larsen was no epic hero but a fatally flawed brute. No more forceful way could be found to demonstrate, as Jack did in the last chapters of his novel, that Supermanship was folly, that it was bound to end in raging futility.*

Yet some fairly acute minds failed to grasp his point, and for that no author, once he recovers from suffering the obtuseness of his critics, can intelligently blame his readers. If they've missed the point, he can only question his own methods of presenting it. Somewhere he has managed to conceal it, perhaps in the confusion of action and conflict. In the case of *The Sea Wolf,* it may be that London erred in making Larsen's fatal flaw physical rather than moral. Larsen was the most memorable human character he created, and what sticks in the memory is his strength, his superiority, rather than his somewhat contrived comeuppance.

Even Ambrose Bierce, his harshest critic, had to concede that *The Sea Wolf* was a "rattling good story," aside from a number of faults which Mr. Bierce was only too happy to expose. Its background was the sealing voyage Jack made as a seventeen-year-old deckhand on the *Sophie Sutherland.* Its characters, aside from the lone female thrust into the story with more artifice than logic, were the kind of men he knew and understood. The workings of the ship, the way its crew lived, the battle against the cold northern seas off the Japanese and Siberian coasts, were brilliantly described; they were, in fact, its

* Later, in defending himself against charges that he was propagating the Nietzschean ethic, he asserted that he wrote *The Sea Wolf* to prove that "the superman cannot be successful in modern life . . ."

main strength and account for its survival as one of the more realistic American sea novels.

His story began with Humphrey Van Weyden, a writer who had always known a life of ease, being cast into the Bay when the ferryboat on which he is a passenger collides with a steamboat.* Van Weyden has the bad luck to be picked up and shanghaied by the sealing schooner *Ghost,* bound for the hunting grounds of the North Pacific. Its captain, Wolf Larsen, refuses to turn back and disembark Van Weyden. Larsen is an awesomely self-educated brute whose "strength pervaded every action . . . it seemed but an advertisement of a greater strength that lurked within, that lay dormant and no more than stirred from time to time, but which might arouse, at any moment, terrible and compelling, like the rage of a lion or the wrath of a storm."

Van Weyden is placed under the greasy thumb of the Cockney cook, Thomas Mugridge (the best drawn of the minor characters), and soon realizes that if he is to survive aboard the *Ghost* — just as Jack himself learned in the forecastle of the *Sophie Sutherland* — he will have to adapt himself to the pitiless environment and crush Mugridge before Mugridge crushes him.

As the *Ghost* sails west Captain Larsen frequently summons Van Weyden to his cabin because he is the only man aboard capable of conducting an intelligent conversation. Larsen unburdens himself of his philosophy that "life is a mess. It is like yeast, a ferment, a thing that moves and may move for a minute, an hour, a year, a hundred years, but that in the end will cease to move. The big eat the little that they may continue to move, the strong eat the weak that they may retain their strength. The lucky eat the most and move the longest, that's all . . ."

Once know as "Sissy," an intellectual who has been sheltered against adversity by a private income, Van Weyden — not too convincingly, perhaps — soon is as tough as the rock-fisted hearties in the forecastle. Larsen observes the change in him with sardonic amusement and promotes him to mate. Van Weyden plunges into the gory seal hunt, "ravaging and destroying, flinging the naked carcasses to the shark and salting down the skins so that they might later adorn the fair shoulders

* This incident was drawn from the sinking of the ferry *San Rafael* on the foggy night of November 30, 1901, when it was struck amidships by the bow of its sister ship *Sausalito* with a loss of three lives.

of the women of the cities." Ven Weyden does not protest Larsen's brutal treatment of the crew because, he believes, "mine is the role of the weak."

After weathering a typhoon, the *Ghost* picks up a lifeboat with survivors from a less fortunate ship, among them a lovely poetess named Maud Brewster whose verse Van Weyden had long admired. Maud, of course, is an infatuated portrait of Charmian Kittredge. (She is literally washed into the story at the halfway mark. At that point in the writing, Jack broke up with Bess. His novel, likewise — it almost makes one believe in retribution — breaks in half at this stage; the first half tough-minded and realistic, the balance larded with sentiment, burdened with a love story more befitting a woman's magazine serial. Mostly because of that love story, presumably, the *Ladies Home Journal* bought several thousand copies of *The Sea Wolf* and distributed them as premiums to new subscribers.) Maud was "a delicate, ethereal creature, swaying and willowy, light and graceful of movement. It never seemed that she walked, or, at least, walked after the ordinary manner of mortals. Hers was an extreme lithesomeness, and she moved with a certain indefinable airiness, approaching one as down might float or as a bird on noiseless wings . . . I have never seen a body and spirit in such perfect accord . . . in her constitution there was little of robust clay."

Inevitably Van Weyden and Larsen are smitten by the girl; Van Weyden's regard, of course, is of a waxen purity while Larsen's is forthrightly carnal. The two men fight over the poetess, and Van Weyden escapes mayhem in that encounter when Larsen is stricken with a blinding, and blindingly fortuitous, headache. Maud and Humphrey flee across the northern sea in an open boat. "Because of her," Van Weyden relates in a gem of Victorian sentiment, "the strength was mine to win our way back to the world." They finally land on Endeavor Island, where they play Mr. and Mrs. Robinson Crusoe and observe the proprieties: ". . . time and place were not met, and I wished to earn a better right to declare my love."

By shameless coincidence, the *Ghost,* with only Wolf Larsen aboard, casts up on the same island. His crew and his hunters have deserted him after his gigantic and even more dastardly brother, Death Larsen, boarded the *Ghost* and offered them more pay. Larsen is in bad shape but still has enough strength and perversity to attempt to defeat their attempts to make the *Ghost* seaworthy again. Van Weyden is about to take a club to him when Larsen suffers another attack — never quite diagnosed by the author, but possibly a brain tumor — and later dies, indicating the fatal flaw in a man who had gloried in his ability to dominate others.

Van Weyden and his ethereal beloved, still "pale but composed" after their ordeal, manage to embark in the schooner. A short time later a U.S. revenue cutter comes steaming over the horizon. The closing lines could have been written by Ethel M. Dell:

" 'One kiss, my love,' I whispered. 'One kiss before they come.'

" 'And rescue us from ourselves,' she completed, with a most adorable smile, whimsical as I had ever seen it, for it was whimsical with love."

The imperfections, the false sentiment, the insipidity of hero and heroine which were to become magnified in his later novels, already manifested themselves in the last half of *The Sea Wolf*. The sinewy prose and poetic simplicity of *The Call of the Wild* had slipped away, and would never reappear except in an intermittent afterglow, in bits and pieces of shorter works.

Instead of resolving to use all his resources to turn out work with the quality of *The Call of the Wild* Jack jumped with both feet into the marketplace. Doubtless his need for money was only increased by the necessity of maintaining a home for Bess and the children, another for his mother and Johnny Miller, and now a third for himself — and there was also the prospect of marrying Charmian. At any rate his attitude toward the commercial possibilities of his work was made clear in an exchange of letters with Brett. After finishing the first half of *The Sea Wolf,* he sent it with an outline of the balance to the publisher, who was rightly enthused — Maud Brewster had barely clambered over the rail of the *Ghost* at that point. Brett recommended it to the *Century Magazine,* which was almost as conservative as the *Atlantic Monthly*. *Century* likewise was impressed and offered four thousand dollars for the serial rights, provided that it would be granted the right to censor anything offensive once Van Weyden and Maud landed without chaperone on that island — none of that Adam and Eve stuff for the *Century*'s sedate readership. Jack agreed at once that the magazine could delete anything it liked. The proviso may also have influenced him to drip glucose all over the relations between his stainless lovers, and thereby destroy the validity of his novel.

Several years later Jack complained to Upton Sinclair about how much he hated writing, principally because sex had to be sugar-coated to fabricate fiction — high-priced fiction, that is. "I loathe the stuff," Sinclair quoted him,[6] "when I have done it. I do it because I want money and it's an easy way to get it. But if I could have my choice about it I would never put pen to paper — except to write a Socialist essay, to tell the world how much I despise it."

For *The Sea Wolf* alone, in spite of such praise as the lordly New York *Herald*'s ("marvelously truthful — poignantly interesting — superb piece of craftsmanship"), Ambrose Bierce would have been glad to advise him to despise himself as a self-made eunuch of the literary harem. "It is a most disagreeable book, as a whole. London has a pretty bad style and no sense of proportion. The story is a perfect welter of disagreeable incidents. Two or three (of the kind) would have sufficed to show the character of the man Larsen . . . Many of these incidents, too, are impossible — such as that of a man mounting a ladder with a dozen other men — more or less — hanging to his leg. . . . The 'love' element, with its absurd suppressions and impossible proprieties, is awful. I confess to an overwhelming contempt for both sexless lovers."[7]

By that time, of course, Bierce's brickbats could barely dent Jack's self-esteem. *The Sea Wolf* became the top best-seller in the country, sold 40,000 copies before publication and eventually 535,507.[8] It was widely translated, rousingly praised throughout the world, accorded an honored place in the vanguard of the New Realism — half-realistic, half-romantic hybrid though it was. Hollywood eventually found it good to look upon, three times over.

While Jack was working on the last chapters of the novel, he and Charmian kept in touch mostly by mail. They met infrequently and furtively, hoping that no one would find out about the affair until they were sure enough of each other to advertise their passion to the world.

The letters they exchanged were, if anything, more passionately platitudinous than those they had written before Jack had broken off with his wife. Charmian's language, sometimes descending to baby-talk, was hardly that of the brisk, comradely New Woman but more that of the violently smitten Victorian maiden. And Jack's replies were couched in the same delirious rhetoric, neo–Robert Browning, instead of the smugly rational accents of Herbert Wace. Charmian declared that she considered herself Jack's sweetheart and wife, if only in a manner of speaking, and Jack actually protested that he considered himself her slave.

For all their pride in being modern, advanced, free of nineteenth-century shibboleths, both Jack and Charmian were children of the Nineties. Nothing could have been more *fin de siècle* than their attitude toward love and sex. Their feverish, ultra-romantic view of how people in love should behave, their passionate wordiness, their hyper-intense conviction that they shared something unique came straight out of the novels of Ouida and DuMaurier, untempered by the cynicism of a Shaw or a Wilde.

The fact that Jack would have to give up his wife and children for Charmian only contributed to the hothouse climate of the relationship, added a novelistic dash of danger and sacrifice, convinced them they were defying the world for each other. It helped Charmian prove that she was emancipated in a time when a woman was expected, as Robert Louis Stevenson put it, to learn only "the arts of a civilized slave among good-natured barbarians," her menfolk. And for Jack it put a still higher value on Charmian, that he would give up so much for her.

A love starting off on such a plane of delirium, though it may have been as much an intoxication of words as emotions, was foredoomed in a sense. No two sane people could have stayed on such a vaulting trajectory for long. And disillusion, when it came, would be all the harder, all the more susceptible to accusations of betrayal.

Jack was recovering from the melancholy he felt just before and after detaching himself from his wife and children — a depression so pervasive that, according to Charmian, he would not keep firearms in his bedroom for fear he might be overwhelmed by the temptation to kill himself. Anna Strunsky, on the other hand, recorded that "there was a time when he kept a loaded revolver in his desk ready to use it against himself at any time." [9]

Jack and Charmian were eminently successful in pulling the wool over Bess's eyes. This was accomplished partly through the hypocritical role enacted by Charmian, who kept visiting Bess and listening to her recital of grief over Jack's abandonment of her. It must have been a curious scene in Bess's parlor: the wronged wife, struggling to keep her dignity, confiding her hopes and fears, and Charmian patting her hand

and exuding sympathy, perhaps secretly vexed that Bess couldn't *imagine* that it was she, rather than Anna Strunsky or some other woman, who had lured Jack away.

Charmian kept Jack informed on what Bess was doing and saying almost from the day they separated until Bess finally learned the truth. On August 11, only a few weeks after the breakup, she wrote Jack that Bess had confided to her that she knew Jack was relenting and would return to his family. With something like a sneer, Charmian added that Bess, in trying to fool her about Jack's intentions, almost succeeded in fooling herself. A month later, beginning to suspect that her role might not be as delicious as it had seemed, she related that Bess had been begging her to stay overnight and was so sweet to her that she actually had to shake off a feeling that she and Jack might be doing wrong. A few days later, however, she was writing Jack that Bess was deep and deceitful, might suspect she was the interloper, and was playing a cat-and-mouse game with her.

Possibly fed up with domestic intrigue, Jack decided to send for his friend Cloudesley Johns and go fishing for a couple of weeks along the Sacramento River. He and Johns wrote in the mornings, fished and hunted ducks in the afternoon, and spent the evenings in their boat talking, smoking, having a few drinks.

The idyllic retreat from his problems was interrupted when Bess wrote that his eldest daughter, Joan, had contracted typhoid fever and was in serious condition. When he arrived at the child's bedside, the doctor said he wasn't at all sure that Joan would survive. Apparently there was something like a reconciliation between Jack and Bess; the Oakland newspapers reported that he was back home for good. Then Joan began to rally and in a few days was on the way to recovery. And Jack, whatever promises he might have made while keeping the vigil at Joan's bedside, slipped away from his family and went back to the *Spray*.

By Christmastime he was working on the last pages of *The Sea Wolf* and hoping that, in view of all the money Macmillan was making on *The Call of the Wild,* his publishers might be giving him a Christmas present. Jack, in fact, wrote Brett suggesting it. The hint was ignored; Jack had made a bargain, was stuck with it and mustn't be encouraged to think a publisher could hand out money on a whim. Brett was an honorable man but he knew that authors had to be kept in their place, especially in regard to money.

New Year's Day, 1904, found Jack broke, his novel finished, no other work in mind. He was at loose ends. What to do next? In a few days he'd be twenty-eight years old, and he had not yet achieved a workable pattern in his life. He was tottering between divorce and remarriage. He and his mother were estranged; she had fought with Bess for three years, but now was bitterly opposed to Jack's abandoning his wife and children and was taking Bess's side in the matter. The hell with everything. He wanted to get away from all the wrangling, find a new perspective on himself and his affairs.

In the past he had seized on outside events as a means of escape from Oakland and its problems — Coxey's army, the Klondike gold rush, the Boer War. Once again he was about to be rescued. The newspapers that New Year's Day were black with headlines sounding the alarm of another war in Asia.

4. *Hearstling*

A few days later Jack went over to San Francisco and posed for a photographer on the roof of the *Examiner* building. Wearing a dark suit, his hair shaggy and tousled, he looked more like a workman in Sunday best than a dashing war correspondent out to compete with the glamorous Richard Harding Davis.

With an outbreak of war between Russia and Japan over the possession of Manchuria expected daily, Jack's services as a war correspondent, despite his lack of experience in either war or foreign correspondence, were eagerly sought. James Gordon Bennett, Jr., of the New York *Herald, Harper's* and *Collier's* all entered their bids, but William Randolph Hearst came up with the highest offer. Jack would cover the war for the San Francisco *Examiner,* the New York *Journal* and other Hearst papers. Hearst, in his most imperial mood, was a big-name hunter at the time. Ambrose Bierce was his Washington correspondent. He had engaged Stephen Crane to expose vice conditions in the New York streets, and later to cover wars or threatened wars in the Balkans and Venezuela; had sent Richard Harding Davis to describe the coronation of Czar Nicholas II and Mark Twain to write about Queen Victoria's Diamond Jubilee. He even coaxed Henry

James into the Hearst stable temporarily when he bought the serial rights to *The Other House* (and brought James to the verge of apoplexy by advertising it as "Henry James' New Novel of Immorality and Crime! The Surprising Plunge of the Great Novelist into the Field of Sensational Fiction!").

Jack was scheduled to leave in a few days for the presumed battlefronts, passage having been booked for him on the S.S. *Siberia* leaving San Francisco for Yokohama on January 7, 1904. In those few days he arranged his affairs in expectation of being gone for months, perhaps a year or two. He wrote Brett on January 7, just before he sailed, instructing that of his $150 monthly stipend from Macmillan, $127.50 was to be sent monthly to his wife and $22.50 monthly to Charmian. On January 14, aboard the *Siberia,* he wrote the *Century* that its forthcoming $2000 installment on *The Sea Wolf* serialization was to be sent to Charmian in her name. He arranged with George Sterling to edit *The Sea Wolf* manuscript and with Charmian to make any corrections she saw fit before it was sent to the publisher. He didn't want to think about the novel or anything else back home, having an amazing ability to drop everything — even a novel that must have been very close to the center of his existence — in favor of something new and exciting, particularly if it was far away and promised adventure.

The fact that he considered himself a pacifist no more inhibited him from rushing off to the battlefields than his Socialist beliefs kept him from joining the stampede to the Klondike. His pacifism was barely skin-deep, something he thought he ought to believe in because it was the humane and Socialist thing to do; it usually vanished at the first hot breath of war coming over the horizon. His own nature was combative, if not aggressive, as anyone who tried his temper soon learned. By the time of the World War he was calling for the extermination of Germany in terms an Allied propagandist would have hesitated to use.

Already he had done considerable thinking about the nature of modern war, though most people then were convinced that there would never be another mass conflict like the American Civil War or Franco-Prussian War. In the March, 1900, issue of *Overland Monthly* he had published an article titled "The Impossibility of War" which was a startlingly accurate picture of what a future world war would be like. His description of such a war, "impossible" only in the sense that it would impose unprecedented hardships on the men who fought it, was a detailed forecast of conditions along the Western Front in World War I. In the future, he wrote, soldiers would burrow into the earth like moles — a view which conflicted with the gallant chromos of the Rough Riders' charge up San Juan Hill two years before — and the fighting would be a laborious "succession of sieges." Instead of decisive vertical thrusts, the pattern of fighting would spread out horizontally in "successive lines of widely-extending fortifications." The greater deadliness and longer ranging of rapid-fire artillery equipped with the newly developed rangefinders would drive the combat troops under ground. He foresaw the development of chemical warfare, such as the poison gas used in World War I. He also predicted, less accurately, the development of steam-driven trenching-digging machines.

Later he would deliver himself of an even more alarming prophecy in the vein of H. G. Wells, the accuracy of which is still to be tested by history. In "The Unparalleled Invasion" [10] he pictured China with her population swollen to desperate proportions, unable to feed her people without conquering other lands and threatening to swarm over all the world. The only alternative available to the West, as he envisioned the situation, was bacteriological warfare, at the end of which China's billion people were completely wiped out.

He believed that Asia was a sleeping giant which, on awakening, would threaten the whole world. Current events only tended to confirm this theory which had engaged many Westerners, including Napoleon, for more than a century. Japan, as the first Oriental nation to modernize itself, had already proved its military capability by a quick victory in the Sino-Japanese War of 1895. Czarist Russia, meanwhile, was bent on expanding in the same direction, making a collision with Japan all but inevitable. The Russians finished building the trans-Siberian railroad and began extending the line southward from their maritime provinces across Manchuria to Darien and Port Arthur. Taking another stride southward, they occupied Manchuria and built a great naval base at Port Arthur to sustain their Pacific fleet. Inoffensive Korea, long known as the Hermit Kingdom, then became the focal point of the struggle. The Russians smuggled soldiers in mufti across the Yalu to prevent the mines of northern Korea from falling into

Japanese hands. In a countermove, the Japanese began colonizing the formerly independent buffer state with twenty-five thousand of their own people.

One fairly earnest effort to evade the clash of interests was made by Japan when it proposed to recognize Manchuria as a Russian sphere of influence if the Czar would grant Japan the same rights in Korea. The Russians refused, believing Japan wouldn't dare challenge a European power. After that rebuff the Japanese began mobilizing, moving their highly disciplined army into jumpoff positions and preparing their first-rate navy for a blockade of Port Arthur and a consequent confrontation of the Russian Pacific fleet.

On the day Jack sailed aboard the S.S. *Siberia,* eager to learn what new shape The Yellow Peril* would take in menacing the white and more or less Christian world, war had not yet broken out. But the Japanese were mobilizing, and that meant war. Foreign observers in Tokyo and St. Petersburg said it was only a matter of days or weeks. For once they were right.

* As he and Hearst commonly designated awakening Asia.

IX

At War with the Japanese

1. *A Non-Diplomatic Incident*

THE WAY to attend a war, for any right-thinking American correspondent, was to watch Richard Harding Davis and try to approximate his distinguished style. You needed almost as many wardrobe changes as a touring matinee idol, since it was necessary to be properly dressed for a legation garden party or scrambling up hills to catch a panoramic view of battle, which you then described in Olympian prose. You drank heartily but with refinement, wore clean collars and conducted interviews with no less than field-grade officers. You remembered it was not only possible but essential that a gentlemanly tone be brought to the practice of journalism. During the Turko-Greek War of 1895 Davis had frowned mightily on Stephen Crane for bringing along his mistress, who had formerly operated a bordello in Florida. Davis had in fact cut her dead. It was a humbling experience to be cut dead by Davis.

Davis may now seem a prig and a stuffed shirt, Mother Grundy's favorite son, but he was the most admired and envied man in America at the turn of the century, casting an aura of romance and respectability around the newspaper business that lasted for years after his passing. He was the square-jawed, steely-eyed Gibson Man. He was braver and handsomer than any general, more romantic than any actor, more publicized than any politician except Roosevelt. His books, glorifying men much like himself, or as he saw himself, were best-sellers. When he went off to cover a war, he got a thousand dollars a week and an expense account suitable for a touring maharajah. "He mounted into celebrity," wrote Thomas Beer, "as gracefully as he might have swung his fine body in its handsome clothes to the cushions of a waiting hansom cab. He rode, a figure of pleasant sophistication and fresh good humor, among passengers who lacked those qualities . . . and boys laboring with manuscripts looked up and saw a star."

Jack London admired him too, but he didn't propose to ape his style or his approach to journalism, which Jack considered a stopgap trade at best. He didn't give a damn about generals or strategies; communiqués were so much gibberish, and he had about as much use for the pomposities of staff officers as for academic critics who tried to tell him how to write a book. Looking more like a steamfitter on holiday than a colleague of the magnificent Davis, he carried a camera instead of a walking stick and proposed to record the sights and smells of war, both on film and on paper, at the level of the infantryman's boots and the cookfires of the cavalry on march.

From the outset he was so determined to plunge himself into the reality of war, regardless of the rules laid down by the secretive and suspicious Japanese, that hostilities between him and the Imperial Army opened almost from the day he landed on Japanese soil.

He arrived in Tokyo on January 24 with a group of English and American correspondents, only to find a still larger group of newspapermen stewing over their inability to leave the home islands for the supposed battle zone. War with Russia had not yet been declared, but every train leaving Tokyo for ports on the Sea of Japan was loaded with soldiers bound for troop transports that would carry them to the Korean peninsula. The atmosphere was febrile with the almost hysterical Japanese brand of patriotism. Obviously the first clashes were only a few days off. But the Japanese War Office, despite the most strenuous protests from the American and European correspondents, refused to provide transportation; all they got was hissing politeness, evasions and invitations to banquets. Japanese staff officers pointed out there was no war to send them to, gave them passes to battle zones which didn't exist and then refused to sign them. Even to an apprentice it was apparent that the Japanese had no intention of permitting any "foreign devils" to reach the scene of their operations.

Jack spent two days in Tokyo, listening to the grumbling of his colleagues and meeting such fellow craftsmen as Davis, who was representing *Collier's* and with whom, against expectations, he formed a lasting and highly beneficial friendship; a young Englishman named

Bill Lewis, representing the New York *Herald,* who as Sir Wilmot Lewis would become a Washington personage as chief correspondent of *The Times* of London; Robert Dunn of the New York *Globe;* Frederick Palmer, destined to become almost as famous as Davis; Ashmead Bartlett, a celebrated English journalist, and Willard Straight, representing Reuter's, who later became a J. P. Morgan partner. At the Imperial Hotel bar he was told about the Hearst correspondent who described the naval battle between the Japanese and Chinese on the Yalu in 1895, claiming to be an eyewitness, though he never moved from his bar stool.

Jack was determined that he wouldn't cover the war from the Imperial bar. After a few interviews at the War Office, he was convinced that the foreign correspondents would be kept hanging around Tokyo while the Japanese armies invaded Manchuria and wouldn't be permitted near the battlefields until after the fighting was over. To hell with the formalities, Jack decided. He'd beat his way to Korea if he had to steal a boat.

He slipped out of the capital on January 27 without saying a word to his rivals and took the train to Kobe, where he learned no steamer would be crossing the straits until February 3. At Nagasaki there was no passenger space available at all. He went on to Moji, down the coast on the Inland Sea, where he obtained passage on a steamer leaving February 1 for Chemulpo, Korea, a staging base for the armies moving toward the Yalu and the Manchurian border.

After buying his ticket, he wandered around the streets of Moji, openly taking photographs of the people and buildings. Secret police came up on the run and hauled him off to the local jail, where he soon was informed that Moji was a fortified town and carrying a camera was strictly forbidden. The police accused him of being a Russian spy. He was questioned for eight hours, then was removed to a higher police headquarters at Kokoura and subjected to more questioning. The police eventually were satisfied he wasn't really a Russian agent, but saved face by taking him into court, having him convicted as a spy and fined five yen. Worse than that, the police confiscated his camera and refused to return it to him. This was too much for the citizen of a sovereign power to bear, especially from a people so lowly regarded as the Japanese; at the outbreak of war, as Frederick Palmer expressed it, Westerners thought Japan would be smashed in a few weeks — "Russia, the mammoth world power with her giant soldiers, against the little fellows who made the pretty lanterns we hung on our lawns for ice-cream parties!" [1]

Jack was determined to retrieve his camera, and wired Richard Harding Davis, still in Tokyo, who immediately interceded with the United States Minister to Japan, Lloyd Griscom, an old friend of his with a rather frisky disposition for a diplomat.

Griscom, as he related the story in his memoir *Diplomatically Speaking*, solemnly marched over to the Foreign Office to place the majesty and power of the United States behind the project of recovering a correspondent's camera. Foreign Minister Komura listened to Griscom's recital, then called in his legal counselor, who affirmed that any weapon involved in a crime became the property of the state. London had been convicted of espionage and his "weapon" was forfeit.

"Does that apply to every crime?" Griscom asked.

"Yes," replied the legal counselor, "to every crime of every description."

Griscom turned to Foreign Minister Komura and said, "If I can name a crime to which this does not apply, will you release the camera?"

"Yes, I will," said Baron Komura.

"Well," demanded Griscom with a straight face, "what about rape?"

The foreign minister's "Oriental stolidity dissolved in a shout of laughter," Griscom recalled, the legal counselor was dismissed, and the foreign ministry ordered that Jack's camera be returned to him.

Ever afterward Jack referred to Richard Harding Davis as "a good old sport," much to the surprise of people who regarded Davis as something of a stuffed shirt, and who could not imagine how Jack, the rough and ready, ever got to be friendly with him.

2. *Open Boat to Chemulpo*

Undeterred by his experiences with the spy-catchers, Jack renewed his attempts to cross over the narrow straits to Korea. He heard reports of soldiers being mobilized in the middle of the night, of regiments being crammed onto everything floatable, and judged that the war would start in a matter of hours. On February 8, he bought passage on a steamer bound for Pusan, at the tip of the Korean peninsula, but the Japanese military requisitioned the ship just as it was about to lift anchor. Finally he caught a steam launch which took him out to a small steamer, with no accommodations but the open decks, bound for Pusan. It was a rough winter night's crossing, which Jack and his fellow passengers spent trying to sleep out on the sleet-driven deck.

On arrival at Pusan, a port which loomed significantly on the battle maps of another Korean war almost half a century later, he took passage on a coastal steamer headed up the line to Chemulpo, stopping at the smaller ports along the way. At Mokpo the Japanese once again requisitioned his transportation, herded the passengers ashore and told them they would have to shift for themselves.

He chartered a native fishing junk, hired three local Koreans for his crew and set off across the Yellow Sea in subzero weather. Gales swept the sea as he navigated the junk up the peninsula toward Chemulpo. His mast was carried away by the roaring winds and his rudder was shattered by the rough seas, but they managed to put in for emergency repairs at Kunsan. He spent a restorative night in a Japanese bath where five maidens assisted him in the rituals of the establishment and admired "my beautiful white skin."

Next morning he resumed the journey, during which he and his crew spent six days and nights battling the knifelike winds and temperatures that dropped to fourteen below, living on a diet of cold rice and fish, warming himself over a charcoal stove that gave off noxious fumes but little heat.

He gave a vivid description of that voyage in recounting the fictional ordeal of Adam Strang, English adventurer, in his novel of ten years later, *The Star Rover*. "We drifted in upon the land in the chill light of a stormy dawn across a heartless cross-sea mountain-high. It was dead of winter, and between smoking snow squalls we could glimpse the forbidding coast . . . There were grim rock isles and islets beyond counting, dim snow-covered ranges beyond, and everywhere upstanding cliffs too steep for snow, outjuts of headlands, and pinnacles and slivers of rock upthrust from the boiling sea."

He arrived at Chemulpo half dead from his privations, but he had beaten the rest of the press corps — except for two English correspondents named Jones and McLeod who had reached Korea before the Japanese halted all travel — and his mood was triumphant. At least the voyage in an open boat proved that he hadn't gone soft in the half-dozen years since he came out of the Klondike.

His English colleagues assured Jack that the shooting hadn't started as yet, so far as they could learn, but the Japanese cavalry undoubtedly were watering their horses in the Yalu and would be leading the invasion any day now.

"Buy everything in sight," the Englishmen advised him, "and get ready to start for Ping Yang."*

The first order of business was to find a horse and a couple of servants, including a *mapu* (groom), a "boy" to handle his personal needs, and an interpreter. The first horse brought around for his inspection proved to be a stallion which bucked like a bronco and left Jack sweating from every pore despite the zero temperature. Another brought around had "the prettiest head and gentlest eyes I had ever seen in a horse" and "I fell in love on first sight." He sought expert advice from a resident cavalryman, Colonel Henry T. Allen, commanding officer of the Philippine Constabulary, official U. S. military observer in Korea, and fourteen years later one of Pershing's better corps commanders in the A.E.F. Allen looked on as the horse was led out for a canter. "Splendid motion," said Colonel Allen. "The easiest riding horse of all, and the hardiest." A short time later Jack learned to scorn expert advice, even in the matter of horseflesh, when his mount bumped head-on into a stone wall. His horse's eyes were not only "gentle" but blind. Jack finally bought a horse abandoned by the Russian consulate when it decamped several days before, a "splendid animal" which had been imported from Australia.

He engaged a Korean youth named Manyoungi as his body servant for $17.50 a month. "He dressed in European clothes," Jack wrote in his first dispatch, "with a white shirt, standup collar, tie, studs, and all complete, and he talked English better, far better, than my provisional interpreter . . . Not only did he know how to work himself and achieve results, but he possessed the miraculous faculty of getting work out of other Koreans. For the first time the hotel boys built a fire in my room and brought hot water before I was dressed and away. And for the first time the fires they built burned." [2] Jack considered Manyoungi such a "gem," in fact, that he brought him back to the United States with him. Manyoungi served him for years despite gibes that a Socialist with a valet was a peculiar breed indeed.

Jack also engaged an interpreter who insisted on being addressed as

* Now Pyongyang, the capital of North Korea.

Mr. Yamada, bought four more horses for his string and hired two *mapus* to take care of them.

Then he struck out for the Manchurian border over roads covered by mud in the daytime and ice at night. On March 5, he was in Pyongyang, the first foreign correspondent to reach that far north, the first to send back a detailed account of the first clash between Japanese and Russian land forces. Scrawled on rice paper, the dispatch told of a cavalry encounter at Pyongyang after a detachment of Cossacks on reconnaissance crossed the Yalu and struck two hundred miles deep into Korea in an effort to determine Japanese strength in the area.

"Three Americans escorting women from the mines of the American concession, fifty miles east of Anjou," he wrote, "encountered the scouting party of Cossacks at Anjou, on the main Pekin road. They traveled with the troop a day and described the Cossacks as splendid looking soldiers, perfect horsemen and mounted on sturdy Russian ponies.

"As an instance of the discipline of the men the following is related: One of the Americans had given a trooper the makings of a cigarette when the command was given for them to break into a gallop. Away fluttered tobacco and rice paper as the soldier instantly obeyed."

The Cossacks met no opposition, he related, "till they reached the ancient walled city of Ping Yang [Pyongyang], the scene of the slaughter of the Chinese by the Japanese in 1894 and a city whose written history leaps boldly back to the centuries before Christ."

He was admirably precise in his details of the first brief skirmish on the battlements of the fortified city: Company 7, 46th Regiment, Twelfth Division of the Japanese First Army opened fire at seven hundred meters. The only casualties were two Cossack ponies. The Russians withdrew, having established that the Japanese held Pyongyang in force.

Jack got his information, he related, from a Japanese lieutenant named Y. Abe, whom he invited to his hotel and "whom I entertained in the Japanese fashion — the only fashion available." He and the officer sat shoeless on straw matting, drinking tea and sake and eating pickled onions with chopsticks. Jack was favorably impressed by his guest, "a typical officer of the new Japan," who spoke French, English, Chinese and was studying German.

Stifling his prejudice in the interests of journalistic objectivity, he wrote that the Japanese "are surely a military race. Their men are soldiers, and their officers are soldiers." He interviewed another officer who told him the Japanese infantry averaged twenty miles a day on the rocky road up from Seoul.

3. *On the Pekin Road*

When the guns began to thunder across the Yalu, Jack pressed north on the Pekin road, his little caravan caught up in the advancing columns of the Japanese First Army. His dispatches were sent back to San Francisco by mail, so there was little value in describing military actions, scant details of which he might have obtained if he had attached himself to First Army headquarters. The press associations would cover such actions in cabled dispatches from Tokyo and other points. Jack aimed to let the American reader know what war was like in this inhospitable country with its barren hills, ice-filled rice paddies and high mountain passes through which Siberian winds blew incessantly.

The glare ice of the roads was a constant threat, particularly when they climbed into the mountains. "The combination of a slippery man and a slipping horse," he wrote,[3] "is not a happy one, while the combination of many slipping horses and men, in a long string, brings out the sweat alike on man and beast. I shall not soon forget such an ice slope we climbed at the rear of a column of infantry. The men were sprawling right and left. Slipping became contagious. My feet were inclined to move in divers directions . . . But my poor Belle, my horse, had four feet sliding in many simultaneous directions. . . . She was pawing and scrambling wildly . . . When we gained the summit — and there was no stopping till we did — all her shoes were loose and two could be pulled off by hand . . ." The suffering of the infantry was even worse, he noted. Footsore soldiers "trailed along for miles behind every marching company . . . Each step is torture, and they must go on, step by step, all day long . . . each step hurting anew the lacerated flesh. To them Paradise would sum itself up in cessation of movement . . ."

They halted for awhile in the town of Sunan, population four or five thousand, most of whom had taken to the hills as the Japanese army approached. By now the Japanese were increasingly annoyed by Jack's presence, and he wrote in his dispatch of March 12 that he couldn't move more than a hundred yards in any direction without being halted by a bayoneted rifle with a Japanese soldier behind it.[4] Jack took over an abandoned house for his quarters, at the door of which a "rapt and admiring" audience gathered throughout the daylight hours.

To the Korean townspeople his activities were like a Japanese play, he said, in that the performance lasted all day. The salient characteristics of the Koreans, he observed, were "inefficiency and curiosity."

Watching the "endless procession" of troops moving up to the front, he knew that a great land battle must be shaping up and he could not linger long.

Back in Tokyo, meanwhile, his fellow journalists were suffering an attack of professional jealousy. They had learned that Jack London had slipped into the war zone and was sending stories back from northern Korea. The other correspondents demanded of the Foreign Ministry that they also be sent to the battlefront. The Japanese authorities decided to pack them off to Seoul, the royal capital, where they would be far from the fighting but unable to continue complaining of their treatment through United States Minister Griscom. As for Jack London, he would have to be prevented from wandering where he pleased.

The army security police picked him up, along with his entourage, and escorted him back to Pyongyang, where he was informed that he was no longer a guest but a prisoner of the Japanese army. Then he was removed to Seoul, two hundred miles from the front, and held for several days in a military prison while the authorities pretended to be investigating whether he was a spy or just an unusually brash American newspaperman.

On release, he was ordered to stay with the rest of the correspondents, who had just arrived from Tokyo, until the Japanese army could arrange a sightseeing expedition into Manchuria. He wandered around the capital, mostly mud hovels inhabited by a quarter of a million people, with little of the fabled glamor of the East about it. The emperor, a terrorized Japanese puppet, lived in a one-story "palace" where coolies dug a cesspool and unloaded brushwood from a packtrain of ponies to heat his quarters. Jack and the other correspondents were fascinated by a German newspaperman's report that the No. 1 imperial concubine, Lady Om, was formerly Miss Emily Brown of

Wisconsin. Most of the time Jack and his colleagues, irked by the smiling refusal of the Japanese to send them to the front, whiled away the days drinking at Martin's bar.

Robert Dunn of the New York *Globe* recalled that once, "after a great deal of vodka," he and Jack went hunting tigers in the caves outside Seoul, an enterprise that might have terminated two promising careers if the man-eaters had existed anywhere but in alcoholic fantasy. "He turned up for lunch next day," Dunn related, "shyly worried because he hadn't been asked. His deep blue eyes never more than smiled; but he said, in the manner of his stories, 'If we ever meet again, Bob, my memory will be your laughing at me and my laughing at you, and your knowing I'm laughing, and my knowing you know I am.'" Dunn said that London's dislike of the Japanese "outdid mine. Though a professed Socialist, he really believed in the Kaiser's 'yellow peril.'" Later, at Martin's bar, Jack lectured his fellow correspondents on Socialism in "a dialectic that few of us then understood," and ended up by grinning suddenly, as though realizing how futile it was to harangue newspapermen about anything, and yelling down the bar, "What are all you bourgeois drinking now?" [5]

For lack of anything more constructive to do, Jack and Dunn rode far beyond the crumbling walls of Seoul one afternoon and got tangled in a marching column of the Twelfth Division. They were indignant over the condition of the ponies hauling packs in the supply train that brought up the rear, many of them lamed on the march or when they were unloaded from the transports at a Korean port.

"Their packsaddles don't fit, either," Jack said. "Look at that for cruel ignorance — God damn him!" He gestured toward a Japanese soldier leading a pony hobbling on three legs; the fourth had been broken and was strapped to his belly. "We slipped from our mounts," Dunn wrote, "cursing the soldier who dragged him by a halter. By some miracle he spoke English. 'All right,' he told us. 'If leg don't touch ground, very soon mend.' And the little yellow brother laughed. We wanted to hit him but we didn't — it would have started an 'international incident.'" [6]

About the only amusement he and Jack found, Dunn said, was in watching the Korean noblemen, "one leading a live stork through bazaars, another hugging the bar in the Foreigners' Club in glowing grass-cloth, a white horsehair cylinder hat, and amber neck amulet.

One such, a Princeton graduate (though his name wasn't Rhee), was in mourning and held before his face a strip of pale fabric on two sticks which he put down to drink his gin swizzle."

Another correspondent, Frederick Palmer, remembered that Jack's upper plate came in handy when they were lunching and the natives would press in too close around them, fascinated by the foreign devils and unacquainted with the methods of modern dentistry. "Jack's front false teeth were attached to a plate. When the staring sheep faces pressed too close, Jack stuck his tooth plate on the edge of his tongue, and the Koreans fell back in disorder for four or five yards. Cautiously and curiously they would draw near again; and again Jack would repulse them." [7]

The Japanese military finally yielded to the combined protests of the foreign military observers and the war correspondents, and allowed them to move up to the Yalu, where General Kuroki's columns were concentrating and preparing for a broad advance into Manchuria once the Japanese Second Army started landing on the Liaotung Peninsula and moved on to the siege of Port Arthur.

The correspondents were placed in charge of a censor named T. Okada, who when hard-pressed would issue his standard communiqué: "All is going according to plan."

Jack, according to Palmer, would smile sardonically and tell Mr. Okada: "Don't forget to tell us if it is not."

The correspondents and the military observers from the United States, France, England, Germany and Italy, who were located in their own camp a few hundred yards away, mingled socially on occasion, though warily, to exchange complaints about their treatment. "They'd *rather* lie to you than tell the truth," Colonel Allen, the United States observer, said. A number of officers with future places in history were among those with whom Jack and his fellows dined, griped and gossiped. Major Caviglia, who was to command the Italian armies on the northern front during World War I, often awakened both camps in the morning by singing opera. The British observer was Sir Ian Hamilton, who was to lead the futile British landing on Gallipoli. One of the Germans was a Captain Max Hoffmann, who drank a quart of Moselle for breakfast every day and who detested the Wagnerian overtones of Prussian militarism so much that he was fond of saying, "If anyone comes near me with a Nibelung's oath of fidelity and offers to die at my side, I shall knock his head off." Hoffmann swallowed his prejudices by the time 1914 came around and was the tactical genius who devised the plans by which the German armies on the eastern front time after time hurled back the numerically superior Russians.

Early in May the correspondents and observers were permitted to move their camp across the Yalu but once again were herded into an isolation center in a temple grove near Antung, Manchuria. On May 8, he wrote George Sterling on a scrap of rice paper that he and his colleagues were sweltering on the edge of a Manchurian city, breathing the dust of the dead and the dust of the living; that he was fed up with his assignment and it was futile trying to describe a war a hundred miles from the fighting.

Two days later he got to a dispatch to the Hearst papers describing how the Japanese had outwitted the Russians in establishing a bridgehead across the Yalu. The Japanese threw three divisions into forcing the crossing against numerically inferior opposition but, he pointed out, "the Japanese had to cross a river under fire and attack an enemy lying in wait for them." He then told how the Japanese did it. "At the mouth of the Yalu the Japanese had two small gunboats, two torpedoboats and four small steamers armed with Hotchkiss guns. Also they had fifty sampans loaded with bridge materials. These were intended for a permanent bridge across the Yalu at Wiju; but they served another purpose — first, farther down the stream. The presence of the small navy and the loaded sampans led the Russians to believe that there was where the bridge was to be built. So right there they stationed some three thousand men to prevent the building of the bridge. Thus a handful of Japanese sailors kept 3,000 Russian soldiers occupied in doing nothing and reduced the effectiveness of the Russian strength by that much."

He described how the Japanese, with three divisions astride the Yalu, faced the danger of being wiped out before they could advance in strength but were spared a disaster through the sluggishness of the Russian counter-measures. The Russians were driven back in a subsequent pitched battle because "The Japanese understand the utility of things. Reserves they consider should be used, not only to strengthen the line . . . but in the moment of victory to clinch victory hard and fast . . . Verily, nothing short of the miracle can wreck a plan they have once started to put into execution. The men furnish the unfaltering bravery, confident that their officers have furnished the precaution . . . 'Men determined to die' is the way one Japanese officer characterized the volunteers who answer in large numbers to every call for dangerous work."

Jack was also impressed by the efficiency of Japanese communications on and behind the battle line. "Every division, every battery was connected with headquarters by field telephone. When the divisions moved forward they dragged their wires after them like spiders drag the silk of their webs. Even the tiny navy at the mouth of the Yalu was in instant communication with headquarters. Thus, on a wide-stretching and largely invisible field the commander-in-chief was in control of everything. Inventions, weapons, systems (the navy modeled after the English, the army after the German) everything utilized by the Japanese has been supplied by the Western world; but the Japanese have shown themselves the only Eastern people capable of utilizing them."

Jack not only made hundreds of pages of notes on everything he observed about the Japanese army — largely, of necessity, the rear area, its supply and communications lines, its care of the wounded and all the other details of military housekeeping — but took hundreds of photographs. His were said to be the first war pictures to reach the United States, and Jack considered himself to be as much a photographer as a reporter.

Complimentary in print as he was about the durability of the Japanese infantryman, he was privately derogatory and commented: "They may be brave, but so are the South American peccary pigs in their herd charges." [8]

He had gone to war like a police reporter chasing a four-alarm fire, but now had adopted an almost stately style of living compared to the communal arrangements of the other correspondents. Jack, wrote Frederick Palmer,[9] was the "most inherently individualistic" and "un-Socialistic of all the Socialists I have ever met," exhibiting a tendency toward lofty isolation that soon would be more marked.

"He preferred to walk alone in aristocratic aloofness, and always in the direction he chose no matter where anybody else was going. He had his own separate mess and tent; general and private of his army of one, he rode in front of his two pack-donkeys, which jingled with bells, the leader bearing an American flag."

He was friendly and cheerful with his colleagues, Palmer observed, but "liked to be the center of conversation."

When his little procession of horses, donkeys, horse-handlers, body-servant and interpreter passed through the camp, Censor Okada would snort:

"The novelist! Noise and color, noise and color!"

By mid-May Jack was thoroughly fed up with being penned in the press camp, and wrote Charmian that he would never cover another Asiatic war again. He hoped to redeem himself as a war correspondent — a part-time career which he obviously intended to follow, like Stephen Crane, whenever he had the opportunity — in some future clash between Caucasian armies. His only compensation for months of frustration, he added, was a better knowledge of Asian geography and people.

Palmer, however, believed that his frustration stemmed partly from having a novelist's rather than a journalist's outlook. "His idea of a fight was one waged by Ed and Pete whom he knew; and he could not know the Japanese Ed and Pete." A study of his nineteen dispatches, not to mention the striking photographs he took, indicates that he did a more than workmanlike job as a correspondent. They reveal better than the accounts of any of his colleagues — none of whom managed to cover himself with glory, incidentally, though many lasted much longer than Jack — just what campaigning was like in that remote war which was to serve as a dress rehearsal for the dreary carnage of World War I.

4. *Too Much* Bushido

Toward the end of May Jack began bombarding his employer with pleas to have him transferred to the Russian side of the battlefront. Before Hearst could act, however, Jack got himself involved in a row which resulted in a revocation of his guest privileges by the Japanese army.

He apparently had adopted something of the sahib attitude toward natives as reflected in Kipling's stories. What became an international incident started when one of his *mapus,* a Korean, claimed that one of the Japanese grooms was stealing fodder allotted to Jack's mounts. Jack headed immediately for the stable area in a high temper. The Japanese groom spoke to him insolently, and Jack knocked him down.

Japanese officers and noncoms continually struck those of lower rank, but they did not propose to extend the same privileges to a Caucasian. The groom's complaints were bucked all the way up to Major General Fuji, Kuroki's chief of staff, who ordered Jack placed under arrest and held for a court-martial. It was his third arrest in four months, which may have contributed to the subsequent habit of Japanese staff officers of referring to the foreign correspondents as "those wild men."

His colleagues, Palmer said, tried to intercede by sending a delegation to army headquarters and "explaining that London was a most gifted writer, with a strong sense of the pioneer American *bushido*, which responded with a blow of the fist to an insult." Not all the correspondents were inclined to take such a tolerant view of his action. One of them, Edwin Emerson, Jr., later stated: "London's row with the coolie, and its prompt consequences, must have revealed to everyone, as well as himself, his chief weakness as a news gatherer among a foreign people. London, according to his own professions, loathed and abominated the Japanese, and who has learned to appreciate their dominant trait of hiding their own feelings, cannot but realize that a man coming among them with such a disposition need never hope to get anything out of them. Not even true impressions." [10]

Richard Harding Davis, still in Tokyo, once again came to Jack's rescue. He sent urgent cables to President Theodore Roosevelt, a personal friend, who responded by making strong representations through the United States ministry in Tokyo. The President was an admirer of Jack's stories — though they later had a well-publicized falling-out over the issue of nature-fakery — and was alarmed by reports that the Japanese might put the author against the wall. Within a few days American pressure resulted in an order from the War Office to General Fuji to release his prisoner. Kuroki's chief of staff agreed only after Jack promised to lose no time leaving Korea.

On his way back to Tokyo, Jack wrote Brett at Macmillan's on June 7 that he was disgusted with the way he had been treated by the Japanese; worst of all, he doubted whether he would be able to wring a book out of his experiences as a war correspondent. He never did, as a matter of fact, except for the sequence in *The Star Rover* which dealt with his open-boat voyage up the Korean coast.

The most permanent effects of his chief brush with the Russo-Japanese War were a heightening of his anti-Oriental prejudices and of his fear of "the Yellow Peril." A short time later he wrote an essay with that title[11] in which he warned that the "yellow" Chinese and the "brown" Japanese might one day collaborate on an "adventure" which could shatter the long domination of the Western world.

"The menace to the western world," he wrote, "lies, not in the little brown man, but in the four hundred millions of yellow men should the little brown man undertake their management. The Chinese is not dead to new ideas; he is an efficient worker; makes a good soldier, and is wealthy in the essential materials of a machine age. Under a capable management he will go far. The Japanese is prepared and fit to undertake this management . . ."

Socialist internationalism extended, so far as he was concerned, only to the brotherhood of the white man, a belief which caused an understandable consternation among many of his fellow Marxist Socialists, who held that class, not race, was what would and should unite the workingmen in the coming revolution. Nor could he be dissuaded that Socialism was reserved for the more "advanced" peoples, at least until the inferior races brought themselves up to the mark.

On his return to the United States, he expounded his views before the Oakland chapter of the Socialist party, one of his auditors, Edmundo Peluso, recalling:

With evident pleasure, he described the wiliness of these "human burnt candles," as he called the officers of the Japanese General Staff, and used stronger expressions with regard to them. But his gorge rose not only at the Japanese General Staff; he cursed the entire yellow race in the most outrageous terms. Some of the comrades present were somewhat embarrassed.

The struggle against race prejudice, especially against hatred of the "yellow" races, was part of the daily work of the Socialist branches on the Pacific Coast and it was hard to conceive of Jack London, one of the foremost members of the branch, evincing race chauvinism.

Convinced that there was some misunderstanding, one of the comrades began talking to him about classes that exist in Japan as everywhere else. Another called his attention to the slogan decorating the wall over the portrait of Marx: "Workers of all countries, unite!" But this did not touch him in the least and only served to increase his passion. Pounding his fist on the table, Jack met their arguments with,

"What the devil! I am first of all a white man and only then a Socialist!"

His comrades might have been forgiven if they wondered just what kind of Socialist Jack was turning into, with his imported valet, his individualism that blazed up at every challenge, his drive for money and fame, and his intense convictions about white supremacy. In those days, however, even Marxist Socialism was fairly tolerant with deviationists, hoping that the misguided comrade could be brought back into the line. In its later evolution into Communism and an insistence on party discipline, Jack would have lasted as a member about as long as his career as a correspondent with the Japanese First Army.

In mid-June he caught the S.S. *Korea,* bound from Yokohama for San Francisco. Richard Harding Davis, now his good friend as well as his protector, came down to see him off. Davis told the departing ex-correspondent that he would be going back home himself as soon as he heard at least one shot fired in anger. Jack replied that it was a lousy war, hardly fit for white men to observe, and he was glad to be going away from there. Had he known what sort of welcome awaited him in San Francisco, he might not have been so eager to scamper up the gangplank.

X

Jack and His "Mate-Woman"

1. *A Suit for Divorce*

JACK may not have expected a civic reception when the S.S. *Korea* docked at the Embarcadero, but he could hardly help being disappointed at the welcome he received — greetings from his wife's lawyers and a bouquet of scandalized headlines. Before the ship docked, in fact, a process server had clambered aboard and shoved Bess's suit for separation and maintenance in his hands. And her charges came as a shock, for she named Anna Strunsky as "the other woman" who had broken up their home. She also had attached all his possessions, including his books, and his earnings, including what the Hearst papers owed him for his war correspondence.

Another dissappointment on arrival was the fact that Charmian, just when he needed her, was not present to greet him. Nor were any friends or relatives. It was as though six months on the other side of the world had cost him love, friendship and honor. About all he had gained was a valet, the efficient Manyoungi, his body-servant during the Korean campaigning.

To reporters who clamored for a statement on his wife's charges — which Miss Strunsky had labeled "merely vulgar," when they approached her — he replied only that "I refuse to say a word about my separation. A man's private affairs are his private affairs."

Immediately on arriving at his quarters in Oakland, however, he wrote Anna Strunsky expressing his regret that Bess had mistakenly nominated her as the cause of their breakup. He hoped that her name wouldn't be linked to any more of his troubles, and wondered why he caused so much injury to people he cared about. He added that the past year or so had changed him, and not for the better. His outlook had been crassly materialistic before, but he believed it was redeemed by his enthusiasm. Now that enthusiasm for life had evaporated.

But what about Charmian? A letter awaited him from that young lady, who was visiting her aunt, Mrs. Lynette McMurray, in Newton, Iowa. Charmian reported that she couldn't meet his ship because her loved ones feared a scandal. She also informed him that she was sick at the thought of all that would happen in the coming months — the inevitable revelation, that is, that it was Charmian and not Anna Strunsky who had come between Jack and his wife. Reading between the lines, Jack could gather that Aunt Netta — Mrs. Eames — had suggested or ordered that she stay away from him for the time being.

Mrs. Eames, however, claimed in later years that she hadn't the faintest suspicion that her niece was involved emotionally with Jack London until it became generally known. Mrs. Eames said that Bess had clung to her in the months after Jack left her and affirmed that she wouldn't give him up. She and Jack had agreed, Bess said, that if either fell in love they would separate but not divorce. Mrs. Eames also declared that Charmian never told her that she was the cause of the Londons' separation, that Charmian and Jack had kept their affair a secret by exchanging letters through a box at the San Francisco *Examiner*. Aunt Netta said she suffered a nervous collapse, in fact, when Bess called and told her that Charmian was the interloper.

Riffling through the letters he had received from her while he was in Japan and Korea, Jack found little consolation in the Charmian he found reflected in them. Was this the woman for whom he was risking divorce — which in 1904 was a serious and shocking matter — irreparably hurting Bess and cutting himself off from his children? There was an unfeeling quality — and less of the soaring phrases about their great love — about many of the letters he had received from her in the Far East. She wanted him to bring certain jewels, more cheaply obtained in the Orient, back for her. She wanted him to buy her a Japanese kimono. She wanted to be given the original manuscript of *The Sea Wolf*. She let him know that she was using part of his money — the balance of the two-thousand-dollar advance for the *Century*'s serialization of *The Sea Wolf* — to rent a piano. She was writing her lawyer to see whether Bess could be prosecuted for opening letters addressed to Jack, which had been sent to Bess by mistake. Was that really any of her business?

It appeared that Charmian's attitude, formerly all fervent protestation of undying love, had taken on a sharp edge of practicality. Jack's egocentric "I like" was being matched by Charmian's self-centered "I want," now that she apparently was confident that he was committed to marry her. And on July 4, when she must have known that he would be agonizing over Bess's suit mistakenly stigmatizing Anna, she wrote him a hardheaded letter advising him on how to beat down his wife's demands for maintenance for herself and their daughters. What right had she to suggest that he turn tight-fisted with those who had a claim on him?

In the days following his return from the Far East, holed up fretfully in his Oakland apartment, Jack was close to changing his mind and going back to Bess and the children. Perhaps only his resentment over Bess's dragging Anna's name into the case held him back. He couldn't set foot outside his apartment without being pounced on by reporters. Once they cornered him long enough to get something like a denial of Bess's charges: "The only feature of the case that stirs me up is that Miss Strunsky's name should be mentioned, for she is an extremely sensitive person." Miss Strunsky had become more definite in her denials, telling newspapermen in New York: "I am astonished. I have seen Mr. London only twice in the past two years, for I have been in New York and Europe. My visit to the London house occurred two years ago, and at that time there was not a breath of rumor that their married life was not a happy one."

First it was necessary to re-establish contact with Bess and convince her to withdraw that separation suit. He wanted a divorce, but one without scandal. Bess must be persuaded to amend her suit and charge him with desertion.

So he confessed to Bess that it was Charmian, not Anna Strunksy, with whom he had fallen in love. Bess heard him out stoically, too proud to show her feelings about what she considered Charmian's double-betrayal, not only stealing her husband but hypocritically playing the role of confidante and listening to Bess's tentative hopes that Jack would return to her.

Joan London says that in her mother's mind Charmian became a "nightmare" figure, all the more horrible because her actions, to Bess, had been incomprehensible. "In my childhood," Joan recalls, "Charmian was a figment of evil, mystery and menace. The foremost rule of my mother's life was loyalty, and what she could never forgive was, not Charmian's stealing her husband, but pretending to be her sympathetic friend. She believed that such two-facedness was utterly reprehensible. Thus, in later years, my sister Bess and I were never permitted to see our father in Charmian's presence. She felt that such a treacherous woman couldn't be trusted for a moment with her daughters."

Joan, on her own initiative, finally met Charmian for the first time when she was a young woman in her twenties. Remembering all that her mother had said about Charmian, Joan expected to meet a Medusa-like creature, slinky and sinister. Instead she found Charmian a middle-aged gamin. "No one could hold any real malice against this pathetic little woman," Joan recalls. "She prattled endlessly; she was a child in adult guise. When I went to see her, overcome by curiosity about her, almost the first thing she said was that she was glad I hadn't inherited my mother's eyes, which, she said, were those of a 'small-minded woman.' After the first shock, you couldn't resent what she said, because you realized that she spoke as thoughtlessly as a child.

"Later, when I was married and had a son, Charmian sent a book to him and inscribed it as coming from his grandmother. She told me that, since she didn't have any children of her own, she'd consider my children her grandchildren, although their real grandmother was very much alive and had never relented in her attitude toward Charmian. You couldn't help being touched by her."

Despite her bitterness over Charmian, Bess came to an agreement with Jack. She would file suit for divorce instead of separation, and would amend her complaint to charge desertion. In return Jack was to build her a new home in Piedmont and provide for her and her daughters. Accordingly, on July 11, Jack wrote Brett asking that his monthly payment from Macmillan be increased from $150 to $250 a month, of which Bess was to receive $75 and he was to be paid $175. (This, of course, was long before the California community-property law, dividing everything equally between man and wife, was enacted.) He also bought a lot, had a house designed according to Bess's specifications, and paid all he had in the bank — almost $4000 from *The Sea Wolf* serialization and what he received from Hearst — to have the house built.

He was deeply depressed, even though he had managed to straighten things out with Bess, and frankly wrote Charmian that he had been wavering in his decision to leave his family. It had taken all his will-power, he wrote, not to give up the idea of divorce and remarriage. What had shaken him so badly, he explained, was seeing his daughters again and marveling at their perfection.

Plunging himself back into his work seemed the only escape from what Charmian later described as "melancholia." Much as he always said he detested writing, much as he hated being tied for hours to a desk, it was the most reliable anodyne. Under the goad of his personal troubles, his productivity reached new heights in the months after his return from the Far East. The progress of his career at least was consoling. In April, Macmillan had brought out *The Faith of Men* (including the stories "A Relic of the Pliocene," "A Hyperborean Brew," "The Faith of Men," "Too Much Gold," "The One Thousand Dozen," "The Marriage of Lit-Lit," "Batard" and "The Story of Jess-Uck"). It was going well enough to warrant a third printing. *The Call of the Wild* was still selling thousands of copies a month. *The People of the Abyss* was selling better than expected. In October, *The Sea Wolf* would be published to general acclaim and would almost immediately achieve best-selling status. Richard Mansfield, the fore-most stage star, was offering one thousand dollars for the dramatic rights to *The Sea Wolf*, as he wrote Brett in July, and Jack thought he was out of his mind because at the moment he couldn't see it as a theatrical success.

Instead of accepting Mansfield's offer, he allowed himself to be swayed by friendship into turning the dramatization over to Joseph Noel, the San Francisco newspaperman who had been an occasional member of "The Crowd." Noel, in fact, was to receive two-thirds of all the proceeds from the production. It was a curious deal which was to cause him considerable grief in the future. Noel claimed that he was given the dramatic rights to *The Sea Wolf* in return for having supplied Jack with the conception of its leading character, Wolf Lar-sen, though Jack indicated more than once that Larsen was patterned somewhat after Captain Alexander McLean, a notorious sailing fleet tyrant whose poaching activities frequently made the headlines in the Nineties.

As Noel told it, however, he showed Jack a copy of a book titled *The South Sea Pearler,* a hair-raising account of the villainies of a slaver operating in the British-governed islands of the South Pacific. Except that he was a sadistic ruffian, the captain in *The South Sea Pearler* bore little resemblance to Wolf Larsen. Noel maintained that the fact that he was given two-thirds of the income from the play was "contributory evidence" that he inspired *The Sea Wolf,* "as in ordinary circumstances the author of the book and the dramatist who converts it into a play divide equally. Where there is a variant, it is to the advantage of the novelist." [1] Noel, in any case, didn't accomplish much with his dramatization. It was given a West Coast production by Oliver Morosco, the leading San Francisco impresario, in which Frank Bacon stole the show as Mugridge, the Cockney cook, playing him for laughs and throwing the whole production out of joint.* The play was never produced in New York.

That unhappy summer of 1904 Jack spent mostly at Wake Robin, Mrs. Eames's summer colony at Glen Ellen, and found himself caught in feminine intrigue.

He kept writing Charmian, who was still visiting her aunt in Iowa, that he wanted her to join him at Wake Robin and sent her a check for eighty dollars for her railroad fare. Charmian neither took the train not returned his money, though Jack informed her that Aunt Netta agreed there was no longer any fear of scandal. He made it plain to Charmian that he considered that there was something odd about her behavior.

As for Mrs. Eames, she was willing to let Charmian return to Wake Robin if she'd promise to behave circumspectly. Aunt Netta later affirmed that she turned gray worrying over "Childie" and her affairs. Charmian, however, protested to Jack that her aunt didn't really want her back because of what people might say. Jack didn't know who to believe. It didn't help that, as Mrs. Eames said later, she was being blamed by Bess for having stage-managed, concealed and encouraged the affair between Jack and Charmian.

Thus Jack found himself caught up in a whirligig of conflicting feminine emotions, chief among them the desire for respectability side by side with a determination to accomplish what would affront most respectable people. Late in August Bess would apply for a divorce, but

* Bacon later achieved fame in the long-touring *Lightnin'.*

only an interlocutory decree would be granted, which meant that a whole year of tightroping stretched before Jack and Charmian. Somehow Jack had to be kept interested in Charmian, seeing just enough of her to whet his desire for marriage but not so much that people would start gossiping.

But it would be months before he saw Charmian again, and he had to be content with the artfully sympathetic company of Mrs. Eames, whom he had taken to calling "Mother Mine." There would come a time when his thoughts of "Mother Mine" would be bitterly unfilial.

2. *Clashes with Critics*

Different as their styles, literary habitats and artistic merits were, there are inescapable parallels between Jack London and Ernest Hemingway. Both wrote most compellingly of adventure in remote corners of the world, both glorified men of action, patterned largely after themselves, and reveled in the more primitive aspects of human behavior. Both were estranged from difficult and domineering mothers. Neither was at his best creating female characters, tending, as many ultramasculine types do, to romanticize them beyond credibility; the Spanish girl who slipped into Robert Jordan's sleeping-bag in *For Whom the Bell Tolls* could have crawled all the way from the snow-covered cabins of London's sub-Arctic world. (Jack was always annoyed by charges that he couldn't create a convincing female character. "I know them too well to write too well about them," he would snap. "I'd never get past the editor and the censor!" Which wasn't quite as effective a defense as he believed.) Both gloried in their masculine strength and vigor, ended their lives the same way and for much the same reasons. The latter works of both suggested that writing had become a sort of sustained reflex, produced long after they had anything that needed to be said, yet containing flashes of brilliance like the retreat of a great electrical storm. And both were fascinated by the prize ring, seeing in the simple brute confrontation of two men with padded fists the elemental theme of survival.

Late in the summer of 1904 Jack began working on *The Game,* a short novel with a prizefighter as the hero.

He didn't expect it to be a financial success, but he wanted to write it as an exercise of his talent, to increase its flexibility. As he often said, he was striving for strength of utterance rather than style of utterance, and a novel with a prizefight background would lend itself to his literary aim. Even with two resounding successes to his credit, he wanted to extend his powers, as he wrote Charmian.

The Game, like *The Call of the Wild,* was well made and tightly constructed. The logical climax was a prizefight, but the underlying theme of the novel was a man's struggle to follow a career of his choosing against a woman's opposition. Genevieve, the heroine, was modeled on a London shopgirl, with a beautiful rose-petal complexion and a completely empty head, whom the author had admired across a candy counter while gathering material for *The People of the Abyss.* It was always one of his favorite novels, and eventually it sold 27,696 copies.

His pride in that bit of work, published in June of 1905, caused him to protest one of the reviews, not because it was adverse but because it suggested he didn't know what he was writing about. This he considered a slander because the prize ring was one of his major interests; before and after writing *The Game,* he attended all the matches at the West Oakland Athletic Club, covering them from ringside as an unpaid volunteer sports writer for the Oakland *Herald;* not only that, he fancied his own ability with the gloves, and extravagantly admired any good fighter.

The review that irked him was published in the New York periodical *Saturday Times,* and complained that *The Game* wasn't realistic enough.

The *Saturday Times* courteously allowed him his say:

I doubt if this reviewer has had as much experience in such matters as I have. I doubt if he knows what it is to be knocked out or to knock out another man. I have had these experiences, and it was out of these experiences, plus a fairly intimate knowledge of prize-fighting in general, that I wrote *The Game.* I quote from the critic in the *Saturday Times:* "Still more one gently doubts in this particular case, that a blow delivered by Ponta on the point of Fleming's chin could throw the latter upon the padded canvas floor of the ring with enough force to smash the whole back of his skull, as Mr. London describes."

All I can say in reply is, that a young fighter in the very club described in my book, had his head smashed in this manner. Incidentally, this young fighter worked in a sail-loft and took remarkably good care of his mother, brother and sisters. And — oh, one word more. I have just received a letter from Jimmy Britt, light-weight champion of the world, in which he tells me that he particularly enjoyed *The Game,* on account of its trueness to life.

A week or two later Jack's wounded feelings were soothed by the New York *Times* review stating that the novel was written "from personal knowledge based on experience," and even more by its subsequent reception in England where it was favorably compared — as well it might have been — with George Bernard Shaw's *Cashel Byron's Profession,* the hero of which was also a prizefighter. Jack was a fervent admirer of Shaw; more as a playwright than as a Socialist, since Shaw was an advocate of Fabian gradualism as opposed to the more precipitous Marxist approach subscribed to by London.

Even before he finished *The Game,* he was thinking about writing a play, wistfully envious, it seemed, of the more gregarious life enjoyed by playwrights, who could watch their creations come to life in the round.

On August 16, 1904, he wrote a woman friend that he would like to turn out a half-dozen plays even if they were not worthy of production — a curious yearning for a professional writer — and expressed his great admiration for Shaw's *Man and Superman.* Several weeks later he mentioned in another letter to the same correspondent that the rising young actress Ethel Barrymore was begging him to write a play for her. He added that he wasn't quite sure how to spell Miss Barrymore's name, which might have come as a shock to the Royal Family of Broadway.[2]

He decided to dramatize one of his own short stories, "The Scorn of Women," a tale with a Klondike background.[3] Its central character was based on Freda Maloof, the kootch dancer he had known in Dawson. It wasn't a major effort, as he wrote Anna Strunsky, but like *The Game* was intended as a sort of exploration of his talent.

He kept tinkering with the play for months, even while working on other things. One leading actress who received a copy was Minnie Maddern Fiske, who had stayed with him and Bess when she played in the Bay area. She liked it, despite the failure of his marriage with her cousin, but apparently her husband-manager Harrison Fiske finally turned it down.

One night in mid-January, 1905, he attended a performance of *The Darling of the Gods,* starring the beautiful and lively Blanche

Bates, at an Oakland theater. For three consecutive nights he watched her from a front-row seat, deciding that she was just the woman to embody Freda in his play. Miss Bates had enacted Cigarette in David Belasco's production of *Under Two Flags,* a role not too dissimilar, as he saw it, from that of Freda.

His interest in Miss Bates, whether it was that of a playwright seeing his heroine come to life or a more personal one, led to a lot of newspaper publicity. Jack called on her, gave a dinner in her honor, and otherwise behaved as though he might be more than professionally smitten. It was during the period of his disenchantment with Charmian, and his eye was roving speculatively in many directions. The papers reported that he and the vivacious Miss Bates were having a fling at romance,[4] and on March 13, he felt called upon to write Brett at Macmillan's denying press reports that he and the actress were going to be married.

Nothing came of either his interest in Miss Bates or her interest in *The Scorn of Women,* and a month later he sent a copy of the play to James B. Pinker, his English literary agent, hoping that an English production might be arranged. The only proviso, he wrote Pinker, was that he wouldn't sell the play for production at a flat fee but would insist on a royalty basis of payment — one of many indications he would not forget all the money he lost on *The Call of the Wild* through not demanding royalties.[5]

Neither in this country nor abroad, however, was there any producer willing to produce the play. Its only production was on the presses of Macmillan's, which published it in 1906, though Jack tried for years to find a leading actress who would like it well enough to cajole her manager into presenting it. His failure as a dramatist, which was to be doggedly repeated in the future, was one of the few major disappointments of his career. He learned to his sorrow that a novelist can rarely cross the boundary between the printed page and the living stage.

After turning out *The Scorn of Women* at top speed, he was forced to return to more immediately lucrative work. Building a home for Bess and his daughters had taken all the cash he could lay his hands on, and he had to write Brett on November 17, 1904, that his wife's lawyers were pressing him so hard for money that he needed a three-thousand-dollar advance. Brett, as was almost invariably the case, sent him the money by return mail. Jack was still strapped and asked Pinker, his English agent, to see whether some of his unused war correspondence could be published in England.*

He then began work on a series of stories based on his experiences as a hijacker of oysters and later as a member of the Fish Patrol, which *Youth's Companion* agreed to publish, seven of them between February and May of 1905. He was hacking out juvenile stuff just at the time *The Sea Wolf* was rocketing to the top of the best-seller lists.

Macmillan, of course, agreed to publish the juvenile tales, despite the usual adverse comment of its outside reader, Professor Carpenter of Columbia, who pronounced the collection published as *Tales of the Fish Patrol* "greatly disappointing." The professor's criticism was cogent, and might have been applied to much of Jack's work. "The author evidently has in mind Kipling's attempt to get the romance out of adventurous real life without the necessity of introducing the love element, but somehow or other, though Mr. London succeeds easily enough in leaving the love element out, he does not succeed in getting the romantic element of real life in." Professor Carpenter, however, included an excerpt from *The Call of the Wild* in his textbook *Modern English Prose,* edited in collaboration with William Tenney Brewster.

Brett also accepted for publication in 1905 a collection of Jack's essays titled *The War of the Classes,* including "The Class Struggle," "The Scab," "The Tramp," "The Question of the Maximum," "Wanted: A New Law of Development," "A Review (Contradictory Teachers)," and "How I Became a Socialist." The collection served to increase his reputation in the Socialist Party, for as the *International Socialist Review* commented, "It would be easy to name a half dozen prominent writers of the last decade who occasionally admitted that they were socialists, but their socialism was generally of such a mild inoffensive sort that it didn't hurt them much with their capitalist friends. London, however, is the genuine, old-fashioned, proletarian, class-struggle socialist."

The outbreak of revolution in Russia early in 1905, abortive as it turned out to be under Cossack knouts, accelerated Jack's activities as a propagandist for Socialism. He signed a proclamation calling

* It couldn't. His war correspondence from Asia and Mexico has never been collected in book form.

on American Socialists to support the revolution along with Eugene V. Debs, Victor Berger (who was to become a Socialist congressman from Wisconsin), and Morris Hillquit. He also took time out from his work, pressed as he was for money to support his wife and daughters, his mother and other dependents, to lecture in various California cities. He told students at the University of California they must join in the class struggle because "here's a cause that appeals to all the romance in you. Awake! Awake to its call!" His trip to Los Angeles in January, 1905, stirred considerable comment in that still sleepy little city.

Julian Hawthorne of the Los Angeles *Examiner* described him as "simple and straightforward as a grizzly bear," and he lived up to the description when the chairman of the meeting he was to address introduced him as "a ripe scholar, a profound philosopher, a literary genius and the foremost man of letters in America." London got up, glowering at the chairman, and announced that he wasn't at all flattered by the introduction. Before fame struck him, he told the audience, he had worked in a cannery, sailed before the mast and spent months in the army of unemployed — "and it is the proletarian side of my life that I revere the most and to which I will cling as long as I live."

He was more coolly received when he accepted an invitation to speak before a businessmen's club in Stockton and, as the local paper commented, "lectured them as though they were unruly schoolchildren." The fact that he chain-smoked cigarets and pounded his fist on the table as he lectured the businessmen on their failings made him seem all the more a dangerous apparition from the lower depths. A cagier propagandist would certainly have adopted a subtler, more conciliatory approach before an expectedly hostile audience, but Jack couldn't resist playing his role to the hilt.

Soon newspapers throughout the country were headlining his inflammatory speeches and reporting that he considered himself a brother to "the Russian assassins," and that he was attacking the Constitution. One of the few newspapers which defended him was the San Francisco *Bulletin,* which said in an editorial, "The hot sincerity and hatred of wrong that burns in the revolutionary heart of young Jack London is the same spirit that characterized the tea-overboard party in Boston Harbor." He was refused permission to speak before the debating society at his quasi-alma mater, Oakland High School.

The furor, with its attendant publicity, delighted him. Nothing pleased him more than to be considered a dangerous radical. It fed his ego, and better still it sold books. *The War of the Classes* would probably have sold a few thousand copies if it hadn't come out at the time of the Russian upheaval and Jack's lecturing, but it had to be reprinted three times before the year was out.

Meanwhile, he was working on a less idealistic project, a book which would be a companion piece to *The Call of the Wild,* though not a sequel.[6] It would deal with the civilization of a dog, a reverse angle on his original theme, he informed his publisher. Obviously it was designed to capitalize on the popularity of the earlier volume. He also wanted Brett to understand, he said in a letter dated December 17, that he would never again agree to a flat payment such as deprived him of his share of the *Call of the Wild* bonanza. A short time later he was boasting to his English agent that he had wangled a better contract out of Macmillan, calling for fifteen per cent on the first five thousand copies sold and twenty per cent on all copies thereafter. The capitalist, of necessity, always lurked just below the Socialist surface.

"I'm always in debt," as he complained to Ashton Stevens, later a prominent dramatic critic, in an interview published in the San Francisco *Examiner*. "Look at that hand. See where the light comes through the fingers? That hand leaks . . . All I'd like to do is to be able to get enough money ahead to loaf for a year — that's my little dream."

"And buy some dress shirts and evening clothes?" Stevens asked.

"Oh, I have them," Jack said. "I've got them. But I'm willing to put 'em on only when I can't get in without them. I loathe the things, but if the worst comes to the worst I've got 'em."

White Fang, as the companion volume to *The Call of the Wild* was to be titled, promised to buy him some of that loafing time if the compulsion that drove him to work constantly would ever let him rest. White Fang was three-quarters wolf and one-quarter dog, born wild but captured with his half-dog mother and raised by men. He heard a different call than Buck, "the call of fire and of man — the call which it has been given alone of all animals to the wolf to answer, to the wolf and the wolf-dog, who are brothers." Reversing Buck's primitive trail, he ends up in civilized comfort on a Santa Clara Valley ranch, where he is called the "Blessed Wolf."

White Fang was twice as long as *The Call of the Wild* and about half as good, the leanness of the former larded with proven commercial ingredients, softer and more sentimental. Published in September of 1906, it eventually sold 438,004 copies and was next to *The Call of the Wild* and *The Sea Wolf* in U.S. hardcover sales of his books.

It also involved him in a controversy with President Roosevelt, who considered his credentials as an outdoorsman superior to all but a few recognized naturalists such as Muir and Burroughs. Roosevelt read *White Fang* and discovered that he disliked London's writing almost as much as his politics.

The President sailed into London with his big stick flailing and called him a "nature faker."[7] Regarding *White Fang*, Roosevelt said: "I can't believe that Mr. London knows much about the wolves, and I am certain he knows nothing about their fighting, or as a realist he would not tell this tale." In particular the President charged that the wolf-dog and a bulldog in his story "fought in an impossible fashion." He also protested that a lynx weighing about twenty pounds couldn't possibly kill a big wolf-dog. On the second count, Roosevelt was mistaken, since in the story the wolf-dog kills the lynx instead of the reverse.

A little sheepishly Roosevelt wrote John Burroughs[8] that he had attacked London as one of the "more preposterous writers of 'unnatural history' . . . I know that as President I ought not to do this; but I was having an awful time toward the end of the session [of Congress] and I felt I simply had to permit myself some diversion."

Mr. Roosevelt was not "diverted," however, when *Collier's* published Jack's reply to the nature-faking charge on September 5, 1908. The article was titled "The Other Animals" and bore a caption which boasted that Jack was "locating the President in the Ananias Club"—that is, calling him a liar. Jack had nothing to do with the impudent caption, of course, and his reply was mild and respectful enough for almost anyone but the sizable ego rampant in the White House.

"President Roosevelt," he wrote, "does not think a bull-dog can lick a wolf-dog. I think a bull-dog can lick a wolf-dog. And there we are. Difference of opinion may make, and does make, horse-racing. I can understand that difference of opinion can make dog-fighting. But what gets me is how difference of opinion regarding the relative merits of a bull-dog and a wolf-dog makes me a nature-faker and President Roosevelt a vindicated and triumphant scientist."

Mr. Roosevelt was so irked that he got off a letter to Mark Sullivan, then editor of *Collier's*, protesting that Jack "deliberately invents statements which I have never made . . . I stated and proved that London knew nothing whatever about wolves or lynxes; that his story *White Fang* would be excellent if it was avowedly put forth as a fable, but as realism it was nonsense, and mischievous nonsense to boot. . . . I have not the slightest intention of entering into any controversy on this subject with London. I would as soon think of discussing seriously with him any social or political reform."

All in all, Jack came off a little better than the President in their exchange of opinions, certainly, and unexpectedly, with more dignity and forebearance.

At the time he was writing *White Fang*, Jack made himself unpopular with a segment of his growing public, particularly those readers who collected autographs and who admired him as a storyteller but not as a Socialist revolutionary. To autograph-seekers he sent a postcard stating that they could have his signature for one dollar, or an appropriate sentiment plus signature for five dollars, their checks or postal money orders to be made out to the Oakland chapter of the Socialist Party. Many of the recipients were outraged, one replying that he had collected the autographs of fifty famous persons, none of whom had demanded payment, and another scrawling on the card Jack sent, "You must take us for asses here in this civilized nation to give even one cent toward promoting that damned viper, Socialism!"

3. *Remarriage*

In the spring of 1905 everything was going smoother for Jack, even his romance with Charmian Kittredge. Charmian returned to Glen Ellen from her aunt's home in Iowa after her long absence; Bess's house was finished, and his mother was established in a house he bought for her in Oakland.

He and Charmian had decided to marry as soon as Bess's divorce became final. They both loved the valley country of Sonoma County so much that, despite Jack's former anti-rural feelings, they were determined to live somewhere around Glen Ellen. When he learned that the 129-acre Hill Ranch, wooded land rising up the Valley of the Moon to Sonoma Mountain, was for sale, he knew he wouldn't be able to rest until he acquired it. And Mr. Brett of Macmillan soon learned that, if he didn't know it already, the vaulting desires of a best-selling author — even a Socialist — could prove to be a considerable strain on a publisher's treasury.

On May 26 Jack wrote Brett that he would like a few thousand dollars on account to buy some real estate, the money to be advanced against earnings on *The Sea Wolf*. On June 7, he advised Brett that he had obtained the property he wanted after paying five hundred dollars for an option; now he needed sixty-five hundred dollars in a few days, or he would lose his option; Brett could advance him the money out of an estimated ten thousand dollars in accrued royalties on *The Sea Wolf*. He gave his publisher a lyrical description of the canyons, streams and springs on the property, the giant redwoods, great firs, maples, white oaks, live oaks, black oaks, madrone and manzanita that must be rescued from the villainous timber-cutters. It was the most beautiful land in America, he affirmed. Brett, of course, came across. Possibly the publisher did not reckon that Jack would soon be expanding in all directions, buying up adjacent land, reclaiming old vineyards, clearing thickets, building, planting, buying livestock. On August 1, Jack demanded an increase on his royalty rate, already more generous than most authors received, but Brett would agree only to a raise in the monthly payments to three hundred dollars — two hundred dollars for Jack, one hundred for Bess and the children.

The publisher also managed to resist Jack on another issue that summer. Mrs. Eames, or "Mother Mine" as he still called her, had been inspired to write a novel titled *Deseret* while playing duenna to the romance between Jack and her niece. In sending Brett the manuscript, Jack emphasized that he was *personally* interested in seeing that it was published. Another publisher had accepted it but went broke just before it could be sent to press. It was a well-written novel, Jack insisted, and he could see no reason why it would not merit publication by Macmillan. Brett did not propose to have even the leading moneymaker of his list telling him what to publish, and firmly rejected Mrs. Eames's manuscript.

By the fall of 1905 Jack had drawn so heavily on his account at Macmillan's that Brett informed him that he would have to pay interest on any new advances made him. For all the financial success of the past year, he was broke, his mother and Bess were asking for an increase in their allowances, Bess wanted a horse and surrey, he owed for ranch equipment, tools and groceries. No matter how much he earned, the demands of others and his own landowner's syndrome with its constant acquisitive tendencies always exceeded his income. The leaky fingers he mentioned to the newspaper interviewer never managed to close tight.

No matter, he could always earn more. In October he set out on a lecture tour of the Middle West and East while Charmian returned to her aunt in Newton, Iowa. They agreed to reunite and marry as soon as Bess's final decree was granted. After the lecture tour was completed, they would return to the ranch at Glen Ellen, which Charmian said they called "our Land of Dear Delight."

They made their plans for marriage confidently enough, considering that a few months before they had almost broken off their unofficial engagement. Charmian accused him of unfaithfulness after attending one of his lectures, during which he had obviously addressed himself to a certain young woman in the audience. Seeing them together after the lecture, Charmian wrote him, she was sure they had slept together the night before. In the same letter, she informed him that she wasn't shocked by his infidelity, that she didn't expect him to be faithful, and she had long ago faced up to his probable unfaithfulness.

Undoubtedly it made him uneasy to be so hastily accused, and on such flimsy evidence, but it probably unsettled him even more that she was so quick to forgive his straying. Would a woman in love be able to forgive so easily, with so little rancor? He was even more shaken when, as Charmian wrote in her biography, some of his friends accused Charmian of "unveracity and disloyalty," the nature of which she did not specify. To disprove the slander, she said, she and Jack checked diaries they both kept and found that they "tallied," apparently proving that Charmian herself had not strayed on a certain occasion. Jack then demanded apologies from the talebearers, and told them, "I love Charmian, not for anything she may or may not have done, but for what I find her, for what she is to me." [9] Still, he had been unsure enough of her to conduct that little investigation before confounding his friends.

On the tour booked by the Lyceum Bureau, Jack was billed as "Daring traveler . . . an original Klondiker . . . an experienced seaman . . . a prominent Socialist . . . the American Kipling . . . Novelist and friend of the underdog." During the first three weeks in November he barnstormed through Iowa, Wisconsin and Ohio, delivering his lecture on "Revolution" or relating his experiences in the Klondike, with Coxey's Army and in the Russo-Japanese War (which the Japanese, as he had foreseen, won with crushing victories on land and sea).

He and Charmian planned to be married November 25, 1905, at the home of her aunt in Newton, following a lecture he was to give at Grinnell College nearby. The plan was changed when Bess's final decree was granted on November 18, several days earlier than expected. He received telegraphic notice of the decree just after finishing a lecture before the People's Institute in Elyria, Ohio, and wired Charmian to meet him in Chicago the next day. They were reunited on November 19, a Saturday night. The problem was how to obtain a special license so they could be married the next day, Sunday. They could no doubt have waited another day but anyone would have done that. Getting married on Sunday, in a flurry which would undoubtedly attract headlines, was more in the dashing London style.

He enlisted the help of the city editor of the Chicago *American*, a Hearst paper, in return for an exclusive story; routed city officials out of bed, finally found one who would accompany him to the home of the marriage license clerk, and bulldozed that sleepy functionary into going back downtown and opening his office at midnight to provide a special license.

They were married by a justice of the peace named J. J. Grant. News of the wedding didn't break until the *American* came out with the story on Monday. Jack and Charmian were returning from Geneva Falls, Wisconsin, two days later when they read the Chicago papers' banner lines reading JACK LONDON MARRIAGE INVALID. They then learned that the Illinois legislature had recently passed a law forbidding divorced persons to remarry in less than a year after a decree was granted. As soon as they checked back into their Chicago hotel, they also learned from the Lyceum Bureau that most of the Middle Western lecture dates were being canceled in a Bible Belt protest at his haste to remarry. Until then, it had been assumed that Jack and Bess were divorcing because they couldn't get along; now it was revealed that he had left his wife and children for another woman. The fact that Illinois authorities were now declaring the marriage invalid only heightened the frenzy of public disapproval.

Jack, of course, was brimming with defiance, and told newspapermen: "I will get married in every state of the Union just as fast as I can get from one to another . . . The State of California provides that a divorced person may not marry within a year, and to encompass this end the courts grant a divorce and one year later a decree, and the decree was granted last Saturday [presumably he meant Friday]. As to whether this divorce is amenable to the laws of Illinois is something I don't know, but it seems that the Illinois law did not go into effect until last July, and it cannot affect my case."

Instead of rushing from state to state to be married, he and Charmian spent several days in Newton at the home of her aunt while preachers fulminated against "this Socialist apostle of immorality," editorial writers decried his unseemly haste, women's clubs condemned them both, and libraries in Pittsburgh, Pennsylvania, and Derby, Connecticut, ordered his books removed from their shelves. Even the Socialists were hard put to defend their most celebrated standard-bearer when one periodical reported scathingly on his mode of travel in Pullmans attended by Manyoungi, his Korean valet, adding in the height of indignation, though somewhat inaccurately, "He even sat in his chair and let that heathen Jap bring him a drink!"

After spending a few weeks honeymooning in Cuba, Jamaica and Florida, Jack and Charmian proceeded north to continue with his lecture tour, the eastern phase of it being sponsored mainly by collegiate groups with a slightly less narrow viewpoint on divorce than the women's and businessmen's clubs of the Middle West which had cancelled him out.

Early in January, 1906, on arriving in New York, he was persuaded by Dr. Alexander Irvine, a New Haven minister and head of the local Socialist chapter, to speak before students at Yale. The Yale Political Union was to sponsor his appearance at Woolsey Hall. At the last minute the older and more conservative members of the faculty launched an attempt to have the use of Woolsey Hall forbidden to a speaker whose topic would be "Revolution." Some of the younger faculty members were enlisted to head off this movement, including William Lyon Phelps, who demanded of his seniors, "Is Yale a monastery?"

So Jack spoke at Woolsey Hall before an audience of more than three thousand students and faculty members, attracted, no doubt, more by his flamboyant legend, his youth and his notorious remarriage than anything he might have to say about the injustices of the capitalistic system which indirectly provided their tuition and paid their bar tabs down at Mory's. As the Rev. Dr. Irvine later reported, Jack "gripped by the intellect and held them," and only one person walked out as he called the proletariat to arms.

Seven million men throughout the world were fighting to overthrow capitalism, the Yale *Daily News* reported him as saying. "They call themselves comrades, these men, as they stand shoulder to shoulder under the banner of revolt . . . The revolution is here, now. Stop it who can!"

He also had attended a university, he said, and found it "clean and noble, but I did not find the university alive . . . And the reflection of this university ideal I find — the conservatism and unconcern of the American people toward those who are suffering, who are in want. And so I became interested in an attempt to arouse in the minds of the young men of our universities an interest in the study of socialism . . . If collegians cannot fight for us, we want them to fight against us — of course, sincerely fight against us. But what we do not want is that which obtains today and has obtained in the past of the university, a mere deadness and unconcern and ignorance so far as socialism is concerned. Fight for us or fight against us! Raise your voices one way or the other. Be alive!"

The walls of Woolsey Hall shook with the ovation he received, more for his passionate sincerity, perhaps, than the persuasive force of his argument.

The next morning, just before he left New Haven, he was interviewed by a gangling, redheaded youth named Sinclair Lewis, who was on the staff of the Yale *News* and recently had read *The Sea Wolf* and wondered whether he was not an "untried Humphrey Van Weyden."

Back in New York, on January 19, it had been arranged for him to address a mass meeting of the Intercollegiate Socialist Society. The I.S.S. had been formed the previous September by a group including Upton Sinclair, Thomas Wentworth Higginson, William English Walling (Anna Strunsky's husband), J. G. Phelps Stokes and Clarence Darrow. Jack London was promptly elected its first president.

Jack was late for the rally in the Grand Central Palace, but when he strode down the aisle and up to the platform, his chunky figure clad in a black suit, white flannel shirt and white tie, the assemblage exploded with enthusiasm; Debs was their leader, as head of the Socialist Party, but London was their hero. It took five minutes for the cheering to subside so Jack could begin his speech. Capitalism, he predicted, would fall before the end of the century. "The crowd that listened so raptly," Upton Sinclair recalled, "was not, I must admit, very collegiate. A few students came, but most of the audience was from the Lower East Side; the ushers were Jewish boys and girls wearing red badges. The socialist fervor of that evening now seems like even more ancient history than it is. A good part of it went into the communist movement, of course . . ." [10]

Next day the adoring young Mr. Sinclair managed to get Jack by himself over a restaurant table, eager to have the advice of the president of the society he had helped to organize. Jack off the platform and on the booze, Sinclair found, was somewhat less inspiring than he had anticipated. Something about New York always profoundly depressed Jack, perhaps because it was too big and bustling and indifferent to be impressed by him. He drank twice as much in New York as anywhere else, and cursed the place as a "man-trap."

London and Sinclair were to be lifelong friends, more on the politico-literary plane than the personal, but the acquaintance was off to a bad start. Sinclair's father had been a drunkard and Sinclair himself was, in reaction, a teetotaler. He was appalled when Jack showed up for lunch already bleary-eyed and proceeded to drink his way through the afternoon. Noticing that he "quailed" at the succession of drinks, Sinclair recalled, Jack was owlishly determined to "have his fun with me . . . Tales of incredible debauches; tales of opium and hashish, and I know not what other strange ingredients; tales of whiskey bouts lasting for weeks." [11]

4. *Plans for a Cruise*

Before leaving New York Jack also spoke before a large audience of well-to-do people eager to be instructed on Socialism's plans for their future. Perhaps they expected him to modulate his views in accordance with the gentility of the occasion, but instead he fired off one of his most inflammatory speeches, calculated to make every worthy burgher and broker in his audience have nightmares for weeks. Before he was through, his audience was "a sea of blasted, purple faces

Young author
on the rise

ɔthers

Brown Brothe

The outdoors
novelist in
his proper
setting

Underwood and Ur

Charmian London goes semi-native in Hawaiian costume

Brown Brothers

London and his dreamboat, the *Snark*, under construction

Charmian and Jack under sail

Brothers

Richard Harding Davis,
"a great big *white* man"

lerwood and Underwood

Underwood and Un

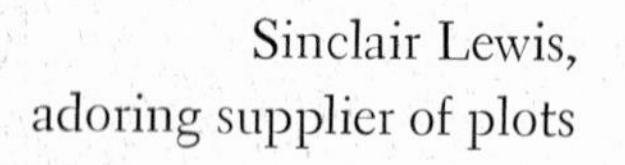

Sinclair Lewis,
adoring supplier of plots

ithers

The House That Jack Built — almost

Underwood and Underwood

Jack and his fellow correspondents en route to the Russo-Japanese War

others

Jack consents to show his passport at Ping Yang

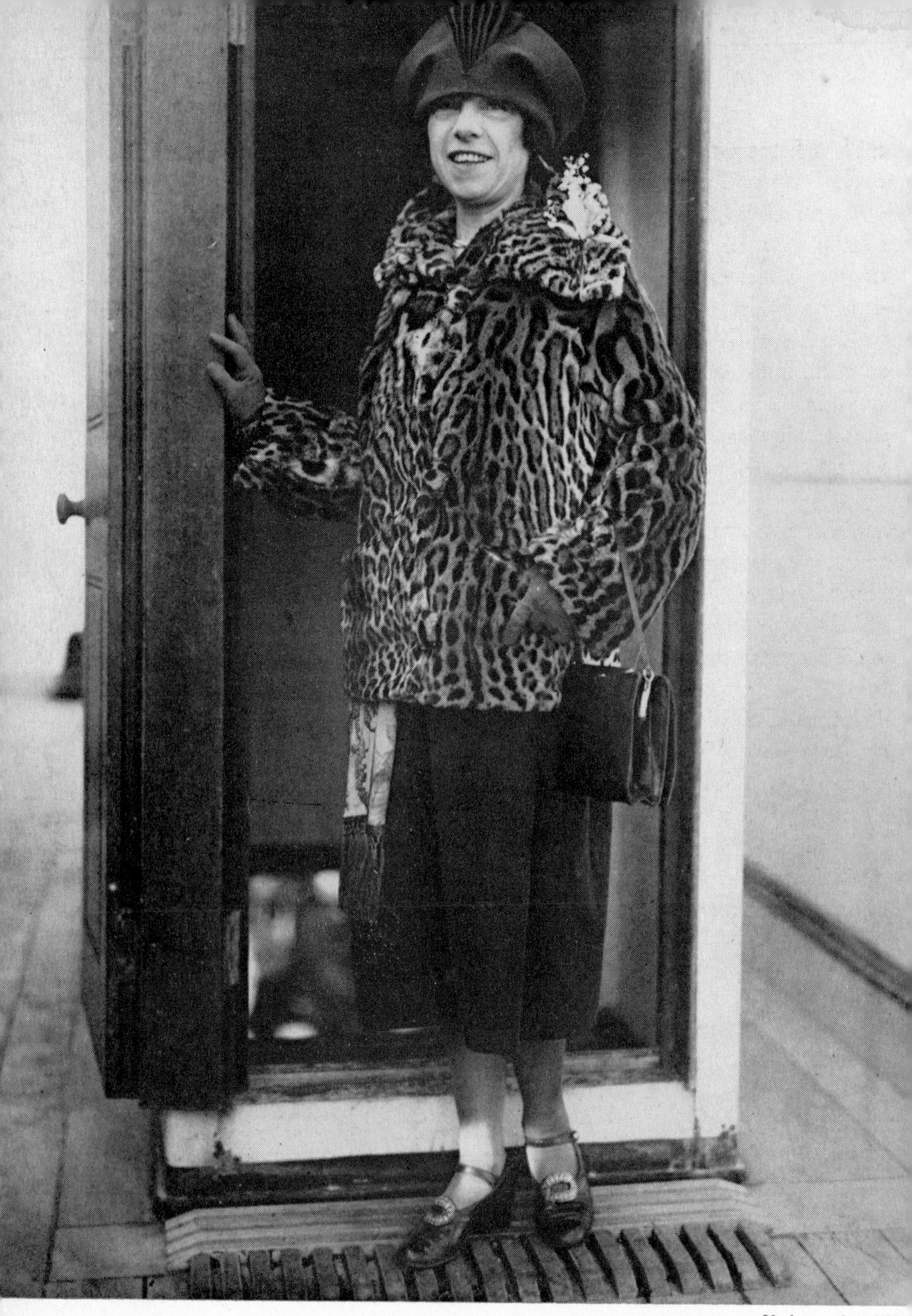

Underwood and Un

Charmian off to Europe on the anniversary of Jack's death

distorted with rage" and some of its members commented that "he ought to be in jail." [12]

Jack told them, "You have been entrusted with the world; you have muddled and mismanaged it. You are incompetent, despite all your boastings. A million years ago the caveman, without tools, with small brain, and with nothing but the strength of his body, managed to feed his wife and children, so that through him the race survived. You, on the other hand, armed with all the modern means of production, multiplying the productive capacity of the caveman a million times — you incompetents and muddlers, you are unable to secure to millions even the paltry amount of bread that would sustain their physical life. You have mismanaged the world, and it shall be taken from you!"

From the impression he gave before returning to California early in February, Jack seemed to be promising a revolution before breakfast. "The revolution is here, now. Stop it who can!" He appeared to be aflame with the spirit of insurgency. Despite his trumpetings from the platform his own plans for the near future included very little revolutionary activity. His only desire was to get away from it all, seclude himself at Wake Robin Lodge, part of which he rented from Mrs. Eames and Edward Payne, and concentrate on his writing career.

His goal now was to build a boat and sail it around the world, far from crowds and causes and cities. He was sick of people, had cut himself off from most of his friends of the pre-1905 period; only George Sterling, Frederick Bamford, Jimmy Hopper and Strawn-Hamilton were still fairly close to him and held in esteem. More and more he was becoming the misanthrope, disgusted with humanity when it came close enough to breathe on him, even while in his public manifestations — temporarily intoxicated by the applause and flattery — he presented himself as a fighter for the rights of all mankind. The Bible Belt reaction to his remarriage may have influenced his attitude toward people; a closer look at his followers may have disillusioned him, but there is also the testimony of Austin Lewis that after 1899 — after he became absorbed in a literary career — his interest in crusading for human rights steadily declined. He had been well paid for his lecture tour, and his only responsibility, he seemed to feel, was to give a good performance on the platform. If people were roused by his prophecies and convinced of the sincerity of his passion, well, that only proved he had given good value for money received.

The idea of cruising the world in his own boat had occurred to him months before his return to Glen Ellen, when he read Captain Joshua Slocum's *Sailing Alone Around the World.* He would duplicate Captain Slocum's feat, except that being more gregarious he would take Charmian and a few others with him. Charmian, whose willingness to follow him into any sort of adventure was her most admirable and endearing trait, was as excited by the proposal as Jack himself. They were encouraged in their plans by Roscoe Eames, who would act as skipper on the basis of seagoing experiences he exaggerated more than slightly, and by Ninetta Eames and Edward Payne, who would not be sorry to have white-whiskered and garrulous old Uncle Roscoe out of their way.

The proposed world cruise would take large sums of money, and since he was all but broke Jack would have to spend months slaving away at books and stories. In addition to building the boat on a sort of naval installment plan, his income was being drained by his ranch-building project, planning a house and planting an orchard, a vineyard and scores of hedgerows.

He hoped that some of the leading magazines would help to subsidize the trip in return for articles sent back along the way, and he circulated a prospectus among a half-dozen editors outlining the projected cruise. He would leave in October that year, would sail first to Hawaii, then to the South Seas, the Philippines and Japan. He would cross the Indian Ocean, beat his way up the Red Sea to the Mediterranean, traverse the Atlantic to New York and then return to San Francisco around the Horn.

Most startling of all, he proposed to spend seven years on this continuous voyage, seven of the most productive years of a writer's life, those of his thirties, during which the world could be turned upside down for all he would know about it. It would be the grandest of all his gestures of contempt for contemporary society; more than just an adventure like running off to the Klondike, it would show what he thought of fame and celebrity — the most talked-about writer in America ditching everything and sailing off into the most remote seas.

That voyage now became his obsession; nothing could be allowed to interfere with it. A magazine asked him to investigate child-labor conditions in the Southern cotton mills, and the San Francisco *Examiner* wanted him to cover Wild Bill Haywood's murder trial up in Idaho, but he turned them both down, though they presented splendid opportunities to play his propagandist's part in the class struggle. Instead, as he wrote his English agent on July 17, he signed an agreement with *Collier's* to cover certain big news stories to be decided on by mutual consent, and turned out more Alaskan tales ("A Day's Lodging," "The Wit of Porportuk," "When God Laughs," "Created He Them," and "Just Meat") as well as collecting the stories for the volumes *Moon Face,* to be published later that year, and *Love of Life,* which was scheduled for the following year. And all this was only a prelude to two longer works which he hoped to finish within a year, *Before Adam* and *The Iron Heel.* In this rigorous work schedule he was sustained by something more valuable than ambition and energy, the habit that would carry him through sterile and fertile years alike, his professional writer's one thousand words a day every day of the year. His talent would never be allowed to lie fallow, though as a farmer he had nothing but contempt for those who worked their fields until they were barren.

By April 8 he had already finished two chapters of *Before Adam,* which he thought would run about forty thousand words and would be more of a juvenile than a regular trade book.[13] Once again he underestimated his market; *Before Adam* sold 65,638 copies. In his communications with Brett he rarely discussed anything but wordage, royalties, sales possibilities, contract provisions, and occasionally more personal matters that might affect his career; never the actual writing or the problems connected with it. His relations with Brett were invariably genial and never descended to rancor even when they disagreed, but he made it clear that he wanted no advice from his publisher on what to write or how to write it. Later Brett remarked on how London "resented" even the most tactful attempts at guidance. From beginning to end, Brett was never his mentor but only the intermediary between manuscript and printed page.

Before Adam, in brief, was the story of a modern boy's nightly dreams of having been born in prehistoric times and told what life must have been like in the days when men lived in caves and confronted the dawn world with only their muscular strength. A note of wistfulness was frequently audible in the clarity and simplicity of its style. The dreaming boy, more often than not, was Jack, sick of the world and its complexities, its demands and disappointments. There must have been something therapeutic about writing *Before Adam* in the midst of his eternally tangled domestic affairs and his constant financial troubles.

It was one more facet of his escapism, once expressed by running away to sea, to hoboing, to the Klondike; later in moving from city to country, then in fleeing the land by cruising to the South Seas, and finally in seeking the last loophole of all . . .

In the middle of writing *Before Adam*, Jack was interrupted by the disaster which all but destroyed his native city.

On the morning of April 18 the floor of Sonoma Valley was shaken by a terrific jolt that almost tumbled Jack and Charmian out of their beds (they slept in the same room but in different beds because Jack was an exceedingly restless sleeper and Charmian suffered from insomnia). Realizing at once, as quake-conscious Californians, that the jolt must have caused severe damage somewhere, they rode up to the crest of Sonoma Mountain. Below, in the direction of San Francisco, there was an immense pillar of fire and smoke.

They immediately set out for the stricken city, carrying only a handbag and trusting that the trains would still be running. It was late afternoon by the time they reached Oakland — Jack pausing only to make sure Flora, Bess and his children had survived — and crossed over to San Francisco on the last ferry permitted to land in the burning city.

All that night he and Charmian walked the shattered streets gathering material for the story Jack would telegraph to *Collier's*. He also took scores of striking photographs of the fire sweeping the city that night and the next day. Several times they were almost trapped by converging walls of flame and by explosions set off by dynamiters hoping to halt the fire.

"At nine o'clock Wednesday evening [April 18]," he wrote, "I walked down the very heart of the city. I walked through miles and miles of magnificent buildings and towering skyscrapers. Here was no fire. All was in perfect order. The police patrolled the streets. Every building had its watchman at the door. And yet it was doomed, all of it. There was no water. The dynamite was giving out. And at right angles two conflagrations were sweeping down upon it." [14]

They walked up Nob Hill as the south wind began blowing the walls of flame toward that summit and the mansions built by the city's magnificoes, all seemingly as doomed as the humbler sections below. The men who had built them were gone, and most of their surviving widows were scattered far from the scene of their husbands' triumphs, but their dwellings still stood for the power and glory of the city's beginnings and their destruction would be more awesome than the ruin of the tall buildings on Market Street. Soldiers guarded the Huntington mansion, and the Crocker butler was supervising the removal of paintings and medieval tapestries. At the Hopkins mansion, whose departed master had once prepared to defend it with a rack of rifles when Kearney was rousing the workers, an army lieutenant had recruited a corps of Barbary Coast hoodlums and barflies to carry off the Hopkins art collection.

Just below the crest of the hill Jack and Charmian stopped to rest on the steps of one of the less stately homes. Its owner, a man named Perine, came out and was about to lock the door. Instead, on an impulse, he asked the Londons to step inside. "Yesterday morning," Perine told them, "I was worth six hundred thousand. This morning this house is all I have left. It will go in fifteen minutes."

Perine suggested that Charmian "try the tone" of his magnificent piano. She played a few chords until, his face contorted by painful memories, he gestured for her to stop. A few minutes later they all left the house and hurried back down the hill.

At Union Square, the heart of the city, they saw a man offering a thousand dollars for a team of horses to haul away a truck loaded with trunks from a nearby hotel. An elderly man on crutches, standing next to them, said, "Today is my birthday. Last night I was worth thirty thousand dollars. I bought five bottles of wine, some delicate fish, and other things for my birthday dinner. I have had no dinner, and all I own is these crutches."

For two more days the fire-storm raged, until San Francisco was "like the center of a volcano" round which were camped the thousands of homeless.

Jack was so deeply affected by the destruction of his native city that he vowed, "I'll never write about this for anyone," but as soon as he returned to Glen Ellen he found a telegram from *Collier's* asking him to rush along twenty-five hundred words and offering twenty-five cents a word, the highest rate he'd ever been paid by a magazine. Brushing sentiment aside, he sat down and wrote the piece, beginning,

"San Francisco is gone. Nothing remains of it but memories and a fringe of dwelling-houses on its outskirts . . . Not in history has a modern imperial city been so completely destroyed . . ."

By midsummer he was hard at work on *The Iron Heel,* which has been called everything from a "blueprint for Fascism" (Maxwell Geismar) to "a forerunner of George Orwell's *1984*" (Max Lerner). It is now a literary curiosity, long out of print, but it was one of the most powerful and influential books written in its time.

From the prehistoric setting of *Before Adam* he moved to the future in *The Iron Heel,* which purported to be the manuscript left by Avis Everhard, wife of the Socialist leader, as a history of the imagined years when the Oligarchy crushed the Revolt of the People. He took his theme from W. J. Ghent's *Our Benevolent Feudalism,* published several years before, which foresaw the "complete integration of capital" into an iron-fisted dictatorship.

In his Marxist-oriented novel, still highly popular in Russia, Jack visualized what would happen when the Oligarchs took over the United States and crushed the Socialist opposition. His hero, Ernest Everhard, organized an underground army called the "Fighting Groups," which were "the one thorn in the side of the Iron Heel which the Iron Heel could never remove." (Everhard, of course, was patterned after the author, or what Jack imagined he would be as the leader of a Socialist counterrevolution. The love story in the novel was his and Charmian's. The scene of Everhard's last-ditch retreat was his ranch in the Valley of the Moon. As a literary Marxist Jack was a one-man cult of personality.)

One of the more stirring scenes was the confrontation of Everhard with the Oligarchs in their San Francisco headquarters. Everhard warns them that he has a following of twenty-five million militant proletarians ready to oppose the Oligarchy of finance and industry. "The cry of this army is: 'No quarter!' We want all that you possess. We will be content with nothing less than all you possess. We want in our hands the reins of power and the destiny of mankind. Here are our hands. They are strong hands. We are going to take your government, your palaces, and all your purpled ease away from you, and in that day you shall work for your bread even as the peasant in the field or the starved and runty clerk in your metropolises . . ."

To which one of the Oligarchy replies, "When you reach out your vaunted hands for our palaces and purple ease, we will show you what strength is. In the roar of shell and shrapnel and the whine of machine-guns will our answer be couched. We will grind your revolutionists down under our heel, and we shall walk upon your faces. The world is ours, we are its lords, and ours it shall remain . . ."

The Socialist counterrevolution goes down to bloody defeat, and the people are driven into serfdom, one of their tasks being the construction of the megalopolis of Asgard, which was completed in 1984—one wonders whether the date stuck in the memory of George Orwell, who read *The Iron Heel* as a boyhood admirer of London's and who considered his books not "well-written" but "well-told."

Avis Everhard's diary ends with the prediction that the "when the Great Revolt breaks out and all the world resounds with the tramp, tramp of millions," the Oligarchy will be overthrown and Socialism will triumph.

The Iron Heel, written with all the revolutionary fire and passion at his command, was published just after the panic of 1907 began and was not immediately a great success. Eventually it sold 66,928 copies in the U.S. hardcover edition. But its influence was far greater than any sales figures could indicate. A whole generation of revolutionaries was brought up on it. In his bibliography of Communist literature, the Russian intellectual Bukharin listed it as the only contribution by an American author. The late Aneurin Bevan, reading it as a boy miner in Wales, wrote in his autobiography that like "thousands of young men and women of the working class of Britain, and as I have learned since, of many other parts of the world," he was converted to Marxism by *The Iron Heel.*[15] Leon Trotsky affirmed that the novel impressed him deeply. "Not because of its artistic qualities: the form of the novel here represents only an armor for social analysis and prognosis. The author is intentionally sparing in his use of artistic means. He is himself interested not so much in the individual fate of his heroes as in the fate of mankind . . . The book surprised me with the audacity and independence of its historical foresight."

Anatole France wrote an introduction to the novel when it was published in France in 1923, praising London for "that particular genius which perceives what is hidden from the common herd" and for possessing "a special knowledge enabling him to anticipate the future."

France believed that one day what Jack predicted would come to pass and "then we will see days like those of the revolts in San Francisco and Chicago whose unspeakable horror Jack London anticipates for us."

In his own country *The Iron Heel* was roundly denounced by most reviewers, an exception being the Baltimore *Sun*'s, who hailed London as "one of the half-dozen Americans with the real story-telling gift." Even some of the Socialist periodicals were derogatory, the *Arena* commenting that his book, with its welter of bloody scenes, would discourage and dishearten the proletariat, and terming it "a detriment rather than a help to the cause of social justice." The *International Socialist Review* thought the book was "well calculated . . . to repel many whose addition to our forces is sorely needed."

Read today, with all its slanging matches between protagonist and Oligarch, it is largely an untempered melodrama peopled by characters who seem to have stepped out of pamphlets, posters and proclamations, ranting and firing papier-mâche machine guns but never coming to life. Perhaps it can happen here. If so, time has already withered its credibility, and it will be remembered only as a curiosity to be set alongside Orwell's much more impressive *1984*, which, if we are lucky, will seem just as much an oddity in 2007.

XI

Twenty-seven Months at Sea

1. *A Seagoing White Elephant*

EVERY logical consideration argued against his building a boat and sailing it around the world. As a writer at or approaching the peak of his powers, he could hardly benefit from an exhausting voyage planned to last seven years. Building the ranch required his close supervision if he did not want to be cheated. As a Socialist who proclaimed the "revolution is here, now," he was placing himself in danger of being called a deserter. As a permanent member of the debtor class, he could hardly spare the more than fifty thousand dollars the cruise was going to cost him, not to mention the incalculable price he would pay for the damage to his health.

None of these considerations, of course, was allowed to impinge upon his determination to undertake the long voyage. He would never check an impulse or quench a desire, no matter how wayward. "When philosophy has maundered ponderously for a month," he explained in *The Cruise of the Snark*, "telling the individual what he must do, the individual says, in an instant, 'I LIKE,' and does something else, and philosophy goes glimmering. It is the I LIKE that makes the drunkard drink and the martyr wear a hair shirt . . . The things I like constitute my set of values. The thing I like most of all is personal achievement . . . achievement for my own delight . . . I'd rather win a water-fight in a swimming pool, or remain astride a horse that is trying to get out from under me, than write the great American novel." Personal achievement, he explained, made him "glow all over. It is organic. Every fibre of me is thrilling with it. It is success."

A tragicomedy of errors, delays, work stoppages, suspected sabotage and swindlings that would have discouraged Columbus himself attended the building of his boat. The *Snark,* as he was to call her,* was being constructed at the water's edge at the foot of Broadway in Oakland. He designed her as a ketch, a craft midway between a yawl and a schooner, and she was to be forty-five feet long at the waterline. The aging Roscoe Eames was placed in charge of construction at sixty dollars a month with orders to spare no money in making the *Snark* as staunch and seaworthy as possible.

The first delay occurred the day the keel was to be laid, which happened to be the day the earthquake struck. From then on, month after month, it was one thing after another. Eames couldn't get along with the fourteen workmen initially hired to build the boat, and there were deliberate slowdowns.

Jack himself caused a number of delays, designing the *Snark* as he went along and thinking up improvements on each new addition. She was to have a seventy-horsepower engine imported from New York. She was equipped with a bathroom that was a seagoing marvel. She was also outfitted with a motor launch, four watertight compartments, Puget Sound planking for the deck to prevent leakage, and a bow designed so that no sea could break over it. It was the greatest toy of his life. On July 17, he wrote Brett that he was so busy with gasoline engines, electric lighting methods, ignition systems and other problems that he wouldn't be able to learn navigation until they put to sea.

As construction proceeded at Anderson's Ways, it became apparent that, as Jack himself said, she was "born unfortunately," by which he meant the timing was bad. If he had been less impatient, the *Snark* would have cost thousands less, and saved him much mental distress. Much of the material that went into her building ordinarily would have been procurable in San Francisco, but the earthquake had caused such shortages of everything used in construction that most of it had to be shipped from New York. And one shipment after another, coming into the tangle of backed-up freight in the Oakland yards, went astray or was shunted to a remote siding. A freight car loaded with oak ribs for the *Snark* arrived in Oakland the day after the quake; it took a month to be located.

Construction, being undertaken at a time when workmen were de-

* He took the name of the imaginary creature in Lewis Carroll's *The Hunting of the Snark,* unlikely though the choice of reading matter appears.

manding "earthquake wages," which must have given Jack second thoughts about the nobility of the common laborer, was so costly that he had to double up on his working schedule. In the mornings, when he was freshest, he turned out his thousand-word stint on *The Iron Heel.* In the afternoons he hacked away at magazine articles and stories.

He had announced that the *Snark* would sail on October 1, but by then the boat was only half finished. It was soaking up money faster than he could earn it. He mortgaged his ranch property at Glen Ellen, then his mother's house at Oakland.

He was also having his problems with Roscoe Eames. Charmian's uncle kept telling reporters that he was the captain of the *Snark,* while Jack insisted that, if he ever learned anything about the science of navigation, he would be co-navigator. Jack himself, the other co-navigator, had not even approached the task of educating himself in how to find his way across the sea. Finally, in December, he wrote Eames an exasperated letter demanding that he stop trying to take over the captaincy. Was Jack himself merely the financial angel of the voyage? No; Jack was paying the bills and Jack would be captain. Finally Eames had to be removed from his post as supervisor of the *Snark*'s construction because the workmen were at the point of mutiny over Eames's constant interference, and Jack had to take over that detail, too, commuting between his desk at Glen Ellen and the boatyard in Oakland.

Eames was instructed to put in all his time at learning navigation, but that didn't work out either. Uncle Roscoe, as Jack explained their divergence of opinion, insisted on ignoring Bowditch and following the navigational theories of one Cyrus R. Teed, who believed that the earth was concave and its people lived inside a hollow sphere. "Thus," Jack wrote in *The Cruise of the Snark,* "though we shall sail in one boat, the *Snark,* Roscoe will journey around the world on the inside, while I shall journey around on the outside."[11]

By New Year's Day, 1907, he had invested twenty thousand in the *Snark.* Two weeks earlier he had finished *The Iron Heel* and sent it off to Brett, who feared its reception, both from reviewers and readers, would be adverse. Brett predicted the press would "come down on the heads of author and publisher . . . but I will publish regardless of consequences."

Jack then plunged into writing *The Road,* an account of his experiences as a hobo, and this idea displeased Brett even more. Brett couldn't understand why Jack would want to revel publicly in the fact that he had once been on the bum; book buyers were generally middle-class, respectable people and would not be interested in the adventures of a hobo.* Jack, as usual, could not be swayed by his publisher's opinion, tactfully phrased though it was. He replied that he considered sincerity the cardinal literary virtue; hoboing had been part of his life, and he would write about it. If all else failed, if his public turned away from him in disgust, he added, he could always devote himself to farming.

Meanwhile, he was having trouble finding a sponsor to share the costs of his projected voyage. *Cosmopolitan* had tentatively offered to help pay for the boat if he would name it the *Cosmopolitan Magazine,* to which Jack agreed, gritting his teeth, then reneged on his agreement. In the end it was arranged that both *Cosmopolitan* and the *Woman's Home Companion* would publish the articles he would send back at stopping places on his voyage, the pieces later to be collected in *The Cruise of the Snark.*

During the early weeks of 1907 Jack stewed and fretted as construction proceeded at a creeping pace and the newspapers began questioning whether he would ever embark. The *Snark,* they said, was "London's Folly," "a sea-going white elephant." When the boat was finally ready for launching, she broke through her ways and sank in the mud at the estuary's edge. Trying to help the tugs haul her out of the mud, Jack started the engine, which promptly broke its cast-iron bedplate and crashed over on its side.

It was about this time Frank Pease and several other University of California students met Jack at a "beer bust" and next day were invited to have a look at his dream boat. He told them of his fears that the *Snark* was being sabotaged, though he could not assign any motive or name the perpetrators, as Pease recalled.[1]

Jack was always at his best with young men, to whom he seemed the epitome of masculinity and, as Pease observed, "the type of man to have commanded other men." His personality was that of "a Kitchener, a

* Brett's opinion was vindicated by the sales figures. *The Road* sold only 5814 copies. His public obviously was willing to accept him as a picturesque adventurer but not as a hobo.

von Hindenburg, a Stanley," with the power to "inflame youth, inspire men, madden women."

The most impressive thing about him, Pease thought, were his unforgettable, blazing, almost hypnotic eyes, "all steel and dew, all sweetness and hidden ferocity . . . eyes common enough, maybe, when the world was young . . . London's eyes changed with the changing color of his soul, and often seemed filled with the anguish of sins impossible to commit." Impressed though he was by the London personality and the vivid quality of his conversation, Pease remarked on his "deplorable modern habit of applying scientific principles to things that do not matter in the least." He also remembered the somehow disheartening way that Jack boasted to his youthful friends of having spent eighteen thousand dollars on the *Snark*'s engine alone, which was definitely an exaggeration.

People tried to persuade him to give up the voyage but he said he couldn't quit, he'd sail the *Snark* to Hawaii if it was the last thing he ever did. The ketch was finally hauled out of the mud and tied up at the Oakland City Wharf. From week to week the sailing date was postponed, shamefacedly, as the workmen labored to make her seaworthy. Finally Jack felt confident enough to announce that, no matter what else happened, they would embark on April 20.

In the freely offered opinion of the experts, the *Snark* would never make it to Hawaii. Arnold Genthe recalled that a group of naval officers discussing the boat at the Bohemian Club agreed that the *Snark* definitely wasn't seaworthy.

"He won't get as far as Hawaii," said a commander. "If he strikes the tail end of a typhoon, that boat will go down to the bottom like a flash."

"The boat may go down," Genthe said, "but Jack London never will." [2]

In the midst of all his vexations, Jack began to have trouble with Manyoungi, his Korean valet, who either had become Americanized too fast or had qualms about sailing with the Londons on a boat everybody said would probably founder a few miles outside the Golden Gate. Until now Manyoungi had always addressed Jack as "Master," which was mightily pleasing to his employer. Now he began calling Jack "Mr. London," and according to Charmian, "His bold black eyes and studiedly nonchalant tongue advertised bid upon bid for discharge." Jack managed to bear up for a time under being addressed merely as Mr. London, because Manyoungi had the "perfect spirit of service" and "could make both Charmian and me ready in half an hour for Timbucktoo," but his patience evaporated one evening when the Korean approached to ask what he would have for his nightcap.

"Will God have some beer?" the Korean asked.

Jack, Charmian said, looked as though he were going to spring out of his chair and assault his valet. One of Manyoungi's successors would address Jack as "Mr. God" without protest, but Jack wasn't in the mood for sacrilege at the moment.

"I don't want anything at all from you, Manyoungi," he finally replied. Next day the insolent young man was sent packing. His successor was a Japanese named Tochigi, who went along on the *Snark* as far as Honolulu, acting as cabin boy until chronic seasickness convinced him that it was time to begin his studies for the Episcopal clergy.

Despite all the publicity given the probable hazards of the voyage, thousands of people wrote Jack pleading to be taken along as part of his crew. Doctors, dentists, lawyers, reporters, students, teachers, engineers, machinists, retired sea captains, electricians and even a number of restless housewives begged to be signed on. The one crew member he needed was a cook, and after sorting through mounds of applicants' letters he found that he was most impressed by the seven-page appeal of a youth in Topeka, Kansas, named Martin Johnson, who wanted to see the world. Jack wired the youth asking whether he could cook. "Just try me," Johnson wired back. Sight unseen and culinary ability untested, he was engaged as the *Snark*'s cook and hastened to apprentice himself to a Greek restaurant in Topeka to learn his job before sailing time. Later Johnson became famous for his books and films about Africa.

Jack had already arranged with Herbert Stoltz, a husky Stanford University student, to act as the *Snark*'s engineer, although the boat's engine was useless and would have to be installed on a new bedplate when they reached Hawaii. Thus the *Snark*'s company would include Eames, as the unschooled navigator; Tochigi as cabin boy; Johnson, as cook; and Stoltz as engineless engineer. The only man aboard with real sailing experience was Jack himself, and he hadn't learned to navigate. Nor, it developed, had Eames. Little wonder that the experts considered the *Snark*'s voyage as fantastic as the expedition of Wynken, Blynken and Nod in their wooden shoe.

2. *Off to Hawaii*

The kinetic energy of Jack's enthusiasms in their early stages was always a wonder to behold. Perhaps it was that expenditure of power at the beginning of a project that invariably drained it of the will to proceed as planned: Jack racing Indian packers to the top of Chilkoot Pass, then returning home in defeat less than a year later without making any real effort to find the gold on which he had staked his stepsister's savings; Jack entering college with all the subjects they'd allow him to take, then dropping out after a semester; Jack rousing the fighting spirit of Socialists in the eastern cities, then returning to Glen Ellen to write for the *Woman's Home Companion*; Jack charging off to join Coxey's Army, then deserting it when they reached the Mississippi; his quick disillusionment as a war correspondent, as a husband, even as a writer. His novels, with the exception of *The Call of the Wild* and *Martin Eden,* reflected that same tendency toward initial enthusiasm followed, about halfway through, with a marked diminishing of creative power. Like a rocket, he always took off with a brilliant burst of exploding energy and burnt out just as he reached the top of his trajectory.

Only that quick-burning determination finally resulted in the *Snark*'s preparing to sail on April 20. It was a Saturday afternoon and the City Wharf was crowded with friends, well-wishers, the idly curious, reporters and photographers, all "thick as coal dust" and raucously enthusiastic about the supposed embarkation. But when Jack and his crew arrived to board her they were halted at the gangplank. A writ of attachment had been served by a United States Marshal on the claim of an Oakland grocer, who had less than perfect faith in the success of the voyage, that Jack owed him a $232 bill for provisions.

Jack reached into a pocket and wrote out a check on the spot, but was told that the writ couldn't be removed that simply. The writ had to be satisfied with due attention to all the legal formalities. That afternoon Jack, his friends and his lawyers chased all over San Francisco and Oakland trying to find the merchant, a federal judge, or the United States Marshal himself — anyone who could legally accept payment of the bill, revoke the writ and allow the *Snark* to sail with the tide. None of those persons could be located, however, because it was a Saturday afternoon.

Fuming with rage and frustration, Jack was forced to wait until Monday before the amenities could be observed, the writ lifted and the red tape unsnarled. Meanwhile, he could read the jibes of his newspaper friends in the Sunday papers.

Finally, on Tuesday morning, April 23, the *Snark* cast off her lines, lifted her anchor and sailed out the Bay and into the open sea. Plowing westward over choppy seas, the *Snark* and its crew found it heavy going at the outset. After serving dinner that evening, Tochigi brought out his flute, as Martin Johnson recalled, "played the most mournful piece I have ever heard and as the last note died away rushed precipitately up on the deck and relieved his deathly sickness at the rail. Mrs. London speedily joined him."*

On the morning of the second day at sea, Johnson recounted, Jack was the only person aboard who had any stomach for breakfast, which amused him no end.

Noting Johnson's greenish pallor on deck that morning, Jack told him with a fiendish smile, "Never mind, Martin, we are not over two miles from land."

"Which way?" the young landlubber eagerly asked.

"Straight down, Martin, straight down."

In the next few days, with the sea fortunately calm, Jack and his crew discovered that things were even worse than they had suspected on departure. The *Snark*'s specially designed and much-prized bow wouldn't heave to properly, the lifeboat leaked, the anchor had to be worked by hand, the motor launch's engine wouldn't turn over, the fresh fruits and vegetables had turned rotten and had to be thrown overboard, the kindling wouldn't burn in the galley stove, the kerosene had leaked all over the more durable vegetables, and the expensive Puget Sound planking on the deck leaked, almost washing Roscoe Eames out of his bunk, where the nominal navigator was lurking with an asserted case of constipation. Martin Johnson, the cook, and Togi-

* It was observations of that sort, undoubtedly, which caused Charmian to denounce his book as inaccurate and presumptuous. She was also irked, judging from letters she wrote Brett at Macmillan, by the fact that Johnson published his account of the voyage, *Through the South Seas with Jack London* [Dodd, Mead], before she finished hers. That made three published accounts of the *Snark*'s cruise. Rarely has one small boat contained so many historians.

chi, the cabin boy, suffered so horribly from seasickness that they too were confined to their bunks. Jack had to take over the cooking as well as sailing the boat with Charmian's and Herbert Stoltz's assistance.

It didn't help that Eames's ability to navigate, despite the study he had undertaken at Jack's expense, turned out to be nil. He was, Jack wrote, "filled with incommunicable information." So Jack taught himself navigation on the spot. "One whole afternoon I sat in the cockpit, steering with one hand and studying logarithms with the other. Two afternoons, two hours each, I studied the general theory of navigation and the particular process of taking a meridian altitude. Then I took the sextant, worked out the index error, and shot the sun. The figuring from the data of this observation was child's play."

Sailing a leaky boat with a crew half seasick and half incompetent should have been enough to occupy any skipper, but as the *Snark* furrowed its way toward Hawaii at a six-knot clip Jack began blocking out in his mind a novel of greater personal interest than any he had written thus far. It would be largely autobiographical, and as he subsequently wrote Pinker, his English agent, it would run about 142,000 words. His title preferences were (1) *Success,* (2) *Star-Dust* and (3) *Martin Eden.* Far from the mean streets in which his novel took place, with the deck of his own twenty-five-thousand-dollar boat beneath him, he relived and re-created the years of his youth. It would not be a very cheerful book, any more than his life had been a happy one. Nor could he convince himself that Martin Eden, given the facts of his existence, would come to a happy end. Looking back on his struggles, Jack could only wonder, as he wrote, whether they had been worth the trouble. Success had a sour aftertaste. All he had waiting for him back in the States was an anxious entourage of dependents. If the *Snark* foundered, their bitterest grief would be for the loss of income. This boat, slung together at three times what it should have cost, was a fair representation of what the world thought of him — somebody to be bled for his last dollar. No, Martin Eden would come to grief, and so probably would his creator.

Twenty-seven days after they left San Francisco, the voyagers aboard the *Snark* made their first landfall, the summit of Haleakala on the island of Oahu. Next day they rounded Diamond Head and sailed into Honolulu harbor. A launch from the Hawaiian Yacht Club came out to greet them, its delegation bringing newspapers from the States which published reports that the *Snark* had gone down with all aboard.

Hawaiian hospitality overwhelmed them. Jack and Charmian were given the use of a cottage on the island of Hilo, were dined and entertained every night and invited to a reception given by Queen Liliuokalani. He fished by torchlight with a prince of the blood, watched a cattle drive on a ranch on Maui, and rode the breakers on a surfboard.

For twelve days he caught up on his magazine writing, turning out articles for *Cosmopolitan* and the *Woman's Home Companion* and one masterly short story, "To Build a Fire," with a Klondike setting.

On the thirteenth day he went back out to see how the *Snark* and its several crew members were doing. Very little, it seemed, but sunning themselves. Stoltz and Eames had neglected to hose down the decks and care for the gear, with the result that both were rotting. He discharged both men and sent them back to San Francisco. Stoltz, in any case, would have had to return in a few months to resume his studies at Stanford. Sending old Uncle Roscoe back to Glen Ellen and Aunt Netta, a failure once again, was harder, but he was deadweight as far as sailing a boat was concerned. Jack had been especially irked to discover that most of the provisions Eames had bought for the galley were the canned health foods he himself fancied. The return of Eames and Stoltz, of course, provided more grist for the newspaper's rumor mills. The newspapers, Jack wrote in an afterword to *The Cruise of the Snark,* simply couldn't tell the truth about the voyage. "When I discharged an incompetent captain, they said I had beaten him to a pulp. When one young man returned home to continue at college, it was reported that I was a regular Wolf Larsen, and that my whole crew had deserted because I had beaten it to a pulp."

While the *Snark* was being repaired and its engine installed on a new bedplate, he and Charmian toured the islands. Their most memorable experience was visiting the leper colony on the island of Molokai, to which all those stricken with leprosy in the islands were sent after being examined by a board of five physicians in Honolulu. Leprosy then was the most dread disease known to humanity, and the colony at Molokai, whose saintly Father Damien had died after contracting the malady, was generally regarded as a lazaretto of unspeakable horrors.

From what they had read, Jack and Charmian expected to find Molokai an island of despair, at best, but were surprised to find it a rather cheerful place. A newspaper writer cited by Jack had recently described — without ever having visited the island — how the superintendent of the colony was nightly besieged in his grass hut by hundreds of lepers wailing for food. They found that the superintendent lived in a wooden cottage and that there wasn't a grass shack on the island. As the superintendent's guest for five days, they watched the brass band and singing societies rehearse, other lepers playing baseball, working farms, going out on fishing boats.

A marine engineer who was installing a steam laundry on the island begged Jack, "For heaven's sake write us up straight. Put your foot down on this chamber-of-horrors rot and all the rest of it. We don't like being misrepresented. We've got some feelings. Just tell the world how we really are here."

Jack did just that, as always at his best when dealing with the outcasts of the world because he identified himself with them.[3]

His article was credited with accomplishing much in changing the medieval attitude toward lepers still prevalent in the world. One of its more effective passages described a match held at the Molokai Rifle Club, with lepers and non-lepers among the contestants. Jack, Charmian and two resident physicians handled the same rifles as the lepers, which he offered as proof that leprosy wasn't as contagious as popularly believed. Most of the lepers shooting for the silver cup were Hawaiians but there was also a Norwegian and a Confederate veteran of the Civil War among them.

Leprosy had to be segregated, he explained, but it was not the "horrible nightmare" described by sensational journalists. "Leprosy," he wrote, "is terrible, but from what little I know about the disease I would by far prefer to spend the rest of my days on Molokai than in any tuberculosis sanitarium."

3. *Across the Pacific*

On October 7, the *Snark* had been refitted, pronounced seaworthy and manned by several new crew members, so Jack and company lifted anchor for the South Seas. Earlier, he had managed to extract a five-thousand-dollar advance from Macmillan to cover the cost of repairs.

Shortly before sailing he wrote Brett that he had rid himself of the last personal friend who would ever sail with him. Recruiting a captain, even on an impersonal basis, had proved bothersome. A Captain Rosehill, called Raisehell by the crew, had tried to fire Martin Johnson on a charge of mutiny and himself had been discharged by Jack after he rammed the *Snark* into an interisland steamer on her shakedown cruise. Another licensed captain named Warren was engaged to help Jack navigate and a Dutch youth named Hermann was hired to help with the sails. Tochigi had decided to return to the States and take up the ministry; he was replaced by a Hawaiian-born Japanese boy named Yoschimatsu Nakata, who was to stay with Jack and Charmian for years.

They were at sea several days before Jack ventured a look at the sailing directions for the South Pacific, upon which he learned that the voyage to the Marquesas on which they were embarked was all but impossible if dependent only on sail power. They had already discovered that the newly installed engine would not turn over properly, which left them at the mercy of the winds. Jack was surprised if not mortified to read that the prevailing winds at this season would be of little help. "There is great difficulty in making this passage against the trades. The whalers and all others speak with great doubt of fetching Tahiti from the Sandwich Islands [Hawaii]."

For days they were becalmed. From October 7 to December 6, their first landfall, they traveled almost four thousand miles, though the distance from Hawaii to the Marquesas was only half that on a straight line. They caught at every breath of wind. Sometimes a brief but violent storm would carry them miles off course. In addition, they had to buck the north equatorial current. According to the *Snark*'s log, she made forty miles westward one day (October 11) and four miles *eastward* another (October 17). It was a jigsaw course dictated by the whims of nature; they were "wedged between the trades and the doldrums."

One day they actually made 103 miles "Westing" and rejoiced in their full sails and foaming wake.

Not for many years had any boat depending solely on sail power attempted that traverse. It was one of the loneliest stretches of the vast ocean and in two months they never sighted another vessel. A disabled ship, Jack said, could drift in that area "for a dozen generations" without being rescued. For the seven persons aboard the *Snark* the memory of land "became like dreams of former lives we had lived somewhere before we came to be born on the *Snark*." Yet they could rejoice in the absence of all the world's intrusions, telephones and telegrams, newspapers, guests for dinner, creditors and advice-seekers bearing manuscripts — or at least Jack could. He insisted that life was not dull even in the doldrums. They fished, told stories, read aloud from Melville and Conrad. And ahead, particularly for Jack, was Nuku-hiva, the scene of *Typee,* which had so enthralled him as a boy reading his way through the shelves of the Oakland Public Library.

Almost every day Jack worked away at the novel which became *Martin Eden*. It was now titled *Success,* ironically, since it was the story of the tragic failure of what man called success. Except on bad days, when rain squalls buffeted the *Snark,* he still averaged his thousand daily words.

Some days they would be caught in the windless doldrums and lie all but motionless in the leaden water for twelve to twenty hours. Others they would be struck by violent squalls, each of which, he said, had to be regarded as potentially capable of wrecking their boat.

The water supply was running so low that it had to be rationed out every morning, one quart to each person aboard and eight quarts to the cook. He noted that as soon as the water shortage became apparent everyone developed a burning thirst. "All of us talked water, thought water, and dreamed water when we slept." Martin Johnson, he observed, would drink his whole quart of water in one feverish gulp as soon as he received his ration.

Even in such straits, Johnson noted, the writer in Jack existed on a plane above the privations of the flesh. In a notable instance of how Jack used the raw material of life, seizing on the immediacy of experience, detachedly considering his own suffering only as an element to be fused into his work, Johnson recalled one day during the drought: "Almost dead with thirst himself, he went into his cabin and wrote a sea story about a castaway sailor that died of thirst in an open boat. And when he finished it, he came out, gaunt and haggard but with eyes burning with enthusiasm, and told us of the story . . ." Later when rain replenished their water supply, in the midst of general rejoicing, Jack was still thinking of that story and said, "I'll not kill that sailor [in his story]; I'll have him saved by a rain like this; that'll make the yarn better than ever!" [4]

Food, at least, was no problem. All they had to do was drop a hook over the side and haul in the fish. The most delicious, they agreed, was a snakelike fish, three feet long, with four fangs in its jaw, which no one had heard of before. Another delicacy was the green deep-sea turtle, weighing a hundred pounds, which they converted into steaks, soups, stews and finally a magnificent curry.

On November 26, they finally caught a trade wind which whipped them along to the southeast under a clear sky with spinnaker and mainsail bellied out. Ten days later they passed to the leeward of Ua-huka, in the Marquesas, and fought their way through squalls into the narrow harbor of Taiohae. It was nightfall by the time they dropped anchor. From the cliffs above they heard the bleating of wild goats, and the air was heavy with the scent of tropical flowers.

Here on Nuka-hiva was the valley of Typee, the scene of Melville's novel, which Jack had dreamed of visiting for almost twenty years.

When they awakened the morning after their arrival, they found themselves in "a placid harbor that nestled in a vast amphitheatre, the towering, vine-clad walls of which seemed to rise directly above the water."

They spent the first day finding their land legs, renting a house said to have been occupied once by Robert Louis Stevenson, and finding horses for a journey inland. The second day they set out for the valley along a climbing jungle trail, entranced along the way by a moss-grown stone idol, a feast to which they were invited by a Marquesan tribe (Jack seemed a trifle disappointed that "long pig" had disappeared from the menu, and in his article "Typee" [5] included a dissertation on cannibalism as locally practiced), by wasps the size of canaries which sent them pell-mell up the trail.

Finally they reached a crest from which they could see the *Snark* anchored in the sleeve-like harbor far below, the deep indentation of Comptroller Bay ahead, and finally the valley of Typee, dropping off a thousand feet.

The valley, which Melville had described as an Eden of fertility, peopled by a strong and graceful race of warriors, was a shocking disappointment. No breadfruit plantations, no orderly rows of grass huts, no warriors on guard with club and javelin to confront the intruders. Jack felt like weeping: all that great valley had been reclaimed by the jungle.

As for the people who survived — once so ferocious that when the French fleet landed in the harbor below, they didn't dare extend their conquest to the valley of Typee — they were human wreckage. Many were lepers, many suffered from elephantiasis, and all were tubercular. Jack saw only a dozen of them, though once the population of the valley, according to Melville's estimate, had been two thousand. Jack mourned that "all this strength and beauty has departed . . . Life has rotted away in this wonderful garden spot . . ."

They spent twelve days on the island, hunting and fishing with the natives, attending feasts and dances, and noting that about all the white man had brought to the Marquesas was disease and an infiltration of his own blood. Most of the natives were part English, French, Danish or German. The slightest exertion caused them to cough and wheeze and moan, so wasted were their lungs from the tuberculosis brought by their white antecedents. As they slept in the native village, Jack said, "all about us the dying islanders coughed in the night."

From the miseries of Nuka-hiva they sailed for the more cheerful atmosphere of Tahiti, reaching Papeete shortly before New Year's, 1908. And there, in the ten weeks of mail which had been forwarded in boxes, awaited all the complications and vexations of his life back in the States. Everything seemed to have gone wrong back home. His finances were a mess; the bank had foreclosed its mortgage on his mother's home, acting on reports that the *Snark* had been lost at sea; eight hundred dollars' worth of checks he had cashed in Hawaii had been rejected by his Oakland bank with the laconic "Not Sufficient Funds" stamped on them; his train of dependents was wailing for support. What the hell had happened? There should have been enough money coming in from his magazine articles and his books, four of them published in 1907,* and *White Fang* still a best-seller.

On leaving the States, he had acted wisely, he thought, in making Mother Mine — Charmian's Aunt Netta — his business manager and disbursing agent. She was given his power of attorney, was to receive all moneys due him and have complete control over his affairs. One

* *Love of Life, Before Adam, The Road* and *The Iron Heel.*

week before leaving on the *Snark,* in fact, Jack had been outraged when Brett started sending Macmillan checks to Mrs. Eames with "For deposit only to the account of Jack London" stamped on the back. Brett, of course, had been trying to protect his interests, but Jack sternly informed his publisher that all checks were to be made out to Mrs. Eames personally and without any rubber-stamped qualifications.

Now it seemed that he was not only broke — a chronic state with him — but his checks were bouncing all over the Pacific.

There was nothing to do but interrupt his cruise and take Charmian back to the States with him on a thirty-day round trip aboard the *Mariposa,* which would be sailing in a few days.

4. *Meanwhile, Back at the Ranch . . .*

Only two days after the *Snark* sailed, Mrs. Eames wrote Brett asking Macmillan to send a five-hundred-dollar advance to cover "small bills" Jack had left behind — this at a time when five hundred dollars was the average annual wage in the United States.

She also immediately, without consulting Jack, raised her monthly stipend from ten dollars to twenty dollars, and later to thirty dollars, which she received in addition to forty dollars a month for rooms at Wake Robin Lodge which he was not occupying.

As Jack learned on arrival in San Francisco aboard the *Mariposa* — an event made lively by the clamor of reporters who demanded to know whether it was true that he was giving up on the *Snark,* that the whole thing had been a publicity stunt, and so forth, all of which he hotly denied — Mrs. Eames had disbursed his money with a liberal hand. In the past December alone, she had paid out fourteen hundred dollars for the support of his various relatives and dependents, to buy supplies for his own ranch and take care of the upkeep on Wake Robin Lodge. She had also spent one thousand dollars for an annex at the Hill Ranch, his own property, to provide quarters for the foreman and his wife. Additionally, there was the one thousand dollars a month it cost him to operate the *Snark.* From Macmillan alone, in December, he had received fifty-five hundred dollars in royalties, and yet he was deep in debt.

Going over the correspondence with Macmillan's, he learned that on October 24, Mrs. Eames had asked Brett for a five-hundred-dollar advance because there were "more bills from Hawaii than I can meet."

Brett had refused because of the bank failures attending the financial panic and his own firm's shortage of cash. "You may perhaps recollect Mr. London recently received from us full payment of the amount that we were owing him," Brett wrote her. On November 4, Mrs. Eames wrote the publisher that she must "urge the serious embarrassment I am under." Brett finally offered his company's note for five hundred dollars, but instead, on December 2, had sent her a five-hundred-dollar advance on royalties.

From all this mass of bills and correspondence, Jack gathered it wouldn't be easy to straighten out his finances. A reporter who interviewed him noted that "The smile that won't come off doesn't half express the London smile" — but it was all a brave front.

For the time being he solved matters by informing Brett that 120,000 words of *Martin Eden* had been completed and received from Macmillan's a five-thousand-dollar advance. This he used to save his mother's home from foreclosure and to pay off most of his accrued liabilities. Current expenses would be taken care of by a series of travel articles which *Harper's Weekly* agreed to publish sight unseen.

Financially he was still dancing on the verge of bankruptcy, and it would have been far wiser to stay home awhile longer and make sure of the immediate future, but he couldn't stand the thought of what the newspapers would say if he didn't return to Papeete on the *Mariposa's* return voyage. And besides he had been happier in the South Seas than ever before. So he finished work on *Martin Eden* on shipboard [6] and was looking forward eagerly to a reunion with the *Snark*. He felt a lot safer on the deck of his ketch, he added, than on the streets of San Francisco.

And while he returned to his adventuring, leaving his affairs once again in Mrs. Eames's hands, the commerical side of his career suffered accordingly. Mrs. Eames peddled his manuscripts in batches instead of sending them out one at a time and holding out for a decent price. He had been receiving five hundred dollars or more for an article, but now the market was glutted with London stuff and editors first beat down the price, then stopped buying. Meanwhile, she kept sending Jack letter after letter complaining how hard her life was and saying that she didn't see how she was going to keep her head above water. Roscoe Eames was a liability (she soon divorced him and married Payne). Finally Jack wrote her to draw on his account at the Bank of Oakland, not realizing how she would take advantage of it. She siphoned thousands of dollars out of his account for doctors' bills, medicines, grocers' bills, clothing, furniture and repairs for Wake Robin Lodge. Later in 1908 she stopped sending him accounts, despite his agonized pleas for word on how he stood financially.

He was used to being tapped, but no one had ever been quite so relentless as "Mother Mine." What would really have irked him was the way she handled the matter of serializing *Martin Eden*. He was pleased, of course, and more than pleasantly surprised, when she managed to wangle seven thousand dollars for the first serial rights out of the *Pacific Monthly*, which had been publishing some of his travel pieces. She also took it upon herself to attempt censoring the manuscript, strictly without his permission. On July 24, she wrote Brett that Charles H. Jones, manager of the *Pacific Monthly*, objected to Chapter 23 in the novel because it was "a covert attack on the *Overland Monthly*." Just why Jones should be exercised over a thinly veiled account of Jack's troubles getting money out of Roscoe Eames and Edward Payne, she did not explain, but it was obvious enough why *she* should want to see it eliminated.

"Our Jack," she wrote Brett, "has obviously made a free and, I fear, ill-considered use of the license of fiction in this case."

Brett agreed that Jack had perhaps been a little hard on the *Overland Monthly*, but tactfully pointed out that he had no right to cut anything from the author's manuscript — a not too subtle suggestion that Mrs. Eames should also refrain from chopping out a part of his story. "I do not think," Brett wrote her on July 29, "that I could very well take up with Mr. London this matter of its revision as, whenever I have in the past suggested to Mr. London changes in his work, he has not been willing . . . to consider the matter at all favorably . . . I feel quite sure that his attitude toward my suggestions in relation to his work is unfriendly, if not actually hostile."

The seven thousand dollars Jack received from the *Martin Eden* serialization would have pulled him out of debt, but just then Mrs. Eames heard that the Lamotte property adjoining the Hill Ranch was for sale and could be bought for ten thousand dollars. Jack already had 129 acres, but the Lamotte Ranch's 110 acres included redwood groves and green valleys he had often coveted. Instead of keeping a cushion against reverses, Jack told Mrs. Eames to make a down payment of three thousand dollars on the Lamotte property. As a man who made his living at writing, he certainly didn't need any more real estate, but when he returned to Glen Ellen he wanted plenty of his own space around him. He already had his eye on the Kohler Ranch, which also adjoined his, despite an asking price of thirty thousand dollars for its 800 acres. If he had to live ashore from time to time, he could only see himself as a member of the landed gentry.

5. *Among the Headhunters*

On returning to Papeete, Jack and Charmian sailed the *Snark* to Bora-Bora, then to Pago Pago, where he was the guest of Polynesian royalty, then to Suva in the Fiji islands. By then he had suffered all he could take of Captain Warren's violent tantrums. Until the last leg of the voyage Warren had performed capably enough. Then he twice went berserk and had to be forcibly subdued.

During one fit of temper, Martin Johnson related, Captain Warren broke the cook's nose and would have inflicted similar damage on Nakata if Charmian hadn't stopped him.* Furthermore it irked Jack that on the voyage from Samoa to Fiji, Warren was unable to point out the *Snark*'s location on her navigational charts when Jack asked for such information. Like most South Seas skippers, Johnson said, he sailed by dead reckoning. And when they reached Suva, Warren compounded his crimes by going on an epic bender ashore.

Taking care of one captain on a small boat, Jack wrote in "The Amateur Navigator," was more trouble than looking after any two small children. "The first captain was so senile as to be unable to give a measurement for a boom-jaw to a carpenter," he said, referring to Roscoe Eames. "So utterly agedly helpless was he, that he was unable to order a sailor to throw a few buckets of salt water on the *Snark's* deck . . . It cost me $135 to recalk it. The second captain [Rosehill] was angry. 'Papa is always angry,' was the description given him by his half-breed son." [7] Warren, as it developed, not only exploded in violent rages but had a hankering for the bottle that made it necessary to keep a close watch on the liquor supply. Although rarely an abstainer on land or sea, he was not overly sympathetic toward the hired help's liquor problems.

* Johnson had been replaced as cook when the *Snark* left Tahiti and was now serving as a deckhand.

From now on, he vowed, he would sail the *Snark* without any supposedly professional navigator aboard. The only available men were on the beach, drunks and incompetents—"the sort of man who beats about for a fortnight trying vainly to find an ocean isle and who returns with his schooner to report the island sunk with all on board."

They sailed from Suva on June 6, once again relying on Jack's self-taught navigation, heading for the Solomons. It was not the place for a pleasure cruise. Armed steamers roved the islands "recruiting"—the Australian euphemism for slaving—native labor for the copra plantations. Many of the Solomon islanders were headhunting sportsmen who kept shrunken heads in their huts. An islander with fifteen heads forming a triumphant frieze around his walls was believed to have acquired the strength of the fifteen men he had slain—and a white man's head was regarded as an especially magical trophy. Despite the value of their heads as trophies, the natives resented the incursions of the white men. In addition the islands were rotten with a variety of tropical diseases, leprosy, malaria, elephantiasis, ringworm, skin ulcers, dengue and blackwater fever.

As an illustration of the perils of life among the Solomon islanders, Jack in later years would often tell of a missionary who was stationed on one of the islands where cannibalism was prevalent. On a journey inland, he was captured by a man-eating tribe, and judging by their menacing appearance he was prepared to end his career as part of a native ragout. Instead, the chief released him on one condition: that he carry a small package to the chief of a mountain tribe some miles away. On the way to carry out this mission, he came across a detachment of sailors from a British warship. They tried to persuade him to accompany them to a safer place, but he stiffly informed the landing party that he was a man of his word and would complete his mission. Just as he was about to continue on his way, an officer from the cruiser arrived and insisted on opening the packet the missionary was carrying. Out tumbled a handful of onions and a note to the mountain chief.

"The bearer," it read, "will be delicious with these."

At Penduffryn on Guadalcanal they met a Captain Jansen of the *Minota*, a teak-hulled converted yacht with barbed wire strung around the stanchions of her deck to discourage hostile boarding parties, which cruised the coast of Malaita picking up plantation labor.

"Why not come along?" asked Captain Jansen. Jack and Charmian nodded eagerly.

"You'd better bring your revolvers along," Jansen added thoughtfully, "and a couple of rifles."

Off they steamed along the savage coast. It wasn't until a day or two later, studying the treacherous, mangrove-studded coastline from the *Minota*'s rail, that Jack thought to ask what would happen if they went aground.

"She's not going ashore," Jansen snapped.

"But just in case she did?"

"We'd get into that whaleboat and get out of there as fast as God would let us."

Captain Jansen explained that in case of mishap he couldn't trust his native crew much farther than the headhunters who lurked in the jungle along the shore.

At first the recruiting mission was a failure. Too many natives had heard of working conditions on the plantations, and were not eager to sign on for three years' labor at six pounds (thirty dollars) a year.

One night, lying in close to shore, they amused themselves by dynamiting fish. Attracted by the explosions, the natives ashore suddenly attacked them with darts, bows and arrows and spears, causing a hasty departure. Day after day went by, and "the *Minota* got no recruits from the bush, and the bushmen got no heads from the *Minota*." But Jack reveled in the constant danger, he was never happier than with the smell of death all around him, and Charmian stood up gallantly to all the tests.

By this time they all suffered from yaws, large skin ulcers that began festering as soon as a mosquito bite was scratched or the slightest cut was left untended, and which Jack treated with corrosive sublimate. Then Charmian came down with Solomon fever, a form of malaria, and had to be packed in blankets and dosed with quinine.

Several days later they entered the anchorage off Malu, which was protected by a narrow, jagged coral reef with an entrance that was treacherous to negotiate, particularly on leaving the anchorage. A party from the *Minota* went ashore, having sighted the beacon fire which signaled the recruiting ship that a number of natives were willing to work on a plantation, and brought seven recruits back to the ship. At that point the *Minota* had only one anchor left, two having been lost along the way at Tulagi. The *Minota* hauled up its anchor and swung around, heading for the exit through the reef. Just as she was about to clear the menacing coral, the wind suddenly changed direction and drove the yacht toward the reef. The sole remaining anchor was let go, but its chain broke just as it hit bottom. Swinging around as though on a pivot, the *Minota* plunged into the breakers and went hard aground.

As the ship rolled and pounded against the coral, Captain Jansen and his crew broke out the rifles, knowing that the helpless vessel would soon be under attack from all directions. Several months before the schooner *Ivanhoe* had run aground down the coast, its crew was forced to flee in the whaleboats and the ship was picked clean by the natives inside an hour.

Within a few minutes, "like vultures circling down out of the blue, canoes began to arrive from every quarter. The boat's crew, with rifles at the ready, kept them lined up a hundred feet away with a promise of death if they ventured nearer. And there they clung . . . black and ominous, crowded with men." Meanwhile on shore the natives flocked down from the hills armed with bows and arrows, clubs, spears and rifles, until there were almost a thousand massed on the beach.

The *Minota*'s crew, under cover of the riflemen on the boat, went ashore for tree trunks to protect her keel and bilges against the jagged reef.

Jack paddled off in a canoe with a message for the captain of the *Eugenie* anchored five miles away but out of sight around a bend in the coastline. He took the message to a missionary named Caulfield, who had come out from the village in a whaleboat when he saw the *Minota* run aground. The missionary was shouting to the natives in the canoes:

"I know what you think. You think plenty tobacco on the boat and you're going to get it. I tell you plenty of rifles on the boat. You get no tobacco, you get bullets!"

Mr. Caulfield was persuaded to take the message to the *Eugenie* in his whaleboat.

Three hours later Captain Keller of the *Eugenie* arrived in his own whaleboat with his fully armed crew and the anchors and hawsers the *Minota* had asked for. "The white man," said Jack later, "the inevitable white man, coming to the white man's rescue."

While the *Eugenie*'s crew and some of Mr. Caulfield's "mission boys" stood guard, the *Minota*'s crew labored to extricate her from the reef. Mr. Caulfield and some of his converts prayed in the *Minota*'s cabin as the boat reeled under the pounding of the surf. Jack recalled it as an impressive scene, "the unarmed man of God praying with cloudless faith, his savage followers leaning on their rifles and mumbling amens."

That night, more than twelve hours after the *Minota* had foundered, there was a great stirring among the natives massed on the beach and it looked as though there might be a general assault on the boat. A member of the crew named Ugi was assigned to harangue them from a whaleboat on the foolishness of such a move. "You kill my captain," shouted Ugi, "I drink his blood and die with him!"

The natives were sufficiently impressed to leave the *Minota* alone and burn one of Mr. Caulfield's mission buildings as an expression of disgust.

After three days and two more tense nights, the *Minota* was finally yanked off the reef and anchored in the smoother water up the coast, her teak hull still sound but much of her insides wrecked by the pounding.

Jack and Charmian sailed off with the *Eugenie* and returned to the *Snark*. They continued cruising the Solomons, though all were afflicted with yaws and sometimes all but one or two were down with malaria. Except when he was too ill with malaria, Jack kept to his writing schedule, producing a novel titled *Adventure*,[8] which detailed with brutal realism the life on a copra plantation in the Solomons, and a number of short stories — few of them in his best manner — with a South Seas background. The stories were later collected in *When God Laughs, The Night Born* and *The Human Drift*. It was evident from their content that Jack was more at home as a writer in the sub-Arctic than in the tropics.

While they were heading from Meringe Lagoon to Lord Howe Island, Jack began suffering from a mysterious skin ailment which was not only exceedingly painful but caused the skin on his hands to peel off layer by layer. At the same time he was seized by a nervous condition which sometimes caused him to stagger and fall on deck. Charmian and the others were ill, exhausted and covered with skin ulcers. The *Snark* had turned into a floating hospital.

Jack decided the cruise would have to be abandoned. The *Snark* was placed in the custody of a retired sea captain, and its crew boarded a steamer bound for Sydney, Australia. After twelve days at sea, they arrived in Sydney and Jack checked into a hospital with his hands swollen to twice their normal size — ten layers of skin had peeled off — and with his toenails growing an inch every twenty-four hours until they were pared off.

He lay in a hospital bed for five weeks while tropical-disease specialists studied his case and admitted their bafflement. Their only conclusion was that the malady was non-parasitic, their only hope that it would clear up by itself in a less savage environment. Jack and Charmian spent five months in Australia, living in an apartment, while he continued as an outpatient at the hospital.

Unable to work because of the racking and continuous pain, he decided that they would have to give up their plans for cruising around the world and return to California, telling Martin Johnson, "It is plain that we are not wanted in the South Seas. California is the place for me." In March, 1909, he sent Johnson and a navigator to bring the *Snark* to Sydney, where it was auctioned off for a mere three thousand dollars, though it had cost him ten times that amount to build and refit, and soon it was plying the Solomons in the labor-recruiting traffic.

On returning from Lord Howe Island with the *Snark,* Johnson went to visit Jack and Charmian at the St. Malo Hospital in Ridge Street, North Sydney. From their conversation he noted an apparent division of opinion on Jack's insistence that the round-the-world cruise be abandoned. Jack emphasized that writing was his profession, his life, and he could not pursue it without returning to California. Charmian, however, "felt so bad she could scarcely speak of the *Snark.*" [9] Abandoning the cruise was the most crushing blow of their marital life; she had reveled in the hardships and dangers even more exuberantly than Jack, which may secretly have annoyed him since he considered himself the foremost adventurer of modern times.

Life was never quite as glowing to Charmian after Jack's illness forced them to abandon the *Snark.* It would have been more tactful for her to have made a show of feminine weakness over giving up the venture, but she couldn't pretend, even though she must have realized he hated to be bested in anything, including the zest for living dangerously. It was a tiny crack in the façade of their romantic legend, so sedulously fostered and embellished, but it would widen.

On July 23, 1909, with Jack still ill, weary and disillusioned, they returned to San Francisco with Nakata. Martin Johnson made it around the world, though he had to work his way as an electrician in Luna Park in Paris and stow away on a cattle boat from Liverpool to Boston, the beginning of an adventurous career. For Jack, on the whole, it had been a costly experience; nothing he published after it quite came up to his pre-*Snark* standards. He had lost his dream of a primitive paradise in the South Seas — the diseased natives, the debased and predatory white men, the rotting jungles, the bloodthirsty howls of the headhunters, the slavery of the copra plantations were its reality. He was badly in debt and had to face up to the fading popularity of his work; the magic had gone out of his byline, and writing had become a worse drudgery than ever before.

On leaving the ship, he told reporters he was "unutterably weary" and only wanted a good rest. The "ineradicable" smile, they observed, was gone; it would never reappear in all its former incandescence. Six months of brooding semi-invalidism in Australia, mixed in with a certain inescapable amount of self-pity, had taught him what he could never believe before, that Jack London was not indestructible. All men learn that at some point in their lives — the "intimation of mortality" — but it was a crushing discovery for a man who atavistically gloried in his strength and who said he would rather win a water fight in a swimming pool than write the great American novel.

BOOK THREE

The Valley

XII

Another Heir Is Apparent

1. *"What Is Plagiarism?"*

AMONG the vexations that awaited Jack's return to the mainland, minor but nonetheless troubling, was another charge of plagiarism. He was beginning to feel that he was a prime target for bruised sensibilities in the literary world. Previously he had weathered similar accusations — those connected with *The Call of the Wild* and *Before Adam* — by admitting that he had used the books in question as nonfictional research which was transmuted into fiction. No one could legitimately deny a novelist the privilege of basing his stories on facts obtained by reading other men's work; in any case the material was processed and refined for his own creative purposes, and the copyright protection of ideas or theories is something less than rigorous.

The newest charge of larceny was caused by a passage in *The Iron Heel* and involved a highly inflammable literary personage named Frank Harris, an Anglo-American almost as determinedly controversial as Jack himself. Harris, the friend and biographer of Oscar Wilde and George Bernard Shaw, had to be taken seriously, if for no other reason than that he generated so much heated vituperation with his charges.

Every successful author is liable to be charged with plagiarism, often from the most unlikely quarters. "What *is* plagiarism?" Jack would demand when the subject came up, as though he didn't know it closely resembled his activities as an oyster pirate. He obviously leaned to the view that it is simply a concentrated form of research.

But Pontius Pilate–like questions wouldn't suffice with Mr. Harris, who claimed that Jack lifted "The Bishop's Vision" in *The Iron Heel* almost word for word from a satirical magazine article he published in May, 1901, titled "The Bishop of London and Public Morality."

Jack's defense was not particularly effective. He told of having read a reprint of Harris's article in an American newspaper and claimed that he had believed it was a verbatim report of a speech actually made by the Bishop of London. Since the "speech" was a corrosive attack on the church as a tool of capitalism, it was considered odd that Jack should have been so obtuse as to miss the satirical point — especially since Harris's satire was about as subtle as a pickaxe. As Jack maintained in a letter to his English literary agent, he had accepted it in good faith.[1] He should be labeled a sucker, Jack said, but not a thief. Either Harris had a terrible temper or he was eager for a lot of unearned publicity. Jack concluded, rather lamely, that the laugh was on him, and the scandal gradually died down.

He and Charmian returned to Glen Ellen immediately after their arrival in the States, and he began the long slow process of rehabilitating himself professionally and physically. His first step was to recall all his manuscripts and turn over their future disposal to a New York literary agent, Paul R. Reynolds. For three months he kept his name off the magazine market while he worked sixteen and eighteen hours a day on fresh material. Mrs. Eames was relieved of her duties as his business manager, her accounts in almost as deplorable shape as his bank balance. He and Charmian lived at Wake Robin Lodge while they planned their own home on the Hill Ranch, and to show there were no hard feelings, despite the muddle she had made of his affairs, he gave Mrs. Eames a five-hundred-dollar wedding present and a seventeen-acre meadow known as the Fish Ranch when she divorced Roscoe Eames and married her business partner, Edward Payne. But she was no longer "Mother Mine" to Jack, and in a few years they would be bitterly estranged.

Meanwhile he was gradually recovering from his painful skin ailment, now that he was no longer baking under tropical suns. The mystery of his affliction was cleared up when he read a book by Lieutenant Colonel Charles E. Woodruff, who had suffered from the same disorder. It was caused by the ultraviolet rays of the sun, Colonel Woodruff said, and was sometimes known as "European leprosy" or "Biblical leprosy." Only Caucasians were afflicted by it, particularly those with light complexions.[2] Jack's skin soon stopped peeling, and he was bothered only by occasional flareups of malaria.

In September, *Martin Eden* was published to a generally disapproving critical reception. The reviewers variously misunderstood his aim, as he claimed, by judging it as a Socialist tract or a further glorification of individualism. Its sales were disappointing at first, but the word-of-mouth appraisal of the book was far more favorable than the reviews and it began to catch on with the public. Eventually it sold 232,606 copies in hardcover, certainly a more than respectable showing, but less than half that of *The Sea Wolf* and only a tenth that of *The Call of the Wild.* He would never recapture the public he held transfixed in his earlier and more vigorous years.

Among young writers, in particular, *Martin Eden* was a sort of guidebook, inspiration, justification and Sacred Writ: their version of the Horatio Alger fable with a bitter, self-pitying twist at the end. For a generation afterward there were hundreds of Martin Edens slaving over manuscripts and choking over rejection slips. The doleful Martin, done in by the Philistines, was their martyr-hero just as George Gissing's aspirant, struggling in the New Grub Street, was that of English writers. (Perhaps it was *Martin Eden* which caused Lewis Mumford to remark that "One cannot help but thinking that the strenuous activities of London's successful years were a continual running away from himself. What was the self from which he ran away? It was the self of an artist, a minor artist, to be sure, but a real one, an artist who might rank with Gissing or Reade." [3])

Martin Eden was so influential among his fellow writers, no doubt, because it rang with the reality of his own youthful struggles to educate himself, to win a girl who was socially superior, and to make his living as a writer. No doubt thousands of his unseen colleagues silently cheered Martin's denunciation of the academic critics who for generations had guarded the canons of "good taste" — or nice-nellyism — behind a façade of beribboned spectacles, scholarly beards and nostrils distended to catch the first unholy whiff of crudity (realism). The more sanctified literary critics, Martin declaimed, "back up your professors of English, and your professors of English back them up. And there isn't an original idea in any of their skulls. They know only the established, — in fact, they are the established."

The love story in Martin Eden, perhaps because of the bitter flavor to it, was more believable than that of *The Sea Wolf;* undoubtedly he could write more realistically of Ruth Morse (Mabel Applegarth) than of Maud Brewster (Charmian Kittredge).

Martin Eden, exactly like his creator, was "starved for love all his life." He fell in love with the ethereal Ruth but soon learned that she was "unsympathetic concerning the creative joy." She even wanted him to enter journalism, which he knew to be "all hack from morning till night." On an eight months voyage to the Solomons — each bit of Jack's personal experience was quickly worked into his fictional life — Martin decided to become a writer and make himself worthy of Ruth.

He had discovered two schools of writing in his pragmatic survey of current literature. "One treated of man as a god, ignoring his earthly origin; the other treated of man as a clod, ignoring his heaven-sent dreams and divine possibilities." Martin would try to find truth — or at least probability — midway between these views.

Ruth agreed to marry him, repelled though she was by his poverty and lack of refinement. Under pressure from her mother and father, however, she broke the engagement when he landed on the front pages of the Oakland newspapers as the leader of the local Socialist party. Shortly after that, his stories and articles began to be accepted wherever they were offered, and an eastern publisher took on his novel. "He flashed, comet-like, through the world of literature, and he was more amused than interested by the stir he was making." Success, however, was a mocking disappointment. He lost his Socialist faith, but had only contempt for the material rewards of his career.

Ruth, with her parents' encouragement, wanted to come back to him, but Martin told her it was too late. "Life has so filled me," he said, "that I am empty of any desire for anything."

Deciding to throw it all over, he sailed for Tahiti, where he would build a grass shack on the shore of a lagoon and trade for pearls and copra. Many days later he came across a volume of Swinburne, read the stanza beginning, "From too much of living . . ." and dove over the side to his death.

That many critics took the message of *Martin Eden* to be a celebration of individualism, a reincarnation of Superman in shabbier clothing, particularly irked him. They'd missed the whole point of the book, he said; he was trying to show the futility of personal success without any idealistic philosophy to give it a firm foundation. "One of my *motifs* in *Martin Eden,*" he wrote on the flyleaf of the copy he sent Upton Sinclair, "was an attack on individualism. I must have bungled, for not a single reviewer has discovered it." Almost as irritating was the carping of several critics that Martin couldn't possibly have educated himself and become a writer in the space of three years. "Yet," he wrote in *John Barleycorn,* "I was Martin Eden." He was still unable to see that if something in fiction is implausible, destroying its credibility, it is no defense to say that what was described actually happened. Perhaps it was all the more a credit to the modest streak in him — so often obscured by flamboyant self-confidence — that he believed his own feats of self-improvement could be performed by almost anyone else.

Shortly after *Martin Eden* was published, he was hitting his stride again as a short-story writer. Some of his earlier vitality flared up again in his work, and the *Saturday Evening Post* paid seven hundred and fifty dollars for "A piece of Steak," and then bought "The Benefit of the Doubt," "Under the Deck Awnings" and "To Kill a Man." He also wrote a number of South Sea pieces sold to the *Sunset Magazine, Pacific Monthly* and *Hampton's.*

Soon he was hitting the stride that would produce a seventy-five-thousand-dollar average annual income until the last year of his life. If imagination and invention flagged — inspiration, of course, never counts with a professional — he fell back upon mechanical tricks of the trade. Let them call him a hack; he could console himself with the Bank of Oakland's statements.

Late in the fall he began to recover much of his old exuberance, and the survivors among the friendships of his pre–Glen Ellen days were invited up for lively weekends — George and Carrie Sterling, Cloudesley Johns and his bride, Frank Atherton, the Partingtons and Xavier Martinez and his wife. Besides his return to health and the brightening financial picture, he had another reason to rejoice. Charmian was with child. This time it was definitely going to be a boy; "Mate-Woman" wouldn't let him down. He referred to the unborn child constantly as Jack, Jr., and a few months hence — for all his scoffing at religion — would be asking Brett to pray with him that a son would be born. It was the most important thing in his life. A son would justify all he had endured.

Among the visitors invited to Glen Ellen was Emma Goldman, the anarchist, and two male companions who were traveling with her on a lecture tour. She had asked Jack to attend her lecture in San Francisco, but he replied that he never went to any lectures but his own and suggested that she come up to the ranch.

Of that visit Miss Goldman recalled in particular how Charmian would "sew on the outfit for the baby while we argued, joked, and drank into the wee hours of the morning," and how joyful Jack was at the prospect of fatherhood. "Here was youth, exuberance, throbbing life. Here was the good comrade, all concern and affection. He exerted himself to make our visit a glorious holiday. We argued about our political differences, of course, but there was in Jack nothing of the rancor I had so often found in Socialists I debated with . . . He did not fail to see the beauties of anarchism, even if he did insist that society would have to pass through socialism before reaching the higher plane of anarchism." [4]

Miss Goldman apparently was unaware of the fact that he viewed her doctrines with more amusement than respect, even after the joke Jack played on one of her male companions. He placed what appeared to be a book, with the title *Four Weeks, A Loud Book,* at his guest's place at the dinner table. The man opened it and it exploded in his face, causing him to leap in the air most satisfactorily. The "book," of course, was a joke-shop production equipped with an explosive device. Jack roared with laughter; nothing pleased him more than a practical joke, and this one was spiced by an anarchist's panicky reaction when placed on the receiving end of violence.

Later he remarked to Charmian, still laughing over his guest's discomfiture, "Never did anyone jump so high as that red anarchist! He must have thought it was a bomb . . . They're such soft people, anarchists, when it comes to actual violence — and when they try to do it, they usually make a mess of it because they're dreamers and haven't learned practical brass-tack ways of doing the very thing they so vehemently preach." If he had ever been seriously swayed by anarchist doctrine, he left no doubt, *his* bombs would have exploded with lethal efficiency.

2. *There's Money in Trees*

The more laborious writing became, the harder Jack sought for a way to escape from his profession. He was wringing his imagination dry for new plots, new characters under the necessity of keeping his market supplied, his dependents happy and his creditors at bay. At various times he would attempt to escape from writing into business on the utterly mistaken theory that all you needed to make money was a little imagination and a lot of enthusiasm, and into agriculture in the belief that the land was meant to support him instead of vice versa.

The first of his gentleman-farmer enthusiasms was aroused by the eucalyptus boom that was sweeping California and a number of other states, something like the ginseng-raising, chinchilla-breeding and other crazes which have seized otherwise sober-minded farmers from time to time with visions of sudden wealth. In back of it, of course, was the inevitable stock promoter. Corporations formed to push eucalyptus-growing, and incidentally their own stock, published brochures claiming that the eastern hardwood supply was giving out. The eucalyptus, which had been imported from Australia a half-century before, would provide a substitute for the furniture and veneer market; it grew much quicker than other trees and thrived on poor soil and rough terrain. One enthusiast wrote that the eucalyptus would make California as gold did back in '49.

Jack's acquisition of the 110-acre Lamotte ranch, which had many barren hillsides and scrubby canyons, made him an easy mark for the eucalyptus boomers. If he could cover his eroded land with the fragrant and fast-growing gum trees, he would not only bring it back to life but would get a quick return on his investment. On April 1, 1910 he wrote Brett that he had planted sixteen thousand eucalyptus trees and was going to plant twenty-five thousand more shortly.

Thereupon he joined the ranks of eucalyptus promoters, as fanatic as dervishes about their mission, and before the fever subsided several years later he had planted a total of two hundred and forty thousand trees.

"I have been trying to get out of the writing game for many years," he was quoted as telling reporters. "I made up my mind some time ago that as soon as I saw my way clear to making money in another direction I would quit pen scratching for good. I think my eucalyptus venture will help me make my getaway in the near future, and it will be a relief for me to get out of the scorching focus of the public eye. One has to burn whole gallons of midnight oil to get ideas and lately it has been wearing on me."

Undoubtedly it was the hope of making a fortune out of eucalyptus trees that propelled him into buying the adjacent Kohler Ranch of eight hundred acres, mostly in vineyard-covered hills. The property would cost him thirty thousand dollars and he was still in the hole financially from his South Seas adventuring. Yet he must have that Kohler land, even though he could only make a down payment and buying it would only increase his already staggering burden. On May 18, 1910 he telegraphed Brett for an advance of five thousand dollars, and the publisher complied without demur. (Jack had finished another novel, *Burning Daylight,* by then.) Now he had joined together three ranches and had more than a thousand acres to call his own. Jack London, Jr., would be born into the landed gentry.

In July he wrote one of the leading eucalyptus boomers, the American Corporation for Investors, asking how much they would pay if he would write them a glowing tribute. Their best offer was niggardly, an opportunity to buy a five-acre eucalyptus tract at half price, but Jack accepted. His fervent endorsement was included in a brochure published by the corporation, but he never received his acreage. He was still a true believer even after most growers, less deeply stung, were disillusioned by an advisory bulletin from the United States Forestry Service, which stated: "Extravagant estimates of the probable returns from planted eucalyptus have been widely circulated, and there is reason to fear that many persons have formed an altogether false idea of the merits of eucalyptus growing as a field for investment."

Jack never regretted his enthusiasm, in any case, because the trees helped to halt erosion and to beautify his domain. He tried to assume the practical farmer's attitude toward his land, undismayed by the fact that previous owners had gone broke trying to make a living off it, certain that he could succeed where they had failed by using more scientific methods. But it was the poet's eye that was really dazzled by his demesne in the foothills, and it was pride of ownership — the slum-born boy's fascination with land that no one else could contest, no one could trample over — that kept him mortgaging his future, kept him drudging at writing and squeezing his imagination dry to maintain himself in the Valley of the Moon. He wanted to be able to ride on horseback in any direction, as he said, and still be on his own land.

That spring, while Charmian awaited childbirth, Jack worked steadily away, back in full stride. He had just finished *Burning Daylight,* a long novel he had begun on his way back from Australia, and was writing a melodrama in four acts titled *Theft.* Olga Nethersole of

Sappho fame, more celebrated for the Nethersole Kiss, a faintly libidinous caress that wreaked havoc with Edwardian blood pressures, than for her acting talent, had begged Jack to write a play for her. He turned it out in his usual headlong style; playwrighting, he told his friends, was a cinch; the dialogue just poured out of him and the situations created themselves. Any experienced craftsman in the field could have told him that scenes which raced from pen to paper usually had to be cast aside or rewritten, but unfortunately he didn't know any practicing playwrights. It wasn't a very good play even by the standards of the Clyde Fitch–David Belasco era when Broadway was ablaze with marquees. The venture, at any rate, came to nothing except that the faithful Mr. Brett accepted it for book publication. Miss Nethersole slithered out of their agreement. On December 23, 1910, Jack wrote Blanche Partington, with whom he had been friendly since youth and frequently used as a confidante, that the actress had just signed a two-year contract with the Shuberts. This made it impossible for her to appear in the vehicle he had written for her. Actresses, he informed Miss Partington, were sleazier in their conduct than women of the street.[5]

Burning Daylight was successful enough financially to make up at least in part for his futile labors over the play. The New York *Herald* serialized it from June 19 to August 28 and distributed its condensed version for publication in other newspapers, working up a highly effective publicity campaign which helped to sell the book. Its total hardcover sale, according to Macmillan's latest figures, was 163,698, which was a more than respectable showing. Yet the sales also demonstrated that even a big book, packed with all the time-tested London ingredients, wasn't gripping the public as before. *Burning Daylight* sold only half as well as *Martin Eden,* which in turn sold only half as well as *The Sea Wolf*. If the halving rate continued, he would soon be back where he started.

Jack was confident enough of the novel to attempt squeezing a large advance out of Macmillan, citing an offer of ten thousand dollars from another firm. On May 19, Brett replied to this indication of restiveness by saying he didn't understand how any firm could make such a large offer. Brett put his foot down rather firmly and added that "it seems probable that you will wish at the conclusion of the present contract not to renew it, and I shall be very sorry for this."

Coming from any other publisher, this might have seemed a bluff; not from Brett. Jack hastily replied that he had no intention of severing relations with Macmillan. A few days later Brett informed him that he had investigated Jack's other offer and learned that the firm which made it was capitalized at only ten thousand dollars so "they were, apparently, going to pay you the whole of it."

Burning Daylight was a conscious effort to recapture his readership, carefully put together and containing bursts of his old narrative brilliance. It suffered, however, from the tendency of many of his longer efforts to start splendidly, then crumple about midway when the romantic interest intruded; the hero and heroine, once again, owed more than a little to Mr. and Mrs. Jack London, who were still able to persuade themselves that they were living the love story of the century.

His hero, Elam Harnish, known throughout the Klondike as Burning Daylight, came to the North Country long before the gold rush, driving a mail sled between Dyea and Dawson. He was the London-Nietzsche Superman in full bloom. Other men "lacked one thing that Daylight possessed in high degree — namely, an almost perfect brain and muscular coordination . . . He had been born with this endowment. His nerves carried messages more quickly than theirs; his mental processes, culminating in acts of will, were quicker than theirs. . . . His muscles were high-power explosives. The levers of his body snapped into play like the jaws of steel traps. And in addition to all this, his was that super-strength that is the dower of but one human in millions — a strength depending not on size but on degree, a supreme organic excellence residing in the stuff of the muscles themselves." On top of all this he possessed a foresight which enabled him to predict that gold in large quantities would be found in the Klondike creeks.

Gambling on this belief, he bought a claim on Bonanza Creek for three pounds of chewing tobacco, and just before the rush began he laid in a large supply of flour for sale to the stampeders.

At thirty-six, he was "King of the Klondike," worth eleven million dollars, and unlike most of those who struck it rich he cleared out of the country with his fortune intact. He plunged into Wall Street speculation convinced that "society, as organized, was a vast bunco game. There were many hereditary inefficients — men and women who were not weak enough to be confined in feeble-minded homes, but who were not strong enough to be aught else then hewers of wood and drawers of water. Then there were the fools who took the organized bunco game seriously, honoring and respecting it. They were easy game for others, who saw clearly and knew the bunco game for what it was."

The financiers of New York and San Francisco were roughly handled by Burning Daylight when they tried to bamboozle him out of his fortune. Three sharklike speculators tried to double-cross him in an intricate financial maneuver, whereupon he confronted them with a pistol and threatened to kill them if they didn't come across, which they did. Back in San Francisco another operator "went over to the enemy in the thick of a pitched battle," and Burning Daylight taught him a lesson by wrecking his company and causing the man's suicide "in a felon's cell." He had learned that "A superman's chiefest danger is his fellow supermen. The great stupid mass of people did not count." Man at the top of the civilized heap "robbed just as cats scratched, famine pinched and frost bit." Though he was falsely accused of glorifying the Superman in *The Sea Wolf*, he could have justifiably been charged with doing the same thing in *Burning Daylight*, which also revealed a growing contempt for the Superman's victims.

Just when it looked as though Burning Daylight was going to undertake a one-man revival of the Vanderbilt-Fisk-Gould golden age of skulduggery, Dede Mason, "a trim little good-looker" and high-minded in the bargain, tripped into his life. She was his stenographer, pert enough to argue over his deficiency in grammar while he was dictating letters, and Charmian should have had no difficulty in recognizing herself in the portrait.

After riding through the Piedmont Hills together, Daylight fell in love with Dede. "He noted the firm, efficient hands — hands that could control a horse . . . that could run a typewriter almost as fast as a man could talk, that could sew on dainty garments . . ." Dede, however, did not approve of his aggressive activities as a financier. She urged him to "do good with all your money," and thus inspired he pledged his entire fortune, now swollen to thirty million dollars, to improving the transit system between Oakland and San Francisco, building suburban roads and improving the water system. But Dede still wouldn't accept him as a husband because "instead of giving yourself to your wife, you would give yourself to the three hundred thousand people of Oakland." She made it plain, moreover, that she couldn't see herself as the wife of a man with all that money.

In the midst of a financial panic he decided that instead of fighting to save himself "I'm wiping the slate clean. I'm letting it all go smash." He and Dede got married and retired to a ranch at Glen Ellen. "As he had prophesied to Dede, Burning Daylight, the city financier, had died a quick death on the ranch and his younger brother, the Daylight from Alaska, had taken his place." Their marriage was idyllic, "all went well with this well-mated pair," and he assured her, "Little woman, even if you did cost thirty millions, you are sure the cheapest necessity of life I ever indulged in." The reader takes his departure as they are seen arm in arm "through the fires of sunset."

Even Brett, gentlest of editors, couldn't resist jibing a little at the idea of his hero tossing away a super-fortune. "When you, as 'Burning Daylight,' gave up that $50,000,000 fortune (or was it $150,000,000?) you might I think have given a poor publisher a chance to benefit by your generosity." [6]

Both the Socialist and the more conservative reviewers agreed, for once, on a London book. His picture of capitalist greed pleased the Socialists, and the others were placated by what several termed his "chastened" mood. Even the staid *Bookman* approved: "*Burning Daylight* has some interesting revelations to make. They show us a Jack London who no longer desires to preach his very amusing radicalism, but who is willing to come back to his power as a storyteller. Also a Jack London who has passed through the sad phase of unrest out of which *Martin Eden* grew . . . and who has attained a calmness of mind by reason of which his glowing, vivid style, with the assurance of ripened maturity, can pour itself into a vehicle of greater pleasure for the reader . . . It reads well as a book, and its author may be forgiven some recent failures for its sake."

Jack would have fewer and fewer shocks for the sensibilities of the bourgeoisie, at least in his writings, during the coming years.

3. *The Muldowney Set-to*

Adela Rogers St. Johns, who often visited the Londons at Glen Ellen with her father, Earl Rogers, the Pacific Coast's master of criminal law, has recalled that Jack's need for a son was "as violent as Henry the Eighth's . . . All he meant to do . . . must have a *son* to carry it on," particularly the magnificent ranch he was building with more loving care than he gave any half-dozen of his books.

Once again his hopes were crushed, and neither his marriage nor his life was ever quite the same. There seemed to be a blight on his chances of getting what he wanted most in the world, a boy whom he could hand over to, a boy who would be better than his father because he could be taught to avoid his father's mistakes. A girl simply wouldn't do, somehow was an affront to his overweening masculinity.

Charmian, on June 19, 1911, gave birth to a daughter. Worse yet, the infant was so sickly that the attending physician immediately informed Jack that she probably wouldn't survive more than a few days.

Much as Charmian must have needed him, much as he depended on her to stand by him in his own crises, he stormed out of what they now called "Beauty Ranch," raging with grief and disappointment. Without waiting to find out whether his daughter would survive, he headed for Oakland and the squalid resorts of the Tenderloin to drink himself blind. Instead of finding oblivion he wound up in jail.

In her biography Charmian related that Jack stayed beside her and did not leave the ranch until after he broke the news of the baby's death, but the cruel truth was that he was arrested on the night of June 21 — and the baby did not die until June 22. A page one headline in the San Francisco *Examiner* of June 22 told the story:

JACK LONDON FIGHTS WITH A SALOON MAN

Jack had wandered into the establishment operated by Tim Muldowney half a dozen blocks from the waterfront. Before Jack could even buy a drink he and Muldowney were swinging away at each other with more passion than skill. "Muldowney's two bartenders and four entertainers of both sexes," the *Examiner* reported, "witnessed the go without paying $50 for reserved seats, and they agreed the big quarrel at Reno on the Fourth [the Jack Johnson–Jim Jeffries heavyweight title fight] probably will not begin to compare with last night's London-Muldowney scrap in the kitchen at the rear of The Tavern, which is Muldowney's music hall and saloon on Seventh Street between Webster and Franklin."

Each contestant came out of the brawl with a bloody nose, black eyes, battered knuckles and torn clothes. When Jack started swinging his fists it was for keeps. Such occasional contenders in literary annals as Theodore Dreiser and Sinclair Lewis, Ernest Hemingway and Max Eastman at least would have had to yield to him as a fistfighter.

The two men, when the police arrived, each insisted that the other be arrested. Both were accommodated, and spent the night at the city jail. Jack was no stranger to municipal hospitality. In addition to his arrest as a boy Socialist, Adela Rogers St. Johns recalls that her father, along with Jack and a professional fighter named Jack Sharkey — not Boston's Jack Sharkey, the ex-heavyweight champion — "got arrested twice the same night for brawling on the Embarcadero, which wasn't considered safe or healthy. Over in Oakland, he [Rogers] and London and George Sterling went to jail and I had to go get them because, when the police apologized and released them, they refused to leave."

Jack charged that Muldowney butted him, otherwise he would have pulverized the 230-pound saloonkeeper, while Muldowney asserted that if Jack hadn't kneed him in the groin he would have made mincemeat out of him.

"I was eating a bowl of soup in my kitchen when this guy comes in and gets gay with me," Muldowney told newspapermen. "He punches me on the nose without giving me a chance to put up my hands, and he says, 'I'm Kid McGrath and you can't monkey with me.' "[7]

Jack's version was somewhat different. He said he wandered into The Tavern with a sheaf of papers under his arm and Muldowney thought he was going into the lavatory to paste signs advertising a venereal-disease cure on its walls.

Both men appeared before Police Judge George Samuels the next day on countercharges of assault and battery. After taking a look at their bruised faces, the judge decided "both will be in a better condition to stand trial after July 4th."

The story, of course, appeared in newspapers from coast to coast and cast Jack in the role of a drunken bum who went out on a spree while his infant daughter was dying.

Jack's reaction to all this was a near-paranoiac frenzy that lasted for weeks and had him claiming that he was the victim of a sinister conspiracy, which was only heightened when Judge Samuels, at the subsequent trial, dismissed the charges against both men. The San Francisco *Examiner* quoted Jack as fuming at the judge, "You treated me like a bully," a remark which could have caused him to be cited for contempt of court, had the judge been less forbearing.

Joseph Noel, who covered the story for the San Francisco *Bulletin*, recalled that he had a liquid lunch with Jack at which the latter pounded the table and railed against Muldowney as "a big Mick, an Irish Kike," and transformed Judge Samuels, a "blue-eyed, pale-haired Nordic" into "a dark, sinister Hebrew judge who, drawing his inspiration from the cruelty of the old scriptures . . . allowed Muldowney to escape punishment for beating up a great man.' *

Then Jack was mistakenly informed that Judge Samuels was secretly the owner of the property on which Muldowney's saloon was located, and because of that had not vindicated Jack. His rage, all out of proportion to the fancied grievance he was nursing, was symptomatic of a growing inability to rein himself in, even when he was making himself publicly ridiculous. From all the evidence, Jack had been fairly treated in Judge Samuels's disposition of the case; the verdict might well have gone the other way, had Jack been a barfly instead of a world-famous author, since he had refused to leave another man's property when ordered. Yet Jack inserted the following open letter to Judge Samuels in the Oakland and San Francisco newspapers:

"Someday, somewhere, somehow, I am going to get you legally, never fear. I shall not lay myself open to the law. I know nothing about your past. Only now do I begin to interest myself in your past, and to keep an eye on your future. But get you I will, some day, somehow, and I shall get you to the full hilt of the law and the legal procedure that obtains among allegedly civilized men."

For all his threats he never "got" Judge Samuels, but he did manage to make literary capital out of the affair, selling a story based on it to the *Saturday Evening Post* and receiving $750 — not bad pay for a night on the town.[8] Poor old Muldowney fared less happily, the San Francisco *Examiner* reporting on October 15, 1911 that the saloon-

* Jack generally, it should be added, was amiably disposed toward the Irish and was, if anything, pro-Semitic, despite racist tendencies in other directions. In a day when anti-Semitism was perfectly respectable, he openly admired everything about the Jews. In a symposium published by *The American Hebrew*, Jack wrote in 1911 that he had "no recollection of having made a Jew serve a mean fictional function. But I see no reason why he should not, if the need and the setting of my story demanded it . . . I am a terrific admirer of the Jews; I have consorted more with Jews than with any other nationality; I have among the Jews some of my finest and noblest friends . . ."

keeper had sold his establishment and "fled" to Fresno. "The question is," said the *Examiner,* " 'Is Muldowney the victim of London's vengeance?' " Judge Samuels, unperturbed, continued to serve in the police court.

After his draw with Muldowney, Jack journeyed to Reno to spend ten days watching Jim Jeffries and Jack Johnson train for their July 4 title fight and then cover the fight itself for the New York *Herald.* Jack had become a star performer in the big-name stable collected by Commodore Bennett, the wealthy eccentric who published the *Herald* and would pay up to a dollar a word for reportage under a famous byline. When he arrived at the training camps, his eyes a gorgeous purple and his face bruised and swollen, he looked more like a sparring partner than a celebrated author. The sweaty turmoil and boozy good-fellowship of the desert town helped to relieve his melancholia over the loss of the baby, whom he and Charmian had decided to name Joy, and over his conviction that he would never father a son.

Reno was churning with excitement over the happy prospect that Jack Johnson would be trounced by Jim Jeffries. Johnson was a Negro, probably the best heavyweight who ever lived, and it was accounted a terrible blow to the white race when he won the title and insisted on keeping it against all contenders, whom he flattened with a good-natured and imperturbable ease. Several years before, a "White Hope" campaign had been launched to find some white man capable of dealing with Johnson. All white hopefuls having been knocked kicking as soon as they presented themselves to Johnson in the ring, there was frenzied enthusiasm when Jeffries announced he would come out of retirement and reclaim the heavyweight title. Jack London, according to newspaper report, bet heavily on Jeffries, though his dispatches to the *Herald* reflected neither any pecuniary interest in the outcome nor any bias against Johnson, despite his own feelings about white supremacy.

At Jeffries's camp at Moano Springs he observed that the ex-champion was "kittenish and frisky in a huge way, full of 'joshes' and bubbling with grim laughter." Those who said Jeffries appeared to be overweight and out of condition were dead wrong: "One might as well call a cat fat because when it is relaxed its muscles become all velvety softness."

He also watched Johnson pulverizing his sparring partners. The

Negro was still full of tigerish tricks, "letting his opponent hit him repeatedly on his unguarded stomach; the old dreaming and sudden awakening to fierce onslaught for three or four seconds . . . passing facetious remarks while at the same time cuffing his opponent . . ."

He also philosophized on the "protoplasmic vigor" possessed by both fighters which "may be our brute heritage, but whatever it is, it is a good thing to have whether one is a prize fighter or not." He recalled that he had once complimented Jimmy Britt, after his fight with Battling Nelson, on having that quality. "I called him an abysmal brute, and he never forgave me. Yet I meant it as a compliment." Jack liked that phrase "abysmal brute" so well that a short time later he used it as the title of a short novel.

Jack was too cagy to predict the outcome of the fight in print, beyond anticipating a long and hard-fought match and noting that Johnson had a talent for "relaxation" while Jeffries was "always more tense."

Six days before the fight he informed the *Herald*'s readership that pugilism was an outgrowth of "the ape and tiger in us," but nothing to be ashamed of. "This contest of men with padded gloves on their hands is a sport that belongs unequivocally to the English speaking race and that has taken centuries for the race to develop. It is no superficial thing, a fad of a moment or a generation. No genius or philosopher devised it and persuaded the race to adopt it as their racial sport of sports. It is as deep as our consciousness and is woven into the fibres of our being. It grew as our very language grew. It is an instinctive passion of race."

When the men met in the ring on July 4, it was quickly evident that the search for a white hope would have to continue, as it did for several more ludicrous years. "It was not a great battle after all, save in its setting and its significance," Jack reported. It was Johnson all the way. "When Jeffries sent in that awful rip of his the audience would madly applaud, believing it had gone home to Johnson's stomach, and Johnson, deftly interposing his elbow, would smile in irony at the audience, play acting, making believe he thought the applause was for him — and never believing it at all." Johnson, after giving the paying customers their money's worth and sardonically showing how futile it was to beat the bushes for earnest bumpkins to get in the ring with him, proceeded to knock Jeffries out in the fifteenth round with a sudden flurry of mallet-like fists. "The greatest battle of the century was a monologue delivered to twenty thousand spectators by a smiling negro, who was never in doubt and who was never serious for more than a moment at a time."

XIII

"The Crowd" Moves South

1. *"A Nest of Anarchists"*

DURING the years in which Jack was establishing himself at Glen Ellen and roaming the South Seas in the *Snark*, "The Crowd," of which he had once been the moving spirit, had re-formed, was reinforced by newcomers and migrated down the coast to the Monterey peninsula and one of the most beautiful sections of coastline in the United States.

First to establish homes at Carmel, a few miles south of Monterey, close to the mouth of the Carmel River and the ruins of the Mission San Carlos Borromeo, were Mary Austin, a serious and prolific novelist; George Sterling, a somewhat less serious poet; James Hopper, the short-story writer; Anna Strunsky and her wealthy husband; Arnold Genthe, the photographer, and several artists of no particular distinction. Carmel in a few years became the most celebrated — or notorious, if you took the sound bourgeois viewpoint — artists' and writers' colony in the country, and eventually included Xavier Martinez, Jack's old neighbor in the Piedmont Hills; John Muir, Edwin Markham, Charles Warren Stoddard, Harry Leon Wilson, Ina Coolbrith, Sinclair Lewis, William Rose Benét, Lincoln Steffens, William Keith, Ray Stannard Baker, Jesse Lynch Williams, Will and Wallace Irwin, Nora May French, and Grace Macgowan Cooke, among about fifty who either built shacks there or paid lengthy visits.

Carmel had many attractions for its colonizers, a broad beach enclosed by rocky headlands, with deep pine woods rising up behind it, and above all a rustic charm which its pioneers swore they would preserve against all the encroachments of a materialistic civilization. It bore little resemblance to the commercialized Carmel of today with its "shoppes" and cocktail lounges and unabashed sprouting of television aerials. The first members of the colony were determined that Carmel would remain a retreat from the clatter and clutter of modern life. The woodland paths would stay unpaved to resist the intrusion of the automobile, now making its appearance in growing numbers. There was no gas for cooking; an open fire, with dining al fresco, was more in keeping with the artistic life. No electricity — candlelight was more romantic, and kerosene lamps were barely permissible. No newspapers — a bulletin board at the post office would serve for communication. There were no stores, and no need for them, since the tradesmen from Monterey came out with their wagons and filled orders, which were left at small wooden stands erected here and there in the woods.

Bohemia had moved outdoors, and it was heavenly. Only a hopeless clod could fail to create masterpieces under the towering Monterey pines, in the fresh sea-washed air, in a free and easy atmosphere isolated from the demands of the marketplace. Here everyone was equal: a college boy like Sinclair Lewis fleeing from the expectations of a middle-class family, and Jack London, who was about as famous as you could get in the days before mass communications had been perfected. The life was communal, almost everyone shared what he had with those who had less; there was no obligation to live up to your neighbor's standard, because he had none. Everyone subscribed to the theory that in Carmel you worked as much as you pleased, so long as it didn't interfere with the enjoyment of life. Under these conditions it was confidently expected that the colony would be a fountainhead of inspiration and achievement, the center of a modern renaissance.

Yet, despite that ingathering of talent, very little of enduring value was produced in the Carmel colony. Perhaps life there was a little too idyllic, too free of incentive; masterworks are more likely to be created in an atmosphere of competition, under the prod of necessity, with life raucous in the streets below and the landlord lying in wait downstairs.

And perhaps it was that balmy, easygoing, playful and carefree climate of Carmel which kept Jack London from ever building his own redwood shack there; he had become increasingly wary of the lures of Bohemia, especially one in the open air with what he described as the "amazing peacock blue" of the bay below. So he and Charmian only visited there, usually as the guests of Carrie and George Sterling.

Perhaps, too, he was aware of an amateurish touch to all the artistic ferment of the Carmelites, something a little too innocent and frisky for a tiring practitioner of his standing. There was, for instance, the sort of invitation Sinclair Lewis received shortly after he arrived at the colony in 1909 as a part-time secretary to some of the local literary ladies, principally Grace Macgowan Cooke. "Moonlight picnic (if Luna will kindly oblige) and Camp Fire; Given by Peggy and Mike Williams and Kid MacNichol to the Carmel Bunch, at Smugglers Cove, 7 January, 1909, in order to Celebrate the opening of the Word Factory of Williams and MacNichol, Perambulating Pen and Pencil Pushers — 'Any Old Literary Thing Tinkered While You Wait' — if you don't mind waiting! — Oyez, Oyez, Oyez! Whoopee! . . . All the afternoon. ENJOY yourselves. Everybody keep their razors in their inside pockets — Enjoy YOURSELVES! Walk — read — chat — and loafe."

With that sort of spirit infecting the bosky dells, Jack must have felt a little out of place, and though not yet thirty-five, more than a little elderly.

Nor could he quite rise to the pitch of poetic enthusiasm cultivated by Sterling and the others, which often seemed excessive in its posturing.

Arnold Genthe told of an abalone party given at the beach by Sterling and Mary Austin.[1] Miss Austin, who was infatuated with Indian life and wrote such novels as *The Land of Little Rain, The Basket Woman, The Arrow-Maker* and *Lands of the Sun*, was wearing a beaded leather dress and the long braids of an Indian princess on this occasion. A short, stocky woman in her mid-thirites, she lived in a wickiup patterned after those of the Owens Valley Indians and worked in a studio built high in the branches of an oak, which she reached by ladder. Usually she roamed the wooden hillsides in a flowing Grecian robe. Sterling, who was "proud of his classic figure and would pose at the top of the cliff in bathing trunks," was diving for abalone — a shellfish so tough it has to be pounded between rocks to make it edible, but at least it was free — with Jimmy Hopper. Later they would broil the pounded steaks over a fire. Miss Austin was gazing westward and quoting Browning on the beauties of sunset, " 'Tis a Cyclopean blacksmith, striking frenzied sparks from the anvil of the horizon."

Jack looked around from the fire he was building and remarked, "Hell, I say this sunset has guts!"

Miss Austin in her memoir[2] wryly recalled that she and Jack "had to shake down a bit before we could get on together."

Unconventional as she was, Miss Austin was affronted at first by his drinking habits and rather uninhibited discussions of sex, particularly his own irresistibility to women. After the death of their only child, Jack was increasingly eager to discuss such matters, even with Charmian present. London and Sterling, Miss Austin said, were "the first men I had known who could get drunk joyously in the presence of women whom they respected."

Then, too, she was neither overawed by his fame nor impressed by his intellect. "There was the difference in type for one thing, and the constantly dissolving and re-forming ring of his admirers, inclined to resent my being unimpressed by Jack's recent discovery of Darwinian Evolution. We were not, at Carmel, inclined to the intellectual outlook, except that there was a general disposition to take Jack seriously in respect to the Social Revolution. But in time, chiefly by way of . . . Charmian, we arrived at Platonic exchanges."

Jack's chestiness about his sex appeal was a trifle more irritating to the spinster. "Jack thought — and Jack had material enough. God wot, on which to base a conclusion — that the assault that men of genius yielded to, or withstood according to their capacities, was the biological necessity of women to mate up, ascendingly, preferring, he thought, the tenth share in a man of distinction to the whole of an average man. Women flung themselves at Jack, lay in wait for him. Knowing primitive women as I did, I thought there might be something in this . . ." yet "I never needed a love affair to release the subconscious in me, nor did Nora May French, who was the only other woman of our circle whose gifts approached Sterling's or London's."

Miss Austin and some of the other more aesthetic types were also taken aback by Jack's fondness for the practical joke, the more violent the merrier. A favorite trick of his was to persuade a man to stand facing a doorway supposedly to have his height measured. While his back was turned, Jack or someone else would hit him over the head with a mallet. Another bit of fun, all the more hilarious since the disaster that struck San Francisco in 1906, was to tie ropes to the victim's bedstead and joggle it from the outside, causing him to race outside in his nightclothes yelling "Earthquake! Earthquake!" Strawn-Hamilton, the philosopher, told Joseph Noel that once, on a picnic, Jack cooked a snake and served it under another name to his guests, several of whom became violently ill. Hamilton thought that the reason for Jack's rude jokes was that "When life becomes too much for us, we laugh it off. 'Laughing it off' by horse-play or a vaudeville quip means reducing the universe to the point where it is a joke. You can't escape the thralldom of reality, so you make a point not to take it seriously. It's a form of rationalization. If that doesn't do the trick, you commit suicide. Suicide is the final laugh."

Suicide, along with sexual freedom and the coming social revolution, was a favorite topic of discussion around the campfires of the Carmelites. It was generally held—and by none more vigorously than Jack—that a person had the right, if not the duty, to make an end of himself when life became boring or painful. And it wasn't, as it turned out, all idle talk. Many of "The Crowd" eventually took the shortcut. Nora May French, the loveliest of all the women at Carmel, killed herself out of frustrated love for Jimmy Hopper, the "only essential monogamist" in the colony. Carrie Sterling killed herself when George left her for another woman. George himself, in 1926, fell ill suddenly in his room at the Bohemian Club while awaiting a visit from his friend H. L. Mencken, for whom he made arrangements for a splendid banquet. The night of the dinner he was too sick and pain-ridden from an ulcer attack to go downstairs and join the banqueters, and took a lethal dose of cyanide from its compartment in an ornate ring he always wore . . . and three blondes wept over his bier. Herman Scheffauer went back to Germany shortly before the World War and served as one of the most vituperative of the Kaiser's propagandists. Soon after the war he killed himself and his woman secretary.

Mary Austin thought that Jack already was "sagging a little with the surfeit of success" and was no longer able to enjoy the simplicity of "tea beside driftwood fires . . . mussel roasts by moonlight . . . and talk, ambrosial, unquotable talk." Instead of rollicking sessions by the campfire he preferred to play cards with his host, George Sterling, whose redwood cabin stood in a pine grove above a field brilliant with lupine. Nearby was a stone altar built by the ex-Catholic pagan to propitiate the gods of the forest, with the skulls of cows and horses fastened to the trees all around. To any wandering stranger coming upon Sterling's temple-like grove it must have looked as though Druidism had established a foothold on the Pacific shore.

Sinclair Lewis, then an eager, shabby, gangling youth in his early twenties, sharing a cabin with the equally impoverished William Rose Benét, met London for the first time since their encounter at Yale while visiting Sterling's cabin. From the professional standpoint they were well-met, it seemed for a time. Jack was drying up on ideas for stories, once complaining to Charmian, "I'm tired of writing potboilers. I won't do another unless I have to" — but he always had to. Lewis, on the other hand, was brimming with ideas. His trouble was that he hadn't learned to put them in a form acceptable to magazine editors.

So they came to an agreement that Lewis would supply London with plots, and Jack would pay a small sum for any he found usable. During 1910 and 1911 Lewis turned out dozens of one and two-page outlines for Jack's perusal. On March 11, 1910, Jack paid him seventy dollars for fourteen such brief story outlines.[3]

One of these, titled *The Assassination Bureau,* he tried to expand into a novel. The story involved an international organization of high-minded killers which, on sober consideration, executed various persons whose removal supposedly benefited society. The plot turned on the conviction of a client of the organization that the president himself, through his activities, had become a menace to society. Eventually he succeeded in persuading the president that he should have himself assassinated by his own operatives.

Jack wrote about 20,000 words and then bogged down.[4] He simply couldn't conceive of a logical ending. Lewis himself wrote a detailed summary of how the story should be carried forward, but Jack didn't like Lewis's ending any better than his own. He abandoned the project. That and a half-done novel titled *Cherry* were the only manuscripts Jack left unfinished.*

Other Lewis plots were more immediately fruitful. On October 4, 1910, Jack bought nine, using two, including the one which became the short story "The Prodigal Father" [5] and "The Dress Suit Pugilist," which Jack converted into a 23,000-word novella, *The Abysmal Brute.*[6]

* The unfinished *Assassination Bureau* was recently exhumed and turned over to novelist Robert L. Fish, who completed it in a style closely resembling London's. It was published in the fall of 1963; a curious addendum to the London legend, considering how sensitive he was about anyone – even the respected George P. Brett – doing anything to his work.

The Abysmal Brute, the title of which he extracted from one of his stories on the Johnson-Jeffries fight, concerned Pat Glendon, a prize-fighter who wrote poetry in his spare time and courted a sophisticated lady reporter who encouraged him to revolt against the corruption of the boxing world. Its climax came when Glendon knocked his opponent out in the first round instead of the eighteenth as arranged by his crooked manager. Thereupon Glendon led the outraged fight fans in wrecking the arena.

On November 15, 1911, Lewis wrote Jack thanking him for a $15 check in payment for three outlines of seventeen Lewis had submitted. The money, Lewis rather pathetically reported, would pay for an overcoat to see him through the New York winter. On another occasion Jack paid $52.50 for nine outlines Lewis submitted, of which Jack reputedly used three. Just how Jack manipulated the plots supplied by Lewis cannot be determined on the basis of existing evidence. For three short stories, one novelette and one unfinished novel the London manuscripts are available but not the outlines concocted by Lewis; for four Lewis outlines extant there are no matching stories written by London.[7]

Despite the rather niggardly pay he received for plots which, on being fleshed out, brought London from $500 to $750 or more (the scale had been set by Lewis himself), he was a London worshipper and at least once accepted an invitation to bask in the masterly presence at Glen Ellen. London was his model as a literary lion in full-throated roar. His temporary infatuation with Socialism was encouraged by London's fulminations, and he even wrote a novel with an Alaskan background, *Mantrap,* which may be traced to the London influence, as well as *It Can't Happen Here,* an anti-Facist novel constructed somewhat along the lines of *The Iron Heel.*

As he recalled later Jack was just a little disappointing in no longer being the embodiment of the "sailor on horseback" of his more adventurous years. "Jack had quit being the galloping adventurer," Lewis wrote of their first meeting, "and had become a country gent, devoted to bridge-playing and pig-breeding. He used to stay with the Sterlings at Carmel, and though the great man was extremely friendly to the skinny, the red-headed, the practically anonymous secretary, it bothered that secretary that Jack seemed content now to play bridge all afternoon, all evening."[8]

The "literary high point" of his Carmel experience, Lewis said, was witnessing Jack's glancing, bewildered encounter with the work of Henry James, which to Lewis represented "the clash between Main Street and Beacon Street that is eternal in American culture." He recalled:

"At a neighboring cabin Jack picked up James's *The Wings of the Dove* and, standing there, short, burly, in soft shirt and black tie, the Master read aloud in a bewildered way while Henry James's sliding, slithering, gliding verbiage unwound itself on and on. Jack banged the book down and wailed, 'Do any of you know what all this junk is about?' "

The course of Lewis's career was tragically similar to London's; he, too, continued to write long after he had anything exciting to say, nothing left but the writer's compulsion to keep producing words and pages and books. He was seized by the same preoccupation with money, the tendency toward alcoholism, the unhappy search for the perfect woman— reflected, like London's, in the heroines of his novels.

Jack was still involved in the intellectual triangle with George Sterling and Ambrose Bierce, an affair that caused much gossip among the Carmelites. Bierce had never given up trying to save his protégé from London's influence, which he was convinced would be the artistic death of him. For years now London and Bierce had been sniping at each other, using Sterling as their medium of exchange. When Jack's *The Road* was published, Bierce wrote Sterling that it was a very bad book indeed. Sterling, who was vastly delighted by the feud and titillated by the fact that two such titans thought him worth contending over, promptly sent Jack a letter quoting Bierce's diatribe. He added that Bierce had demanded that he give up his friendship with London — which, as Bierce's biographer Carey McWilliams determined after a search of their correspondence, was simply not true.

In reply, assuming a specious magnanimity, London advised Sterling not to quarrel with his old patron over him and declared that Bierce was really a splendid old gentleman who hadn't had access to the latest scientific knowledge. Bierce, Jack added, had stopped growing mentally long before he and Sterling were born. If he'd been born a generation later, Jack was certain, Bierce would also have been a Socialist — or more likely an anarchist. About all he was good for now was long-range vituperation.

Once, as a joke, Jack composed an "article" denouncing Bierce which he showed to Sterling and said he intended to publish. The outrageously libelous piece identified Bierce as "a skunk that stinks in the pay of William Randolph Hearst" — a service which Jack himself had performed on occasion. Further, Bierce had acquired Napoleonic delusions from having served for a time as Empress Eugénie's press agent in England. "No doubt he [Bierce] will be as much of a Napoleon as a Waterloo creates, and no more." Bierce's Waterloo, Jack charged, would come through his leaning toward plagiarism, "in which he is so expert on his own account that he can detect it in the works of others where it does not exist." Just in passing, and for good measure, Jack cited the report that Bierce was claiming that a certain young actress of growing prominence was his illegitimate daughter.

London and Sterling almost came to blows, and did arrive at the point of threatening each other with mayhem, before Jack admitted he had no intention of publishing the article.

Bierce, of course, was more than able to match invective with London any time the latter was willing to risk open warfare. During Jack's voyage on the *Snark*, when the newspapers reported that the boat had been lost at sea, Sterling wrote to Bierce — a curious choice if he was looking for sympathy — concerning his fears for Jack's safety. Jack was in no real danger, Bierce replied, because even if his boat was wrecked "the ocean will refuse to swallow him."

When Bierce returned to San Francisco in 1910, Sterling invited him to come down to Carmel for a visit — then fretted over the possibility that Jack might happen to drop in the same weekend. Sterling, according to Mary Austin, went around the colony telling everyone how fearful he was that the two enemies, who had never met, might collide under his roof. He was still afraid, Miss Austin wrote, that Bierce would find out how closely linked he was to London.[9]

Then Bierce appeared, but Jack did not. The old iconoclast spent an evening listening to Sterling and his friends talk on their favorite subjects, which Oscar Lewis has quoted a Carmelite as saying were "the true meaning of art with a capital A, the themes of the poems and stories and novels on which they were engaged, and the lamentable pigheadedness of editors and publishers." [10]

Observing him as he glowered at the youthful aspirants across the gap of two generations, Mary Austin thought Bierce was "a man secretly embittered by a failure to achieve direct creative power, a man of immense provocative capacity . . . always able to forgive any shortcoming of his protégés more easily than a failure to turn out according to his prescription . . . something of a poseur, tending to overweight a slender inspiration with the apocalyptic." The irony of Miss Austin's observation was that Bierce, "slender" though his inspiration and his purely literary output, survives today through his Civil War stories, which is more than can be said for Miss Austin or any of the others around that campfire.

After that visit, she added, Bierce and Sterling "drifted into a slightly veiled antagonism."

Bierce made no secret of the fact that he wholeheartedly detested Sterling's associates, even without the presence of Jack London, and somewhat ungraciously informed his host that he would never come back again.

"A nest of anarchists" was Bierce's final judgment on that colony of innocents gamboling under the giant pines.

2. *Encounter with the "Eminent Tankard Man"*

Despite George Sterling's efforts to keep the two men apart, Jack London and Ambrose Bierce finally met face to face—and drink for drink—during the latter's visit to San Francisco in the summer of 1912. It was widely predicted that when the two antagonists met in person there would be a brief, formal exchange of insults followed by an Embarcadero-style assault and mutual mayhem. The experts gave London the edge on youth and general competence as a waterfront brawler, but pointed out that Bierce was larger and had a ferocious temper.

Both men attended the summer encampment of the Bohemian Club on the Russian River, the Annual High Jinks at which members and their guests were supposed to relax, contemplate and enjoy the beauties of nature. Any sort of feuding or bickering was regarded as unseemly. It was definitely not the proper setting for a meeting between Bierce and London.

Bierce heard that London was attending the encampment and asked Sterling to introduce him. Sterling, as he recalled in an article,[11] demurred on the grounds that it would not be good clubmanship to bring the two enemies together and disturb the sacred fellowship of the Grove.

"Oh, you mustn't meet him," Sterling said. "You'd be at each other's throats in five minutes."

"Nonsense," Bierce replied. "Bring him on. I'll treat him like a Dutch uncle."

Sterling said he "disentangled London from the poker-game to which he gave his forenoons," and early that afternoon presented him to Bierce in the rustic but well-stocked bar. The stage was set for a historic drinking bout. London's alcoholic capacity was notorious, and Bierce prided himself on being an "eminent tankard man." Bierce was seventy years old but had never been bested in any drinking contest; his feats at the bar of the Army and Navy Club in Washington were part of a heroic legend.

Word spread through the Grove that a famous feud was about to be resolved either in a flurry of fists or a challenge at tipping the bottle. Among those who gathered to watch the encounter was J. B. Cassell, associate editor of the San Francisco *Bulletin,* who reported in his newspaper the following day that "Mr. Ambrose Bierce, the reddish-haired vivisector of local reputations, met Comrade Jack London, special counsel for the enforcement of the United States Constitution, in a three-round bout at Bohemian Grove yesterday afternoon."

Jack, according to Cassell's somewhat hyperbolic account, opened by inviting Bierce to have a drink, which was accepted.

"Here you are, Bierce, if you don't mind taking a drink from the wildcat of literature."

"Thank you, London," Bierce replied, "but why drag in literature?"

"Because," Jack said, "you're a good judge of verbal tatting, having indulged in it all your life. Have another drink?"

"Here's good health, London, and I'm sorry I wasted even an impoverished pattern on one who thinks civilization is a slum."

"Here's how, Bierce, and I think civilization's a slum only when it's cluttered up with critics. Then it smells bad. Have another drink?"

"Thank you, London, this is good liquor. Very good. If I were sure it would have the improving effect on your manners that it obviously has on your repartee, I should recommend it. By proper indulgence you might in time become a gentleman."

"Even if you should patronize the same bar all your life, you'd never become that."

Bierce turned to Sterling, who was standing by in the role of referee, and growled, "Call him off, Sterling, I'll kill him, if you don't."

Both men, Cassell reported, were showing signs of wear from the hastily downed drinks.

"I'll tie your breastbone in knots if you start anything," Jack replied. "Have another drink."

And so it went for hours. Till late that night epithets were exchanged and insults bandied, but it was booze and not blood that flowed. Unfortunately the witnesses, including Sterling and Arnold Genthe, joined freely in the drinking and were never able to give a detailed account of the slanging match, but if Cassell's story of the initial exchanges was accurate no great flashes of wit were lost to posterity. Writers are not at their best ad-libbing. If they had had time to compose their diatribes on paper, it might have been one of the great verbal slaughters everyone expected, but the combination of alcohol and extemporaneity kept the encounter on a level not much above that of any barrelhouse set-to.

Later that evening London, Bierce, Sterling and Genthe adjourned to Sterling's camp to sit around the fire talking and drinking until (as Genthe recalled) "none of us quite knew what we were talking about." Bierce was wearing a derby, "the first and last ever seen at the Grove," and it was tipped at an "alarming" angle as the night wore on. From verbal sparring, he and Jack had proceeded to a wary respect and finally to an alcoholic fellowship. "The two men conversed in the friendliest manner," Sterling recalled, "though signs of an armed peace were not lacking to my anxious eye." Whiskey, in fact, had worked such wonders that Jack couldn't bear to be separated from Bierce and insisted that they would all accompany him to his brother's camp, where he was staying, a mile or two away.

It was a perilous journey for four men as tipsy as they, since they had to cross the Russian River in a rowboat, then walk along the railroad tracks on a steep embankment that followed the river. Somehow they got across the river all right, despite "the ocean of our potations," as Sterling said. The four men proceeded along the tracks singing lustily, with Bierce's arm around Jack and his hand nestling fondly on

Jack's shoulder. Then suddenly the other three realized that Bierce was no longer with them.

"Why, where the hell's Ambrose?" Jack asked.

Backtracking, they found that Bierce had stumbled against a tie, smashed his lantern under him and slid headfirst down the twenty-foot embankment to the water's edge. Bierce was curled up in a fern bed and "seemed content to lie" there, Sterling recounted, but his fellow roisterers hauled him to his feet and continued on their way to Albert Bierce's camp.

Sterling and Genthe promptly went to sleep, but Bierce and London sat outside the cabin and drank the night away, as Sterling recalled, "consuming a bottle each of Three Star Martell. God knows of what they talked! I was to awaken at seven with the worst headache of my life. Truly they were made of the stuff of heroes." Bierce slept against a tree with his battered derby jammed down over his ears, and Jack was sprawled nearby.

Despite that convivial night in the Bohemian Grove, Jack and Bierce never became friendly but continued to exchange potshots through Sterling. Bierce was convinced that Sterling had escaped from his patronage and would ruin himself through association with Jack — and Bierce could never forgive the loss of a protégé.

3. *House of the Wolf*

Jack was growing away from his old friends, it was observed, despite his occasional appearances in Carmel and forays to Oakland and San Francisco where he immersed himself for a night or two in the old familiar low life. Many attributed his growing isolation to Charmian's influence, more out of a dislike for her than any concrete reason. It was their theory that she encouraged the baronial style of living at Glen Ellen out of an instinct for social climbing, with Jack dragged unwillingly behind her, but the truth was that he was following his own inclinations, as always.

Joseph Noel wrote Sterling about Jack's new outlook: "However he may express it, his clutching at the illusion of great possessions is for no other purpose than to impress people he would have brushed aside as of no importance in the old days. He is going the way of all wedded middle-class flesh. At thirty-six he is edging into a scheming middle-age, and we may as well realize it. He is lost to us." In his reply, George said, "I forgot to comment on something you said in your letter as to our eventually losing Jack. I think I see what you mean (so does Carrie) and have a notion that you're correct." [12]

As his fortunes recovered from the slump they had undergone while he was cruising on the *Snark,* Jack began living on a scale he considered suitable to his eminence and prosperity. During this period he devoted himself largely to magazine writing, which brought the quickest returns, and signed a contract with *Cosmopolitan* to provide them with a series based on an adventurous character named Smoke Bellew, for which he received seven hundred and fifty dollars a story. The first *Cosmopolitan* contract was non-exclusive and he continued to supply *Collier's* and the *Post* with other stories from time to time. He did not delude himself as to their value. "All hack," was his comment on this output.

His growing list of possessions was of more importance to him than the quality of his work. He brought a thirty-foot yawl, the *Roamer,* on which to sail San Francisco Bay with Charmian, his valet Nakata and his cook Yamamoto. He was spreading out in all directions on his ranch, and its operation was becoming so complicated that he brought his stepsister Eliza, who had just separated from her elderly husband, up to Glen Ellen to manage it for him. Eliza was a shrewd, practical woman, completely loyal to him, and brought order into his affairs whenever his own extravagance was temporarily curbed.

Undoubtedly what most disturbed his friends, particularly those of the Socialist persuasion, was his plan for building a magnificent house in a redwood grove on the Hill Ranch overlooking the Valley of the Moon. Actually house was too humble a word for the establishment he envisioned; it was more like a castle, almost Hearstian in its splendor. Forni, an Italian stonemason who considered himself such an artist that he used only his surname, and who was engaged to superivse construction, had in fact been employed in the building of Mrs. Phoebe Apperson Hearst's castle, Wyntoon, up on the McCloud River. This, he told his friends, would be his "historic home." It would be called Wolf House. He liked to be called Wolf, had used it twice in book titles, and it was a sort of motif threading through his ego and intertwined in his storytelling.

He called in San Francisco architects to draft the details but designed the place himself. It would be built to last a thousand years out of the plentiful indigenous materials, red volcanic rock from the boulders strewn throughout the valley for the foundation and first floor, with a superstructure of redwood above it. There would be a huge library to contain his thousands of volumes, a music room for Charmian, a dining room capable of seating fifty guests, and in the basement an expansive playroom where Jack and his male friends could play poker and shoot pool, argue politics and indulge in the strenuous horseplay he loved. He would have a large workroom with space for a secretary and dictating equipment, and a redwood-timbered master bedroom with a massive night table. (He always retired with a row of Thermos bottles containing water, buttermilk and grape juice, with a mass of books, papers and letters, and with boxes of his favorite Russian cigarets, Imperiales, fitted with paper mouthpieces, which he chain-smoked night and day. Often he dropped off to sleep with a burning cigaret in his mouth, and Charmian would find holes burned through the sheets and pillows or his celluloid eyeshade consumed in a flash. He was never living more dangerously than when he retired for the night in a haze of cigaret smoke.) There would be half a dozen fireplaces scattered through the house large enough to roast oxen. At least twelve of the rooms must be set aside for his guests.

He was willing to spend a fortune, he said, to create the most beautiful home on the continent. By the time it was finished it cost a total of eighty thousand dollars, according to the Oakland *Tribune,* and that was a lordly sum indeed before World War I.

He was not in the least dismayed by Socialist protests that he was setting himself up as a feudal baron, nor would he have been perturbed by the comment of Maxwell Geismar that he "continually squandered the money that he had slaved so obsessively to earn" and that the main drive of his life was to "establish a feudal and technocratic dynasty" on his ranch.[13] He was giving jobs to thirty deserving workmen, he pointed out, and when Wolf House was completed it would shelter the best radical brains in the country, gathered under his stately roof to foment the revolution. Weren't William English Walling and J. G. Phelps Stokes both millionaires, and yet considered perfectly respectable Socialists? Was there anything wrong about a Socialist making himself comfortable, particularly if he worked hard to pay for it? He also pointed out to an interviewer from the Los Angeles

Record, when he visited Southern California in January, 1911, with Charmian, her Aunt Netta and her new husband, that his socialist beliefs were "costing him several thousand dollars a year." A short time later he wrote a businessman stating that boycotting and blacklisting of his work by his capitalistic opponents actually had cost him hundreds of thousands of dollars.[14]

His attitude toward the men working on Wolf House was more paternalistic than comradely. At times he rode over to the construction site and drank wine with the workmen. Out of earshot of his hirelings, however, he would refer to them as "my inefficient Italians," with a sort of exasperated benevolence. And long before Wolf House was roofed over, he would be quoted as saying, "The reason a man works for me is because he cannot work for himself. Stupid boobs, most of them!"

While Wolf House was being built, he moved out of Wake Robin and into an abandoned ranchhouse on the Kohler property which he had bought, renovating it at considerable expense, adding a dining room, enlarging the kitchen, building on verandas and sleeping porches.

He converted one of the bedrooms into a workroom lined with books, pamphlets, souvenirs of his travels, and his collection of prankster's paraphernalia, including glasses that dribbled when tilted, water pistols, coins with two heads or two tails, decks of cards with more than the usual allotment of aces, and other devices with which to put his guests at ease and amuse their host. The barn was converted into a dormitory for guests with nine rooms, which were occupied most of the time, and other callers were accommodated in cabins and tents surrounding the ranch house. Down in a nearby eucalyptus grove there was a sort of hobo camp tenanted by an assortment of indigent philosophers, often including Strawn-Hamilton. They were known as "the five sages of the eucalyptus grove," as Louis Stevens, a young protégé of London's latter years, recalls, and were generally so ill-kempt that Charmian discouraged them from coming up to the main house.

Here George Sterling, James Hopper and Cloudesley Johns, among the surviving friends of his youth, came to visit the Londons for varying lengths of time. So did Mabel Applegarth, who apparently held no grudge for the way she had been portrayed in *Martin Eden,* but she was in such failing health by this time that often she could not come to the table and Jack would bring a tray to her cabin. Other guests included many of the people he had met through the years, in the Klondike, in Korea or the South Seas, people of all classes and occupations. He chose isolation from the cities but kept the place well stocked with people, until the last year or two, when even his oldest friends wriggled out of accepting his invitations. The motto of the Ranch House was "The latchstring is always on the outside." Many guests stayed for weeks at a time. On a fairly typical evening his guests included Ula Humphrey, the actress who had played Maud Brewster in Noel's dramatization of *The Sea Wolf;* Luther Burbank, the plant wizard, with whom Jack was consulting on new methods of agriculture, and assorted neighbors, writers and a sailor who'd just returned from a voyage to the Far East.

The traffic to Glen Ellen was so heavy that he had a schedule printed which he sent to prospective guests who must be made to understand that they would have to fit into the routine ordained by their host. "We rise early, and work in the forenoon. Therefore, we do not see our guests until afternoons and evenings. You may breakfast from 7 till 9, and then we all get together for dinner at 12:30. You will find this a good place to work, if you have work to do. Or if you prefer to play, there are horses, saddles, and rigs. In the summer we have a swimming pool."

After the morning's work and dinner at noon with his guests, he went riding across the hills. He prided himself on his horsemanship, though Adela Rogers St. Johns says that he "wasn't really as good a rider as he thought, because it's something you have to start in childhood." Hunting had no attraction for him. He told Finn Frolich, the sculptor, a frequent guest at Beauty Ranch, that he got no pleasure out of killing animals ever since he'd shot a bird in the Klondike and watched it dying in the snow. Tears rolled down his cheeks, Frolich said, as he recounted the bird's death agonies. "Now when I think about hunting," Jack told him, "I'd rather go out and shake the dice for a drink."

Notoriously hospitable as he was, throwing his ranch open to anyone who appeared at the gates, he would not allow hunters to roam his spread. "You may call it sport, if you please," he told Bailey Millard, a *Cosmopolitan* editor, who visited the ranch, "to take out into the forest a machine and a beltful of cartridges and proceed to pump away at any animal you may happen to see but to me it is no longer sport.

I hate the idea of it. It would be all very well and perfectly fair to go out with a club and kill a jack rabbit for food, but it isn't fair to take along a hundred brass cartridges." [15]

Such views did not, however, drive him to the humane extreme of becoming a vegetarian. He welcomed all gifts of game birds for his table, and his gormandizing during the duck season was legendary.

Since becoming the hearty, hospitable squire of Glen Ellen, he was surrounded by his stepsister Eliza and her son Irving Shepard, and his stepsister Ida's husband, Jack Byrne, who was given a job as secretary after Ida died. He seeldom saw his mother any more. His relations with her were often strained and difficult, though she lived in modest style in her own house, with a fifty-five dollar a month allowance and Mammy Prentiss to look after her. He was embarrassed on several occasions when her unquenchable spirit of enterprise, or perhaps it was only a desire to humiliate him, flared up. Once she started operating a home bakery and peddled her loaves in the neighborhood from door to door, claiming that Jack refused to support her. Subsequently she tried to buy a newsstand in downtown Oakland, at which her complaints might have been given even wider circulation. Jack, however, managed to halt both enterprises as soon as he heard of them. Flora had never quite forgiven him for replacing her as his hostess, first with Bess, then with Charmian, and was even more outraged by his divorce and remarriage. There is nothing of record to indicate that she ever visited her son at the ranch on which he lived for the last seven years of his life.

He drew closer to his daughters after the death of Charmian's baby, apparently convinced that they would be the only flesh and blood to survive him. Every few weeks he visited them in Oakland, but Bess wouldn't let them visit him at any home he shared with Charmian. Louis Stevens recalls that once the two girls came up to Glen Ellen and he chatted with them at the railroad station until the next southbound train arrived and took them back to Oakland.

His attitude toward his daughters, as Joan recalls, was sternly moralistic. When he heard that Mrs. Fiske had invited one of them to join her theatrical company on tour, he was as outraged as any mid-Victorian papa, angrily forbade the venture and declared that actresses were a bad lot — an opinion dating back to Olga Nethersole's termination of an agreement to appear in *Theft*. Joan today considers his paternal piety an "over-compensation" for his own wayward youth. She and her father did not get along particularly well. Joan, reflecting something of her mother's bitterness, was defiant when she was not reserved and unresponsive to paternal gestures.*

Her sister Bess's recollections of her father are somewhat sunnier. Now Mrs. Percy Fleming, living in the Oakland area, she recently recalled an outing on which she and Joan were taken by their father. They went to Idora Park to ride on the scenic railway. "He never wanted anyone in his family to be afraid of anything, so he handed out $5 and said, 'We'll ride until this is used up.' By the time the money was used up both my sister and I were bored with the ride. It was just like walking down the street. He was always out for a grand time and never disciplined us." [16] She also remembered his habit of carefully saving burnt matches. He hated to turn down the page of a book to mark his place, so he used the matches as book marks. Many of the books he used most for reference looked "like porcupines" with all the burnt matches sticking out.

As early as the spring of 1911 Jack evidently decided that his daughters would never be very close to him, that they were too thoroughly dominated by their embittered mother to accept him as he believed a father should be.

On May 24, 1911 he signed his name to a mean-spirited and curious document, containing some of the most unfeeling phrases ever attributed to him — his will. Significantly perhaps, it was drawn up by Willard L. Growall, who was married to Charmian's cousin Emma. The document named the attorney, Eliza and George Sterling as his executors. Charmian was to inherit all his money and property except for forty-five dollars a month to be paid Flora, fifteen dollars a month to Mrs. Jennie Prentiss, thirty-five dollars a month plus twenty-five hundred dollars outright to Eliza. His first wife was cut off with five dollars plus the use of the home he built for her but "the instant she marries, all use and occupancy of said house must automatically cease." His daughters were to receive twenty-five dollars a month until they were married. "Any additional help they may obtain shall not be from my estate, but from my present wife, Charmian Kittredge London.

* Joan now regards her relations with her father as a tragedy of misunderstanding and unnecessary bitterness, and is writing a book vigorously advocating that divorced fathers have the legal right to visit their children any time they want.

Whatever additional may be given them shall be a benefaction and a kindness from Charmian Kittredge London."

And he malignantly added, "I recommend that my daughters . . . be personally housed, cared for, and managed by my beloved wife, Charmian Kittredge London, of whose fitness and goodness for this duty I am amply confident."

That last bedeviling provision, "recommending" that his daughters be removed from their mother's custody and turned over to the care of a stepmother whom they had been taught to look upon as a monster of deceit, was an all but incomprehensible gesture of malice. After Jack's death, however, legal action had to be threatened before Charmian would comply with the terms of his will concerning his daughters, though the value of his estate was estimated at one hundred thousand dollars. The action was called off when Charmian agreed to pay the girls the twenty-five dollars a month provided for in the will. Neither would accede to the "recommendation" that their stepmother take over their custody.[17] His daughters have not shared in the hundreds of thousands of dollars which have flowed into the London estate from motion picture producers and publishers all over the world.

Joan London is still unable to comprehend exactly why he made out such a will, though she is glad now that she was virtually disinherited because "it taught me not to rely on money." She believes that "the will was foreign to his nature. He was not a vindictive man. It was made out during the period when he was drinking heavily, in the year after the death of Charmian's baby. Alcohol must have driven him to the edge of insanity. Undoubtedly he meant to change the provisions of the will." In the five years between the day he made out the will and his death, however, there was no recorded effort on his part to change or rewrite it.

Undoubtedly the motivation behind that uncharacteristically spiteful document was to be found partly in his resentment of the estrangement between him and his daughters, which he blamed largely on their mother, and the increasing effects of alcohol on his mind and spirit.

4. *The "Long Sickness"*

One afternoon in October, 1911, Jack rode back to the Beauty Ranch from Glen Ellen and announced to Charmian that he had just cast his vote for women's suffrage. Charmian was surprised that he had turned enthusiastic over women winning the right to vote. The main reason for his vote, he explained, was that "women's suffrage means Prohibition." Women hated what liquor had done to their fathers, brothers, husband, sons. When they acquired political power — he accurately forecast — the first use they would make of it would be to outlaw liquor. Later, in a local-option election, he voted for closing the saloons in Glen Ellen, though he was their best customer, because "it might save some of the young people from falling victim to John Barleycorn."

Many of the changes in Jack noted by his friends, some of which they attributed to the spoiling process of success and big money, were traceable to his heavy drinking, to what he called his "long sickness."

Until recent years, of course, there was little effort to understand the alcoholic in this hard-drinking nation, no scientific approach to rooting out the psychological causes of his addiction. Dipsomania was merely a violent form of self-indulgence, and the victim was consigned to the Keeley Cure, jail and Skid Row. Jack's book *John Barleycorn,* published in 1913, was the first honest, self-revelatory effort to understand the drinker and his compulsion.

His heavy drinking was looked upon with disgust or ridicule, something he could quit if he really wanted to. Yet there is no doubt that he was using it, not as an expression of high spirits and manly hell-raising as he once had, but as an escape from moods of deep depression in which he brooded over his illegitimacy, his domestic problems, his declining ability to make use of his talent.

Was he an alcoholic? Jack thought not, observing in *John Barleycorn* that though he was occasionally blinded by the "white logic" of alcohol, he could quit any time he wanted. He never drank for weeks on end while the *Snark* was cruising the South Seas. Drinking was a bad habit, but he could lick it any time he wanted.

The typical alcoholic personality, according to an experienced worker with Alcoholics Anonymous, is "highly emotional, ultra-sensitive, egotistical, easily bored, restless, and has an exaggerated sense of his own importance coupled with an inferiority complex rooted in his childhood."

That description fitted Jack to the last syllable.

Whenever he felt the walls closing in on him, when the vexations of dealing with his numerous entourage at the Beauty Ranch grew too much for him, he hitched up his horses and buggy and drove at the gallop to Glen Ellen. That village had a dozen saloons going full blast, and each one of them would see him — hearty, jovial, laughing, buying drinks for the house — before the night was out. The cry would go up that Jack was in town, and barkeeps rubbed their hands in glee over a certain upturn in business. He would tie his horses to the nearest hitching post and push his way through the bat-wing doors of the nearest saloon, to which every barfly in town headed immediately.

Jack would stride to the bar shouting that he was buying a round for the house. After a few drinks and a recital of the latest stories he had heard — he never told a dirty joke, according to his neighbors in Glen Ellen, but he particularly admired and constantly retailed the "gallows humor" of his Jewish friends — he would push on to the next saloon, hold court and buy drinks. Sometimes he would deliver political orations, which may have been one reason that Glen Ellen, tiny as it was, had a Socialist local.

Before he hightailed it back to the ranch, he would have consumed a quart of whiskey, but he held it well and was generally taken for just another convivial drinker. People who served him at the bar or who drank with him said he could handle more liquor than anyone they knew, that he never lost his dignity or got himself involved in fights.

Around Glen Ellen, of course, he held himself in, conscious of his position as the local patroon.

When he ventured outside the valley, his conduct was likely to be unbuttoned, to put it mildly. Dr. Frank Topping, a Carmel physician and nephew of Frank M. Pixley, the editor of the *Argonaut*, would always remember the uproar Jack caused at a Bohemian Club encampment when the thirst was upon him. "Jack wanted to open the bar at 2 o'clock in the morning and rouse the whole camp to drink with him. I wouldn't let him." Dr. Topping was in charge of the bar, at which closing hours were strictly enforced by request of a majority of the membership, who did not want wassail to get out of hand. Jack threatened Topping with assault and mayhem if he didn't open the bar and let him awaken his sleeping friends. "He was pretty mad," Dr. Topping recalled, "but he got over it the next day."

The first time Louis Stevens, who became a novelist, partly through Jack's guidance and encouragement, and later a highly successful screen writer, saw him he was on a sizable bender in San Francisco.

At the time Stevens was a newsboy in his early teens, selling the bulldog editions of the morning papers at Kearney and Sutter Streets. He saw a hansom cab up the block trailed by a growing and excited throng. On the driver's seat atop the cab was Stanley Ketchel, the high-living middleweight champion, who was throwing money to the people on the street. Inside were Willus Britt, his manager, and Jack London. All three were exhilarated enough to have hijacked the cab from its driver. The cab halted in front of Louis Parente's saloon at Pacific and Kearney, part of the still uproarious Barbary Coast, and the three men went inside followed by their admirers. Stevens, joining the contingent, went up to the bar stool occupied by Jack and tugged at his coattail.

"I want to be a writer," he announced when he finally caught Jack's attention, expecting that the writer, whose interest in struggling tyros was well known, would be overwhelmed by the news.

"The hell you say," Jack commented, and went back to his drinking. Later, when he won a newspaper essay contest, which must have recalled Jack's own initial step as a writer, Stevens wrote to him and enclosed a clipping of his prizewinning effort, and Charmian, on Jack's behalf, replied that they'd like him to come up to Glen Ellen for a visit.

Adela Rogers St. Johns vividly recalls the anguish she shared with Charmian one time when Jack and her father, Earl Rogers, disappeared from the ranch in Jack's buggy to make a drinking tour of Glen Ellen, Santa Rosa and other points of alcoholic interest in the Sonoma Valley. It turned out to be a five-day spree, during which the teen-aged Miss Rogers and Charmian kept a despairing vigil. Not a word came from the two men during those five days.

"This was the first time I'd kept this vigil with another woman," Mrs. St. Johns writes in her biography of her lawyer-father.* "Now I was astonished at the way Charmian London took it as a personal insult. *What he's doing to me.* Her laugh fluttered higher and higher and broke like a light globe. . . . Charmian was sharp and bitter. Nothing was ever said between us about drink. A man's family did not discuss this, nor admit it. Now I knew she *hated* Glen Ellen. Her longing was to be back on the *Snark,* breathing the high seas again, seeing strange places, new horizons. I saw that she was about as domestic as a mountain

* *Final Verdict.*

lioness, of which she kept reminding me more and more . . . I began to say my prayers again . . . God was a last resort but something—*something*—I had seen in Jack London drove me to it. On my knees."

Late on the afternoon of the fifth day, bedraggled but hilarious, Jack and his drinking companion returned to the ranch. They were riding two burros so small that their riders' feet dragged on the ground; just what happened to the horses and buggy in which they left would have to be sorted out later. From inside the ranchhouse Rogers's daughter heard their giddy conversation.

"I am a little confused," she heard her father say. "Why am I riding this burro?"

"You are confused," Jack told him, "because at this moment you are not sure whether you are a man dreaming you are a burro or a burro dreaming you are a man. We all have these moments."

"I think," Rogers replied, "I should prefer to be a burro dreaming I am a man."

They joined their womenfolk out on the terrace and "Jack went over and kissed his wife and she gave him a flashing, narrow-eyed smile I'd rather not have had myself . . . All too plainly neither of the prodigals had slept *or* bathed *or* changed their shirts since they left."

Charmian remarked in a brittle voice that Jack had had "a long visit this time with your friend John Barleycorn."

Jack replied, "I am friend to John Barleycorn. I am, I was, I never was. But he is no friend to me. I am never less his friend than when he is with me and I seem most his friend. How can I be his friend when he is my enemy? He is the king of liars . . . He is also in league with the Noseless One [Jack's favorite designation for death] . . . He gives clear vision and . . . muddy dreams. He is the enemy of achievement and the teacher of wisdom beyond man's vision. He is the red-handed killer and he slays our youth."

Jack's voice "got deeper as the light faded around us, he had the same sense of theater that Papa did . . . they were *hams,* they were *great* actors . . . They were ruthless yet they gave themselves as I have never seen anybody else except a few others like them—as Ernest Hemingway did also." It was excruciating to watch Jack "laying bare his soul. Jack did this often, he was without ambush or concealment, at least he had a soul fit to bare in all its fighting anguish."

Her last memory of that melodramatic evening was Jack trying to persuade her father and George Sterling, who had come up to the ranch just before the dinner, to form a "compact" with him. "When our work is done, our life force spent, exit laughing. Is it a promise? We hereby agree not to sit up with the corpse."

Morbidly but always eloquently, and with a raging despair that he never hesitated to share with others, Jack was facing the prospect of disintegration. He could halt the process temporarily, but felt himself doomed, helpless as Prometheus chained to a rock and being torn by birds of prey.

XIV

Dreams of a Gentleman Farmer

1. *Swearing Off*

CHRISTMAS was the one time of the year Jack detested with a passion. The sentimentality of that holiday, contrasted with his memories of the joyless Christmases of his boyhood, made him moody and restless. As a non-Christian he could hardly celebrate Christ's birthday — though Christ, he said, was one of his two heroes — with any religious feeling. That would be hypocrisy. At the same time he resented any sort of celebration in which he couldn't wholeheartedly participate. His remedy, as usual, was to flee what he found distasteful, generally with John Barleycorn as his faithless companion.

As Christmas, 1911, approached he suggested to Charmian that they get away from it all, go to New York, and then return home via Cape Horn on a sailing vessel. The prospect of a new adventure under sail excited her almost as much as it depressed her to think of the weeks they would spend in New York before sailing, during which Jack would take care of business matters and predictably drink more heavily than usual. There was, however, a codicil to his proposal for the trip that raised her hopes that Jack might soon abandon his reckless jousting with the bottle. Once they boarded the sailing vessel bound for California, he promised, it would be "Goodbye, forever, to John Barleycorn" — a farewell which he would memorialize in a book telling the raw truth about his lifelong grapple with the enemy.

The trip started gaily as they shared a bottle of champagne at Jack's favorite restaurant in Oakland, the Saddle Rock, and then boarded the Western Pacific Limited for the East. They made only one stop, at Salt

Lake City, where they took an excursion to Fort Douglas. Charmian's father, Captain Willard Kittredge, had served as provost marshal at the fort during the Civil War years.

Once in New York Jack was sucked into the vortex of restless pleasure-seeking. He was the rare San Franciscan who stood in awe of New York. He always felt the need to deaden himself against the grinding confusion of the metropolis, which somehow made him feel insignificant and excited the suspicion that he was not living up to his potentialities.

This visit was made uneasy, too, by the necessity of negotiating a new book contract. After a solid decade of mutual profit and generally amiable relations, he had decided to break away from Macmillan. The publisher's correspondence files give no particular reason for the move, except that Jack apparently felt that he might be published to greater advantage, with more promotional excitement, by another house. Undoubtedly he suspected that Macmillan was beginning to take him for granted. Other houses, he had learned, were paying higher royalty rates to their star attractions. On Macmillan's part there was no evident disposition to hang on to Jack at all costs; the house had published four of his books that year, *Adventure,* the short South Seas novel; *The Cruise of the Snark,* and two short-story collections, *When God Laughs* and *South Seas Tales,* none of them particularly successful. The trouble, from the publisher's standpoint, was that he had to publish London's unproduced plays, essays and documentaries like *The Road* . . . and his set pieces, such as the recent *Burning Daylight,* had fallen off sharply in quality and salability. Macmillan simply failed to make an all-out effort to keep him.

During this period, Sinclair Lewis, who had become a junior editor at Frederick A. Stokes Company, contributed in no small way to Jack's discontent with Macmillan. He and Jack continued corresponding even after Lewis stopped supplying ideas for stories; mostly the exchange was of a trivial nature, including repeated pleas from Jack to Lewis to steal a Jack London Cigar poster for him. Lewis did not hesitate to capitalize upon his friendship with Jack at Stokes which, he facetiously revealed to Jack, caused him to be considered quite a hellion, if not a dangerous anarchist. People ducked under tables, Lewis said, every time he reached into his pocket for a handkerchief. After he was promoted to publicity director for Stokes, Lewis evidently was encouraged by his superiors in a rather sneaky campaign to lure London away from Macmillan.

Lewis first broached the matter in November of 1910, when he was still concocting plots for London, but the latter brusquely replied that there wasn't a chance of his leaving Macmillan for Stokes.

On January 21, 1911, Lewis jolted him out of his complacency with Macmillan by casually remarking that Robert Hichens received a twenty per cent royalty on *The Garden of Allah*.[1] Apparently this caused Jack to wonder whether the payment he was receiving for magazine articles as well as the royalty rate at Macmillan were compatible with his standing as a writer. He was receiving a fifteen per cent royalty from Macmillan. Irked at the possibility he was being downrated by magazine and book publishers, he suggested that Lewis act as his spy in the literary marketplace and find out how much other writers were getting for their work. Lewis was only too eager to comply, knowing that his standing at Stokes would be greatly enhanced if he could lure Jack London into the firm.

By November 20, 1911, Jack had already begun negotiating for a new publisher, according to a telegram he sent Lewis. One publisher had offered a seventy-five-hundred-dollar advance for *Smoke Bellew Tales,* but the deal fell through because the firm wanted first refusal on his next two books. Rand, McNally had offered a three-thousand-dollar advance for *The Abysmal Brute*. If Stokes wanted to join in the bargaining, he informed Lewis, it would have to realize that only a sizable offer would be considered and would have to be forthcoming immediately because Jack needed the money.

Lewis whetted the edge of Jack's dissatisfaction with his present publishers by detailing, in a letter dated December 1, 1911, how he had pumped both Charles Hanson Towne, the editor of *The Delineator,* a woman's magazine, and William Morrow, the editor-in-chief at Stokes, who probably needed very little priming, for information on how much the big names were getting for their work.

Lewis's espionage provided very little comfort for Jack, who was then receiving five hundred dollars to seven hundred and fifty dollars for short stories, or ten to fifteen cents a word. According to Lewis's gleanings, Theodore Roosevelt was getting one dollar a word from *Scribner's Magazine* for his African travel pieces; Kipling, fifty cents a word;

Richard Harding Davis, one thousand dollars a short story, and the same for Edith Wharton and David Graham Phillips; Conan Doyle, fifty cents a word from *Collier's* for his Sherlock Holmes stories; Gertrude Atherton, ten cents a word; Robert W. Chambers, ten thousand dollars minimum for his serials.

Lewis also passed along the information from Morrow that some authors were receiving a twenty per cent royalty. Furthermore, Morrow revealed with what Lewis described as an almost cloak-and-daggerish demand for secrecy, that a very few were getting as much as twenty-five per cent.

The telegraphed news that Jack was coming to New York just after Christmas "excited" Lewis, as he wrote Jack, and evidently raised his hopes that Jack could be maneuvered onto the Stokes list. It was not to be, for all Lewis's sly hints that his present publishers weren't doing right by Jack. All he had succeeded in doing was to make Jack disgruntled with the best publisher he ever had. Stokes, apparently, was unable to come up with an offer alluring enough to capture his interest, for all those insinuations from editor-in-chief Morrow about twenty-five per cent royalties.

Instead, Jack signed on with another publisher. The major credit for that move obviously belonged to Sinclair Lewis, who had aroused his dissatisfaction and caused him to wonder why the most famous writer in America was so ill-rewarded financially. Undoubtedly it also contributed to the savagely discontented mood which caused Jack to drink so much that winter in New York. He went over to the Century Company with more misgiving than hope, if for no other reason than that it was not headed by the patient, understanding George P. Brett, whose only fault was that he refused to raise the ante. His forebodings were justified in the event. Century published *Smoke Bellew Tales* in 1912 and in 1913 *The Night Born,* a short-story volume; *The Abysmal Brute,* his short prizefight novel, and *John Barleycorn.*

By the time he had written *Barleycorn* he was trying every trick to be released from the Century contract. Century insisted, despite insulting letters from Jack, on publishing *Barleycorn,* which the *Saturday Evening Post* serialized to the dismay of some of its more priggish readers. Then, with relief and gratitude, he returned to Macmillan and stayed there. The Century Company had irked him in particular by refusing to pay him a thousand dollars a month, for three months, while he worked on *Barleycorn.* Brett, on the other hand, had always understood his need for a continuous supply of cash.

"One wild maelstrom" was the way Jack himself described the several months of that New York winter. He plunged into night life, sometimes dragging Charmian after him, and sometimes not. In her biography Charmian seldom even hinted at any troubles in her marriage, but the concern he caused her that winter showed through her forget-me-not prose like an exposed nerve-end. "It was the old story," the big city "plucked to light the least admirable of his qualities," nine-tenths of the time they spent in New York "he was not his usual self"— and his "usual self" was no model of uxorious behavior.

On arrival, she recalled, he had warned her that he was going on one last, farewell fling with John Barleycorn, then he would settle down as a sober and dignified man of letters. From all accounts, he lived up to his word in one respect: that binge in New York was a stem-winder. He did practically no work, for the first time in years, though he had started writing *The Valley of the Moon* before leaving the ranch. Every night he was out on the town, often *all* night, wandering with friends from saloon to cabaret to Jack Dunstan's near the Hippodrome for the rounders' favorite breakfast at dawn, Irish bacon and eggs.

"Rome in its wildest days," he told an interviewer from the New York *World,* "could not compare with this city. Here making an impression is more important than making good. In this great city woman does not care for woman friends. She will boldly tell you so. She does not trust them. The average so-called woman of New York City will not introduce her attractive men friends to her women friends."

Charmian recalled that she was intuitively aware of his extramarital activities that winter when he left her alone night after night in the apartment they were occupying on Morningside Heights, and more was revealed to her later. She consoled herself with the assurance that when he got off the Manhattan merry-go-round she would be able to "welcome back the sane and lovable boy."

On that New York visit he met a number of distinguished contemporaries, including Victor Herbert, who surprised him with a pedantic discourse on the value of having a prominent nose; Dr. Charles P. Steinmetz, the unexpectedly witty and mordant electrical wizard, and

John Butler Yeats, the portrait painter and father of William Butler Yeats. He also spent a number of afternoons at the infant Authors League, helping its officers draft plans for a campaign to obtain stricter laws to protect copyrights.

At least one meeting with a writer of near-equal rank, feeding his sense of inferiority among the more polished and elegant type of New Yorker, came off rather badly. Bailey Millard, the editor-in-charge-of-Jack-London at *Cosmopolitan,* insisted that he meet David Graham Phillips, the ex-newspaperman, ex-muckraker and author of *Susan Lennox* and other highly successful novels, in the belief they would have much in common. Phillips was celebrated for his fastidious dress; Jack defiantly wore a flannel shirt when he met Millard and Phillips for lunch. The atmosphere, as Millard said, was "hostile," frigid with a mutual suspicion between the two writers.

After London left them, Phillips complained to Millard, "London did not like me because he did not approve of my clothes. He mistook me for a dude and would not open up."

Several days later Millard met London on the street, and the latter immediately burst out, "I am afraid that your friend Phillips was disappointed in me. He did not like the way I was gotten up. Well, let it go at that. I'm not going to change my style to suit these smart dressers!"

Most of his time that trip was spent among the night-crawlers of metropolitan life, often with Joseph Noel, who was now working in New York and who joined Jack in another venture they both hoped would make them rich.

At the Flatiron Building one night they watched the parade of homosexuals who congregated at the intersection of Broadway and Fifth Avenue. Michael Monahan, the editor of *Papyrus,* a literary magazine, who was with them, remarked that Rimbaud had been corrupted by homosexuality and offered the opinion that all sexual deviates ought to be summarily tried and sentenced to the gallows. Jack's attitude was more tolerant. "Sailors are that way, too . . . Wherever you herd men togeher and deny them women their latent sexual perversions come to the surface. It's a perfectly natural result of a perfectly natural cause." He paused thoughtfully, and added, "A man should love women, and lots of them." At dinner that evening he met Henry Gallup Payne, editor of the *Sunday Magazine,* a newspaper supplement, and within five minutes made an agreement to sell him twelve short stories at one thousand dollars apiece, more than he had been getting from *Cosmopolitan* or the other slick magazines. Payne soon regretted the deal. He complained that Jack sent him rejected stories written early in his career without "even bothering to shake the dust from their pages."

On another evening, Noel said, Jack insisted on being accompanied to a cabaret called the Burlesque Club at Seventh Avenue and Broadway, where they met several hard-eyed friends of Jack's whose "lips drooled obscenities as casually as if a group of scavengers had gathered together to discuss sewage disposal."

When Charmian accompanied them on their forays, Noel recalled, her resentment of his activities and his local acquaintances came out in the open. She ventured to upbraid him for his conduct, and he warned her to mind her own business — hardly the kind of talk Mate-Woman was accustomed to hearing from Mate-Man, especially in public. Noel observed that Charmian's face turned gray and "she seemed suddenly old." She was aware of the appraising eye he turned on other women, glancing at her, then at her "slim-ankled potential rivals." Her smile "withered" as the long weeks of Jack's almost nightly debauches went on, and her eyes had "an apologetic upturn." Noel could only conclude that being the wife of a literary lion, particularly one with Jack's appetites, was utterly exhausting.

Jack's feverish dissipations in New York came to an end, as he had promised, when it was time to leave for Baltimore and board the four-masted bark *Dirigo* for the trip around the Horn. Unwittingly perhaps, Jack let slip the reason for those weeks of wassail when he returned home and was interviewed by an Oakland *Tribune* reporter. "No big city for me, and above all not New York. I think it is the cocksure feeling of superiority which the people of the metropolis feel over the rest of the country that makes me rage . . ."

2. *Under Sail Again*

On March 2, 1912, they sailed from Baltimore on the *Dirigo,* with Jack sober and "very subdued," as Charmian observed. He had had his head shaved, presumably while still under the weather. His explanation was that he wanted to "give it a good rest." Charmian was so appalled at the result that she wept for three hours, and later claimed that she refused to look directly at him until a half-inch of hair had grown out.

As they waited to board the vessel shortly after dawn that cold gray morning a little three-month-old terrier, apparently a homeless mongrel, kept nuzzling against Jack's ankle. Jack impulsively decided to take the dog along on their voyage, and gave him the name Possum. It turned out better than most of Jack's impulses, for Possum was his constant companion from then until his death. The little terrier would sit outside his workroom window while he wrote, patiently waiting for his master to join him. He was a character in both *The Valley of the Moon* and *The Mutiny of the Elsinore*.

The *Dirigo*, the whole voyage delighted him. Their passage cost a thousand dollars from Baltimore to Puget Sound, and since the vessel had no license to carry passengers Jack had to sign the articles as third mate, Charmian as stewardess, and Nakata as cabin boy.

They put out to sea in a winter gale, and the early stages of the voyage were rough and storm-buffeted. There was nothing to do aboard but work, read, walk the decks. Under the cold sea winds his face recovered its ruddy glow and something of his old creative vitality came back. He finished writing *The Valley of the Moon* during the 148-day voyage, began making notes for *John Barleycorn* and thinking about the books he would write in the years ahead. Among the works he planned — but never got around to writing — were what he called "a Christ novel," to which he gave a lot of thought and which later was compressed into a sequence in *The Star Rover;* another with the Middle Ages as the background, another tentatively titled *The Far Future*, which would deal with the "perfected and perishing human race." Another projected work would concern the "farthest distant" — a science fiction novel which envisioned the use of atomic power. In his notes for this he wrote, "Radium engines, etc., for energy — See Atoms and Evolutions in Saleeby's 'The Cycle of Life' " and outlined the possibility of the earth colliding with a "dark body from out of space." [2]

More important, it seemed to Charmian that Jack was taking stock of himself and what she called the "abominations" of his recent weeks in New York, and was deciding to live more sensibly. She was also sure that he was sorry for all the pain he had caused her that winter. Perhaps some of the tenderness arose from the fact that she was pregnant again, which briefly allowed him to hope for the arrival of a

Jack London, Jr. She lost the baby through miscarriage after they landed in Seattle.

Night after night in their stateroom Jack read aloud — everything from Robert W. Chambers to Eugene Sue's *The Wandering Jew* to John Masefield — while Charmian lay in her bunk, and embroidered lingerie. He acted as ship's dentist, pulling sailors' teeth, having brought along a portable case of dental equipment he had carried on the *Snark*. When the sea was calm, he and Charmian, to the amazement of the crew, put on boxing gloves and sparred — surely not the best exercise for a pregnant woman.

They were closer, aboard the *Dirigo,* than they had been since sailing on the *Snark.* At sea Charmian had no rivals either in bottles or skirts; it was only on land that their married life became complicated and unhappy. She hoped that, shaken by his uncontrolled drinking in New York and prodded into self-knowledge by conceiving the autobiographical *John Barleycorn,* he now realized that he had to leave alcohol strictly alone.

Yet it seemed he was still capable of self-deception. She was depressed by a conversation he had on the subject of drinking with the *Dirigo's* first mate, Fred Mortimer, who happened to mention at dinner one evening after they had rounded Cape Horn that he never drank to excess, "just a glass now and again on shore with the fellows."

Jack nodded approvingly and said he was "reviewing the whole question of alcohol with reference to myself" after three clear-headed months on the wagon and that he was "working toward" a life of sobriety. But he had also concluded to Charmian's recorded dismay, that "I am not an alcoholic in any sense of the word." He was confident, he said, that he could drink "occasionally, deliberately, not because I have to have alcohol in the economy of my physical system, but because I want to . . . for social purposes. It has never mastered me . . . it never shall . . ."

His delusion that he could control his drinking, Charmian foresaw, would have tragic consequences. She had observed enough of his reactions to alcohol, his susceptibility to it, to know that he could never become a moderate social drinker. Liquor excited him, sucked him in like a whirlpool, caught him up in violence. He could never master it; it had always, in the end, mastered him.

Something of that self-delusion was plainly visible in the pages of *John Barleycorn,* in which he repeated his assertion that he could spar with his old enemy and yet not succumb to a knockout punch. He wrote almost wistfully — considering that the book was planned as an attack on alcohol — of the warm comradeship engendered by drinking, of the exhilarating atmosphere of the saloon. The romantic attitude of the American writer toward the oldtime saloon, including many of O'Neill's plays, would make an instructive monograph.

People who knew him, Sterling and Whitaker among them, privately criticized the book for romanticizing certain episodes of his life, especially those indicating a belief in the generosity of saloonkeepers. Sterling was quoted as commenting, "You must remember that Jack was the public's male Cinderella. This public likes to think that a pumpkin of a saloonkeeper has been turned into a Fairy Prince who dispensed largesse for the benefit of mankind instead of rotgut."

Jack claimed in *John Barleycorn* that Johnny Heinhold, proprietor of the Last Chance, loaned him fifty dollars to continue his education, an episode that aroused much sardonic laughter along the Oakland waterfront, where Heinhold was regarded as notably tight-fisted. Spider Healey, whom Jack had known in his oyster-pirating days, wrote him that Heinhold was "estimated according to Bradstreet's to be worth about one hundred and sixty thousand dollars," while Jack's old friends and Heinhold's old customers, including Healey himself, Soup Kennedy and Joe Goose, were on their "last legs." Healey added that "Soup is very much enthused when I told him that I was about to ask you for a small bit of assistance."

When it was serialized in the *Saturday Evening Post,* from March 15 to May 3, 1915, and later came out as his last book under the Century contract, *John Barleycorn* created a sensation almost comparable to the muckraking books of a decade before. It was credited with being an important factor in the campaign which succeeded six years later in bringing Prohibition to the United States: Jack's one victory over his old enemy.

Ministers waved the book in front of their congregations and used it as the text of sermons against intemperance, the liquor industry denounced it, thousands of problem drinkers had it thrust into their trembling hands as an object lesson. It virtually became the textbook of the Anti-Saloon League, the Women's Christian Temperance Union, the clergymen, educators, propagandists, professional crusaders and others who joined in the Prohibition movement.

Such reviewers as Floyd Dell, Joyce Kilmer and Elbert Hubbard agreed that the vitality of its argument, the self-revelatory frankness of his encyclical against liquor made it a work of classic proportions. One dissenting, and very perceptive voice was that of Andre Tridon,[3] who saw *John Barleycorn* not so much the *J'Accuse* of the temperance movement or a straightforward autobiography, but an indication of why his talent was fizzling out. "I knew there was something wrong with London's stuff. The vocabulary was apparently gone, his imagination seemed to be failing him, he repeated himself frightfully, his stories were becoming as safe as those of any popular novelist." *John Barleycorn,* Tridon wrote, was an indication that "he does not even seem to know how far he has gone." The critic advised Jack to "cease to abuse alcohol. It isn't alcohol that is troubling you, it's people, the small, nice, human, uninteresting, hearty, loyal, trashy people with whom you drink. Alcohol may have something to do with your temporary downfall, but people have and are having more to do with it. . . . May I suggest a cure for London's ailment? To live in some large city where 'people' are so cheap a commodity that we don't go to their houses nor let them come too often to our lodgings, and we enter sociability under the heading of dissipation or profit and loss . . ."

A review headed " 'John Barleycorn' Under Psychoanalysis" must have annoyed — or troubled — Jack even more. The reviewer, Wilfrid Lay, charged that Jack's masculinity was suspect. A psychoanalyst, wrote Lay, would find "traits of Sadism-Masochism, homosexuality and extraversion to a high degree" in the London personality.

"To Jack London . . . being a man means accepting what fate has given him," Lay wrote, "but not without plenty of outcry at the time . . . A man's man, among other characteristics, rates women, horses, dogs and other animals on much the same level . . . looking at them all as animals . . . In his pages his dogs live; his women do not . . . He does not appreciate a woman . . .

"Jack London appears to have been more grown up as a boy than he was as a man . . . By being a man's man only, he thought he was becoming a complete man . . ."[4]

Hundreds of thousands of people read *John Barleycorn.* It was necessarily sketchy as autobiography but definitive in its exploration of how alcohol can influence behavior, the mind and spirit; a searing indictment of the price exacted for the temporary "white logic," the illusory brilliance of the insights which can come out of a bottle. "Suicide, quick or slow, a sudden spill or a gradual oozing away through the years, is the price John Barleycorn exacts. No friend of his ever escapes making the just, due payment." Perhaps many drinkers were "saved" through reading the book. The tragedy was that its author was unmoved by his own stark admonitions and still believed that he could handle John Barleycorn, given the discretion he mistakenly believed he had acquired.

3. *Squire of Glen Ellen*

George Sterling once said of his friend that Jack was two people — "One is a mixer, a go-getter. The other is heart-hungry for an ivory tower where he can be an artist. His error lies in thinking that an ivory tower as large as the San Francisco Ferry Building is necessary. Danger lurks in the division of Jack's mind."

Actually Jack's ivory tower — the Beauty Ranch, as he called it — was a lot larger than the ferry building. It had become an obsession with him, destructive in that it demanded financing that could be supplied only by turning out the "stacks of hack" he detested, as compelling as the urges that sent him to the South Seas or the Klondike . . . or the bottle.

Much of his mystic feeling for the soil, particularly that expanse of the Sonoma Valley which he owned, was compressed into *The Valley of the Moon,* which had enough popular ingredients to be serialized by *Cosmopolitan,* including the usual sticky love story, and was the first book to be published by Macmillan on his return to Brett's paternal care in 1913. It was his first full-length effort since *Burning Daylight,* and once again he hoped that it would restore his public to him.

The hero of *The Valley of the Moon* was Billy Roberts, a brawny teamster and part-time prizefighter cast in the familiar London mold; the heroine Saxon Brown, who worked in an Oakland laundry. Her odd first name was supposed to symbolize the purity and strength and grace of the peoples who founded the English race. She was, her creator emphasized more than once, conscious of the "great hegira of the land-hungry Anglo-Saxons" and nourished on the tradition of the wagon trains, the pioneers and Indian fighters, and their bitter fate after reaching the Promised Land west of the Rockies. Billy, too, was embittered by the harshness of the lot of the citified descendants of the pioneers. "It's a dirty world — an unfair, lousy world. I can't make it out. There's no squareness in it . . ."

For more than the first third, the novel is an exploration of the proletarian life of Oakland and the labor strife of the Nineties. Billy and Saxon met at an Irish picnic in Weasel Park on a blind date. During their first, rather incredible conversation Billy and Saxon informed each other of the fact they possessed pure Anglo-Saxon blood. Their exchange of confidences was interrupted when the Irish picnickers, lacking the proper admixture of Anglo-corpuscles, turned the picnic into a gigantic brawl when a tug-of-war contest got out of hand. One of the best scenes Jack ever wrote, in fact, described the Donnybrook involving hundreds of joyous combatants battering each other in a vast panorama of flying fists, boots and brickbats.

Billy and Saxon eventually married and settled down in a four-room cottage near the Southern Pacific yards. Soon after that, disaster struck them from every quarter. Billy lost his job when a general strike broke out. Saxon lost her child through miscarriage when she was caught in a mob of rioting strikers. Billy was thrown in jail. Eventually they decided to quit the city, with all its squalor and violence, and seek the freer and cleaner atmosphere of the countryside.

In their wanderings they paused at Carmel, observing the fresh-air Bohemians at play, then continued their "pilgrimage" into northern California, seeking what Saxon, with remarkable prevision, called their "valley of the moon."

En route they came across a famous writer named Jack Hastings and his fascinating wife Clara. The reader did not have to guess who the charming and glamorous Jack and Clara were modeled after.

Hastings generously directed them to the Sonoma Valley, where they acquired acreage and settled down to raise horses and vegetables. Billy and Saxon then were able to congratulate themselves, in the usual closing scene bathed by an overpowering sunset, that though "We're the white folks that lost out . . . that was too busy being good to be smart" they had finally attained their pioneer heritage.

The novel was a fervent statement of the mystic bonds of "race, blood and soil," a hymn to his own kind which has caused Maxwell Geismar to condemn it as "racial paranoia." Harsh as it sounds, the verdict would appear to be just, viewed in the context of mankind's subsequent experience of racial problems. A few years later Jack would renounce his former hopes for universal brotherhood and declare, "I believe my race is the salt of the earth." Earlier, in his essay on "The Yellow Peril," he had been explicit in stating why he believed that the Anglo-Saxons deserved to inherit the earth. Granted that they had committed many crimes of conquest and brutality against less developed races, "there is a certain integrity, a sternness of conscience, a melancholy responsibility of life, a sympathy and comradeship and warm human feeling, which is ours, indubitably ours, and which we cannot teach to the Oriental as we would teach logarithms or the trajectory of projectiles." Despite his own non-Christian views, he believed that "The colossal fact of our history is that we have made the religion of Jesus Christ our religion . . . We are pre-eminently a religious race, which is another way of saying that we are a right-seeking race." The chosen people, he made clear, were the English-speaking, not the whole white race, not even western Europeans.

Nor was there anything in *The Valley of the Moon* to comfort any doctrinaire Socialist. The only Socialist character in the novel was a dreamy and ineffectual weakling. As for its protagonist, Billy Roberts, he deserted the working class in the middle of a general strike and went off on his own to become a "scientific" farmer exploiting the labor of others.

Democracy itself was attacked as "the dream of stupid peoples . . . democracy is a lie . . . an enchantment to keep the work brutes content, just as religion used to keep them content." Individualism, it seemed, was the only answer. A man like Billy Roberts, stronger and more independent than his fellows, could find personal salvation only by going off on his own and carving a place for himself in the isolation of the countryside. Unconsciously, no doubt, he had come perilously close to Ambrose Bierce's futilitarian philosophy that the common man was an underserving dolt and the capitalist a predatory varmint — and a plague take both their houses.

His disgust with the world, his disenchantment with humanity in the abstract was clearly stated in that novel. The only way he could live in a reasonable amount of contentment was to shut them out. This was a dangerous attitude for a writer with any ambition of retaining his influence and keeping in touch with the times.

His hedge against all that he repudiated in *The Valley of the Moon* was the boundaries of his ranch, his property, his soil. Those boundaries were again extended when he bought the five-hundred-acre Freund Ranch adjoining his property, for which he scraped together all the cash he could find. He had invested close to fifty thousand dollars in planting a total of 140,000 eucalyptus trees, which cabinet-makers called "Circassian walnut" when it was finished and which he was confident would be worth a fortune in another score of years. He was making seventy-five thousand dollars, on a rough average, every year but spending a third again as much on developing his property, entertaining his guests, and supporting his train of dependents, employes, sycophants and resident philosophers. Once Charmian made a determined effort to have the latter evicted from their grove, but Jack said they gave him more pleasure than it cost him for their simple needs and wouldn't hear of it. His stepsister Eliza later estimated that from one-third to one-half of his income went toward supporting relatives and friends.

He wouldn't consider cutting down on the expense of operating and expanding his ranch. He told a young radical who came to interview him. "I dream of beautiful horses and fine soil. I dream of the beautiful things I own . . . And I write for no other purpose than to add to the beauty that now belongs to me. I write a book for no other reason than to add three or four hundred acres to my magnificent estate. I write a story with no other purpose than to buy a stallion. To me, my cattle are far more interesting than my profession."[5] It was no statement to make the professional guardians of English prose clap their hands with delight, not to mention any surviving believers in his Socialism. When and if the revolution came, he added, he would stay at Glen Ellen and "let it go to blazes."

Earn and spend — the motto could have been carved on the rooftree of Wolf House, still under construction with its payroll of twenty to thirty masons and carpenters.

A letter to Brett on March 1, 1913, indicated how he was constantly spending money faster than he made it. He was building a new home for Bessie and his daughters in Piedmont Hills, another on the ranch for Eliza and her son. Another house was under construction on the ranch, remote from the main house, which would (he hoped) be rented to vacationers at fifty or sixty dollars a month. He had just bought an English shire stallion for twenty-five hundred dollars and a mare in foal of the same breed for seven hundred and fifty dollars. The letter wound up with a request for thirty-five hundred dollars which Jack needed for the Spanish tile to be used in roofing Wolf House.

He became a scientific breeder, convinced that the livestock in the Sonoma Valley had gone to "scrub." Attending stock shows, he began buying purebred cattle, a prize bull for eight hundred dollars, eight heifers for three hundred fifty dollars apiece. He journeyed to Southern California to find the heavy draft horses he required for clearing his fields of volcanic rock. He built a piggery and imported prize Duroc Jersey hogs for it, along with a herd of eighty-five Angora goats.

He envisioned an agricultural Eden in his Valley of the Moon, and crammed himself on the subjects of animal husbandry, farm management, breeding, and reviving worn-out soil just as he had prepared in a few months to enter the University of California. His workroom was crowded with books and government pamphlets on those subjects. His name became more prominent, both as a byline and a subject for interviewers, in agricultural journals than in literary magazines — especially since he was no longer regarded as a member of the literary vanguard but a commercial writer whose work was designed for the mass-circulation magazines.

If the high priests of contemporary literature would no longer take him seriously, he professed to be more interested in the fact that the Beauty Ranch was celebrated for having the first manure spreader in the vicinity, the first concrete silo (forty-three feet high and eleven feet in diameter) ever built in California, for the stone barns and water troughs which he said would last a millenium. Everything was made as hygienic as possible. Before entering the piggery, it was observed by Bailey Millard, on his visit to the ranch, the visitor had to step into a little pagoda and rub his feet on a "sticky carbolized mixture" so he wouldn't carry any stray cholera germs on the soles of his shoes.

Millard said Jack called it "the Ranch of Good Intentions," and explained his appetite for land-buying, "I want to be able to go all up and down those beautiful green ridges and always to be upon my own land. In order to get the uplands I had to buy the lowlands." [6]

Much of his time was spent conferring with Eliza, who was superintendent of all his holdings, his various foremen, and the stockmen, Hazen Cowan and Thomas Harrison, two of the best wranglers in the country, who were in charge of his horse herd, as well as inspecting the work being done in his barns, fields and pastures. He remarked, only partly in jest, that he spent two hours a day on his writing and ten hours on his ranching.

A blacksmith shop in Glen Ellen was bought and moved up the steeply climbing road to the ranch on rollers. ("Good boy, Jack!" snidely commented the Sonoma newspaper. "Take a couple more loads and move the whole town up there.") A crew of twenty-two men was set to work reviving his tangled acres of vineyard. A crop of the spineless cactus developed by his friend Luther Burbank, over the objections of University of California agricultural experts that it was ninety per cent water, was planted to provide feed for his stock. He planted some of his newly cleared fields with Canadian peas, rye and vetches to be plowed under for three years, which would increase the humus content and build up the starved soil.

He believed in scientific tillage rather than artificial fertilization, he told Millard, and in "grading the land, making it over into rolling contours and abrupt terraces. It's the only way that such land should be cultivated anyway, as it gives a chance for good, long furrows along the hillside. But the big thing about it is that by these new contours I keep the moisture in the soil and do not let it dissipate itself by seepage or evaporation."

Jack London on the New Agriculture became a favorite topic for newspaper and magazine writers who journeyed to Glen Ellen. He told a Los Angeles reporter he had been studying why California farmers destroyed the fertility of their land in forty or fifty years while the soil of Asian lands had been tilled successfully for thousands of years. In ten years, he warned, "the mouths to feed in the United States have increased by sixteen millions. In that ten years the number of hogs, sheep, dairy cows and beef cattle have actually decreased on account of the breaking up of large ranches into small farms." He told another interviewer, Henry Bland Mead, that the trouble with American agriculture was that, through scientific study, it knew *why* certain things must be done, but not *how*, while in Japan, China and Korea the farmers, depending only on tradition and the knowledge passed from father to son, knew how to conserve the soil even if they couldn't give learned reasons why it must be done.

He propagandized for a "return to the soil" to the extent that he seemed to be proposing that the clock be turned back a century and America be reconverted to the rural paradise of sturdy yeomen envisioned by Thomas Jefferson.

Within the enclave of his valley, as Jack dreamed of it in the years to come, he would be the master of a self-sufficient barony. Everything he needed or wanted would be raised on his own land. Let the revolution come, let wars rage, let his countrymen herd themselves into the cities — he would be isolated from all the world's clamor in Glen Ellen. His private colony — and no nonsense about communal living, no confusion over who gave the orders, no pretense that he wasn't the number one Adam of his Eden — would be sufficient unto itself.

With that great aim in mind, what did it matter that, according to Eliza, he was always at least twenty-five thousand dollars in debt, no matter how much "brain merchandise" he produced, and that by 1913 he had a monthly payroll of three thousand dollars? It was worth it, he told everyone, worth every penny of it.

4. *J. London, Businessman*

Ever since he had been the sharpest boy trader on the Oakland waterfront Jack was convinced that he had the makings of a keen, shrewd and potentially successful businessman. All the evidence to the contrary, he believed that he had handled himself well in dealing with book and magazine publishers; the switch from Macmillan to Century was an aberration, soon corrected, and some of his magazine deals had been ill-considered, but that was because he split himself between artist and entrepreneur. He had turned over his affairs to be botched by "Mother Mine" during the *Snark* cruise, but any man could be led astray by sentiment. He was gypped, hoodwinked, overcharged and outbargained wherever he went, but the illusion of fiscal capability would not die. Like Mark Twain, and along much the same lines, he was tempted to beat the businessmen at their own game and make himself independent of any income from writing.

When Burning Daylight, in the novel of that title, invaded Wall Street and faced down the thimbleriggers, when he ruthlessly made millions on the San Francisco stock exchange, he was merely acting out the daydreams of Jack London. It was safer doing it on paper, but unfortunately he was lured more than once into acting out his wolf-of-Wall Street fantasies.

The new technology, with its possibilities of quick millions for any new labor-saving device, attracted him and his money into the marketplace, where men could be almost as dishonorable as any of his deepest-dyed villains. Just as Twain was drawn into the linotype manufacturing business, though with much less disastrous effects, Jack was attracted by the possibilities of color lithography, which would be a great boon to the booming advertising business.

One day in 1910, while hanging around the Oakland bureau of the San Francisco *Bulletin* where his friend Joseph Noel worked, he was introduced to a man named Miller who had just developed a three-color lithographic process. Jack took samples of his work to an expert in San Francisco, who pronounced them closer to perfect than he had ever seen.

Within a week, perhaps to distract himself from the recent loss of Charmian's baby, he was caught up in a whirlwind of plans to develop and market the process. Noel suggested that the process be tested in San Francisco first to determine how feasible it was commercially, but Jack said the local sharks would tear them to pieces and it would be wiser to transfer all activities to New York, establish a plant and go into production.

Capital was hastily raised for the venture. Jack mortgaged his mother's home again for four thousand dollars and Noel invested his seven hundred dollars in savings. George Sterling's uncle was persuaded to put in a thousand in George's name. Smaller sums were raised among other people they knew.

Miller and his wife were persuaded to sell their Oakland home and packed off to New York with the eleven thousand dollars raised to establish the Millergraph Company. Then Noel was persuaded by Jack to give up his job with the *Bulletin* and move to New York with the assignment of keeping an eye on Miller and their capital.

In New York, as they would have learned through preliminary investigation had Jack not been so eager to get the project rolling, there were a number of lithographic processes in vigorous competition. Instead of spending their capital recklessly, Miller set up a shop in his Brooklyn home and went to work on further perfecting his process. Experts were called in to make a survey of the competing processes and the potential market. The only way they could make a success of Millergraph, Jack and his associates were told, was to reincorporate and issue two million dollars in stock and five hundred thousand dollars in bonds.

Jack was delighted. The talk of millions made it seem as though *Burning Daylight* was being translated into real life. The fact that he came to New York that alcoholic winter of 1912 in a rather feverish state of mind probably had a lot to do with the erratic course of Millergraph on and off the Big Board. Jack himself would be president because his name on the stock certificates would cause a stampede among investors. He would borrow twenty-five thousand dollars — no, fifty thousand dollars — from Macmillan to increase their working capital. Noel, however, proposed that they turn the job of financing the company over to the Wall Street professionals, to which Jack reluctantly agreed. A man who had participated in the organization of the Western Pacific Railroad was called in, though Jack was apprehensive that once Millergraph was consigned to the manipulations of the Wall Streeters they'd all be frozen out.

In the process of reorganization Jack was offered his money back or stock equivalent to holdings in the new company. Jack elected to take the stock in spite of his apprehensions. Later he had Eliza send up a barrage of letters demanding to know what was going on with the company he had more or less founded. About all he got in reply was soothing letters, explaining the difficulties in obtaining patents and buying machinery. Before the year was out, the Millergraph Company went bankrupt amid rumors of stock-juggling.

Jack, however, still had his dreams. Making money was a game, so it was said, and he liked games. He was sucked into a Mexican land deal in which the promoters said all he would have to do was sign his name to a few papers. Business contracts and stock certificates were boring as reading matter. Pretty soon money was being demanded of him as a result of his hasty signature. Shortly after that he was trimmed on a fidelity loan deal, again having carelessly signed papers at the request of eloquent rascals. The two transactions cost him approximately ten thousand dollars. Jack shrugged them off, explaining to Charmian that he had entered them in the spirit of a man taking a fling at roulette. The wrong numbers had come up, that was all.

Another fling at high finance was the Jack London Grapejuice Company, which he formed with one Oliver Dibble, whose rustic New England name was all too reassuring.

The idea behind this venture was that Jack's vineyards would furnish the grapes while Dibble and his associates would process and market the grape juice. All agreed that with Jack's supplying the brand-name, along with the quality of the grapes, of which Jack was exceedingly proud, they had a veritable bonanza.

While Jack was in Glen Ellen or elsewhere, however, his associates were busy trying to make the company into something more than a mere purveyor of grape juice. The company was capitalized at two hundred and fifty thousand dollars, but few investors chose to buy stock. Jack knew nothing of the stock flotation scheme, though it was undertaken with the idea of attracting capital on the strength of his name. Somehow, whatever capital was raised disappeared before any grapes could be squeezed.

The next thing Jack heard of the Jack London Grapejuice Company he was being sued for forty-one thousand dollars by irate investors who believed that he had made off with their money. Eliza engaged legal counsel immediately, and they were able to establish proof that only Jack's name and his grapes were involved in the scheme and he had no responsibility for the stock issued. The case never came to trial.

Jack was still not dismayed. His failures in the business world were blamed, with some accuracy, on a poor choice of associates. Hereafter he would avoid taking in partners. His last venture was a plan to market the dairy products of the Beauty Ranch, again using the Jack London brand-name to lure customers, but he died before it could begin operating.

Early in 1913, as a businessman of letters, he was still maintaining his high level of income, having signed a five-year contract with *Cosmopolitan* which gave that magazine the right to publish all his fiction, including novels as well as short stories. On January 30, he wrote Sterling[7] that he had agreed to supply *Cosmopolitan* with two novels and twelve short stories of six thousand words each annually; a difficult schedule to maintain even for a writer with his energy and discipline. Apparently George had been supplying him with story ideas recently; the letter informed Sterling that Jack couldn't use the plot outline just sent. *Cosmopolitan,* it seemed, had insisted on the right of approving his choice of material in advance; in other words, he was submitting to the editorial formula of the magazine — a giant step backward for a man who had always prized his independence and would not let even George Brett advise him on what to write. To cushion the blow, Jack wrote Sterling a few weeks later that he thought his friend had a splendid talent for the short story and — small comfort to a man struggling to make ends meet in his cottage at Carmel — his letters were so amusing that Jack always had Charmian make five copies and circulate them among their mutual friends.

Jack was working hard on a sea novel using much of the background acquired on the journey around the Horn aboard the *Dirigo.* The novel, an all-out melodrama, was designed as a protest against the way the American merchant marine was being allowed to founder. It was serialized later that year as *The Sea Gangsters* and published by Macmillan as *The Mutiny of the Elsinore.* Once again it would prove that both his talent and his readership were slipping away from him.

The big excitement in his life that spring and summer was the proposed production of a film based on *The Sea Wolf.* Jack, of course, saw great possibilities in the motion-picture industry, both as a source of income and a storytelling medium. Had he lived longer, he might well have ended his career in a Hollywood writer's cubicle, provided he could have found a producer easygoing enough to put up with his temperament. He was so enthused in fact that he started negotiating with a short-lived film-making firm, the Balboa Amusement Producing Company, to have the exclusive motion picture rights to all his stories signed over in return for a share of the profits. Some of the films would be made in the Valley of the Moon. And according to a story published in the Los Angeles *Express* in May, 1913, he intended to lend his considerable, though unproven, dramatic talents to the venture. He considered himself as handsome as any matinee idol imported from the New York stage, and a lot more rugged. "I shall appear as the leading actor in all my own short stories and novels dramatized into motion pictures," the newspaper quoted him as saying. "Will it mean a fortune to me? Well, I'll buy two or three Jersey cows for my Valley of the Moon ranch with the proceeds."

That deal fell through, along with his ambition to play his own heroes on celluloid, but a week or two later Hobart Bosworth, who had once been Minnie Maddern Fiske's leading man and now was an actor, director and producer in Hollywood, came up to Glen Ellen with the proposal to film *The Sea Wolf*.

Jack was "gruff and business-like," Bosworth recalled many years later, and growled at his caller, "Bosworth, your money will talk." [8]

Bosworth was operating on a shoestring and said all he could offer Jack was fifty per cent of the net profits. Until then he had been a director under contract to Selig Brothers, for whom he had turned out 112 one-reelers in the space of a year. Now, Bosworth explained, he wanted to make a long film with real artistic merit: *The Sea Wolf* would be the first eight-reel film ever produced. Bosworth himself would play Wolf Larsen, as well as directing and producing the film. Jack liked Bosworth's forthright manner and agreed to his proposition.

Late in June Jack suffered an attack of appendicitis and had to be removed to an Oakland hospital. His appendix was removed. Four days later he was holding story conferences with Bosworth and others associated with *The Sea Wolf* production at his bedside. In a letter to Brett, sent from the hospital on June 29, he expressed his amazement at the fact that Hollywood was actually going to spend six thousand dollars on making the picture, with one thousand dollars allotted to renting a vessel on which most of the action would be filmed. He expected to earn from ten thousand to fifty thousand dollars on the film, he informed Brett, sublimely innocent of Hollywood sleight-of-hand methods of dealing with profit and loss.

Before he could start collecting that anticipated windfall, however, he was involved in a series of court actions to determine whether — under the antiquated copyright laws then in effect — he really owned the motion picture rights to *The Sea Wolf*.

Towering above all the vexations of the moment, the troubles over the film rights, his mounting debts, the necessity of mortgaging everything that wasn't already in hock, was one matter of great joy. Wolf House, four years in the building at a cost of eighty thousand dollars, was finally aproaching completion. A lot more than time and money went into its construction: this was the seat of the London dynasty which he hoped would dominate the valley it overlooked for a thousand years, the greatest of all monuments to his ego. Joaquin Miller had his stone funeral pyre in the Piedmont Hills, George Sterling had his altar in the grove, and Jack had his neo-Gothic pile at the head of the Valley of the Moon. There was no question which was the most magnificent. Many of his visitors assured him it would be the most beautiful home in America.

The bank holding the mortgages on the ranch and its various improvements had covered part of their potential loss with insurance policies, but Wolf House was not mortgaged, nor was it insured. Everyone agreed that insurance wasn't really necessary. Much of it was constructed of rock and concrete, and the rest was extensively fireproofed. All pipes were covered with asbestos. All its beams and siding and paneling had been coated with a supposedly fireproof paint. The roof was built of tile, and the roofing paper under it was fireproofed. The only way a fire could start, Jack was assured, was by setting a torch to it in a dozen places. And who would want to do that to Jack, who felt himself loved from one end of the valley to the other?

On August 22, Forni's workmen had finished their job and were clearing the waste materials out of the house. The wiring was also finished. Jack and Charmian expected to be able to move in before winter, with only the interior decoration to be completed. Late that night Jack and Forni took a last look at that magnificent pile limned against the moonlight — this, too, would last a thousand years. He felt an immense satisfaction. Here was one perfect thing he had created.

He went to bed at midnight a happy man.

Two hours later Eliza hurried into his bedroom and shook his shoulder until he awakened. Wolf House was on fire. Over the wooded knolls, a half-mile away, the whole sky was leaping with flame.

A team was harnessed, and Jack drove over the trail toward Wolf House with Charmian and Eliza. When they urged him to whip up the horses, he shrugged and said, "What's the use? If the big house is burning, there's nothing we can do about it."

And there was nothing to be done. The whole wooden superstructure was on fire, and no water was available. They could only stand and watch it burn down to the rock and concrete shell.

Forni, who had been roused before Jack and was the first to arrive on the scene, said that Jack stood at his side and wept.

All that he could recall Jack saying was, "We will rebuild."

Arson obviously was the cause of the fire, otherwise it could not have blazed up, against all the safeguards, and burned so quickly. There was a lengthy investigation in which a workman whom Jack had discharged a few days before for laziness and insolence was accused of having started the fire out of revenge, but nothing was proved against him. Various other suspects were questioned. A favorite official theory was that a Socialist, outraged by Jack's style of living, had set the fire.

But the investigation, which went on for months, failed to turn up the arsonist, if there was one, or even to establish exactly how the fire started. Jack lost interest in the matter completely; he was certain now that whatever he wanted the most and worked the hardest for would be denied him. You had to become a fatalist or crack up. Occasionally he talked of rebuilding Wolf House but never did anything about it. Sometimes he would ride over the trail from the ranch house and stare at its ruins, over which moss rapidly grew until it looked like an old English abbey.

Three days later he was in San Francisco watching Bosworth directing the first scenes of *The Sea Wolf* aboard a rented yacht in the Bay. The film was finished in a few weeks and a rough cut was shown Jack in a projection room. Unlike many authors in the subsequent history of Hollywood, he was most pleased by the result, thought Bosworth was the embodiment of Wolf Larsen as he had imagined him, and told him, "Great Scott, man, I'm amazed that you've stuck to my story. I thought the movies always changed everything."

Despite that initial satisfaction, *The Sea Wolf* film involved him in a long dispute in the courts, which kept him traveling between the ranch and Los Angeles and New York. Two producers made "pirate" versions of *The Sea Wolf*, so a suit was instituted to test just what legal control an author had over the motion picture rights to his work. Very little, he soon learned. In Los Angeles, where he sued the two producers, the courts determined that the film rights to any work that had been serialized belonged to the magazine which first published it, rather than to the author. Thus, without his knowing it, the rival companies which filmed *The Sea Wolf* had acquired their rights by paying small sums to the magazine. The copyright laws simply hadn't caught up with the development of motion pictures.

Then he learned that he would also have to clear up the matter of the dramatic rights to *The Sea Wolf,* which he had given Joseph Noel years before. Noel's dramatization had been a flop on the Coast and never opened in New York. Noel had sold the rights to Henry B. Harris, the theatrical producer, who went down with the *Titanic* the previous year. Since then, they had been acquired by Ben Stern, formerly Harris's general manager, who announced his intentions of presenting it on Broadway.

In order to clear his title to making a film of his own book, he had to buy back those rights and settle with Noel. The latter, however, wanted his play produced and the movie released two years later. After a heated wrangle, the two former friends agreed to submit the dispute to the executive council of the Authors League, to which they both belonged, for settlement. Jack withdrew at the last moment and "said he'd fight me through every court in the country," Noel recalled in later years. "He reminded me that he had the money to do it and that, as I had none, I would be unable to fight back." Jack's position was that he wanted back what he had given away; Noel's that he had labored over the dramatization and felt he had something coming for it.

According to the tale later related with gusto by Jack, he holed up in a rundown theatrical hotel off Times Square in October of 1913, deciding to stage a small melodrama of his own to convince Noel to sign the release. He had let his beard grow before calling Noel and asking him to come over and discuss the matter. He also took his upper plate out of his mouth, put on a tattered pair of pajamas and assured himself in the mirror that he looked desperate and decrepit enough to wring anyone's heart. When Noel showed up, the way Jack told it, he was so alarmed by Jack's appearance that he signed the release immediately.

Noel himself does not mention any such hoked-up scene in his memoir *Footlose in Arcadia,* but only says that he finally agreed to release the dramatic rights in exchange for Jack's promise not to permit the film to be shown in the theaters for two years. "And he did not live up to his pledge," Noel added.

Macmillan's correspondence files show that Jack obtained thirty-five hundred dollars in advances to pay off the owners of the theatrical rights to *The Sea Wolf* and another one thousand dollars to be sent Noel for an unstated purpose. No doubt it was that thousand dollars rather than any private melodrama he might have staged which resulted in a final clearance of the rights to distribute the film. After all that trouble, in and out of court, he never made a dollar on the film version of his book because there was never any net profit to be distributed, thanks to Hollywood-style bookkeeping, a trap into which many writers have fallen.

During all this in-fighting in New York Charmian stayed on the ranch and fretted over his heavy drinking, reports of which reached her from friends willing to provide intelligence of her straying husband.

One night Jack and one of his Burlesque Club friends were taking three of the girls in the cabaret's floor show home in a taxicab. The cab collided with two others, and Jack found himself at the bottom of the pile in the overturned automobile with the four other passengers on top of him and his mouth full of broken glass. It was a narrow escape from death, according to the newspapers.

But there was no way he could short-circuit a telegram which Charmian received from a friend who signed herself "Amy" reporting that Jack was spending most of his time with a woman who lived in a hotel on West Forty-eighth Street, just off Times Square. His new romance, according to gossip reaching his friends back home, was an actress.

That fall of 1913 Jack was also spending much of his energy helping to organize the Authors League of America. He was among the founders of the League, which included Rex Beach, Booth Tarkington, Ellen Glasgow, Arther Train, Gertrude Atherton, Samuel Hopkins Adams, George Barr McCutcheon, Will Irwin, Ida Tarbell, Kate Douglas Wiggin, the American Winston Churchill and Meredith Nicholson. Former President Theodore Roosevelt, himself as prolific as any of the professionals, also joined the League. Jack worked with Arthur Train, the lawyer-author, and others in obtaining changes in the copyright law to afford better protection to authors' rights. One of the main purposes of their campaign was to insure that an author had full control of his dramatic and motion picture rights and prevent such abuses as that which vexed Jack when three different versions of *The Sea Wolf* were showing on one Los Angeles block. The motion pictures, Rex Beach, an early president of the League, wrote, "grew into long pants but with them [they] put on the sweater and cap of a hoodlum . . . became a neighborhood nuisance, a disorderly character . . . robbed peanut stands, upset pushcarts and jeered at the police." And play producers "blackjacked dramatists, rifled their pockets, then dropped them down dumb-waiter shafts." [9]

Thanks to a sustained effort by London, Train and others, Congress was persuaded to change the copyright laws, establish a writer's ownership of any story published in a magazine or in book form, and end the piracy of stage and film producers. Jack attended the annual banquets of the League at which, Beach recalled, the writers "assembled with plume, shield and assagai to stamp our heels and shout for bigger royalties."

The 1913 banquet was notable for the spectacle Jack made of himself in objecting to the honored presence of the Secretary of State. President Wilson had been invited to give the principal after-dinner speech but instead sent William Jennings Bryan.

Jack, always restless when other men were speaking, showed up well fortified against the anticipated ordeal, according to the recollection of Will Irwin. He sat at a corner table in the banquet room with a bottle of gin and a box of cigarets in front of him. When Secretary of State Bryan rose to lecture the assemblage on its responsibility for elevating the standards of American literature, which he and other moralists believed was succumbing to coarseness and levity, Jack offered a highly audible commentary.

"Young writing men and women of America," thundered the statesman from Nebraska, "do you realize your re-spon-si-bil-ity?"

"Bunk," snorted Jack, shaking off the attempts of other people at his table to shush him.

Undeterred Bryan launched into an impassioned denunciation of tendencies toward alcoholism among writers, with a portentous glance at the corner table, and impurity in what they purveyed.

Jack filled every orotund pause with "Oh, hell!," "Hohum!," "Blah!," and other expletives which affronted the Secretary of State and embarrassed his hosts. The tactful among those present, by no means a majority, began applauding every time Bryan paused in an attempt to drown out Jack's remarks.

A few days later the executive council of the League, under pressure of some of its more sensitive members, met to draw up a letter of apology to Mr. Bryan asking his pardon for "the interruptions by a small minority of the audience"—namely Jack London. Irwin recalled, however, that he and his fellow council members "giggled" as they composed the letter because Jack had given "great though secret pleasure" to most of those attending the banquet.[10]

XV

The Face of Revolution

1. *"On to Mexico City"*

AFTER YEARS of talking and writing about revolutions, London finally got a chance to study one at first hand. The Mexican Revolution was conveniently located, and he considered himself an expert on its background and motive force. His ultimate reaction, so far as his Socialist comrades were concerned, was surprising.

During the early years of revolution and counterrevolution, Jack, as a good Socialist, was hopeful that Mexico wuld succeed in establishing a just and stable government. Early in 1911 the oligarchy of Dictator-President Porfirio Díaz and his clique of wealthy landowners were overthrown after more than three decades of ruling Mexico as successors to Juárez and the war of liberation which ended the "empire" of Maximilian and Carlotta. A liberal, Francisco I. Madero, assumed the presidency. Jack was overjoyed. Now the great haciendas would be broken up and distributed among the land-hungry peasants, and the quicker the Mexicans expropriated the oil, land and mining concessions in the hands of foreigners the better.

In February, 1911, Jack wrote an open letter widely reprinted in the Socialist press and addressed to his "brave comrades of the Mexican Revolution," which left no doubt that he identified himself with the revolutionaries:

"You will notice that we are not respectable in these days of property. [He will not mention that he himself was the proprietor of a *hacienda* and the largest employer of labor for miles around.] All the names you are being called, we have been called. And when graft and greed get up and begin to call names, honest men, brave men, patriotic men and martyrs can expect nothing else than to be called chicken thieves and outlaws."

He ended his call to arms with, "I subscribe myself a chicken thief and revolutionist. Jack London."

To further the cause he wrote a short story titled "The Mexican," one of the best of his later years, which was exciting enough for the *Saturday Evening Post* to publish despite its obvious propaganda content.* It was a beautiful example of how to combine ideology with a crackling action story.

"The Mexican" of the story was Felipe Rivera, a boy with eyes that "burned like cold fire" with revolutionary zeal. He worked for the Junta in Los Angeles, which was dedicated to raising money and buying weapons for the coming revolution against the Díaz dictatorship. That event waited on the first gunfire: "The border was ready to rise. . . . And clear across to the Atlantic, the Junta was in touch with them all and all of them needing guns, were adventurers, soldiers of fortune, bandits, disgruntled American union men, socialists, anarchists, rough-necks, Mexican exiles, peons escaped from bondage, whipped miners from the bull-pens of Coeur d'Alene and Colorado who desired only the more vindictively to fight — all the flotsam and jetsam of wild spirits from the madly complicated modern world. And it was guns and ammunition, ammunition and guns — the unceasing and eternal cry."

The other members of the Junta didn't quite trust Felipe Rivera at first, believing him to be an agent of Díaz's secret service. Then he was given the mission of re-establishing the lines of communication between Los Angeles and the rebel underground in Baja California, which had been disrupted by the ruthless suppressions of Díaz's military commander in the state. Felipe's remedy was to bury a knife in the commander's chest. "To me," said one awed member of the Junta, "he is the primitive, the wild wolf, the striking rattlesnake, the stinging centipede."

The time came when the Junta needed five thousand dollars to buy the last shipment of arms to touch off the revolution. All along Felipe had been contributing smaller sums from purses won in the Los Angeles prize ring. Now he arranged a winner-take-all bout with

*Collected in *The Night Born,* 1913.

Danny Ward, a far more experienced fighter who was being built up for the championship.

Everybody expected Felipe to be knocked senseless in a round or two when he faced Ward, but the boy was inspired. "He saw the white-walled, water-power factories of Rio Blanco. He saw the six thousand workers, starved and wan, and the little children, seven and eight years of age, who toiled long shifts for ten cents a day. He saw the perambulating corpses, the ghastly death's heads of men who labored in the dye rooms. He remembered that he had heard his father call the dye rooms the 'suicide holes,' where a year was death . . ."

The fight was a toe-to-toe brawl from the beginning, with Felipe's hatred making up for his opponent's superior skill and strength. "It was all of a piece. They were the hated gringos and they were all unfair. And in the worst of it visions continued to flash and sparkle in his brain — long lines of railroad track that shimmered across the desert; *rurales* and American constables; prisons and calabooses; tramps at water tanks — all the squalid and painful panorama of his odyssey after Rio Blanco and the strike . . . The guns were there before him. Every hated face was a gun. It was for the guns he fought . . ."

The two men fought on fairly even terms for seventeen rounds (though any realist of the prize ring would know that even the most impassioned club fighter could hardly last that long, let alone beat a contender for the championship). And then the miracle happened: Felipe laid out his opponent and won the five thousand dollars. "The guns were his. The revolution could go on."

In the three years between 1911 and 1914 there was a murderous struggle for power in Mexico. Madero, the pathetic and ineffectual idealist, was murdered and succeeded by Huerta, a brutal general of the Díaz stripe and a master of the doublecross. Despite his harsh methods, despite the backing of British oil interests, Huerta could not pacify the country. A series of counterrevolutions broke out. Zapata led the peasant revolt in the south. In the north three rebel leaders were contending for supremacy. Carranza had the widest support, appealing to those who wanted a constitutional democracy. Subsequently he was joined by General Obregón, who had commanded his own following in the north. Pancho Villa, the third contender, was a colorful brigand who lived like a Chinese warlord, traveled in an armored train and kept northern Mexico and the United States border towns terrorized by his raiding horsemen. Another and more Socialist-oriented revolutionary was a workers' leader named Magón, whose efforts were short-lived. Magón, with the help of American radicals and adventurers, captured Mexicali and established the "Socialist Republic of Lower California" but it collapsed soon after Magón was arrested while on a mission in the United States and sent to a federal penitentiary.

During the later stages of this upheaval, Jack apparently lost interest in the revolutionary struggle south of the border. The events of 1911 had excited his imagination, but the problems of supporting his ranch and building Wolf House absorbed him to the exclusion of outside events. Or at least there were no more pronunciamentos from the self-styled chicken thief. His attitude toward the revolution had cooled considerably by the fall of 1913 when William Randolph Hearst asked him if he would be willing to go to Mexico as a correspondent if large-scale fighting broke out or the United States intervened. Hearst, with his vast holdings in Mexican land and mineral properties, wanted the country pacified, forcibly if necessary, and his correspondents were not expected to file dispatches favorable to the revolutionaries. Jack, however, was ready to accept his offer. It was finally turned down only because they couldn't agree on the price for Jack's services.

In the spring of 1914, five months before Europe slid into a conflict that raged for four years from the Belgian coast to the plains of the Ukraine, war fever swept the United States. Hatred had been focused for several years on our troubled neighbor to the south, and an armed invasion was widely prescribed as a corrective. Few paused to consider that our attitude was more that of a neighborhood bully than an anxious big brother. Behind the anti-Mexican sentiment was the intrigue of United States oil interests which wanted Carranza in and Huerta, the British favorite, out and the desire of the large American property owners to protect their holdings from the threat of expropriation, which would certainly occur if a wild man like Villa or a fanatic like Zapata managed to seize Mexico City.

A splendid excuse for interfering cropped up late in March 1914, at Vera Cruz. A junior paymaster from the American naval squadron lying offshore was arrested by General Huerta's officers while buying supplies. The United States immediately demanded that the officer be released and that the Vera Cruz garrison tender a thirteen-gun salute to the American flag to demonstrate its regret for the incident.

Huerta, seeing in American intervention an opportunity to unite Mexico behind him, refused. Washington decided that Huerta would have to be unseated.

On the morning of April 21, President Wilson authorized the seizure of the customs house at Vera Cruz by naval landing parties, four members of which were killed and twenty wounded in the assault. This was followed up by a United States Army occupying force of four regiments under Major General Frederick Funston, which took over the whole port city. "In a moment either of policy or pique," as Walter Millis has written, "the President had snatched up the tremendous engines of brute power lying always ready to the hand of those who control the modern state."*

Two days later the regular army was being mobilized for an invasion of Mexico from the northern border. "On the Mexico City!" went up the cry from thousands in San Francisco as two regiments from the Presidio paraded down Market Street to entrain for the border. The country was gripped by an urge to straighten out the Mexicans at bayonet point.

Six days before the landing at Vera Cruz took place, Jack had been telegraphed an offer from *Collier's* to cover whatever campaigning might occur. He was to be paid eleven hundred dollars a week. Since his contract with *Cosmopolitan* gave that magazine exclusive rights only to his fiction, he was able to accept. He was eager, he said, to prove himself as a war correspondent "after what I was held back from doing by the Japanese Army" ten years before in Korea and Manchuria.

He was to proceed to Galveston, Texas, where an army transport would take him and other correspondents to Vera Cruz.

Charmian, determined to keep an eye on him even in a potential war zone, accompanied him to Galveston. From there she would take passage on a commerical steamer to Vera Cruz, though no other correspondents were taking their wives.

Jack agreed only with the proviso that she would have to stay behind in Vera Cruz "when we go on march to Mexico City." Once he had raged at his own country for imprisoning Mexican rebels, including the Socialist Magón. Now he was eagerly anticipating an armed excursion to the Mexican capital.

Before he could obtain his credentials from the War Department

* *The Road to War: America, 1914-1917.*

and board the transport to Galveston, his radical reputation caught up with him. Some bureaucrat in Washington had clipped and filed an article which appeared in the October, 1913, issue of the *International Socialist Review*. It bore Jack London's byline and was headed "The Good Soldier." It read:

Young men: The lowest aim in your life is to become a soldier. The good soldier never tries to distinguish right from wrong. He never thinks; never reasons; he only obeys. If he is ordered to fire on his fellow citizens, on his friends, on his neighbors, on his relatives, he obeys without hesitation. If he is ordered to fire down a crowded street when the poor are clamoring for bread, he obeys and see the gray hairs of age stained with red and the life tide gushing from the breasts of women, feeling neither remorse nor sympathy . . .

A good soldier is a blind, heartless, soulless, murderous machine. He is not a man. He is not a brute, for brutes only kill in self-defense. All that is human in him, all that is divine, all that constitutes the man has been sworn away when he took the enlistment roll. His mind, his conscience, aye, his very soul, are in the keeping of his officer.

No man can fall lower than a soldier — it is a depth beneath which we cannot go. Keep the boys out of the army. It is hell.

Down with the army and the navy. We don't need killing institutions. We need life-giving institutions.

Because of that diatribe against the armed forces, Jack's war-correspondent credentials were held up while Jack fumed and listened to the polite evasions of General Funston's staff officers at the embarkation headquarters in Galveston. He wasn't even told why they were being withheld.

Once again Richard Harding Davis came to his rescue. Learning of Jack's difficulties, he was informed by Funston's staff that the credentials were held up because of "The Good Soldier" article. Davis then asked Jack if he had written it.

Jack vehemently denied authorship of the piece. He insisted that the article had been published without his knowledge, that he never wrote a word of it. (Yet there is no record of his having demanded a retraction of the *International Socialist Review*, though the article had appeared more than six months before. He must have seen it or heard about it, since it was widely reprinted, caused much comment and provoked demands for a Congressional inquiry. Perhaps he had grown weary of denying what he called "canards.") The War Department might have been forgiven for suspecting that he wrote the fulmination: the shotgun phraseology was certainly an excellent imitation of his polemic style. By 1913, however, his views on militarism, as on many other matters, had changed considerably. It would have been out of character for him, in any case, to have denied authorship of anything he had actually written.

After hearing Jack's indignant denials, Davis passed them along to the general's staff. Later that same day, lunching at a Galveston hotel, Jack was summoned to General Funston's table by an aide and was assured that he would be provided with credentials before the transport sailed for Vera Cruz.

Once again Davis, beefy and red-faced now, no longer the slim and dashing adventurer but looking "like a cavalry colonel," as one of his colleagues observed, had bailed him out of trouble. "People can say what they damn please," Jack proclaimed, "but Davis is a great, big *white* man!" [1]

Initially eager as he was for a glimpse of action, he found Vera Cruz as peaceful as his own county seat, pacified by the guns of the American soldiers patrolling the streets. Robert Dunn, representing the New York *Post,* a friend from the Korean campaigning, thought he "looked less cocksure . . . I saw an inner softness." He wasn't greatly impressed by Charmian with her "possessive eyes above a thin mouth . . . full of girlish laughter." They spent six weeks in the old port city, which had seen so many conquerors arrive from overseas and many depart in bemused haste, with Jack fretting over the army's restrictions against travel into the interior. In Korea he had prided himself on evading such restrictions, and even the portly Richard Harding Davis made it to Mexico City on an end run, but Jack was no longer so venturesome. He contented himself with griping, exchanging rumors with his fellow correspondents, including Frederick Palmer and Jimmy Hare, both of whom he had known in Korea; Ford Madox Ford, representing a London newspaper on a sabbatical from more literary efforts; Vincent Starrett, John T. McCutcheon, Stanton Leeds and Arthur Ruhl.

Although he had been strongly anti-militarist in his youth, he was pleased by what he saw of the American army and navy, praised their clean-cut efficiency and admitted that he now believed that war was part of the human condition. "Although I am a man of peace," he said,

"I carry an automatic pistol. I might meet somebody who would not listen to my protestations of friendship and amity. And so with nations . . . It looks as though we shall need armies for a weary while to come . . ."

Except for a brief excursion to the oil port of Tampico, Jack spent most of his time drinking, nursing a low-grade fever and talking about his plans for future writing. Dunn recalled that he boasted of having "an idea every day" but "none was ever written, as far as I know, and he looked peaked, yellow." [2]

His only real interest seemed to be drinking. Years later Dunn remembered his "wistful mid-morning look" of the compulsive drinker hoping someone would join him at the bar.

Ford Madox Ford, whose World War I novels won him an honored place in English literature, accompanied Jack when they hitched a ride to Tampico on a tanker on five minutes' notice. "Let's go and see what oil smells like," Jack suggested. Ford was fascinated by him and afterward wrote that Jack was Celtic to the core, "small, dark, full of movement, with eyes that could glow like topazes when something exciting was happening . . . I shall always think of him as the most lovable child I ever met . . . Like Peter Pan, he never grew up, and he lived his own stories with such intensity that he ended by believing them himself." [3]

Ford said that London mentioned his plans for writing a novel with the Mexican revolution as the background and made desultory attempts at absorbing local color. "He rode out from Tampico for a couple of days or so — a quaint figure in a Palm Beach suit of ducks and a Panama hat — with a body of insurgent horse." He also explored the oilfields for firsthand information on their methods of operation. But the novel never was written.

The two writers spent most of their time in the bars of the oil port where Americanos from the nearby fields drank up their pay.

Once two drunken oilmen drew revolvers in a bar and it looked as though a Dodge City–style gun battle was about to break out. Jack, Ford recalled, sat at their table with a look of "childish glee" on his face: this was the sort of local color he regarded as priceless. Ford thought they ought to step in as peacemakers before someone got hurt, but Jack pushed him back into his chair. The two gunfighters fired, both missed, and with honor apparently satisfied the tension dissipated with the last wisps of gunsmoke. Everyone in the bar went back to their drinking. "Now," asked Jack with a curator's pride, "what do you think about *that?*"

In his own account of the excursion to Tampico, Jack defended the "pernicious activities of American adventurers" in the oilfields, as those who favored expropriation labeled them, and cited the great installations they had erected. Only three of the eighty-nine producing companies, he pointed out, had paid a dividend on their local investments because they were plowing so much of the income back into developing the fields. Still it was a bonanza town, and he quoted an old sourdough whom he had known seventeen years before in Dawson as saying, "It's got the Klondike faded . . . we're taking out $90,000 a day in gold from a mere eight-inch hole in the ground . . ."

Jack believed that the United States should have landed troops at Tampico as well as Vera Cruz. A short time before mobs had beseiged American citizens in their hotels, torn down and spat upon the American flag. The captain of a German warship in the harbor had proposed to the Dutch and English naval commanders that shore parties be landed to protect the Americans in Tampico, but his suggestion was refused. General Zaragoza and four thousand Federal troops had been driven inland by the Carranza forces and could have fired the oilfields in their retreat, Jack pointed out. "A wad of cotton waste saturated with kerosene and ignited and tossed into the oil could have started a $2,000,000 bonfire. General Zaragoza could have started it. So could any drunken peon." The only trouble with the American intervention, he indicated, was that it hadn't been forceful enough.[4]

Whatever his difficulties with the old demon in the bottle Jack turned out his weekly pieces for *Collier's* on schedule, seven articles appearing in as many weeks from May 16 to June 27, "The Red Game of War," "With Funston's Men," "Mexico's Army and Ours," "Stalking the Pestilence," "The Trouble-Makers of Mexico," "The Law-Givers" and "Our Adventurers in Tampico."

In every one of them he revealed a startling change of mind about Mexico and the Mexicans, a reversal which shocked those of his fellow Socialists who still considered him one of them. Many of the freedom-fighters, he said, were simply bandits and robbers. The peon with a gun in his hand was merciless to the weak and helpless, obsessed with loot and murder, a man bent on destruction rather than building a stable society. "He is not fighting for any principle, for any reward. It is a sad world, in which witless, humble men are just forced to fight, to kill and be killed."

The revolution itself was a fraud, he maintained. "The phrases and slogans of the Mexicans do not mean what they seem to mean. Countless Americans think the present revolution is an expression of the peon's land hunger." That, he held, was all nonsense, propaganda put out by Madero before he was assassinated, now by Villa and Zapata. "What peon with any spunk in him would elect to slave on a hacienda for a slave's reward when, in the ranks of Zapata, Carranza or Villa, he can travel, see the country, ride a horse, carry a rifle, get a peso or so a day, loot when fortune favors, and, if lucky, on occasions kill a fellow creature — this last a particularly delightful event to a people who delight in the bloody spectacles of the bull ring."

His most searing remarks were saved for the mestizos, the "half-breeds" as he called them, of mixed Indian and Spanish blood. They should be kept out of any future government. They were comparable to Eurasians who, he said, "possess all the vices of their various commingled bloods and none of the virtues." The mestizos, forming a fifth of the population, were the class that "foments all the trouble, plays childishly with the tools of giants, and makes a shambles and a chaos of the land. These 'breeds' represent neither the great working class, nor the property-owning class, nor the picked men of the United States and Europe who have given Mexico what measure of exotic civilization it possesses. These 'breeds' are the predatory class. They produce nothing. They create nothing. They aim to possess a shirt, ride on a horse, and 'shake down' the people who work and the people who develop."

The Mexican people would continue to be "mismanaged and ill-treated" unless the United States took over the country. The United States was the "big brother of the countries of the new world" and had its duty to "police, organize and manage Mexico." Responsible Mexicans, he held, would "hail American intervention with delight."

Even more surprisingly, and with scant evidence at hand, he considered General Huerta the possible savior of the republic once he had undergone big-brotherly tutelage by the United States. "Huerta is the flower of the Mexican Indian. Huerta is brave. Huerta is masterful." He conceded that Huerta had never "betrayed possession of high ideals nor wide social vision" — a classic understatement — but the other potential leaders were either adventurers like Villa or "child-minded men, incapable of government" like Zapata.

Delivered of these hasty impressions, Jack devoted himself to amusement and sightseeing and helping Charmian buy heirloom jewelry of coral and gold filigree from "decayed Spanish gentlemen."

He was best remembered by his colleagues for his luck with the dice, particularly a marathon crap game in which he cleaned out all the newspaper correspondents plus the ambassadors of Spain and France.

On May 30, he was scheduled to go up in one of the two Curtis flying boats attached to the occupation force, which would have been his first flight in an airplane. Instead he came down with amoebic dysentery, having picked up the bug either from unwashed food from the ktichen of the Diligencias Hotel or on his trip to Tampico. He was nursed by Nakata — who had accompanied Charmian by steamer, making Jack the only newspaperman in recent history who went to war attended by a valet — and his wife. An army doctor and a resident American physician were in almost constant attendance until he passed the crisis. The attack of dysentery, complicated by pleurisy, almost killed him. He no longer possessed the kind of stamina which carried him through an open-boat voyage across the Yellow Sea ten years before. When he was operated on the previous year, Dr. William S. Porter of Oakland, who removed his appendix, warned him that he would have to stop gorging himself on half-raw meat, cannibal sandwiches and undercooked duck, and cut way down on his drinking. The advice had been disregarded.

Robert Dunn related that once he went up to the London's room and caught a glimpse of Jack "under a white sheet, against a ratty lattice." Charmian, he said, "shooed me out before any word came from the bed." She cooked his food and boiled his water on an electric plate in their room.

Nine days later he had recovered sufficiently to be taken aboard the cattle transport *Ossabaw* for the voyage back to Galveston.

He was still recuperating at the ranch when war broke out in Europe. *Collier's* and other periodicals wanted him to cover the fighting on the Western Front, but he turned them all down. The day of the war correspondent, in his opinion, was over. War had become so complicated the journalist could do little but rewrite the communiqués, and "I would be unable to get what I went after."

Apparently he was undisturbed by — or at least made no reply to — the Socialist and liberal reaction to his reportage from Mexico. The *Nation* considered his attitude toward the revolution "somewhat disconcerting." A year later, in the *Appeal to Reason,* John Kenneth Turner, a leading Socialist intellectual, described his own journey to Tampico. The oil-company representatives there, he reported, tried by flattery and persuasion to convert him to their point of view that Mexico was created for its exploiters.

Jack, he implied, had been induced through the same sort of flattery and good-fellowship to broadcast the exploiters' propaganda, to "turn out a brief for the oilman, a brief for intervention, a brief for what the Mexicans call 'Yankee imperialism.'" This, of course, was utter nonsense. It took more than a few free drinks and a slap on the back to make Jack London change his mind about anything. He had simply started to look upon threats to the rights of property from the viewpoint of the squire of Glen Ellen rather than that of the "chicken thief and revolutionist."

2. *Marxian to Freudian*

Jack's name on a magazine cover attracted a mass readership, otherwise the circulation-conscious *Cosmopolitan* wouldn't have signed him to an exclusive contract. Book-buyers, however, were wary of his merchandise. It was one thing to pay a dime for a magazine with Jack's name plastered all over the cover, and another to invest two dollars in a book which had already been serialized. By the end of 1914 he was wondering whether he would ever again regain his place with the book-buying public.

He wrote Brett the day after Christmas that he was depressed because none of his recent novels had been best-sellers, while Rex Beach's Alaskan thrillers were selling by the hundreds of thousands. His only recent success in the fictional line was *The House of Pride* (1912), of which Macmillan sold 98,305 copies, and that was a collection of short stories with Hawaiian backgrounds. A month later he was writing Brett mockingly deploring that he couldn't write like Harold Bell Wright, whose pious works automatically rocketed to the top of best-seller lists as soon as they were released. Even if Macmillan spent a hundred thousand on advertising, he wistfully remarked, his novels wouldn't sell like Wright's.

The last several major efforts of his career met with a comparative indifference from critics and book-buyers alike. Theodore Dreiser, despite the glacial immobility of his prose, was the current white hope of literature. He wrote of the cities, and the people who struggled for existence in them or fought to dominate them. Graceless and elephantine though his style was, his work was meaningful to his contemporaries. Jack, on the other hand, was out of touch. For ten years he had isolated himself from the main currents of American life, first on the high seas, then in the Valley of the Moon. He had virtually no contact with other writers, except the dabblers at Carmel, which wasn't necessarily a bad thing in itself, but his insularity was extended to the whole contemporary scene. He had simply lost interest in the country and its people at a time when the most significant changes in its history were coming to pass, the years when it took its first tottering steps as a world power, conscious of its surging force yet hesitant to accept a Roman destiny. Now was the time for a novelist of Jack's inherent grasp to be intensely alive and aware. Yet he was trapped in nostalgia, in a fierce love of the land as it was and of the sea in the sailing days, like a wasp imbedded in amber. Not yet forty, he thought of himself as an oldtimer and referred to himself as "the ancient." His attitude was that of a man who had come west with a wagon train. Once in the vanguard, he was now eating dust well back in the literary procession, a weary and aging trekker who wondered whether the journey would ever end.

Just before covering the expeditionary force to Vera Cruz he had completed *The Star Rover*. It was a strange work, full of murky metaphysics, yet contained passages of great force and imaginative power; and its phantasmagoric quality suggested that he had inherited some of the mystic tendencies of his parents — his mother's Spiritualism, his presumed father's guidance from the stars — and was finally putting them to use. The idea for the novel came from an acquaintance of his, Ed Morrell, who had recently been released from San Quentin state prison partly due to Jack's work on his behalf. Conversations with Morrell, whom he frequently met at the Saddle Rock in Oakland, about the men in solitary confinement for weeks and months gave him the realistic basis of the work. *The Star Rover* also included great chunks of work he had contemplated but never got around to putting on paper.

His hero was Darrell Standing, a professor of agronomics at the

University of California's college of agriculture, who had been sentenced to life for having killed a fellow professor over a "purely private matter." Standing was placed in solitary after having been falsely accused of participating in a plot to smuggle dynamite into the prison, and was tortured by the brutal warden, who had him laced into a canvas jacket so tight it almost crushed the life out of him. Others in solitary instructed Standing in the art of releasing himself from suffering by traveling backward into another dimension of time and reliving experiences of the past. "My method of mechanical hypnosis," Standing explained, not very convincingly, "was the soul of simplicity. Sitting with folded legs on my straw-mattress, I gazed fixedly at a fragment of bright straw which I had attached to the wall of my cell near the door where the most light was. I gazed at the bright point, with my eyes close to it, and tilted upward until they strained to see . . . And when I felt myself away out of balance backward, I closed my eyes and permitted myself to fall supine and unconscious on the mattress." He wandered "through the stored memories" — an echo of the Nietzschean theory of eternal recurrence.

Thus he relived the experiences of Jesse Fancher, the son of a wagonmaster whose train was wiped out in the Mountain Meadow Massacre; of a nameless hermit on the Egyptian desert who had fled the persecution of Arian heretics; of Count Guillaume de Sainte-Meuve fighting a duel in medieval France; of Adam Strang, an English adventurer in the Orient who married the Lady Om* of a Korean noble house; of a captured Dane serving as a Roman centurion during Pontuis Pilate's administration of occupied Jerusalem, who considered his friend Pilate a well-meaning politician caught in the cross-currents of Jewish intrigue and who yet was moved by "the serenity of Jesus in the heart of the tumult and pain."

In his journey through time Standing learned that "the morality we practiced in those old days was a finer morality than we practice today . . . We were clean . . . We did not dream of such depths of depravity."

On his return from Vera Cruz, Jack worked steadily away at *The Little Lady of the Big House,* another hymnal on the back-to-the-land

* A flashback to reports he had heard while a correspondent in Seoul that Lady Om, one of the Imperial concubines, was formerly Miss Emily Brown of Wisconsin.

theme. Basically it was the story of a love triangle, with the heroine in love with her husband and his best friend, a story which emerged from a dry mulch of information on modern farming and stock-breeding methods. The hero, Dick Forrest, was the heir to a fortune which he invested in a huge ranch and in Mexican mining properties ("Old Diaz was a robber, but he was a decent robber," in his unenlightened opinion) and the author of a number of agricultural classics such as "Silage Practice" and "Humus Destruction." A friend declared that "Dick is to the domestic animal world what Burbank is to the domestic vegetable world" — exactly the role Jack fancied for himself. His wife, Paula Desten, was the daughter of his father's mining partner.

Once again there was a definite autobiographical tinge to his story. Dick was the physical image of London, with a "mouth girlish and sweet to a degree that did not hide the firmness to which the lips could set on due provocation." Charmian-Paula suffers from insomnia, loves lacy caps and gorgeous costumes, and plays the piano divinely. They keep a kennel of tame philosophers they call "the seven sages of the madrono grove," whom Paula views with a "certain definite aloofness . . . compounded of sheerest democracy and equally sheer royalty."

The interloper in their agricultural Eden was an old friend, Evan Graham, "good stuff, old American stock, a Yale man."

Unintentionally, and with all the anguish which would make the characters acceptable to a middle-class magazine public which didn't mind being titillated but couldn't stand being shocked, Paula and Evan fall in love. The trouble is, she also loves her husband. She "tingles with pride" at the thought of "these two royal men suffering for her and because of her," and reminds herself that "there had been other women in that wild career of his [Dick's] over the world." She admits to herself that she is in love with both men, "only I don't know which I love more."

Dick gently insists that she make a choice between him and his rival, and all three behave with the impeccable nobility of characters in a nineteenth-century novel. The dilemma is too much for Paula, so she shoots herself. While dying, with both men at her side in a death scene almost as lengthy and lyrical as that in *La Bohème,* she refuses to allow the doctor to give her morphine until Evan sings *The Gypsy Trail* to her and Dick follows with a rendition of *The Song of Ai-kut,* an Eskimo lament. Once the concert is over, she permits the doctor to ease her pain from the gunshot wound and delivers her hardly memorable curtain speech: "Sleepy, sleepy, boo'ful sleepy . . ."

Little wonder that Sterling could hardly conceal his nausea at the relentless cuteness of *The Little Lady,* not the least of which was the names given the Chinese servants, Oh Dear, Oh My, Ah Ha, Oh Joy and Oh Ho. Sterling criticized the book so sharply it almost ruptured their friendship. Jack was definitely not at ease creating characters of the upper class. He could think of no classier way of describing a character than making him a bona fide graduate of Yale University.

Underlying it all, again, was the urge to break away from the modern world. Once his heroes had escaped into adventure in remote places; then, as in *Burning Daylight* and *The Valley of the Moon,* they fled from the crushing complexities of city life to the eternal verities of life on the soil. If *Little Lady* was any indication, Jack no longer believed in the efficacy of rural escape. His heroine, like Martin Eden, committed suicide.

The *Mutiny of the Elsinore, The Star Rover* and *The Little Lady of the Big House,* all published from 1914 to early 1916, along with such lesser works as the short novel *The Scarlet Plague* and the short-story collection *The Strength of the Strong,* were as varied as any author could be expected to produce for his readership. His hopes for *Little Lady* were especially high. Shortly after he finished it, on December 10, 1914, Charmian wrote Brett that Jack was so proud of the novel that he hoped the publisher would read it himself in manuscript. But the sales figures on the three major efforts only provided further demonstration of his declining popularity in the bookstores if not the offices of the magazine publishers. *Mutiny* sold 49,181 copies, little more than half as many as *The Valley of the Moon; Star Rover,* 30,634, and *Little Lady,* 21,679.

Possibly alarmed by these indications that he was losing his grip on the public's reading tastes, he was reaching for a new method, a new approach that would vitalize his work. If he was living in self-willed isolation from the contemporary world, he was still avidly exploring the realm of ideas. Charmian wrote that his "princely ego" was never satisfied by any of his attainments of the past. Success went sour, money slipped away from him, even recognition was ephemeral, and romantic love was the greatest fallacy of all; yet he kept searching for something that would give his life, and therefore his work, a new and more significant direction. His intellectual curiosity, at least, had not been stultified.

Somehow, unlikely as it may have seemed for a wanderer of his type, a writer largely occupied by the physical aspect of things, he began delving into the new science — or cause, as it soon became — of exploring the psyche. He devoured the works of Freud, Prince and Jung, fascinated by what he could grasp of their claims for psychoanalysis.* Something of a Freudian approach may be detected in parts of *The Little Lady of the Big House*.

Evidently he came to believe that by using the methods of the psychoanalyst — a belief which anticipated a trend in literature still running its course — he could devise a whole new and more penetrating approach to writing. He had always been seeking a method; the Marxist scheme had failed him, or vice versa, and now he thought he had discovered a design to replace it. If he was no more than a minor literary prophet himself, with credentials based largely on the visions embodied in *The Iron Heel*, at least he could recognize a major prophet when one appeared on the distant horizon. He was convinced that the theories of Freud and Jung, when put into wider practice, would drastically and permanently change humanity's way of thinking about itself, its purposes and its destiny.

"Mate-Woman," Charmian quoted him as saying, "I tell you I am standing on the edge of a world so new, so terrible, so wonderful, that I am almost afraid to look over into it." [5]

3. *The Sands of Waikiki*

In February of 1915, in the midst of a bleak and brooding winter, he decided that he and Charmian needed a change of scene and would go back to Hawaii, which they had enjoyed during their stopover on the *Snark* cruise (despite an interview reported in the *Pacific Commercial Advertiser* of Honolulu in January, 1910, in which he condemned that city as "provincial" and invited a scalding reply by the editor in the same issue). Charmian accepted the proposal with relief.

For months he had been going to "startling lengths," as she put it,

* An English translation of Freud's *The Interpretation of Dreams* was published in 1900; of Jung's first work in 1902.

"in this risky game of 'playing with souls'" by analyzing her, himself and the people they knew. His conclusions about them all, as a Freudian amateur, were "saddening in the extreme."[6] It only deepened his disillusionment with mankind, she believed, and excited a state that would later be identified as manic depressive. His morbid probings were throwing them both off balance, and "the test of my endurance was severe." So she was greatly relieved when he suggested the trip to Hawaii and outlined his plans for working on two dog novels, *Jerry of the Islands* and *Michael, Brother of Jerry*, back to back. By March 19, he was writing Brett that he had already finished twenty-seven thousand words of his first dog novel, though mindful of the criticism he always received from dog lovers and animal psychologists.

They rented a bungalow on Kalia Road along Waikiki Beach, and for a time he seemed to have arrested the decline in his health. They swam, surfed and rode horses daily. He seemed engrossed in his story of Jerry and his adventures in the New Hebrides, perhaps recalling how Buck of *The Call of the Wild* had made him famous, and that even *White Fang* had sold almost half a million. Dogs were good luck, and besides they took his mind off people, whose murkily sex-motivated depths he had so recently come to suspect.

Even in that balmy climate and peaceful atmosphere his body would not mend; the stomach and internal organs which he had formerly boasted were made of "cast-iron" now seemed to be composed of the most delicate and painful tissue, easily affronted by his curious diet. Except for breakfast and an occasional papaya, he lived off *aku*, raw bonito, with an occasional gorging of pork barbecued at a luau. He steadfastly refused to eat the vegetables his doctors back in the States had urged on him.

One night he was seized by abdominal pains and cramps in his legs that made him cry out and turned his face gray with agonizing pain. The doctors summoned by Charmian diagnosed his attack as a calculus caused by his kidney condition. He was suffering from nephritis, an inflammation of the kidneys which could turn into Bright's disease, and uremia, a toxic condition traceable to a malfunctioning of the kidneys. His kidneys, unable to eliminate wastes, flushed them back into his system. The renal insufficiency was complicated by the fact that he was suffering from pyorrhea, his remaining teeth having been infected for several years, and that only increased the toxic condition of his blood.

The doctors relieved his pain with narcotics and pulled him through that attack by keeping him on a diet as long as he was in bed. Once on his feet he shrugged off their advice and went back to gormandizing on raw fish and meat. He stopped exercising, only occasionally going for a dip in the ocean. When he wasn't working, he read or played poker and joined in the Honolulu social life. The local smart set lionized him, and he and Charmian went out almost every night, attending dinner parties, dances (though Jack never ventured on the floor), theater parties and luaus.

He drank much less than formerly, but this was not so much a concession to his physical condition as to the fact that a few drinks affected him now as a bottle or two did before.

Disillusioned as he was with everything life had to offer, physically ill and mentally depressed as he was during this period, and always surrounded by Charmian's possessiveness, it would seem unlikely that he was capable of falling in love again.

At the time he was thinking of writing a book to be titled *Jane Barleycorn,* which he would sign under the pseudonym Jack Liverpool, a disguise which only the most witless reader could have failed to penetrate, to reveal the treacherous nature of women as he had ruthlessly exposed the designs of John Barleycorn. The influence of women, he believed, was as destructive as alcohol on any man of susceptibility.

Some of his plans for *Jane Barleycorn* were disclosed to Upton Sinclair, who recalled that Jack planned to reveal "his tragic disillusionment, and his contempt for woman as a parasite, a creature of vanity and self-indulgence . . . I have heard one of his best friends say that he is glad Jack never lived to write it." Sinclair believed that Jack's "too easy" conquests resulted in his contempt for women. "Like most fighters he despised an unworthy antagonist. The women who threw themselves at his head came from all classes of society, drawn to him as moths to a flame; but it is evident that his philosophy was to blame for the fact that there were so few among them he could respect." [7]

Despite all this, Jack fell in love again.

Who the woman was, whether she was married or single, was never disclosed. Considering the circles in which he was traveling at the time, it seems likely that she was a woman of some position. Adela Rogers St. Johns recalls that from conversations she heard at Glen Ellen later that year it was apparent that Jack had fallen hard. Had he been younger and healthier and more hopeful, he would probably have divorced Charmian and remarried. Yet he was also attached to Charmian, felt protectively toward her, more than any other woman he had known. In this dilemma, he hoped for the impossible. He "wanted Charmian to agree that they separate," as Mrs. St. Johns recalls, "but couldn't bring himself to demand it." Somehow he expected Charmian to agree to self-extinction in the only role she valued, as mistress of Glen Ellen, wife to a famous author, keeper of the flame. With all the contempt he professed to feel for women, he could not bring himself to detach his life from Charmian's, with a final act of ruthlessness which might have saved him by giving him a reason to live. By way of confirmation, Upton Sinclair in his autobiography wrote that "Jack's own theories brought him to a situation where he could not have his wife and another woman at the same time."

His daughter Joan, having heard rumors of this last frustrated love in Jack's life, asked George Sterling about them years later. "George," she recalls, "told me that he fell in love with a woman he met in Honolulu. That was all he would say. George was a prodigious talker, often gossipy, but he had a habit of suddenly cutting off his recollections. This was one of those times. He wouldn't tell me the woman's name or anything else about her." Joan London, however, considered it significant that he planned to go on a trip to Norway, where he would do research on a book based on the old Norse legends, leaving Charmian behind for the first time.

That last love, whose anonymity Jack was unusually careful to preserve, was not quite strong enough to keep alive his appetite for life, once the most striking feature of his character, now extinguished for good.

4. *Search for a Daughter*

Saddened by the spectacle of his disintegration, his friends and former admirers, who once eagerly sought invitations, were staying away from Jack and his fiefdom at Glen Ellen, to which he returned in the spring of 1915. Upton Sinclair, who said he owed more to Jack than any other writer, was living in Pasadena, only an overnight train journey from Glen Ellen, but he could not be persuaded to come up for a visit. "I did not go up because George Sterling told me that Jack's drinking had become tragic." Sinclair remembered the last time he had seen him in New York "with a flask of gin before him, and the stumps of many cigarets in his dinner plate, and his eyes red and unwholesome-looking." On June 3, Sinclair Lewis wrote Jack mentioning a ruckus the latter had raised over a note Lewis had written him. Lewis couldn't remember what the note might have concerned but soothingly confessed that "Prob'ly I done it all right." Jack had fallen into the embarrassing habit of dredging up old grievances everyone else had forgotten about.

To George Sterling went many letters beginning "Dearest and Only Greek," urging him to visit Glen Ellen. Before going to Hawaii he and George had quarreled bitterly over the merits of *The Little Lady of the Big House,* with Jack proclaiming it the greatest novel ever written and George replying it was mediocre at best.

George was depressed enough with his own emotional problems and the disappearance of Ambrose Bierce. Bierce, sick, weary of life, had crossed the Mexican border with a vague plan of joining Pancho Villa, the last word from him a letter reading, "If you hear of my being stood up against a Mexican stone wall and shot to rags please know that I think it's a pretty good way to depart this life. It beats old age, disease or falling down the cellar stairs. To be a Gringo in Mexico—ah, that is euthanasia." No American, so far as can be determined, ever saw him again. Almost as many rumors cropped up around his disappearance as that of Judge Crater. One of the more persistent was that he joined Villa's forces as sort of a military adviser, got in a row with Villa and was shot. One investigation after another ran up a dead end. No doubt Bierce, as determined a legend-maker as London himself, would have been pleased by that final aura of mystery; it would have suited him better than the tallest memorial in Arlington National Cemetery. It was ironic that Bierce, the arch-foe of anarchy and disorder, should be swallowed up by a revolution while London, who had styled himself a revolutionary for most of his adult life, turned his face from that same revolution and opted for a quieter passing from the scene.

One letter from "Wolf" to "Greek" complained, with a pathetic attempt at joshing, because George and Jimmy Hopper hadn't come up to the Valley of the Moon for a long time and suggested that if the Southern Pacific had raised its fares they could walk it from Carmel to Glen Ellen. A short time later, loneliness apparent between every line, he wrote Sterling urging him to join them at Glen Ellen and make a long stay of it. A quiet room would be set aside for Sterling's working hours. He would be able to produce better work at Glen Ellen than amid the distractions of Carmel.

Jack didn't seem to realize his old friends were avoiding him in their distress over his uncontrolled eating and drinking, his testiness of manner, his new habit of turning belligerent without warning.

Professionally it was a frustrating period for Jack. His machinelike tempo of production faltered; he didn't get around to finishing *Jerry of the Islands* until after his return to Glen Ellen. One of his unfulfilled ambitions was to write the Grove play presented by the Bohemian Club at its annual encampment. Earlier that year he had written *The Acorn Planter,* a drama in verse celebrating the merits of the soil-tillers and life-breeders by contrasting them with the warriors and death-makers.* Writing the Grove play was accounted a great honor among San Francisco literary men, though the work of amateurs was often chosen over that of professional writers. Jack's play was turned down, much to his disappointment, but Macmillan loyally published it.

Though annoyed by the rejection of his play, Jack attended the High Jinks on the Russian River that summer, ate and drank in reckless style and somehow persuaded Xavier Martinez and George Sterling to return home with him when the encampment ended. They were greatly depressed by his drinking, his tendency to turn an impersonal discussion into a quarrel, his attacks of despondency. Uremia was making its deadly inroads — the poison dripped into his system as from a faulty internal filter — yet he could not stop drinking.

During that fall he suddenly renewed his efforts to win over his daughters, particularly Joan, who resembled him and possessed the high spirit of his youth. Then in her early teens, Joan had written a play and asked for his professional opinion. He complied at once and

* A review in the *Nation,* August 17, 1916, commented on its monosyllabic verse "moving with a celerity that leaves the question of purely poetic gift in a possibly fortunate abeyance."

wrote her that he could hardly believe that he was old enough to have a daughter who could write such a good play. Evidently he hoped that this would mark the beginning of a thaw in their relationship, but Joan had, after all, asked for his professional rather than his paternal opinion of her work. He wrote many letters pleading for her understanding, somehow expecting the child to develop an adult viewpoint overnight and on command, and to her implacable mother asking her help in effecting a closer relationship with the two girls. Bess, who could be hardheaded, believed he had abandoned his rights as a father — and that was that.

Once, according to Rose Wilder Lane, Joan replied to his plea that she come to live with him at Glen Ellen, "I don't want to leave my mother. I love her."

"But don't you love me?" Jack pleaded.

"Why, Daddy," Joan said. "How could I love you? I don't know you." [8]

Adela Rogers St. Johns has recalled the day she and Jack were riding along a trail on the ranch and he brought up his newest plan for winning his daughters' devotion. "Turning off onto a narrow trail, we came to a little valley in a circle of oaks. Right here, he said, he was going to build a home for Bessie and the girls. At first he had me so swept away that this seemed a wonderful idea, then there entered a chill little doubt. Charmian might not be enthusiastic about this? I asked him how she felt about this and he said cheerfully, 'Oh, there won't be need to see much of each other.'

"That the man who had written *Martin Eden* could say such a thing when even a half-baked girl like me could feel its plain lunacy, held me in stunned silence until he turned and glared at me. He said, 'It seems to me this would benefit everybody.' "

Adela bluntly remarked, "It won't work. They're all women. You know how women behave."

Jack then related his troubles trying to overcome Joan's resentment, and complained that she wouldn't even answer his letters at times. "I ask her to give me a chance to make her know me. Is that too much?" What right did she have to judge her father, Jack wanted to know, forgetting that he had been judging his mother for years. "How can a child know what a man feels? What he needs, the measure of his temptations, the obligations to his work — he must venture into the unknown because he is afraid of it, he lives in another dimension, he fights wars and sails the seven seas, dares death —"

Adela, who was about Joan's age and also came of a broken home, tried to make him understand how his daughter felt. "She would blame you for what you did to her mother, leaving her, marrying somebody else. She would want to defend her mother. You have to think about Joan the way she is, the way she has grown up. She's made a choice . . . I don't think she can be expected, the way you treated her, to understand you the way I do Papa."

Later that day Jack, still marveling at the girl's gift of understanding, told her father that he wanted to become Adela's godfather. "Papa and I both knew he wanted to substitute me for Joan, because I loved my father the way he was now determined Joan should love him. Charmian looked at me quickly, her eyes narrowed to golden slits . . . and said, 'I shall be godmother.' "

Charmian, the girl was certain, didn't know of Jack's plan to bring Bess and his two daughters up to the ranch but "she sensed it, her claws went in and out and her ears went flat back like a mountain lioness."

Later Bess and her two daughters did come up to the ranch with several friends, apparently to test the emotional climate at Glen Ellen, and Jack took them on a picnic in a secluded corner of his property. Just as the lunch was laid out, Charmian appeared on horseback on the horizon, rode toward them like a whirlwind, circled the picnic scene at a mad gallop and kicked up enough dust to ruin the outing. Bess declined Jack's offer to build a cottage on the ranch for her and their daughters, even though he offered to change his will so that his daughters, instead of Charmian, would inherit the property if she would accept.

By now the relations between Jack and Charmian had cooled perceptibly; they were business partners, collaborators in Jack's career, a mutual protection society, rather than participants in what they had proclaimed was a great romance. During John Barleycorn's more desperate sieges, they were patient and nurse-keeper. His protégé Louis Stevens, who often stayed at the ranch during that period, recalls that they slept in different wings of the house and "there was very little emotional contact between them."

She too was subject to moods, sometimes indifferent, sometimes sullen and demanding, sometimes openly possessive and jealous. Except for the secretarial chores which she shared with Johnny Byrne, she lived a largely self-centered life at the ranch: most of their guests were Jack's friends, and many of them disliked her, men as well as women. Some, undoubtedly, were motivated by self-interest. Without Charmian acting as watchdog, Jack's openhandedness would have ruined him twice over. Charmian herself possessed a wide streak of generosity but it stopped short of any willingness to be trimmed. Her manner was often that of a wayward child. One neighbor (female) described her as "a homely little thing, always posing, demanding attention."

Yet to the teen-aged Adela Rogers St. Johns she was a woman of glamor, dash and originality, with her "flowing velvets for evening, her picturesque Chinese costumes around the house, her elegant riding habits, her queenly air of ruling Glen Ellen." Mrs. St. Johns believes that "If she loved him, no woman could have survived as Jack London's wife, at the level of the greatest love story of all time, which they had consciously joined together to create." Trying to live at Jack's pace, keeping up with his exhausting and volatile temperament, "putting up with his infidelities and never letting on she even knew of them," all strained her resources to the limit.

"Some of the things that Papa found embarrassing were, I think now, pure hysteria," Mrs. St. Johns believes. Her girlish efforts to imitate Charmian in dress and manner infuriated her father. " 'Don't imitate her,' he would yell at me, and insisted she was the wrong wife for London, once he had decided to settle down. There was, Papa said, no settle down in Charmian, she might be great before the mast in a storm but not in a quiet country life."

Mrs. St. Johns, recalling her visits to Glen Ellen of forty years ago, said recently that Charmian was "spoiled rotten" by her indulgent husband. (Jack once told Eliza that "Charmian is our little child—we must always take care of her.") Her tragedy was that they could not have kept cruising distant seas forever on the *Snark*. But the Beauty Ranch was important to Jack. "Like most great writers," as Mrs. Johns has said, "he was an actor, an exhibitionist, and the ranch was his stage."

London, she said, "lived in a box—he never saw anything unconnected with himself." Despite his record of sexual conquests, he "never saw women as *people*. Women weren't really important to him, nor was sex. I never saw Jack particularly attentive to or engrossed by a woman. He was more interested in the men in any gathering." (In a letter to Blanche Partington dated August 30, 1904, he stated bluntly that his only interest in women stemmed from nature's demand that he reproduce himself. And when people around the ranch heard him threatening to bring another woman on the ranch, even with Charmian there, it wasn't the Honolulu lady whom he was referring to but "any woman who can give me a son.")

One of her more vivid recollections of life at Glen Ellen was Jack's continually bringing up the subject of suicide. "The whole Carmel crowd," she remembers, "discussed suicide almost voluptuously." Jack always carried a gun, an automatic pistol or a revolver, wherever he went on the ranch, she said, and "I always thought he would shoot himself one day when he got sick of it all."

During the last year or so of his life, his literary production-line slowed down to the extent that it took months for him to finish the two dog books which once he would have turned out in rapid succession and sent off to New York. Yet he would not let illness or drink or despair interfere with his daily schedule. It was the last discipline of his life; without it his life would fly apart. And he kept to it despite increasingly severe attacks of insomnia which permitted him only a few hours of sleep at best.

Louis Stevens recalls that Jack's invariable daily routine was as follows:

At 5 A.M. his valet awakened him with his first cup of coffee.

At 5:30 the valet brought a second cup of coffee and Jack went to work on his correspondence, writing replies to the letters he received on the back of their envelope to be typed up later by Charmian.

At 9 A.M. he began work on whatever novel or short story engaged him at the moment.

At noon he quit writing and joined his guests for a long, conversation-filled lunch.

At 1:30 P.M. he took his guests out for a long ride along the ranch trails.

At 4 P.M. they returned to the ranch house and had drinks until 5:30.

From 5:30 to 6:30 he adjourned to his workroom to plan the next day's work and make notes.

At 6:30 he and Charmian presided over the dinner table.

At 10:30, after four hours of talking and drinking with his guests, he retired to his bedroom and wasn't seen again until the following noon.

From 10:30 to about 2 A.M. he read the mail he had received that day, then began his nightly grapple with insomnia.

The way he gave himself to other people, his patience and generosity even with complete strangers, his unquenchable sympathy for struggling writers, or strugglers of any kind, was the most remarkable virtue he possessed. As may be gathered from the above schedule, he spent much time on his correspondence — most of it concerned with other people's troubles — even while fighting to get a grip on himself and win his way back to public esteem as a writer. Thousands of letters poured into the workroom on the Beauty Ranch, and none went unanswered. He sent monthly checks to unknown writers struggling to finish a book. He contributed automatically to strike funds and bail-raising efforts on behalf of union organizers under arrest. An Australian woman who lost both sons during the early battles of the World War received a fifty-dollar monthly check from him until he died. When he was broke himself and received begging letters he couldn't withstand he asked Brett to send money and take it out of future earnings. All this in addition to the demands and appeals of people he knew, of the members of his entourage, who clung to him until he drew his last breath.

Even more amazingly, perhaps, he read every manuscript sent him by writers who couldn't understand why their stuff wasn't selling, edited them, scrawled advice on their margins and wrote long letters trying to put them on the right track. An exchange of letters with Donald D. Horne, whom he had only met once or twice, was typical of his labors with those less talented or fortunate. Letter after letter came from Horne insisting on advice on how to market his essays. Jack kept replying that he couldn't sell his own serious essays, that he had just had one rejected by every leading magazine in America. Long after most men would have lost patience, he was sending Horne a three-page letter analyzing the flaws in an article the man had just written.[8]

Often, if he thought something submitted to him was publishable, he took on the job of trying to sell it himself, sending the manuscript to a magazine or book publisher with his recommendation. Every day's mailbag brought at least one manuscript to be assayed and criticized, anything from a few stanzas of verse to a full-length novel. And he kept pouring his energy, enthusiasm and experience into other people's lives, even though most of his supplicants possessed little talent, and few exhibited even the faintest signs of gratitude; his efforts were taken for granted, yet were continued with unflagging zeal.

Advice poured out of him unendingly, he never lost his missionary's enthusiasm for good writing, his eye for promising or unfulfilled talent. In the depth of illness and despair he busied himself promoting Joseph Conrad's *Victory,* which he had just read and considered one of the greatest novels ever written. His wholehearted appreciation of other men's work was a true measure of his size as a man. After reading Conrad's *Personal Record,* he had rushed up to a friend and said, "There! Look at that! Here's Conrad saying a thing about a dog in two words that I've been trying all my life to say, and couldn't!" He wrote Conrad telling how he had started reading him when he was beginning his own career and how much he had learned from him. He seems never to have communicated with other great contemporaries, such as Dreiser and Norris, with whom he might have been expected to have much in common. Norris, of course, died in 1902, just as his own career was getting under way, and Stephen Crane two years before that. Dreiser's laborious style, perhaps, was too much for him.

To most aspirants seeking advice he warned against self-pity, told them not to dream of being literary artists while hoping someone else would lick their work into shape — that was the sure road to mediocrity. He especially decried the typical writer's plaint that his work was as good as someone else's — you had to make your own work so much better there would be no reason for comparison.

When his protégé Louis Stevens asked for guidance, Jack told him simply to read and reread the King James version of the Bible until its simplicity and force of expression influenced his own style. Adela Rogers St. Johns first started thinking about becoming a writer after listening to an impassioned discourse, complete with "great sweeping gestures." He told the girl: "Strength, be careful not to prune away all the strength. To polish and prettify all the blood and bones and flesh out of the work. The world will always buy *strength.* The writer who did most to influence his times — Dickens, he is not afraid of sentiment, of great slashing smashing strokes, of power, an exaggeration to prove a point. More than life-size, more than mountain high. He makes the reader weep and shriek with terror and laugh with glee. He was an echo to no man and puppet for no critic. Nor am I. I tell you —

look at the strength of Jane Austen. Look at the suspense. Hers is a different style — a different canvas — but it's *strong*." [10]

The dream of a model community on his fifteen-hundred-acre ranch still obsessed him, still claimed a large share of his income even as it dropped from seventy-five thousand to forty thousand dollars a year in 1915 and 1916. His hope was that it would not only become self-supporting, in perhaps a half-dozen years, but would sustain his colony of relatives, more or less permanent guests (including the "sages of the eucalyptus grove"), and deserving workers. The latter, he specified, must love the soil they worked. Their children would attend a school on the ranch, their wives would shop at a non-profitmaking general store on the property. He would build a slaughterhouse and refrigerating plant. The Beauty Ranch would be his greatest creation, his legacy and monument.

His hopes would not be extinguished despite every disaster that could strike a gentleman farmer. Perhaps his greatest pride was what he called the "Pig Palace," a stone-floored piggery with a private cubicle and outdoor runway for each family of porkers, complete with running water and feeding troughs. For all the planning that went into their accommodation, the whole lot died of pneumonia contracted from sleeping on those expensive stone floors. His prize shorthorn bull slipped and broke its neck. The prize stallion of his stable died. Disease killed every one of his Angora goats. At last it seemed the only animal on the place that didn't succumb to disease or accident was his little mongrel, Possum, the dog he had picked up on the Baltimore docks.

About the only relief he found in his daily routine, now that liquor was more of a necessity than an occasionally exhilarating pastime, now that he was becoming increasingly dependent on opiates to deaden the pain of his uremic condition and ease the burden of insomnia, was the rigging of elaborate — though not very original — practical jokes. One of his favorite gags was the ancient snipe hunt.

Louis Stevens, having been brought up on the sidewalks of San Francisco, had never heard of that trick played on greenhorns. He remembers:

> Jack spent a week building up to the snipe hunt, talking about it at the dinner table, expanding on the excitement of the chase, and so forth. It had to be a moonless night, he said, as the snipe were very shy and elusive.
>
> So one moonless night Jack, several of his friends and some of the ranch

workers took me out on the hunt. We went deep in the woods, far from the ranch house. Jack gave me a lantern and a net and stationed me at the end of a path. I was supposed to wait there and drop the net over the snipe when the others, after beating the woods, drove him toward me. The others were making a lot of racket in the woods, and I was trembling with anxiety. I wanted to make good, after all, on my first snipe hunt.

A while later Jack came back and said I was supposed to wait there until the snipe came tearing down the path. It might take a few hours, but the others would be widening the drive and eventually they'd scare up a bird.

Hour after hour I waited there. No snipe. No more sounds from the so-called beaters. Finally, a little before dawn, damp and bedraggled, I trudged back to the ranch house. When I walked into my cubicle in the guest house, I was greeted by a roar of laughter. Jack and four or five of his friends had waited up all night, sprawled on the floor and passing a bottle around, just waiting for me to show up . . .

But that wasn't all. The next day I took Beth Wiley [a niece of Charmian's], whom I had a crush on, down to Glen Ellen. I wanted to make an impression on Beth and erase the memory of that humiliating night in the woods. I'd never patronized a saloon before, but I was determined to prove how manly and sophisticated I was. I took Beth into a bar. The first thing the bartender asked was — not the question I feared, whether I was old enough to buy a drink — "How was the snipe hunt?" Jack knew I'd be seeking alcoholic solace for my bruised ego, and had sent word down from the ranch to every barkeep in town to ask me that question as soon as I walked through the swinging doors.

Stevens, like Mrs. St. Johns, was one of those few visitors to the Beauty Ranch who sympathized with its chateleine, even admired her for a streak of gallantry visible underneath all the willfulness, the posturing, the odd taste in costuming, the habit of frequently dominating the conversation at table with her chatter when most of the guests had come to listen to Jack.

Finn Frolich, the sculptor, who executed a statue of Charmian on horseback still on display at the museum into which her House of Happy Walls was converted, said that she was desperately afraid of losing Jack, conscious of her failure to provide him with a male heir (which may well have been one of the primary causes of his disillusionment with his first wife), worried sick over his threats to impregnate some other woman and raise an illegitimate son on the ranch to inherit all his holdings. As during his fling at psychoanalysis the previous year, he would not spare her one pang of the torment he was enduring himself. Generous to strangers, he was always hardest on those around him, especially those who could make some claim on his loyalty or compassion.

Doubtless it was in a desperate attempt to recapture his interest, to show that she could play the sexual game as ruthlessly as he, that she became glancingly involved with several other men. She had annoyed Jack by laying down the rule that workmen couldn't start their chores around the ranch house until nine o'clock in the morning because she got little enough sleep as it was. His rage was all the greater, because of that labor-wasting ukase, when he found her one morning (according to one of his relatives) watching the sunrise on a haystack with a young male guest.

Charmian, as Mrs. St. Johns recalls, "had a couple of romances on the side — not very nice ones."

No longer was there any pretense of the great love they had paraded for the envy and admiration of the world. They were two middle-aged people doing their time, living out their sentence, trying to put up with each other. To Charmian it must have seemed only a question of time before she became a widow or a divorcee — and she was determined that it would never be the latter.

Toward the end of 1915 Nakata, the Japanese-American whom they had picked up in Hawaii as a thirteen-year-old cabin boy, decided to leave their employ now that he had reached manhood. The parting, on both sides, came with a heartfelt wrench. He had literally grown up in their household and had unquestioningly followed and served them in the South Pacific, on the voyage around the Horn, in Vera Cruz. He was not only Jack's valet but the major domo of the establishment; he took charge of the house and its several other servants as Eliza superintended the ranch; and when friends came to Glen Ellen the first thing they usually asked was, "Where is Nakata?" More than that, he had become part of their lives.

Now he wanted to make something more of his life than being a servant, even a highly privileged one. He had decided to study dentistry, and eventually would establish a prosperous practice in Honolulu.

The gap he would leave in Jack's life, especially, would never be closed. In the last years he was as close to Jack as any other human being. Usually he called his employer "Master," but sometimes, having heard how his predecessor had been fired, he would impishly address him as "Mr. God," and without objection from Jack.

Nakata's was the first face he saw in the morning, the last he saw at night. One of his prime duties was seeing to it, under Charmian's supervision, that Jack didn't overdo the drinking while locked in his workroom or after he retired for the night. Beside his bed and his desk a large container of ice was kept with tall drinks imbedded in it, whiskey mixed with fruit juice. It was one of Nakata's duties, delegated by Charmian, to keep the whiskey content low and the fruit juice high, since Jack swigged down three of those glasses an hour.

When he left the Beauty Ranch, Jack wanted to give him something that would express his gratitude in no common way, but found that his finances wouldn't permit any lordly gesture. He had to borrow money from the bank to advance Nakata enough money to enter dental college, and also gave him a portable typewriter which the Corona company had sent him for a promotional plug ("Famous Author Uses a Corona!").

Jack was inexpressibly sad the day Nakata was driven down the road to the Glen Ellen station. The youth thanked him and Charmian for having taught him to read and write, for having stayed up all night with him on the *Snark* when he almost died of food poisoning. "You have treated me as your son," he told them, and it was the loss of a son Jack felt on his departure.

XVI

Death's Horses

Satiety and possession are Death's horses; they run in span.
— JACK LONDON

1. *On War and Socialism*

ON MARCH 7, 1916, Jack London began a letter with the old revolutionary's salutation "Dear Comrades" and ended it with "Yours for the Revolution" for the last time. It was addressed to the Glen Ellen local of the Socialist Party but was immediately given prominent display in newspapers throughout the United States, for it announced:

I am resigning from the Socialist Party, because of its lack of fire and fight, and its loss of emphasis on the class struggle.

I was originally a member of the old revolutionary, up-on-its-hind-legs, fighting, Socialist Labor Party . . . My fighting record in the Cause is not, even at this late date, already entirely forgotten. Trained in the class struggle, as taught and practiced by the Socialist Labor Party, my own highest judgment concurring, I believed that the working class, by fighting, by never fusing, by never making terms with the enemy, could emancipate itself. Since the whole trend of Socialism in the United States during recent years has been one of peaceableness and compromise, I find that my mind refuses further sanction of my remaining a party member . . .

My final word is that liberty, freedom and independence, are royal things that cannot be presented to, nor thrust upon, races or classes. If races and classes cannot rise up and by their strength of brain and brawn, wrest from the world liberty, freedom, and independence . . . they never in time can come to these royal possessions . . . and if such royal things are kindly presented to them by superior individuals, on silver platters, they will not know what to do with them, will fail to make use of them, and will be what they have always been in the past . . . inferior races and classes.

Although Jack had never been very close to the realities of the class struggle, had in fact escaped from them at every opportunity, and so far as the actual leaders of the movement were concerned was merely one of an echelon of literary trumpeters — inspirational but noncombatant — his resignation naturally caused a stir in the party's ranks. His militancy had been taken for granted even though there was no record of his having participated in a strike, walked a picket line or skirmished with strikebreakers and company detectives. His had been one of the pictures hoisted icon-like at rallies and conventions along with those of Eugene V. Debs, Victor Berger, Meyer London (a congressman from New York and a Socialist, but no relation), Upton Sinclair and Morris Hillquit.

Few who knew him were surprised by his resignation; they were astounded at the reason he assigned for it. If he had quit the party because it had moved too far to the left, they would not have been astonished in the least. Obviously Jack had shed his Socialist skin a long time back. Twenty years later, Austin Lewis, his old mentor and one of the several San Francisco intellectuals who had recruited him into the Socialist Labor Party, stated that from 1899 on Jack "stood with one foot in social democracy and the other in the philosophical teachings from which have sprung Fascism." He added that Jack and Mussolini had a lot in common. Mussolini "was by nature more ruthless. He brutally solved his contradictions [Mussolini had been a Socialist before turning to Fascism] in terms of his own interest. Jack was in reality much more tender. He broke under the contradictions." Only up to the turn of the century, Lewis believed, could Jack "wear that inimitably beautiful smile of his without a touch of insincerity." After that he was interested only in himself and his career.

His Socialism had always been of a sentimental or romantic nature, his few actual contacts with the movement after 1899 generally arranged on his own terms. He would argue Marxist doctrine, but only if the debaters came up to Glen Ellen. He would address meetings occasionally if the audience was sizable and the occasion important enough. He would serve as president of the Intercollegiate Socialist Society but his only activity in furthering its aims was to speak before its first mass meeting. He was more an ally than a member of the party.

Socialism touched his consciously created legend with a halo of fire, a hint of wrath, a suggestion of danger. He believed in it as an actor believes in the lines he is declaiming.

He was "Yours for the Revolution" yet turned away in repugnance from the first actual revolution that confronted him. Socialism had provided him with a podium when he could attract attention no other way. A "Boy Republican" would have gone unnoticed in Oakland's City Hall Park, and certainly could not have got himself arrested.

There was more than a suggestion of theatrics in the recollection of Georgia Bamford, the wife of another of his early mentors, that Jack was "terrifying" — that he "boiled" with fanaticism — when he began speaking of the revolution to come.[1]

Even in his fiction the elements fused in him that made him a Socialist in name only were visible to that most professional of all revolutionaries, Lenin, who ordered his wife to read London to him on his deathbed. Nadezhda K. Krupskaya recalled: "Two days before his death I read to him in the evening a tale of Jack London, 'Love of Life' — it is still lying on the table in his room. It was a very fine story. In a wilderness of ice, where no human being had set foot, a sick man, dying of hunger, is making for the harbour of a big river. His strength is giving out, he cannot walk but keeps slipping, and beside him there slides a wolf — also dying of hunger. There is a fight between them: the wolf wins. Half dead, half demented, he reaches his goal. That tale greatly pleased Ilyich. Next day he asked me to read more Jack London. But London's strong pieces are mixed with extraordinarily weak ones. The next tale happened to be of quite another type — saturated with bourgeois morals. Some captain promises the owner of a ship laden with corn to dispose of it at a good price; he sacrifices his life merely in order to keep his word. Ilyich smiled and dismissed it with a wave of his hand."[2]

London, however, continues to be one of the several most popular American writers in the Soviet Union. Thirteen million copies of his works have been distributed in Russia, though recent critics have complained of his "bourgeois individualistic motives which are alien to us."[3] He is now officially defined as a "petty bourgeois rebel," a victim of the "unstable position" of his class, whose Socialism was merely a "promised land." *Martin Eden* and *The Iron Heel* have been published in large editions in recent years, both of them selling out almost immediately. In 1955 an eight-volume set of his fictional works, with a printing of 600,000 copies, was subscribed in its entirety within five days of the announcement of publication. *The Iron Heel,* incidentally, is presented to Communist readers as "a picture of contemporary America." Vil Bykov, a Russian exchange student at the University of California, has explained that "The Soviet reader feels that Jack London helps him to understand the national traits of the American people, their energy, persistence and will to emerge as the victor." [4]

The real reason Jack quit the Socialist Party early in 1916 had nothing to do with that given in his letter of resignation. He was motivated by disgust for the official Socialist position on the World War; from the first he had been violently pro-Allied. In Europe most of the Social Democratic parties lined up with their governments along strictly nationalistic lines, thus deviating from the Marxist-Leninist doctrine that it was a capitalistic war, that Socialists should refuse to fight, that the war must be seized upon as an opportunity for overthrowing the governments engaged in the struggle. This stand was enunciated by Lenin himself in his Swiss exile and by other hard-core Marxists, most of whom later became Communist leaders in Russia and Germany.

In neutral America, Socialist opinion was sharply divided. Victor Berger, the Socialist congressman from Wisconsin, was so vigorously opposed to intervention that he was later imprisoned as a seditionist. Eugene Debs also sided with the Marxist-Leninist position. Many others believed the Socialists must support any action taken by the administration in power. To decide which stand to take, the National Executive Committee of the party submitted a referendum to the membership on whether to oppose the appropriation of money for building up the army and navy. The membership voted to oppose, thus taking what amounted to an anti-intervention position.

The results of the vote were announced in December of 1915, triggering Jack's resignation in March of 1916 and those of a number of other prominent Socialists, including Upton Sinclair, Robert Hunter and J. C. Phelps Stokes, later the same year. The pro-Allied group charged that their opponents were pro-German, and the party was split by bitter factionalism.

Jack's letter of resignation came from the peaceful shore of Waikiki, he and Charmian having returned to Hawaii in January. They hoped that the sun and the sea would help arrest his steady decline in health, but his drinking and his defiance of the diets prescribed for him continued. A prescription compounded of camphor, hyoscyamine and opium deadened the pain of uremia, though it could not quell such side effects as insomnia, irritability, melancholia, and a tendency to fly into rages when his opinion was disputed.

He labored meanwhile to finish *Michael, Brother of Jerry,* the companion piece to *Jerry of the Islands,* the former a trenchant argument against training dogs for vaudeville acts. The book, published in 1918, posthumously launched a crusade. As he had suggested in his preface, Jack London Clubs were formed throughout the world to protest the cruelty of training dogs for the stage; by 1924 they had enrolled four hundred thousand members. In the United States dog-lovers would rise and leave the theater when a dog act — as much a staple of vaudeville as the Japanese acrobats who opened the bill — was announced. The movement eventually died out, along with vaudeville itself, but Jack with that one book, far from his best work, converted more people to a cause than all his books dealing with Socialism, just as his dog books outsold his people books.

He loved Hawaii, the balmy ease and dreamy atmosphere of the island life, and spoke of establishing a permanent home there. Not the least of its attractions, perhaps, was its remoteness from the scenes of his more vigorous years; the cobalt surf washed out memories of his threadbare youth in the Oakland streets, the frozen wastes of the Yukon, the frustrations of estate-building at Glen Ellen, the clamor for social justice in smoke-filled halls, the drunks and brawls and escapades — everything that he was and especially everything that he had hoped to be. Here was the place to forget the vain ambitions of youth and console himself with the milder, saner present.

The most intense preoccupation of the final months of his life was the Allied cause in Europe. Jack, though anti-militarist and at least nominally pacifist in his earlier years, was now hotly interventionist. No British propagandist exceeded him in the violence of his proclamations that Germany must not only be defeated but annihilated. Not even Theodore Roosevelt was more vehement in urging that the United States join the Allies.

"I am with the Allies life and death," he said in a statement to the press.

Germany today is a paranoiac. She has the mad person's idea of her own ego, and the delusion of persecution. She thinks all nations are against her. She possesses also the religious mania. She thinks that God is on her side. These are the very commonest forms of insanity, and never before in history has a whole nation gone insane.

I believe that the World War so far as concerns, not individuals but the entire race of men, is good.

The World War has compelled men to return from the cheap and easy lies of illusion to the brass tacks and iron facts of reality.

The World War has redeemed from the fat and gross materialism of generations of peace, and caught mankind up in a blaze of the spirit.

The World War has been a pentecostal cleansing of the spirit of man.[5]

Much of his pro-Allied sentiment was grounded in his belief that a superior destiny awaited the Anglo-Saxon peoples. His pride in his English ancestry — though so far as he knew he was Welsh on his mother's side and only by presumption English on his father's — was the one constant of his life. In his pro-Allied jeremiads he rarely mentioned France, Russia or other members of the Entente.

He was enraged at the "Safety First" attitude of his countrymen, at their general opposition to becoming involved in Europe's war, at the wide support of President Wilson's view that American efforts should be directed at trying to end the war, to feed the starving children and to plead the cause of humanity, rather than taking one side or the other. He refused to flinch at the casualty lists which would result from American entry on the European battlefields. His argument, as Olympian as any staff officer coolly planning an offensive that would cost a hundred thousand lives, was that "As regards a few million terrible deaths, there is not so much of the terrible about the quantity of deaths as there is about the quantity of deaths that occur in peace times in all countries in the world, and that has occurred in war times in the past."

Charmian said that he "suffered unendurably" over the war fought by other nations on the other side of the world. Germany was the mad dog of Europe. To defeat her would require a war of attrition, but it would all be worthwhile if Germany was crushed.

The execution of the English nurse Edith Cavell before a German firing squad in Belgium caused him to rage for days. He readily complied with a request from Hall Caine, the English novelist turned propagandist, to contribute a piece on the heroic resistance of Belgium to the German invaders for *The King Albert Book*. "Belgium," he wrote, "is rare, Belgium is unique. Among men arises on rare occasions a great man, a man of cosmic import. Such a nation is Belgium. Such is the place Belgium attained in a day by one mad, magnificent, heroic leap into the azure. As long as the world rolls and men live, that long will Belgium be remembered."

Despite what a number of his former comrades believed — many of them, after all, workingmen of German descent — he argued vociferously that it was not a capitalistic war but a crusade to uphold the principles of civilization — though it was a civilization which he had often decried as founded on the dominion of the weak and crafty and corrupt. "I believe intensely in the Pro-Ally side of the war. I believe that the foundation of civilization rests on the pledge, the agreement, and the contract. I believe that the present war is being fought out to determine whether or not men in the future may continue in a civilized way to depend upon the word, the pledge, the agreement, and the contract." Perhaps it was just as well for his self-confidence as a prophet that he did not live to see the results of World War I and the crusade for civilization, including the rise of a dictatorship in Russia and a disarray among nations that may yet be solved only by destroying their earthly habitation.

When the newspapers asked him for a statement on his preference of the nominees in the 1916 election, with Woodrow Wilson campaigning for re-election against the Republican candidate Charles Evans Hughes, Jack spoke in the outraged tones of a member of the Union League Club fretting over his French and British investments:

> I have no choice for President. Wilson has not enamored me with past performances. Hughes has not enamored me with the promise of future performances. There is nothing to hope from either of them, except that they will brilliantly guide the United States down her fat, helpless, lonely, unhonorable, profit-seeking way to the shambles to which her shameful unpreparedness is leading her.

The day is all too near when any first power or any two one-horse powers can stick her up and bleed her for bankrupt. We stand for nothing except fat. We are become the fat man of the nations, whom nobody loves.

My choice for President is Theodore Roosevelt, whom nobody in this fat land will vote for because he exalts honor and manhood over the cowardice and peace lovingness of the worshippers of fat.

Both his illness and his concern over the war and the American complacency about not plunging into the conflict conspired to keep him from working at his usual pace. He had turned out a short potboiler titled *Hearts of Three* for magazine serialization and subsequent production as a film, had managed to finish *Michael, Brother of Jerry* on returning to Honolulu, and was working halfheartedly on a novel with a Eurasian girl named Cherry as heroine, which he never finished. The previous year only his short novel *The Scarlet Plague* and *The Star Rover* had been published; in 1916 only *The Little Lady of the Big House, The Acorn Planter* (the play rejected by the Bohemian Club) and a short-story collection, *The Turtles of Tasman*. Most of this work had been done in the previous several years. The machine was running down. He had turned forty the previous January. He spoke frequently of being old and outdated, of being sorry he ever "opened the books."

2. *A Question of Water*

"Our Jack," said his stepsister Eliza, "has not come back to us." He had, of course, physically. He and Charmian returned to Glen Ellen in August, 1916, to prepare for a predictably unpleasant court action their neighbors had brought against him, also to consider what to do when his contract with the *Cosmopolitan* expired. What Eliza meant was that there was something disturbing about his lackluster eyes; she had known him longer than any of them, and she was worried. He was gray-faced, flabby, and weighed two hundred pounds, thirty-five pounds more than he should have. His ankles were swollen, and he was suffering severely from rheumatism, another side effect of uremia.

A calculus resulting from the undiminished strain of excessive eating and drinking on his diseased kidneys brought him all but unendurable pain, dulled only by massive doses of morphine. Later he was laid up by rheumatism for a week, and that time in bed apparently convinced him that he should pull himself together before it was too late. He stayed on a diet largely composed of boiled vegetables and salads, and his condition began to improve. It wasn't too late, if he had the will to live, as his doctors put it, "sensibly."

He went down to Oakland and took his daughters to see Henry Miller in *The Great Divide*. Later, at dinner, he reached over and took the hand of each of them. "I want you to remember that I'm your rock," he told them. "No matter what happens I'll always be there."

On the voyage home from Hawaii he had started a short story, "When Alice Told Her Soul," [6] in which he used the psychoanalytical approach derived from his reading of Jung and Freud. His heroine was a woman burdened with guilt who confesses all to a wandering evangelist. He had begun to value the ease afforded Catholics through the confessional, he said. Once again he saw psychoanalysis as a means of relieving his own soul-sickness, if only he could find (as he underlined a section of Dr. Beatrice Hinkle's introduction to Jung's *Psychology of the Unconscious*) "the character and intelligence which makes it possible . . . to submit . . . to a facing of his naked soul, and to the pain and suffering which this often entails." And once again he returned to psychoanalyzing himself and Charmian, which was particularly hard on the lady, who believed she should be allowed to keep a few secrets to herself. Jack kept demanding that she "let go completely," and she would flare up in resentment. The scenes between them would have been high comedy — the self-taught psychoanalyst and the rebellious subject with her feminine evasions — if there had not been that desperate undercurrent in Jack's probings, in his trying at the last moment to make the transition from Marxist to Freudian and thereby save himself, like a man sliding down the face of a cliff and grabbing at rocks and bushes to stay his fall.

His state of mind was so troubled that he feared he was going insane, brooded over his mother's occasional oddity of behavior, and begged Eliza to promise that if he cracked up she wouldn't have him committed to an institution. Charmian, in her biography, said that the mental strain of his last weeks on earth was so great that she believed his mind would have broken if death had not intervened.

This inner tension was greatly increased by the legal battle over water rights in the valley, particularly since the Superior Court in Santa Rosa, the county seat, kept pushing it back week after week on the court docket. Something of the strain it inflicted on him was visible in a letter he wrote George Sterling on October 28, the kind of letter he could never have written anyone, let alone his closest friend, a year or two before. He bitterly reproached George for not having kept his promise to come up to the ranch and cited all the inconvenience he had caused the servants by his failure to show up as scheduled. His excuse for not coming, Jack added, was so trivial George wouldn't swallow it himself. It was the last word George ever heard from his friend, a peevish curtain-line to what had been a Damon and Pythias legend of Pacific letters.

The trial of the water rights suit was finally called on November 8 and lasted six days. A number of his neighbors in the valley, headed by Ninetta Eames Payne, for whom Jack no longer felt any filial affection, and her husband, were suing for an injunction to prevent Jack from diverting the waters of Graham Creek. The plaintiffs also included Henry J. Chauvet, who operated a reservoir partly fed by Graham Creek; Elizabeth C. Wiley, a cousin of Charmian's; J. G. Cromwell, Mrs. Anna A. Cromwell, G. W. Thompson, A. E. Clark, Nina Watson, Margaret Belden, and J. Wegener. The bitterness of the dispute was only increased by the fact that most of them were old friends of the Londons, and that the former "Mother Mine" and her reverend husband were believed to have organized the campaign against them.

Jack, it was charged, had tapped Graham Creek with a four-inch pipeline and diverted part of its waters for a lake on his property, thereby endangering the riparian rights of his neighbors. Jack contended that he had paid a high price for the ranches he acquired only because he had been assured that he had the primary water rights to the creek, which flowed through his land; furthermore that the amount he diverted from the creek wouldn't appreciably lower the level of the reservoir or deprive anyone else of water. Most of the impartial witnesses agreed that he wasn't being too greedy in the amount of water he took from Graham Creek for his artificial lake.

On November 16 Jack himself took the witness stand for four hours. The strain of testifying was intensified by pain from a series of uremic attacks which had begun shortly after the trial started. A few hours after his appearance as a witness the court ruled in his favor and denied his neighbors the injunction they sought.

Jack was magnanimous in victory, eager to end the hard feelings over the suit. A few days later he invited a number of his opponents in the water suit to have lunch at the Beauty Ranch and inspect the lake. "I wanted them to see the lake they had been worrying about," he told the San Francisco *Bulletin*. "Most of them hadn't seen it. If they had they wouldn't have sued me." The *Bulletin* man reported that Jack "merely smiled" when asked if water would be the "main feature of the entertainment."

In the past several weeks, perhaps because of the nervous strain of the court action, Jack had gone off his vegetable diet and also tumbled off the wagon. He was drinking hard and his usual meal was two large wild ducks cooked for eight minutes. One guest at the reconciliation feast said that he "very conspicuously demonstrated that he was able to out-eat any of them."

Finn Frolich, the sculptor, who visited Glen Ellen during this period in November, later remarked on how much Jack seemed to have changed. "He wasn't himself, he was in a nasty mood, he criticized his friends, was suspicious of everybody. There was no longer that gleam in his eye. He didn't laugh any more."

Time after time he would say, "It's a pretty picayune world." He was referring not only to the court action over water rights, he would add, but the fact that "every person I've done anything for . . . has thrown me down." Charmian noted that there was a sort of "deadness" about him, an indifference to everything but his occasional bouts with pain. He refused to stop eating the underdone mallards or canvasbacks at every meal; it was the duck season and he meant to have his fill of them, and he was, he said, "naturally a meat eater."

Yet in the last few days of his life he was busying himself with plans for the future. He would continue to make improvements on the ranch, including a school for the children of ranch workers, and in a few months he would start marketing the Jack London brand dairy products. He wrote Hughes Massie, now his London agent, that he would be going to New York late in November to discuss with magazine editors his plans for a fifty-thousand-word autobiography.* He wanted Massie to find out how much the *Wide World Magazine* would pay for first serial rights in Britain. The money he would receive from the autobiography would pay for the ranch improvements he planned.

He also was working on notes for an eighty-thousand-word historical

* Which he intended to title *Sailor on Horseback.*

novel dealing with the discovery of America by the Vikings — "love — hate — primitiveness."

Weary and ill though he was — intermittently racked by rheumatism in his legs, dysentery, the edema which swelled his ankles, dull headaches that pounded for hours, all symptoms of the kidney disease that was poisoning his system — he was determined to get his career rolling again. On November 22, he would leave the ranch and go to Oakland; a week later he would leave for New York, stopping off in Chicago to attend the livestock show and buy more cattle for the ranch; after a few weeks in New York he would leave for the Scandinavian countries, where he would do research in the old Norse myths for the historical novel he planned. Charmian would not accompany him. He would return some time in February.

On Tuesday, November 21, he arose after a mostly sleepless night, complaining of fatigue and a renewed attack of dysentery. Charmian wanted him to call Dr. Allan Thompson in Glen Ellen, but he refused. He slept most of that afternoon and had considerable difficulty in rousing himself for dinner that evening.

At dinner — half-raw ducks as usual — he talked of his plans for the ranch with Eliza and Charmian.

Next day he would be leaving for Oakland, and he retired early, before nine o'clock, hopeful of a decent night's sleep.

The last they saw of him was as he walked down the hall toward his sleeping porch. Possum was frisking at his heels, eager for a romp, but for once his master did not respond.

A little later that night Charmian left the house for a stroll under the stars, and when she returned she noticed that Jack's light was still burning on the sleeping porch. Later several of the men employed on the ranch told George Sterling that they thought they heard Jack walking restlessly around the house late that night. It was a beauiful night, clear and bright with stars, with a hint of frost in the air — the last night of his life.

3. *The Last Battle*

At seven o'clock the next morning, November 22, his valet, Sekine, a young Japanese who had replaced Nakata, brought the usual cup of coffee to Jack's sleeping porch. But Jack couldn't be aroused; he was lying on his side and bent double, and his face was constricted. Sekine ran to Eliza's quarters, awakened her, and brought her to Jack's bedside. Eliza took one look and went for Charmian. Together they raised him to a sitting position on the bed and tried to pour black coffee into him, without success. Jack obviously was in coma.

At eight o'clock Dr. Thompson was summoned, and it was immediately evident to the physician, from the dark blue color of his face, that Jack was unconscious from an overdose of narcotics.

Some time during the night he had been stricken by a calculus, with its all but unbearable agony. Even after the drugs he had poured into himself, before he lost consciousness, he was still doubled up from the pain. The malfunctioning of his kidneys had caused his legs to swell twice their normal size. And after a quick look around the room Dr. Thompson knew that he had deliberately taken enough narcotics to kill himself.

On the floor near the bed were two empty vials labeled "Morphine sulphate — 1/4 grain, with atropine sulphate, 1/150 grain." Each prescription was for twenty-five pills.

On the table at his bedside was a pad with figures scrawled on it indicating that Jack had calculated how much a lethal dose of morphine sulphate would be.

A daylong fight to bring Jack out of his narcosis thus began. Dr. Thompson summoned Dr. W. B. Hays of Sonoma to assist him, and together they washed out his stomach with a potassium permanganate solution, the antidote for morphine poisoning. They administered stimulants, massaged his arms and legs, did everything they could to bring him out of the coma.

On a table in the room, where he left mail to be picked up by Sekine and sent out in the morning, was a letter he had written the night before, perhaps just before he was stricken, which was clear evidence that he had not intended — until the unendurable pain began — to make an end of his life.

The last words he ever wrote were to his daughter Joan, with whom he had struggled for years to arrive at a proper father-daughter relationship. He had often been harsh and impatient, as when he scolded her for charging her schoolbooks to his account at an Oakland book store. She had been unforgiving, dominated as she was by her mother's bitterness. Given a few more years, they would probably have grown to understand each other. But time had run out for them, even as he wrote asking Joan and Bess if they would have lunch with him the coming Sunday. If the weather was good they would go for a sail on Lake Merritt; if it wasn't they could attend a matinee.

Then the constricting agony began, obliterating everything else . . .

By eleven o'clock Dr. J. W Shiels and Jack's surgeon, Dr. W. S. Porter, had arrived from San Francisco and Oakland, but there was little to do that Dr. Thompson and Dr. Hays hadn't done. Jack could not be shocked out of his coma. Only once they noted a flicker of consciousness. About noon his eyes fluttered open, and his lips moved. Dr. Thompson thought he might have said "Hello." Then he lapsed into coma again.

Some of the ranch hands gathered outside the sleeping porch made a try at rousing him by yelling, "Wake up, wake up! The dam has bust!" The workers thought that only a threat to his beloved ranch would bring him out of the coma.[7]

But he still lay in his leaden stupor, almost as though defying the efforts to haul him back over the precipice.

He had always contended that a man possessed one inalienable right, the "anticipating of the day of his death . . . the individual's right to cease to live." He had lived as he pleased, in a way most people found egocentric; had taken what he wanted out of life, and now he had no more use for it. Perhaps he could have endured a continuing decline in his fortunes, even the steady evaporation of his powers as a writer, but the physical pain hardly made the struggle worthwhile. It was impossible to imagine himself nibbling like a rabbit on vegetables and sopping up milk toast just to keep his kidneys happy. His only choice was to live as Jack London, a hedonist enjoying life to the hilt, or to die, quite shamelessly, at the moment of his choosing.

If any consciousness remained to him, invisible to those attending him, he voted in favor of death.

Those at his bedside almost could feel his resistance to all attempts to bring him out of narcosis. He could not or would not be roused from the sleep which would slide into death.

The shadow of Sonoma Mountain was lengthening. Well away from the house his ranch hands huddled in small groups, watching as the doctors worked in relays over Jack, massaging his limbs, on the lighted sleeping porch where he lay. People came up from Glen Ellen and Sonoma and other valley towns to join in the vigil.

The sun set on the harvested fields, the upland pastures, the groves of eucalyptus, the ruins of Wolf House, the stone outbuildings, the trails he rode into the redwood forests, the artificial lake which had excited the suspicions of his neighbors, the empty "Pig Palace," the little meadows where his blooded cattle grazed, the shanties where his resident "sages" dwelled — everything he had built and would leave behind him.

His breathing was increasingly labored as night fell, rattling and wheezing in his clogged lungs. It was time to go wherever men — pagan, hedonist, agnostic, or not — went when they died.

He died at 7:45 that evening.

Physicians and relatives left the deathbed. There were still the formalities to be observed, the paper work to be done. Charmian, according to a later statement by Dr. Thompson, argued that death must be attributed to natural causes. Whether the attending physicians were swayed by her pleas or not, they joined in concealing the cause of his death; it remained a secret, so far as the public was concerned, until 1938 when Irving Stone's *Sailor on Horseback* was published.

A bulletin was issued for the press and signed by all four doctors, which stated: "At 6:30 P.M. Nov. 21, 1916 Jack London partook of his dinner. He was taken during the night with what was supposed to be an attack of indigestion. This, however, proved to be a gastro-intestinal type of uremia. He lapsed into coma and died at 7:45 P.M., Nov. 22."

Dr. Porter alone signed the death certificate stating that Jack had died of uremia following renal colic, with chronic interstitial nephritis as a contributing cause.

Later that night the newsboys in Oakland, outside the waterfront saloons he had patronized, and in San Francisco, along the Barbary Coast and outside the low-life hangouts where he had freely spent his time, money and health, shouted the news that John Barleycorn had finally claimed a favorite son. Next morning the news would reach all over America and shoulder war dispatches off the front pages; he had not delayed his departure, like other diminished literary giants, so long that the world would shrug it off as overdue. His comparative youth made his death all the more dramatic, even though attributed to disease. In Europe many newspapers gave his obituary more space than that of Franz Josef of Austria, who died the day before Jack.

Charmian, from all accounts, took his death with remarkable self-possession. Still calm, composed and dry-eyed she went to bed that night and slept the clock almost twice around. In her biography of Jack, she attributed her long sleep to her complete nervous exhaustion. "The night he died," said Finn Frolich, "Charmian slept for the first time, slept for a day and a half because she knew at last that no other woman could take him."

She decided against attending the funeral services down in Oakland because, as she explained, his first wife and his two daughters would be there and she didn't want to cause any embarrassment.

The day of the funeral Louis Stevens, then a reporter on the San Francisco *Bulletin* despite Jack's warnings against journalism as a bad training school for the serious writer, came up to the ranch to offer his condolences. Charmian was still dry-eyed and seemingly unaffected. She asked Stevens to go riding with her, and they took the trail leading over to the ruins of Wolf House.

As they dismounted, she noticed that something was floating in the tree-shadowed pool near the charred shell of the stone castle. They walked over to see what it was. Floating on the surface was the body of Possum, Jack's little mongrel. He had disappeared immediately after Jack died.

Charmian was convinced, Stevens recalls, that Possum had drowned himself in grief over his master's death.

For the first time, apparently, the reality of Jack's death struck her, almost with the impact of a physical blow. They had not really been happy for years, not since the death of the daughter they were going to call Joy; yet they would probably never have parted, for all the imperfections they had found in each other. Charmian never married again. "Mate," obstreperous and lovable, demanding and indulgent, terrifying and endearing, was gone. She broke down and wept.

On Friday, November 24, six of Jack's ranch workers hoisted his coffin to their shoulders and carried it down the winding road to

Glen Ellen, where it was placed on the train for Oakland. Nakata, his former valet, was waiting there to accompany it to the crematory where memorial services were held that afternoon. Among the small group of mourners were Bess and her daughters; his mother, who had left a sickbed to be there, Dr. Porter, George Sterling, and Nakata.

At Charmian's request, Edward Payne, so recently involved in the water rights dispute and possibly the last man Jack would have wanted to say anything over his corpse, delivered the eulogy. Jack had always dealt harshly with Payne's views on practically everything, but especially metaphysics, and "held in contempt," as Payne wrote, "any mind that could wander about in any such bogey world as he conceived the metaphysical realm to be." In *The Soul of Jack London*, published in London ten years after his death, Payne and Aunt Netta obtained their posthumous revenge, telling of "spirit messages" received from a now repentant Jack through a medium in Santa Cruz. The spirit of Jack London informed them that "I have said much, much that I must undo . . . I followed the lost trail of materialism and sickened in the foul mists of error . . . I take orders now. In my earth life I gave them." Mr. and Mrs. Payne said they transmitted a message to Jack reminding him of "the appeal to the higher manhood in you," evidently dealing with money problems, in a letter they sent him while he was on his last visit to Hawaii, which Jack had neglected to answer. Back came the message from Jack, "I am evil . . . I wronged you . . ." Even in the great beyond, the way the Paynes told it, Jack was not spared the treacly reproaches of "Mother Mine."

The eulogy Payne read was in verse hastily composed by George Sterling, beginning "Farewell! Although thou know not, there alone . . ." and maundering on in a funereal style which Jack would surely have snorted at with derisive laughter. There were no prayers; Jack had sternly forbidden anything verging on the religious at the last formalities.

Just before they all turned to go, leaving Jack to the crematory fires, Nakata stepped forward and slipped a pad of paper into the coffin.

Dr. Porter was about to remove it when Nakata moved up beside him and begged, "Don't, please. The master always carried a pad. It should go with him. I wrote the words. They are my goodbye."

On the pad Nakata, with more eloquence than anyone else had mustered for the occasion, had written, "Your words were silver. Your silence now is golden."

Two days later, on Sunday, a copper cylinder containing his ashes was buried on the knoll above the ranch house among the manzanita and white oaks. Several tons of concrete were poured on top of the cylinder, and a reddish-brown boulder rolled over it. Jack had asked that he be buried in this manner near the pioneer Greenlaw children who died in infancy the year he was born. Oak leaves drifted over the grave as Charmian, Eliza and the workmen walked away. Jack couldn't have written a more appropriate closing scene for himself. It was sunset, the hour of the ending of his novel *The Valley of the Moon,* which celebrated the beauty of his resting place.

There is no inscription on the boulder which marks his grave. That was the way he wanted it: his life and his work would speak for him. The terse indignity of the epitaph was not for him. One contemporary thought that Pegeen Mike's farewell in the J. M. Synge play would have served beautifully: "Oh my grief, I've lost him surely. I've lost the only Playboy of the Western World." But he was no playboy, not even in the rural Irish sense of the word. There were too many contradictions in the man to submit him to the hasty summations of cemetery wit.

He survives today chiefly as a storyteller with a vigor and freshness that carries over, with a recurring sense of discovery, to each new generation of readers. Undoubtedly that appeal will increase. In the appallingly overcrowded world predicted for the near future, his vivid word-pictures of empty seascapes and uncluttered lands, and of the free and self-reliant individuals who contended with them and each other, will be a breath of fresh air from the simpler past. No one excelled him as a reporter-participant on the retreating remnants of our frontiers. As a self-made intellectual, he will be interesting only as a curiosity, as an example of the social ferment in the early part of the century. His Socialism shrivels into absurdity against the searing light of Soviet reality. His prophecies — the triumph of a capitalistic oligarchy in *The Iron Heel,* for instance — appear no less doomed in the dry air of actuality.

Although the last ten years of his life were artistically an anticlimax, he will endure through *The Call of the Wild,* parts of *The Sea Wolf* and *Martin Eden* and at least a score of superb short stories. His own life story, his consciously created legend, was an even greater artistic work than any he committed to paper. Surely, Jack London, "for history it is enough."

A Partial Verdict of Posterity

"No American writer has had a career more representative of his time . . . lacking poise and moral background, he must be passed as an ephemeral sensation as regards all but a handful of his stories."

—Frederick Lewis Pattee, *The Cambridge History of Literature*

"His books are very uneven, but he wrote many a hard-muscled, clean-cut page."

— Bliss Perry, *The American Spirit in Literature*

"He mastered the outward circumstance of life, and then played with the toys. The world was his by physical and intellectual possession; but he preferred to live in a nursery . . ."

— Waldo Frank

London, Frank Norris, and Upton Sinclair were "reporters, or, if they thought of themselves more pretentiously, social scientists; their novels were photographs, or at any rate campaign documents . . . In attack, in criticism, they did able work; but when it came to offering a genuine alternative, their picture became a negative one: industry without millionaires, cities without graft, art without luxury, love without sordid calculation. They were ready to upset every aspect of modern industrial society except the fragmentary culture which had brought it into existence."

— Lewis Mumford, *The Golden Day*

". . . enjoyed enormous prestige, quite out of proportion to the literary merit of his story-telling."

— J. B. PRIESTLEY, *Literature and Western Man*

". . . a bugle, an awakener, an annunciator, a wall-shatterer, a herald of the dawn . . . He intuitively understood the spirit of California and gave it voice; also intuitively, like a woman, he understood America through California and the West, and spoke for her."

— STEPHEN GRAHAM, *The Death of Yesterday*

"He is of value for his immense, driving energy, for his intelligent concern over social evils, for his ability to convey the thrill of clean-limbed action, and for his poetic response to the beauties of primitive landscape."

— WALTER FULLER TAYLOR, *A History of American Letters*

His literary vogue was based upon "a thoroughly discredited interpretation of the survival of the fittest theory."

— LUDWIG LEWISOHN, *Expression in America*

"He was the true king of our story tellers, the brightest star that flashed upon our skies. He brought us the greatest endowment of genius and of brain, and the story of what America did to him is a painful one."

— UPTON SINCLAIR, *Mammonart*

"There occurred a conflict between social ideals and personal ambition which he was never able to resolve. It left a deep fissure in his moral nature, and produced a startling inconsistency in his life and his writing."

— LLOYD MORRIS, *Postscript to Yesterday*

"By Jack London's death, American letters suffer a heavy loss, as by his life they incurred a heavy debt . . . He had truly amazing powers of observation and interpretation, and though he often dealt with the impossible, he rarely, if ever, missed what in art is far more important than possibility — plausibility."

— New York *Times* editorial, November 24, 1916

"Like Peter Pan, he never grew up, and he lived his own stories with such intensity that he ended by believing them himself."

— FORD MADOX FORD

"Where did he get his hot artistic passion, his delicate feeling for form and color, his extraordinary skill with words? The man, in truth, was an instinctive artist of a high order, and if ignorance corrupted his art, it only made the fact of his inborn mastery the more remarkable . . . There was in him a vast delicacy of perception, a high feeling, a sensitiveness to beauty. And there was in him, too, under all his blatancies, a poignant sense of the infinite romance and mystery of human life."

— H. L. MENCKEN, *Prejudices: First Series*

"He was a captive of beauty — the beauty of bird and flower, of sea and sky and the icy vastness of the Arctic world."

— ANNA STRUNSKY, *The Masses,* July 1917

"A potential naturalist in his amoral attitude and his underlying pessimism, but carried away by zeal of revolution. Lacks restraint and finish."

— V. L. PARRINGTON, *Main Currents in American Thought*

Afterword

"Why should I care whether or not my name endures for a flicker of time after I'm dead?" Jack London once asked in a conversation with friends. "I want the rewards of my work while I can enjoy them. Give me the money now, and other men can have the fame. What is fame? A flash of light that goes out in darkness . . ."

Nevertheless London left a mass of material, practically every scrap of paper relating to his career, to help any future biographer set off that "flash of light": letters, notes on work in progress, rejection slips, journals, account books and manuscripts. Equally important perhaps he lived vividly in the memory of his contemporaries — many of them also writers — who recorded their impressions with a frankness he would probably have encouraged. He lived out in the open, and was the least secretive of men.

The first London biography was written by Rose Wilder Lane and published in serial form in *Sunset Magazine,* October, 1917, to May, 1918, but was never issued between hard covers. His second wife Charmian produced a two-volume official biography in 1921, a widow's monument, pious, romantic and sentimental, with only occasional disillusioning glimpses of what life with a self-absorbed writer was like. Irving Stone's popular *Sailor on Horseback* was written at a time when many of London's contemporaries were still alive and available, and published in 1938. For some reason a reprint edition of Stone's biography, brought out later the same year, was subtitled "a biographical novel," but it was obviously nonfictional. The last full-dress biography was *Jack London and His Times* (1939), an admirably candid and coolly objective work by his elder daughter Joan.

None of the above is what book reviewers lovingly label as "definitive." Nor, it must be regretfully conceded, is this one. London's heir and literary executor, Irving Shepard, refused permission to examine the London collection in the Huntington Library on the grounds that he is bringing out a revised edition of Charmian London's book and also a collection of London's letters. Both Charmian London's and Irving Stone's books made extensive use of that collection. I was permitted to use the London collections at the University of California (both at Berkeley and Los Angeles, the latter including the notes Irving Stone made for his biography), Stanford University, the California Historical Society and Yale University.

London was such a prolific writer that it was not possible to discuss everything he produced in the sixteen years — and fifty volumes — of his professional career. Many of his stories and articles are of little interest today except to his most ardent admirers and specialists in his period.

I wish to acknowledge in particular the assistance and generosity of three persons who knew London in their early youth, Adela Rogers St. Johns, who provided a brilliant portrait of him in her recent *Final Verdict;* Joan London (Mrs. Charles Miller), who took time out from her own work in progress, and Louis Stevens, an old friend of mine who was London's protégé in his boyhood and youth and later became a novelist and screen writer. Mr. Stevens died several months after this book was finished.

I also appreciate the assistance of the following:

R. L. De Wilton, recently retired as a senior editor at Macmillan, for providing the correspondence between London and his principal publisher.

James T. Babb, librarian, and Donald C. Gallup, curator of the Collection of American Literature, at Yale University Library, for letters and telegrams exchanged by Jack London and Sinclair Lewis.

For help in research, Jack Wallace, executive editor of the San Francisco *Examiner,* which London served as a special writer and war correspondent.

Agness Underwood, Tom Caton, Neison Himmel and Ben White of the Los Angeles *Herald-Examiner.*

Jack Smith of the Los Angeles *Times*.

Frank Scully, the writer, of Palm Springs, California.

Samuel Stark, of San Francisco, the theater historian and collector.

James de T. Abajian, of the California Historical Society, San Francisco.

Mrs. Frances Buxton of the California Room of the Oakland Public Library.

Dr. Paul Jacquelin of Los Angeles, for spending months tracing an old friend of London's.

J. R. K. Kantor, reference librarian, Bancroft Library, University of California at Berkeley, for permitting me to examine the London correspondence in the Joaquin Miller, Gelett Burgess and Blanche Partington Letters.

Ralph W. Ashley, curator of the Charlotte Ashley Felton Memorial Library at Stanford University, for London's letters to his British literary agent.

Hensley C. Woodbridge, librarian at the Murray State College Library, Murray, Kentucky, who has compiled the first complete bibliography on London, soon to be published, and who was exceedingly generous and helpful in pointing out sources which would never have occurred to me.

Albert E. Hise, curator of the Masillon Museum, Masillon, Ohio, for information on Flora Wellman London's early life in Ohio.

Herbert T. Silsby, attorney-at-law in Ellsworth, Maine, for digging out much new material on London's presumed father, who practiced law, among other things, in Ellsworth.

Selected Bibliography

Altrocchi, Julia Cooley, *The Spectular San Franciscans,* New York, 1949.
Austin, Mary, *Earth Horizons,* Boston, 1932.
Beach, Rex, *Personal Exposures,* New York, 1940.
Berton, Pierre, *The Klondike Fever,* New York, 1960.
Bevan, Aneurin, *In Place of Fear,* London, 1952.
Braybrooke, Patrick, *Peeps at the Mighty,* London, 1927.
Brooks, Van Wyck, *The Confident Years,* New York, 1952.
Brown, Deming, *Soviet Attitudes Toward American Writing,* Princeton, 1962.
Byington, Lewis F., and Oscar Lewis, *The History of San Francisco,* San Francisco, 1931.
Chaney, William H., *Primer of Astrology and Urania,* St. Louis, 1890.
Dunn, Robert, *World Alive,* New York, 1956.
Foner, Philip S., *Jack London: American Rebel,* New York, 1947.
Geismar, Maxwell, *Rebels and Ancestors,* Boston, 1953.
Genthe, Arnold, *As I Remember,* New York, 1936.
Gilliam, Harold, *San Francisco Bay,* New York, 1957.
Goldman, Emma, *Living My Life,* New York, 1932.
Graham, Stephen, *The Death of Yesterday,* London, 1930.
Grattan, C. Hartley, *Bitter Bierce,* New York, 1929.
Hardinge, Emma, *Modern American Spiritualism,* New York, 1869.
Hicks, Granville, *The Great Tradition,* New York, 1933.
Hofstadter, Richard, *The Age of Reform,* New York, 1955.
Irwin, Will, *The Making of a Reporter,* New York, 1942.
Johnson, Martin, *Through the South Seas with Jack London,* New York, 1913.
Johnston, Alva, *The Legendary Mizners,* New York, 1953.

Langford, Gerald, *The Richard Harding Davis Years,* New York, 1961.
Lewis, Oscar, *Bay Window Bohemia,* New York, 1956.
Lewisohn, Ludwig, *Expression in America,* New York, 1932.
London, Charmian, *The Book of Jack London,* New York, 1921.
London, Joan, *Jack London and His Times,* New York, 1939.
Lynn, Kenneth S., *The Dream of Success,* Boston, 1955.
Marcosson, Isaac F., *David Graham Phillips and His Times,* New York, 1932.
McDevitt, William, *Jack London as Poet* (a pamphlet), San Francisco, 1947.
McWilliams, Carey, *Ambrose Bierce: A Biography,* New York, 1929.
Mencken, H. L., *Prejudices: First Series,* New York, 1921.
Millis, Walter, *The Road to War: America 1914-1917,* Boston, 1935.
Morris, Lloyd, *Postscript to Yesterday,* New York, 1947.
Mumford, Lewis, *The Golden Day,* New York, 1926.
Noel, Joseph, *Footloose in Arcadia,* New York, 1940.
O'Connor, Richard, *High Jinks on the Klondike,* Indianapolis, 1954.
Palmer, Frederick, *With My Own Eyes,* Indianapolis, 1932.
Payne, Edward B., *The Soul of Jack London,* London, 1926.
Roosevelt, Theodore, *The Letters of Theodore Roosevelt* (edited by Elting E. Morrison), Cambridge, 1952.
St. Johns, Adela Rogers, *Final Verdict,* New York, 1962.
Schorer, Mark, *Sinclair Lewis, An American Life,* New York, 1961.
Seidler, Murray B., *Norman Thomas: Respectable Rebel,* Syracuse, 1961.
Sinclair, Upton, *Mammonart,* Pasadena, 1924.
Sinclair, Upton, *The Autobiography of Upton Sinclair,* New York, 1962.
Stone, Irving, *Sailor on Horseback,* Boston, 1938.
Wickham, Gertrude, *Pioneer Families of Cleveland,* Cleveland (undated).
Williamson, Thames, *Far North Country,* New York, 1944.

PERIODICALS

American Hebrew
American Mercury
The Argonaut
Atlantic Monthly
The Bookman
Collier's Weekly
Cosmopolitan
The Editor
Everybody's Magazine
Home Magazine
Huntington Library Quarterly
International Socialist Review
Living Age
The Masses
The Nation
New England Quarterly
Outing Magazine
Overland Monthly
Pacific Monthly
Saturday Evening Post
Seven Arts Magazine
Sunset Magazine

Town Talk
Variety
The Wasp
The Wave
Woman's World
Youth's Companion

NEWSPAPERS

San Francisco *Chronicle*
Examiner
Call
Bulletin
Los Angeles *Herald*
Examiner
Express
Times
Record
New York *Times*
Herald
Tribune
Journal
Call
Chicago *Tribune*
Examiner
American
Inter-Ocean
Cleveland *Plain Dealer*
Buffalo *Express*
Oakland *Enquirer*
Tribune
Times
Herald
Ellsworth (Me.) *Herald*
Honolulu *Advertiser*

BOOKS BY JACK LONDON

The Son of the Wolf, 1900, Houghton Mifflin.
The God of His Fathers, 1901, McClure, Phillips.
A Daughter of the Snows, 1902, Lippincott.
The Cruise of the Dazzler, 1902, Century.
Children of the Frost, 1903, Macmillan.
The Call of the Wild, 1903, Macmillan.
The Kempton-Wace Letters, 1903, Macmillan.
The People of the Abyss, 1903, Macmillan.
The Faith of Men, 1904, Macmillan.
The Sea Wolf, 1904, Macmillan.
The Game, 1905, Macmillan.
War of the Classes, 1905, Macmillan.
Tales of the Fish Patrol, 1905, Macmillan.
Moon-Face, 1906, Macmillan.
Scorn of Women (a play), 1906, Macmillan
White Fang, 1906, Macmillan.
Love of Life, 1907, Macmillan.
Before Adam, 1907, Macmillan.
The Road, 1907, Macmillan.
The Iron Heel, 1907, Macmillan.
Martin Eden, 1909, Macmillan.

Lost Face, 1909, Macmillan.
Revolution, 1910, Macmillan
Burning Daylight, 1910, Macmillan.
Theft (a play), 1910, Macmillan.
When God Laughs, 1911, Macmillan.
Adventure, 1911, Macmillan.
The Cruise of the Snark, 1911, Macmillan.
South Sea Tales, 1911, Macmillan.
The House of Pride, 1912, Macmillan.
A Son of the Sun, 1912, Doubleday, Page.
Smoke Bellew Tales, 1912, Century.
The Night Born, 1913, Century.
The Abysmal Brute, 1913, Century.
John Barleycorn, 1913, Century.
The Valley of the Moon, 1913, Macmillan.
The Strength of the Strong, 1914, Macmillan.
The Mutiny of the Elsinore, 1914, Macmillan.
The Scarlet Plague, 1915, Macmillan.
The Star Rover, 1915, Macmillan.
The Little Lady of the Big House, 1916, Macmillan.
The Acorn Planter (a play), 1916, Macmillan.
The Turtles of Tasman, 1916, Macmillan.
The Human Drift, 1917, Macmillan.
Jerry of the Islands, 1917, Macmillan.
Michael, Brother of Jerry, 1918, Macmillan.
The Red One, 1918, Macmillan.
On the Makaloa Mat, 1920, Macmillan.
Hearts of Three, 1920, Macmillan.
Dutch Courage, 1922, Macmillan.

Of the last four of his posthumously published works, three were collections of short stories. *Hearts of Three* was a short novel, serialized in *Cosmopolitan*. It was designed to form the basis of a motion picture, but was never produced.

Notes

BOOK ONE: THE BAY

I. THE CHILDHOOD THAT NEVER WAS

1. Deming Brown, *Soviet Attitudes Toward American Writing.* Sources referred to in these footnotes may be found in the bibliography at the end of the book.
2. Lenin's widow, Nadezhda K. Krupskaya, *Memories of Lenin.*
3. Quoted in a notable feat of scholar-detective work by Fulmer Mood, *An Astrologer from Down East,* in the *New England Quarterly,* Vol. V, No. 4, 1932.
4. Herbert T. Silsby II, *Ellsworth: A Brief History.*
5. Published in St. Louis in 1890.
6. Joan London, *Jack London and His Times.*
7. Gertrude Wickham, *Pioneer Families of Cleveland.*
8. Emma Hardinge, *Modern American Spiritualism,* a definitive work published in 1869.
9. *The Spectacular San Franciscans.*
10. The pseudonymous "Burlington Hawkeye" in the *Argonaut,* April, 1877.
11. *McKenney's Oakland, Alameda and Berkeley Directory* for 1887-1888.
12. Recalled in *John Barleycorn.*
13. From *John Barleycorn.*
14. Letter dated December 13, 1906 and now in the possession of the California Room of the Oakland Public Library.
15. *Bay Window Bohemia.*
16. Judging from a layout of photographs of Jack London's various homes published in the Oakland *Tribune,* March 16, 1952.
17. *John Barleycorn.*

II. MAN AMONG MEN

1. From accounts he gave in *John Barleycorn* and biographical sketches for Macmillan and Houghton Mifflin.
2. Joseph Noel, *Footloose in Arcadia.*
3. Biographical sketch for Macmillan.

4. According to an article in the San Francisco *Chronicle*, August 18, 1906, published after London had brought out *The Sea Wolf*.
5. *The Human Drift*, 1917.
6. In the biographical sketch written for Macmillan.
7. *John Barleycorn*.
8. *With the Procession*, published in 1895.
9. Published in 1907.
10. In *The Road*.
11. *Revolution and Other Essays*, 1910.

III. A GIRL WITH GOLDEN HAIR

1. *Revolution and Other Essays*.
2. *The Dream of Success*.
3. Georgia Loring Bamford, *The Mystery of Jack London*.
4. *John Barleycorn*.
5. Seattle *Post-Intelligencer*, July 18, 1897.

IV. SELF-DISCOVERY IN THE KLONDIKE

1. From an article for *Home Magazine*, June, 1899, titled "Through the Rapids on the Way to the Klondike."
2. Quoted in Beach's *Personal Exposures*.
3. In *Burning Daylight*, published in 1911.
4. In the biographical sketch for Macmillan.
5. *The Klondike Fever*.

BOOK TWO: THE SEA

V. "CLUBBED INTO FORTUNE"

1. *Far North Country*.
2. As he recalled the conversation years later in *John Barleycorn*.
3. Recounted in his article published by the *Editor*, March, 1903.
4. One fairly recent exception was Philip S. Foner's *Jack London: American Rebel*.
5. Quoted in Oscar Lewis's *Bay Window Bohemia*.
6. *The Making of a Reporter*.
7. *Footloose in Arcadia*.
8. *Ibid*.

VI. "SEVEN STURDY SAXON SONS . . ."

1. *The Making of a Reporter*.
2. Emma Goldman, *Living My Life*.
3. Published by Macmillan in 1903.
4. *The Golden Day*.
5. *Rebels and Ancestors*.
6. *Mammonart*.
7. *The Making of a Reporter*.
8. *As I Remember*.
9. *Jack London and His Times*.
10. Arnold Genthe, *As I Remember*.
11. *Footloose in Arcadia*.

VII. A DOG NAMED BUCK

1. *The Autobiography of Upton Sinclair.*
2. *Earth Horizon.*
3. *Footloose in Arcadia.*
4. Quoted in Joan London's *Jack London and His Times.*
5. *Footloose in Arcadia.*
6. Upton Sinclair in *Mammonart.*
7. Published in *Cosmopolitan,* June, 1902, as "Diable, A Dog," and included in the collection, *The Faith of Men,* published by Macmillan in 1904.
8. Macmillan correspondence, March 10, 1903.
9. *The Great Tradition.*
10. Letter to the Oakland *Enquirer* in 1905; clipping otherwise undated in Oakland Public Library scrapbook.

VIII. ENTER MISS KITTREDGE, EXIT MRS. LONDON

1. *Footloose in Arcadia.*
2. Published by *McClure's,* August, 1906; collected in *Love of Life,* 1907.
3. *Footloose in Arcadia.*
4. London to Brett, September 2, 1903, Macmillan correspondence.
5. In *The Golden Day,* published in 1926.
6. In *Mammonart.*
7. Bierce to George Sterling in a letter dated February 18, 1905.
8. At Macmillan's latest count.
9. *The Masses,* June, 1917.
10. Published by *McClure's* in July, 1910, and included in *The Strength of the Strong,* 1914.

IX. AT WAR WITH THE JAPANESE

1. *With Kuroki in Manchuria.*
2. San Francisco *Examiner,* dateline February 26, 1904.
3. Dispatch dated March 7.
4. Published in the San Francisco *Examiner,* April 17.
5. *World Alive.*
6. Ibid.
7. *With Kuroki in Manchuria.*
8. Quoted in Frederick Palmer's *With Kuroki in Manchuria.*
9. In his autobiography, *With My Own Eyes.*
10. *Sunset Magazine,* October, 1905.
11. Published in the San Francisco *Examiner,* September 25, 1904, and later made part of the collection titled *Revolution.*

X. JACK AND HIS "MATE-WOMAN"

1. *Footloose in Arcadia.*
2. Letters to Blanche Partington in the Bancroft Library of the University of California.
3. Collected in *The God of His Fathers,* 1901.
4. Oakland *Tribune,* January 27, 1905.
5. Letter in the Charlotte Ashley Felton Memorial Library, Stanford University.
6. London to Brett, Macmillan correspondence, December 5, 1904.

7. In an interview with Edward B. Clark, published in *Everybody's Magazine,* June, 1907.
8. *The Letters of Theodore Roosevelt,* Vol. VII, edited by Eltinge E. Morrison.
9. *The Book of Jack London.*
10. *The Autobiography of Upton Sinclair.*
11. *Mammonart.*
12. Joshua Wanhope in the New York *Call,* November 24, 1916, an article written shortly after London's death.
13. London to Brett, April 8, 1906.
14. *Collier's,* May 5, 1906.
15. *In Place of Fear.*

XI. TWENTY-SEVEN MONTHS AT SEA

1. *Seven Arts Magazine,* March, 1917.
2. Genthe's *As I Remember.*
3. In an article titled "The Lepers of Molokai," published by *Woman's Home Companion,* January, 1908.
4. *Through the South Seas with Jack London.*
5. Published by the *Pacific Monthly,* March, 1910.
6. As he wrote Cloudesley Johns February 17.
7. *Pacific Monthly,* May, 1910.
8. Published in 1911.
9. Johnson, *Through the South Seas with Jack London.*

BOOK THREE: THE VALLEY

XII. ANOTHER HEIR IS APPARENT

1. London to James B. Pinker, July 1, 1909.
2. *Effects of Tropical Light on White Men.*
3. *The Golden Day.*
4. *Living My Life.*
5. Letter in the Partington collection, Bancroft Library, University of California at Berkeley.
6. Brett to London, January 9, 1911, in Macmillan correspondence files.
7. San Francisco *Examiner,* June 22, 1911.
8. The story was "Benefit of the Doubt," published by the *Post* November 12, 1910.

XIII. "THE CROWD" MOVES SOUTH

1. *As I Remember.*
2. *Earth Horizon.*
3. According to Lewis's account books, cited by Mark Schorer in his *Sinclair Lewis: An American Life.*
4. As he wrote Lewis on October 4, 1910.
5. Published by *Women's World,* May, 1912, and collected in *The Turtles of Tasman,* 1916.
6. Serialized in *Popular Magazine* and published in book form in 1913.
7. Professor Franklin Walker's article, *Huntington Library Quarterly,* November, 1953.

8. Quoted in Professor Schorer's *Sinclair Lewis: An American Life.*
9. *Earth Horizon.*
10. *Bay Window Bohemia.*
11. *American Mercury,* October, 1925.
12. *Footloose in Arcadia.*
13. *Rebels and Ancestors.*
14. Joan London, *Jack London and His Times.*
15. "Jack London, Farmer," *The Bookman,* October, 1916.
16. Interview in the Oakland *Tribune,* May 7, 1950.
17. San Francisco *Examiner,* Feb. 6, 1919.

XIV. DREAMS OF A GENTLEMAN FARMER

1. Lewis correspondence files, American Literature Collection, Yale University Library.
2. Charmian London, *The Book of Jack London.*
3. *New Review,* November, 1913.
4. *The Bookman,* March, 1913.
5. Quoted in Joan London, *Jack London and His Times.*
6. Millard, the *Cosmopolitan* editor, described his visit in "Jack London, Farmer," *The Bookman,* October, 1916.
7. Letter in the Oakland Public Library's California Room.
8. Los Angeles *Times,* March 24, 1941.
9. Beach's Memoir, *Personal Exposures.*
10. *The Making of a Reporter.*

XV. THE FACE OF REVOLUTION

1. Quoted in Gerald Langford, *The Richard Harding Davis Years.*
2. In his memoir, *World Alive.*
3. *Living Age,* January, 1917.
4. "Our Adventurers in Tampico," *Collier's,* June 27, 1914.
5. *The Book of Jack London.*
6. *Ibid.*
7. *Mammonart.*
8. *Sunset Magazine* serialization of Mrs. Lane's biography, April, 1918.
9. Letters in the Bancroft Library, University of California at Berkeley.
10. *Final Verdict.*

XVI. DEATH'S HORSES

1. *The Mystery of Jack London.*
2. *Memories of Lenin.*
3. Deming Brown, *Soviet Attitudes Toward American Writing.*
4. *Quarterly News Letter,* Book Club of California, Winter, 1958.
5. Statement to the Pathé Exchange, June 16, 1916.
6. Published by *Cosmopolitan,* March, 1918, and collected in *On the Makaloa Mat,* 1920.
7. Oakland *Enquirer,* November 23, 1916.

Index